5. 24-73

Portuguese Settlement on the Zambesi

Exploration, Land Tenure and Colonial Rule in East Africa

M. D. D. Newitt

Africana Publishing Company · New York

Published
in the United States of America 1973
by Africana Publishing Company,
Holmes & Meier Publishers, Inc.
101 Fifth Avenue
New York, N.Y. 10003

© Longman Group Ltd 1973

Library of Congress catalog card no. 72–86888
ISBN 0–8419–0132–5

Printed in Great Britain

Contents 1769869

Maps and Illustrations

Plates

Preface

When this book appears, it will be over three years since most of it was written. A number of important advances have been made in the field of Moçambique history in that time and some of these I would like to mention. Dr H. Bihla's thesis on Manyika and the Portuguese was accepted by London University in 1971 and contains a great deal of original material on Portuguese trade with Manica. Important work has been done by Mr S. Mudenge on Zumbo and the Rosvi empire, upsetting many of the accepted ideas on the subject. In 1968 Allen Isaacman published the preliminary results of his research on the *prazos* in *Studia* under the title 'The Prazos da Coroa 1752–1830 – a functional analysis of the Political System'. For those who want a short introduction to the *prazos* in English, this is by far the best thing available. I have also had the privilege of seeing unpublished work by Professor Isaacman and Father W. Rea SJ on the Chicunda and the Jesuit *prazos* respectively. Finally there is the highly important publication of a book on the *prazos* by Giuseppe Papagno, *La Questione dei Prazos da Coroa nel Mozambico alla fine del Secolo xix*, Biblioteca Einaudi, (Turin 1972).

Acknowledgements

I would like to acknowledge the very generous financial assistance I received from the Calouste Gulbenkian Foundation, which enabled me to make two journeys to Lisbon and carry out the research necessary to complete this book.

I would like also to thank Professor Dauril Alden, Herr Gerhard Liesegang and Professor C. R. Boxer for the help and advice they gave me at different stages of this work, and my sister, Hilary, who impersonated the general public and painstakingly went through the text making me explain myself clearly.

The publishers are grateful to the following for permission to reproduce copyright material:

Cambridge University Press for the Plan of Massangano from 'The "Aringa" at Massangano' by M. D. D. Newitt and P. S. Garlake, *Journal of African History*, VIII, I (1967) and the Royal Geographical Society for the paintings by Thomas Baines 'Manufacture of Sugar at Latimo: making the panellas or pots to contain it' and 'Part of Tete looking up the Zambesi river'.

Photographs have also been reproduced from the following books: *Relatorio da guerra de Zambesia* by A. de Castilho (Plate 1); *Relatorio da viagem da Canhoneira Rio Lima de Lisboa a Mocambique* by A. Castilho (Plate 7); *Memorias de um Velho Marinheiro e Soldado de Africa* by Joao de Azevedo Coutinho (Plates 8 and 9); *Narrative of an Expedition to the Zambesi and its Tributaries* by David and Charles Livingstone (Plates 3, 10, 11 and 12); *Historia das Guerras no Zambeze* by F. G. Almeida De Ea (Plates 15, 16 and 18) and *Zambezia* by R. C. F. Maugham (Plate 17). Plates 2, 4 and 5 were taken by the author.

1 The Background to the Portuguese Settlement in East Africa

Land tenure in medieval Portugal

Portugal began her expansion overseas in the middle of the Hundred Years War and towards the end of the prolonged social and economic depression which lowered over the fourteenth century. Her problems were mirrored by those of most other European countries of the time. Henry V of England would certainly have understood the difficulties of the Portuguese monarchy, beset by the interest groups of under-employed and often landless knights, and preoccupied with the growing problem of land falling out of cultivation and vagrancy among the rural population. He might also have understood the deference paid by the king, *Dom* João I (1385–1433) to the merchant community of the capital, for, while agriculture had been increasingly depressed in the fourteenth century, Lisbon had prospered as a port of call for ships passing from northern Europe into the Mediterranean (*345*).

The agricultural depression was the backdrop to much of the restlessness of late medieval society. The profits from arable farming declined and on the noble and ecclesiastical estates land fell out of cultivation. The attendant social ills of 'bastard feudalism' and vagrancy became increasingly serious and food production fell. In the latter part of the century the government was forced to intervene to revive rural prosperity and underpin the crumbling fabric of society.

In 1375 the then king, *Dom* Fernando, published the famous *Lei das Sesmarias*—the law of the uncultivated lands. This was designed to legislate the peasant class back onto the land and the land back into cultivation. By this law all owners or lessees of land had to find men to cultivate it. The royal justices were empowered to see that anyone who was prepared to farm vacant land could obtain draught oxen at a reasonable price. If a landowner did not co-operate the local authorities—*concelhos*—could intervene, find cultivators and sequestrate the rent for the royal coffers. All *sesmarias* had to be confirmed by the crown. This law was encorporated in the first great compilation of Portuguese law, the *Ordenações Affonsinas*, which was completed in 1446 (*360*, vol 3, 699–702).

The *Lei das Sesmarias* was a document as much of social as of economic policy. It could be used by governments to constrain landlords to let their lands and to force the rural unemployed back into productive labour. It could also be used by the landless to lay claim to land on which to settle. Its objective was probably to free land for easier cultivation and to encourage owners to rent or lease small peasant plots. It was one of the first overt attempts to deal with the menace of the great *latifundia* which has become an obsessive problem for Iberian statesmen up to our own day. Both in Portugal itself and in its overseas empire, *sesmarias* were only partly effective in arresting the seemingly organic growth of great landed estates. They were only partly effective because they ran counter to the massive social and economic forces emanating from the whole Portuguese system of land tenure. Of the various land tenures which existed in Portugal, emphyteusis came to be the dominant and most persistent form.

Emphyteusis is a contractual form of land tenure which was first clearly defined in the late Roman empire. Its purpose was to attract cultivators to land which the owner found difficulty in exploiting. Its prevalence in the late Roman empire, when rural depopulation was widespread, was not accidental and the imperial government went out of its way to encourage it (*432*, vol. 1, 26). By a contract of emphyteusis land could be leased in perpetuity or for some long but limited period, which was usually three generations. The person who leased the property acquired extensive rights in it, and some jurists were to maintain that these rights were superior to those of the owner (*339*, 62). He could leave the land to his heirs, and he could sell it. He could sub-lease the land, though not subdivide it, and he could develop it as he pleased. Moreover, he could not be dispossessed so long as he fulfilled the contract. In this way the reluctant cultivator was lured by what virtually amounted to full ownership and security of tenure. The original owner retained the reversion of the land if the lessee should die without heirs, and he could intervene to secure payment of his rent. In some cases he could also intervene if the land was being ruined. The contract of emphyteusis was terminated therefore 'by lapse of term, destruction of the land, death of the holder without successors, and forfeiture which might be for irretrievable damage, or non-payment of rent or taxes' (*328*, 275).

2

Sir Henry Main in his book *Ancient Law* suggested that the Roman idea of dual ownership, as expressed in the contract of emphyteusis, passed directly into the law codes of the barbarian tribes and thence to the feudal land law of northern Europe (*399*, 175–8). In the same way continuity has been claimed for Spain and Portugal. It was argued that emphyteusis was adopted by the Visigothic kings of Spain who incorporated it into the *Breviarium Alaricianum* of A.D. 506 from where it passed directly into the legal heritage of the Iberian peoples (*475*, 21). This continuity is, however, illusory. It was, in fact, in the medieval law schools of Italy that Portuguese churchmen learnt of emphyteusis and, in the thirteenth century, used this Roman model to impose order and system on the variety of land contracts already in common usage in Portugal (*295*, 161, 164).

Two kinds of land contract had already been in existence in Portugal for a hundred years. These were the general contracts called *carta de foro*, made between the owner of some great *latifundia* and all the inhabitants of it collectively, and individual contracts between man and man (*339*, 45). After the church began to use Roman models in drawing up land contracts the Roman legal usage spread among other landowners.

Three types of contract of emphyteusis became common. There were perpetual leases called *fatiotas*; there were leases for a number of lives called *emprazamento*; and there were short-term leases (often for ten years) called *arrendamento*. The grant made for one or three lives became increasingly popular in Portugal. After three lives were completed the lessee—called in Portuguese *foreiro* or *enfiteuta*—could petition for renewal, though the insecurity resulting from this was to prove a major objection to this form of land tenure and was complained of by the Evora Cortes of 1490 (*295*, 152, 171).

So successful did *emprazamento* prove, that its use spread beyond land tenures so that tolls, taxes, market rights and even movable property came to be leased in this way. The thing leased was called a *prazo* after the Latin *placitum*. The fact that in Portugal the *prazo* could not be subdivided greatly contributed to the excessive size of estates and the large number of landless men.

The quit-rent paid to the lord was called *foro* in Portuguese. It might be paid either in money or in services, which prompts some kind of comparison with the manorial economy of feudal northern Europe. Service in battle, service in ploughing, transport, harvesting, the obligation to use the wind-mills, ovens, salt-pans and winepresses of the lord are very reminiscent of the manorial economy. Emphyteusis, however, remained a written contract; it lacked the personal bond between lord and man which was so important an element in northern feudalism. It was a contractual economic arrangement enforceable in law which greatly restricted the ability of the lords of the land to exploit their inferiors. It created a large class who lived on their rents and sub-leased their property, though the long tenures made it difficult to adjust rents, which often failed completely to represent the value of the property. In this way the seigneurial class was divorced from the land and from the rural population.

As a result of the spread of French ideas in the early nineteenth century, belief in the virtues of unimpeded economic processes and unencumbered land ownership prevailed, and in 1832 Mousinho da Silveira extinguished the rights of the *senhor* in all royal estates leased under contract of emphyteusis. This type of land contract still thrives, however, and today is almost always perpetual.

Portuguese knights and the overseas conquests

Throughout most of the fourteenth century there was peace between Chrstian and Muslim in the Iberian peninsula, but the class of knights (*fidalgos* in Portuguese) who looked to such conflicts for employment had been engaged in frontier warfare. Regularly Portugal and Castile had raided each other in defence of shadowy dynastic and territorial claims, and imperceptibly this raiding had merged with the Hundred Years' War. However, in 1385 a large Castilian army was defeated at Aljubarrota by an Anglo-Portuguese force and the Portuguese claimant, João of Aviz, who now found his throne secure, was drawn into an alliance with England. This was concluded at Westminster in 1386 and was sealed by the marriage of the king to Philippa, daughter of the Duke of Lancaster. This was to be the beginning of an era of frontier peace, for although João accompanied his father-in-law on an abortive invasion of Castile, in 1389 Juan of Castile died and his successor, Henry III, was for many years not in a position to revive the Castilian claims to Portugal. The two kingdoms were to confront one another again in the fifteenth cenury, but chiefly in the Atlantic as each strove to monopolise the islands and coastline of northern and western Africa.

The cessation of hostilities between Portugal and Spain and England and France for a generation after 1389 imposed severe strains on the stability of late medieval society forced to absorb the energies of an unemployed warrior class. It is no coincidence that in 1415 both the Lancastrians in England and João I had to reopen hostilities. The year of Agincourt was the year in which a large Portuguese army stormed the Moroccan city of Ceuta and established a new frontier where honour, wealth and advancement were to be won.

In a century of warfare the Portuguese hold on North Africa extended. Tangier resisted attack in 1436 but Alcazar fell in 1454, Arzila and Tangier in 1471, Targa in 1490, Agadir in 1505, Safi in 1508, Mazagão in 1509 and Azamor in 1513. This placed the whole coastline west of Gibraltar in Portuguese hands (433). Into these North African campaigns the Portuguese monarchs poured far more resources in men, money and ships than they ever invested in their eastern enterprises, yet the Moroccan conquests never yielded any economic returns. One reason for this policy undoubtedly was to prevent any other European power dominating this stretch of coastline, but the really important consideration must at all times have been the popularity of the North African battlefields with the Portuguese *fidalgos*.

A knight ambitious for advancement entered royal service in one of the Moroccan garrisons. There he learnt the profession of arms and learnt also to hate the Muslim as enemy to his faith and to his country alike, heedless of the fact that it was he who was invading the land of the Muslims. From North Africa he might return to enter the royal household where, as the Portuguese empire grew, the most bountiful patronage was distributed— captaincies in the royal fleets, commands in one of the royal fortresses or official posts in the factories of the east. It is hardly surprising that he took with him to the east his prejudices in favour of an embattled front towards all Muslims and a belief that the fruits of this world are to be won by deeds of arms. The fleet which sailed for the east in 1515 had on board, according to a contemporary memorandum,

> more than seven thousand able-bodied men ... including many gentlemen, knights and wards of the king our lord, thanks be to God, well used to routing the Moorish fleets and to taking by force of arms their cities, towns and lands and to subject them to the service of His Highness (259, 21).

If North Africa, and later the East, were frontier regions where military prowess could be displayed, there were other possibly

5

more lucrative openings for *fidalgos* in the field of maritime enterprise. Captains in Portuguese service reopened the sea-route to Madeira and reached the Azores by 1439. The Canary Islands had been rediscovered in 1402 by Jean de Bettencourt who did homage for them to the Castilian king.

For twenty years after the rediscovery of Madeira, Portuguese and Castilians fought to control the islands of the North Atlantic. Portugal based her claims on the actual occupation and colonisation of the islands reinforced by Papal Bulls obtained periodically from Rome. The islands were granted to Prince Henry, *Dom* João I's fourth son, who was governor of the military Order of Christ. The Popes granted the Order ecclesiastical jurisdiction and the receipt of tithes throughout the Portuguese overseas empire. When Manuel became king in 1495 the governorship of the Order was absorbed by the crown and the tithes became little more than a royal tax. A Papal Bull of 1496 permitted members of the Order to marry and from that time membership of the Order became a coveted reward for men who had distinguished themselves in royal service, carrying with it rank, a pension and judicial immunities.

In order to settle the Atlantic islands Prince Henry turned them into captaincies—or fiefs. The lure of empty land on the fertile and sub-tropical islands was very strong for men of all classes in medieval Portugal.

As more of the coastline of West Africa was charted, however, Madeira and the Azores became mere stopping places for more adventurous spirits. The mapping of the Sahara coast was largely completed during the regency of *Dom* Pedro between 1440 and 1449 and probably under his inspiration (*370*, 141). In 1441 Antão Gonçalves, one of Prince Henry's captains, brought back the first prisoners from the Sahara and the following year returned with slaves and a little gold dust, thereby confounding the sceptics who had always held that the African voyages were a waste of money. The slaves found a ready market in Portugal and to meet the demand the Portuguese built the first European trading fort in Africa on Arguim island in 1448. The slaving voyages are described by Gomes Ennes de Azurara in language which was intended to invoke the ideals of Christian chivalry. Here was occupation for the Portuguese knights which was certainly lucrative but also honourable. Antão Gonçalves was, in fact, knighted on the African shore by Nuno Tristão for a feat of arms which included capturing a camel driver and a slave woman (*315*, 147).

The class of *fidalgos* who were so prominent in the early phase

6

of Portuguese expansion were not, of course, the only people interested in the new empire, but their attitude and their outlook on life explain many of the peculiar features of Portuguese imperialism. After the example of Azurara the chroniclers cast the deeds of their contemporaries in a heroic mould, and the great biography of Afonso de Albuquerque, published by his son as late as 1557, is one of the greatest of these chivalrous epics. There are signs that some Portuguese became so bemused by contemplating their empire in the distorting mirror of chronicles such as these that, like Don Quixote, they lost all sense of reality. The army which the king, *Dom* Sebastian, led to disaster at Alcazar in 1578, some thirty years after sounder political judgement had already begun to shed the North African fortresses, is but one example. Francisco Barreto is another. To lead an army of seven hundred men equipped with cannon, camels and armour into the depths of the African low veldt was hardly the result of hard-headed and rational policy making.

To this early phase of expansion, when European society was still influenced by 'bastard feudalism', also belongs the habit of regarding colonial offices, military commands and even the captaincy of ships as the legitimate spoils of the noble families, and the habit of binding commerce in monopolistic straitjackets and using these monopolies also to reward the service of the noble class. To it belongs the aristocratic manners and the contempt for work—even work not of a menial nature—which the Portuguese assumed overseas, and the idiom of bombastic exaggeration which so many Portuguese writers have used up to the present to describe their imperial history.

Colonisation and the captaincy system

By the end of the fifteenth century the Portuguese had secured four groups of uninhabited islands in the Atlantic. Madeira and Porto Santo were settled in the years immediately following their rediscovery in 1418; the Azores were settled by the Portuguese under a charter of Afonso V dated 1439; the Cape Verde Islands discovered in 1458 or 1459, were settled in the 1460s; and S. Thomé, Principé and Fernando Po in the Gulf of Guinea were discovered by captains in the service of Fernão Gomes about 1472 and settled in the following decade. In addition to colonising these islands, the Portuguese committed themselves to securing a monopoly of the trade between West Africa and

7

Europe, which was being challenged by Italians, Flemish and Castilians.

To succeed in this formidable task Portugal needed a strong position in international law. The Bulls issued by Popes Eugenius IV and Nicholas V went a long way to establishing Portugal's rights. The last of the series, the Bull *Romanus Pontifex*, published on 8 January 1454, specifically confirmed Portugal's monopoly not only over the lands already discovered, but also over all future discoveries *usque ad Indos* (*455*, 14–18).

A partition treaty in 1479 which gave Castile the Canary Islands and Portugal a monopoly of the Guinea trade strengthened her position which was underwritten further by the famous Tordesillas agreement of 1494 dividing the world along a longitudinal line running 370 leagues west of Cape Verde. When in 1500 Cabral sighted the Brazilian mainland, this was found to lie east of the Tordesillas line, thereby bringing the whole of the south Atlantic within the Portuguese sphere.

To administer and defend these vast possessions was difficult enough, to colonise and exploit their economic potential was far beyond the capacity of a medieval king with limited resources and no reserves of manpower. The Atlantic islands and the Brazilian coast were all months away from Portugal and they could only be effectively protected if they were peopled by a self-reliant and self-supporting community. This situation was not without precedents for medieval administrators, for all the frontier regions of Europe had presented similar difficulties of communication, defence and settlement, and it was certainly the experience of the crusades and the *reconquista* which suggested the system of *capitanias* (captaincies) adopted by the Portuguese in their earliest experiments in colonisation.

The captaincy system was confined to the Atlantic and its seaboard. The earliest captaincies were those granted in 1440 to Teixeira and Zarco on Madeira, 20 years after the first settlements had been made. The last captaincy was that granted to Paulo Dias de Novais in Angola in 1571. The Atlantic islands then known had been granted to Prince Henry in 1433 and it was he who initiated the captaincy system. He granted the islands by means of charters to his followers. The grantees were called *donatários* or *capitaes-donatários*. Like the 'marcher' lord of feudal northern Europe the *donatário* was expected to administer, defend and settle his territory out of his own resources. His lordship was both a bastion of defence and a frontier of advancing religion and civilisation. He had civil and criminal jurisdiction subject to

8

certain cases being removed to the royal courts. By virtue of the *Lei das Sesmarias* he was obliged to lease his lands to settlers—usually for a probationary period of five years—and to guarantee their rights with a *carta de foro*.

To recompense him for these obligations, the *donatário* enjoyed extensive financial rights. The settlers paid a *foro* to him for the use of their land and he could claim from them extensive seigneurial rights familiar in the manorial economies of the later middle ages. These are well illustrated in the confirmation issued by *Dom* Manuel in 1496 of the captaincy of the northern part of Santiago in the Cape Verde Islands to Rodrigo Afonso.

He is to have rights in

> all wind mills, prohibiting anyone else from building one without licence of the *donatário* . . . likewise no-one may have a water mill without a licence; that he shall have from all the sawmills one mark of silver *per annum* or an equivalent value or the mills shall pay one-tenth of the planks sawn each week as is paid in other things; and there shall be tithe on all engines for exploiting mines; he shall be able to hire bread ovens, other people being allowed to have them but not to hire them; in the same way, as long as the *donatário* has salt to sell no-one else may indulge in this commerce . . . (*451*, vol 1, 47).

Most captaincies were hereditary, but the king reserved the right to exclude unsuitable persons. A woman, *Dona* Branca d'Aguiar, daughter of the original captain, Antonio da Noli, succeeded to the captaincy of the southern part of Santiago in 1497 and *Dom* Manuel was careful to make the proviso that she should marry the man of his choosing (*451*, vol 1, 51).

The *donatários* successfully developed their islands. By the end of the fifteenth century Madeira had a prosperous agricultural population and had become an archbishopric. It was the first great sugar island of the modern world. The Cape Verde group also prospered for a time. Trade with Guinea developed and the islands became regular stopping-places for the Africa fleets. Santiago received special privileges as a royal town and a cathedral church was constructed on the island. S. Thomé, which became a captaincy in 1485, also developed as a sugar island and as a base for trade with the Congo. Until 1535 it was a penal colony and received many of the Jews exiled under *Dom* Manuel's persecution. It developed a sugar industry and it was illegal traders from S. Thomé who founded the settlement that was eventually to grow into the great city of Luanda. The successful colonisation of the islands suggested an extension of the system to mainland areas, but this was soon discovered to raise problems of a wholly new dimension.

Along the Brazilian coast the vast distances were forbidding and the presence of Indians an unknown hazard. The fifteen captaincies established in 1534 on the advice of Martim Afonso de Sousa each had a coastline of fifty leagues and a hinterland undefined and as yet unconquered, but extending in theory as far as the Tordesillas line. The terms of the donation charters (*cartas de doação*) did not, however, differ in concept from the earlier island charters. The crown reserved to itself certain commercial and fiscal rights and the cognisance of certain criminal cases which included treason, heresy, forgery and sodomy and all serious charges brought against privileged persons. Beyond this the *donatário* had full jurisdiction, including the right to inflict the death penalty. The crown also reserved the right to send a royal official to investigate the conditions within the captaincies.

The *donatário* made grants of land and received *foros* from the settlers; he could impose monopolies over salt pans, mills, etc.; he could tax river transport, slaves and fish. He could found towns and villages and appoint their administrators and he was bound to defend his captaincy. Although the rights of the settlers were guaranteed in a *carta de foro*, they could seek redress for grievances only from the man most likely to be their oppressor.

After a false start trading dye-wood, the colonists of Brazil began to develop sugar and struck up their disreputable alliance with the slavers of West Africa and Angola. However, the scale of operations proved to be too great for the limited resources of the *donatários* and only four of the captaincies grew beyond struggling coastal settlements.

The last and largest of the captaincies was also the greatest fiasco. Paulo Dias de Novais, a grandson of Bartholomew Dias, had travelled in the service of the king of Portugal to the Congo and the court of the Ngola. There he and his companions had been detained for five years. Dias' charter was born out of a welter of conflicting motives; *pietas* to the memory of the greatest of the Portuguese navigators; a reward for Paulo's own services; the militancy of the Jesuit missionaries, tired of fruitlessly waiting on the devious whims of African monarchs; the lust for silver and the desire to close the Cuanza to the contraband traders from S. Thomé.

Dias' captaincy ran for thirty-five leagues south of the Cuanza.

Of these Dias himself could acquire twenty as his own domain, but the charter was unusual in that it also appointed him captain for life of a further stretch of coast between the Dande and the Cuanza rivers. Dias' charter also contained very specific obligations. He enjoyed privileges similar to those of the Brazilian captains but undertook to settle four hundred soldiers and one hundred families, to breed horses, build forts and churches and explore the African coast southwards.

Paulo Dias had first to conquer his captaincy and he was faced by a skilful and well-organised enemy very different from the Brazilian Indian. After fifteen years he died, having made little progress and having failed to fulfil the terms of his contract (*320, 42-48*).

The captaincy had been pioneered by the Portuguese royal family as a way of settling and defending its vast new territories. It was continued only so long as it served royal interests. The greatest danger clearly was that the crown might lose control of the captaincy once it was successfully established. There was never any chance of the island captaincies asserting their independence of Portugal. They were too vulnerable to attack by sea. When the captains of S. Thomé began to harbour and encourage illegal traders, the crown moved in swiftly and extinguished the captaincy in 1522.

Similar action was taken when it was realised that the captains in Brazil and Angola were not the peaceful harbingers of Christianity and colonial development that the king had hoped. In 1549 a governor was sent to Brazil to take over some of the powers of the captains. In Angola Paulo Dias' charter was not renewed after his death and Angola was ruled by a royal governor. The extent to which freebooters from S. Thomé and Angola had undermined the policy of peaceful co-operation in the Congo made the Portuguese very wary of allowing mainland colonies to develop under the independent control of a *donatário*.

The Portuguese captaincy bridged two worlds. Originating in a 'bastard feudal' society pre-occupied with the problems of land and the concepts of chivalry and the crusade, the captaincy was a feudal institution to the extent that it was conceived as a set of personal relationships linking individuals through land grants, services and rents. Yet it looks forward to the great chartered companies of the Dutch and the English, for in Brazil and Angola the economic objectives of the captaincy are as pronounced as the military and political (*400*).

The captaincy was a fruitful experiment in government and

organisation on a world scale. It shows the great creativity of the Portuguese in the era of the discoveries, and a mentality adaptable, expansive and capable of response to environment and changing conditions, in marked contrast to the rigidity and corrupt inefficiency of later years.

Empire in the East

In 1628 *Dom* Nuno Alvares Pereira petitioned the royal council for the grant of a captaincy to extend from the Cape of Good Hope to Inhambane (*282*). The request was refused and this remains the only occasion an attempt was made to extend the captaincy system to the East. From the very beginning Portugal's empire in the East had been a totally new conception.

Down the west coast of Africa the Portuguese had felt their way like a blind man, advancing often painfully slowly and with little idea of what they were looking for or where they were likely to find themselves. The first voyage to India was quite different. Elaborate preparations were made lasting nearly a decade and information was gathered and sifted before Vasco da Gama eventually sailed.

Pero da Covilhão and Afonso de Paiva set off in 1487 to spy out the way and their letters sent back to Lisbon via Cairo described the Muslim trading system of the Indian Ocean. When the monsoon began to blow towards Africa in October, fleets of lateen-rigged dhows set off from the Hadramaut, the Persian Gulf and the west coast of India. Brass-ware, glass, porcelain, cloth and beads were landed at one of the scores of little Swahili ports stretching from Melinde in northern Kenya as far south as Sofala and Inhambane. Most of the dhow captains belonged to the cosmopolitan Muslim culture of the Indian Ocean and the Portuguese referred to them simply as *mouros*—a term more all-embracing than the courtesy title of Arab which English-speaking writers confer on them.

Covilhão also visited India, Calicut, Goa and Cananor where he learnt the details of the spice trade and the close commercial connections of western India with Persian Muscat and Ormuz. He travelled to the Persian Gulf and Arabia and became the first Christian known to have visited Mecca. He eventually settled in Ethiopia where he married and lived out the last thirty years of his life (*303*, 369–76). His reconnaissance, and the empire that was successfully built upon it, were exactly copied a century later when Jan Huygen van Linschoten visited the Portuguese towns in the East and reported back to the rebel Dutch provinces. Unfortunately Covilhão left no record comparable to the *Beschryvinge ven verscheyde Landen* . . .

On the west coast of Africa the Portuguese had achieved a considerable diplomatic success in forming alliances with African rulers and using their favour to establish commerce. *Dom* Manuel hoped that this tactic could be repeated in the East. What should have been a purely commercial venture, however, became confused with the expectation that the kingdom of Prester John would be found and that the projected alliance would be first and foremost a religious one.

If this was the king's idea, it received a rude blow through Vasco da Gama's conduct on his first voyage. The great navigator was no diplomat. He quarrelled his way up the African coast and across to Calicut, alienating most of the rulers with whom he had relations. The trade goods he brought found no market in the East and he discovered that the Muslim trading community had a far closer alliance with the Hindu Samorin of Calicut than he could ever obtain. Even his report of the discovery of a Christian community with their elaborate churches turned out later to be a Portuguese Catholic's first experience of Hindu religion. Cabral's voyage to the East in 1500 was, if anything, still more disastrous and ended with the Portuguese bombarding Calicut.

The commercial failure of the early voyages to India profoundly influenced the development of imperial strategy. If the Portuguese could bring little from Europe which would repay transport to the sophisticated markets of the East, they would have to take over the role of middle-men from the Muslims and trade East African gold and ivory for the spices which fetched such a high price in Europe.

It was with this objective in mind that *Dom* Francisco de Almeida was sent in 1505 as the first governor of Portuguese India with orders to 'prevent any more spices from passing to the lands of the Sultan and persuade all the peoples of India to put aside the fantasy that they can ever again trade with any but ourselves' (*258*, 227). Almeida and his immediate successor, Afonso de Albuquerque, evolved a simple and daring strategy. Portuguese commerce in the East was to rest on sea-power. One fleet was to remain permanently in Indian waters driving Portugal's competitors from the sea-routes and protecting the trading ships, while an annual voyage to and from Europe took home the spices and brought out the munitions, manpower and supplies.

The success of this plan rested on the superiority of the Portuguese at sea. By the early sixteenth century the *nau* was replacing the *caravella* on the major ocean routes and Portuguese shipwrights made use of the magnificent timbers of the tropics to construct ships in India. These very soon outstripped contemporary European ship design and the great India-built carracks secured for Portugal control of the eastern seas for a hundred years. The only serious challenge in the sixteenth century came from the Turks, the spread of whose power through Egypt and Mesopotamia towards India was contemporaneous with the rise of Portuguese power in the East. The Turkish galleys with their shallow draught and independence of the monsoons made excellent commerce raiders but were not powerful enough to challenge the Portuguese on the high seas.

The weakness of Almeida's plan had been his reluctance to commit the Portuguese to garrisoning their own ports, though he did establish forts at Sofala and Kilwa. Albuquerque had a better understanding of the precarious position of a Portuguese fleet dependent on the goodwill of an Indian or Muslim ally but in his turn seemed not to count the cost of his enterprises. By the time he died in 1515 Portuguese bases had been constructed to dominate the Persian Gulf at Ormuz and Muscat, the west coast of India at Goa, Cochin and Diu, and Indonesia at Malacca. Only Aden and the Red Sea eluded Portuguese control, though Socotra was occupied for a short time and the alliance with the Christian emperor of Ethiopia helped to control this outlet.

The Portuguese empire in the East was a bureaucratic and military structure in marked contrast to the feudal and commercial elements in her empire in the Atlantic. At the head of the administrative hierarchy was the viceroy or governor of the State of India resident at Goa, whose term of office was usually only three years. Directly beneath him were the captains of the fortresses. In the sixteenth and seventeenth century it was common for the captains to purchase their commands, though sometimes these were granted as rewards for service or even as compensation to the widow or orphan of a dead servant of the crown. During his tenure of office—which in Moçambique was three years—the captain had a commercial monopoly from which he was expected to derive profits sufficient to pay for the expenses of the garrison, fort and administration of his command and to recoup his own private fortunes. No greater temptation could

14

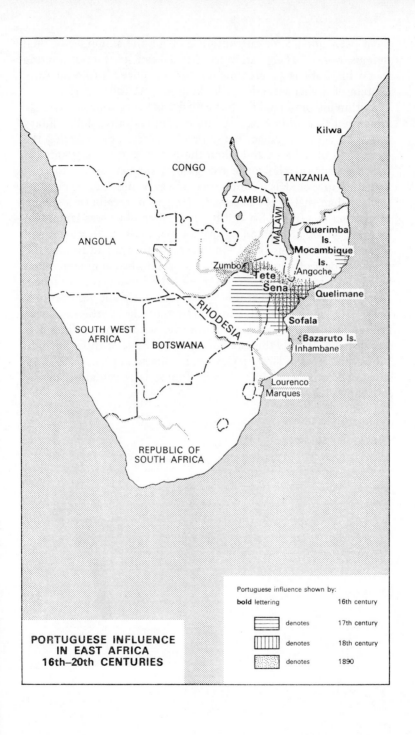

PORTUGUESE INFLUENCE
IN EAST AFRICA
16th–20th CENTURIES

Portuguese influence shown by:

bold lettering	16th century
denotes	17th century
denotes	18th century
denotes	1890

CONGO

TANZANIA

Kilwa

ZAMBIA

MALAWI

ANGOLA

Querimba Is.
Mocambique Is.

Zumbo **Tete**
Sena Angoche
Quelimane

RHODESIA

Sofala

SOUTH WEST AFRICA

BOTSWANA

Bazaruto Is.
Inhambane

Lourenco Marques

REPUBLIC OF SOUTH AFRICA

have been offered for corruption and for the skimping of vital defence works. 'The greatest proof a man can give for not wanting to do his duty is to give money for an office,' wrote an early captain of Sofala severely to the king in 1518 (*262*, *573*).

Within his command the fort captain had very wide powers. He appointed to a wide range of minor administrative and military posts, he acted as judge in the first instance, he controlled the commerce of his area and when there was land to be granted it was the captain who made the grants, subject always to confirmation in Goa. His position was, however, much more circumscribed than that of the *donatário*. He was in receipt of a stream of instructions from Goa and his general conduct was laid down in the *regimento*, or standing orders, with which he was issued when he took up his post. Moreover, he always had to face the near prospect of a judicial investigation into his command when he surrendered it to his successor, and the faction rivalries in the State of India meant that this was a not infrequent occurrence.

For the most part the jurisdiction of the Portuguese was limited to their own nationals and slaves within the confines of a fort or town. In only three regions did the 'State of India' include substantial areas of land, in Ceylon, in Goa and in Zambesia. The story of Portuguese settlement in Zambesia is contained in the following chapters.

2 The Environment

The river

The Zambesi flows nearly two thousand miles from its source on the Zambian border with Angola to the Indian Ocean. Its upper reaches cross the Kalahari sands of the Barotse plain, and it is possible that at one time the waters of this system drained southwards to the Kalahari Desert and Lake Ngami. Every year the river floods the Barotse plain, causing a migration of farmers from winter to summer villages and gardens, but in spite of the problems caused by these floods this area of the upper Zambesi has always attracted settlement and has endured through the rise and fall of many African state systems.

At Livingstone the Zambesi plunges three hundred feet into the Batoka gorge which zig-zags for sixty miles along a fault in the basalt and takes the river across the Batoka plain. From there to the Luangwa confluence the river again follows a geological fault—the Gwembe trough. On this stretch the Zambesi is often confined between narrow walls of rock, but the valley itself is not a single groove cut by the floods in their passage over the Karoo sands. Instead it winds through a belt of broken country as much as twenty miles deep on each side, and this broken escarpment in some areas effectively prevents easy access to the Zambesi for those living on the high veldt. At Mpata and Kariba the river is blocked by intrusive granite barriers through which it has cut a passage of rapids and racing water impossible to navigate. The climate here is hot and humid with little rainfall (477, 388–427).

At the Luangwa confluence the river enters Moçambique. It crosses two more granite barriers at Cabora Bassa and Lupata where the river is once again confined between narrow walls and reduced to a breadth of 300 yards. From Lupata, the Zambesi, now immensely swollen by the waters of the Luangwa and the Kafue and shortly to be joined by those of the Shire, spreads out over a vast sandy bed extending in places up to five miles across, but with a mean width of between one and two miles. The escarpment recedes north and south and where the valley is wide the settlement is thicker while the easy flow of the river makes navigation in canoes possible over long stretches.

The Zambesi drains half a million square miles of central African grassland. Seasonal rains falling from November to April on the high veldt drain rapidly into the valley so that by April the river has swollen to ten times its October volume. In the narrow confines of the Batoka or Cabora Bassa gorges this rise in the waters may be quite dramatic. David Livingstone thought that at Cabora Bassa the floods lifted the river eighty feet above its dry season level.

In its wider reaches, however, the floods spread out over the whole breadth of the river bed, drowning islands and sand banks and hiding the main channel of the river. Although the depth of the water may rise anything from five to ten feet at this time, navigation is made little easier, for river craft have difficulty finding the channel and have to battle against a stronger current. Livingstone observed that, although a sudden rise in the water level would bring down mud and other matter, the water of the Zambesi was at all other times 'almost chemically pure, and the photographer would find that it is nearly as good as distilled water for the nitrate of silver bath.' (390, 70) It is widely believed today that the Zambesi is free from bilharzia.

The immense volume of the Zambesi's waters has relatively little impact on the climate of its valley, where the annual rainfall is lower than that of the high veldt. At Tete the mean annual rainfall is twenty inches compared with the notoriously drought-prone area of Bulawayo which has a mean rainfall of twenty-four inches. For six months of the year no rain falls at all and down to the very margin of the river the vegetation is the familiar parkland and bush-veldt of Rhodesia, although baobabs flourish in the slightly greater humidity. Surprising as it may seem, it is a frequent occurrence for the Zambesi valley to be devastated by drought and famine. The explorer Lacerda recorded in 1798 that men dropped dead in the very streets of Tete after a famine that had lasted for four years, and Filipe Almeida De Eça records the famine that struck Zambesia between 1917 and 1919 as the result of the dislocations of war and, on this occasion, an exceptional flooding of the river. 20,000 deaths he records as the toll of famine in those years (298, 61).

The coastal region and the delta are, however, quite different.

At Quelimane the annual rainfall is fifty-two inches—one of the highest in southern Africa—and rain falls continuously throughout the year. The vegetation of the delta and coastal regions is correspondingly more luxuriant. Tall forest trees flourish, palms, papyrus and ferns, banana and sugar as well as a great variety of aquatic plants are all in marked contrast to the dry grasslands fifty miles in the interior.

Although the lower Zambesi is fairly thickly settled, the hot, dry valley does not encourage human civilisation. The low and unreliable rainfall makes agriculture difficult. Crops grown on the river bank or on the islands, which would have all the water they require, are at the mercy of sudden rises in the river and of marauding hippopotami. Cattle which thrive on the grasslands of central Africa are destroyed by tsetse fly once they descend the escarpment. Tsetse fly seems to have been a very ancient inhabitant of the Zambesi valley, for Francisco Barreto lost all his horses at Sena in 1572 through some mysterious disease which was probably sleeping sickness. Malaria and other fevers carried by mosquitoes or water weaken man and sap his energies and, although in fishing and hunting the Zambesi compensates for its lack of generosity in other ways, the advantages which the river offers for trade and human communication are largely nullified by the extreme difficulties of navigation.

As they cross the Kalahari and Karoo sands of the upper river, the Zambesi floods lift and carry with them thousands of tons of sand. Where the river broadens and the flow decreases the sand is dropped to form islands and sand banks. Above the Victoria Falls, for example, the river splays out on a front a mile wide and the stream is broken by a maze of islands covered with dense vegetation, the resort of all kinds of wild game. These wide stretches of the river are cut short by the gorges and rapids caused by the intrusive granite blocks. Here the current quickens, the sand is lifted and carried on, and it is not until the Moçambique plain is reached that the full impact of the silting of the river is felt. As the water falls in May and June what was once a wide river becomes an immense bed of sand dunes, pools and tortuous streams which dry up one by one. By July and August the main channel may have sunk to a hundred yards in width and even this is blocked by sand-bars covered with only one foot of water.

Every year the main channel alters and in five years the whole bed and course of the river may become completely unrecognisable. E. D. Young, who led the mission of the Free Church of

Scotland to Lake Nyasa and who had visited the Zambesi in 1863, found that

> the course of the Zambesi had altered a great deal in the neigh-
> bourhood of Mount Morumbala since I was last there . . . The
> land lying in the fork of the junction of the two rivers (Zambesi
> and Shire) is at the best of times, little more than a swampy
> plain sacred to buffaloes and waterbuck and mosquitoes. Two
> years ago an extraordinary flood occurred, and the mighty
> torrent of the Zambesi put forth all its power. One consequence
> is that it no longer keeps its even course from Sena, but takes a
> turn through a great shallow lake to the confusion of those who
> now almost despair of finding the waters of the Shire in the
> various currents that mingle there. (*480*, 29–30.)

This capacity of the Zambesi to metamorphose itself is bad enough on the upper river; near the delta it makes navigation a nightmare. The delta covers two thousand five hundred square miles and has a sea frontage of fifty miles. It is probable that in the sixteenth century the Qua Qua river was one of the mouths of the Zambesi, but centuries of Zambesi floods have choked the exit so that in Livingstone's day only exceptionally high floods opened a way from the main river to the tidal Qua Qua opposite Quelimane town.

In the seventeenth century the Portuguese sometimes used the Luabo mouth at the southern end of the delta and this kept a reputation for being the best entrance to the river (*351*, 305–8). However, the bar was dangerous and in the eighteenth century the only direct access from the sea to the Zambesi for a boat was through a series of tortuous channels, blocked by trees and under-growth. In 1858 Livingstone discovered that the Kongone, or Inhamissengo, mouth would take fairly large vessels but he recorded that the river was so rapidly altering its course that it would soon be closed.

> During the period of our acquaintance with the Kongone,
> about eighty yards were washed away on one side and deposited
> on the other. A navigable channel by Nyangalule was quite
> filled up, and Pearl Island nearly all washed away. As nothing
> is done to preserve the channel, it will soon be as shallow as
> the Lilambe, and entirely useless for navigation. (*391*, 32.)

In 1889 Daniel Rankin discovered that the Chinde river had

a bar of three fathoms. This was greeted as a great discovery by those who did not know the river. A town grew up and the British obtained a concession on the water-front and built offices and warehouses. Within two seasons the Zambesi had almost totally consumed the foreshore. Chinde town was hastily dismantled and moved further from the reach of the floods. For five brief years Chinde flourished as a port of entry, though it was found that steamers drawing more than eighteen inches had great difficulties navigating the river. By 1894 Chinde bar was closing and the development of Beira as a port led to the virtual abandonment of any attempt to use the Zambesi as a port for central Africa.

To take any boat larger than a canoe up the Zambesi, therefore, presented almost insuperable problems. From Tete to the sea trade could be carried on small river boats; above Tete the way was not only closed to navigation by the Cabora Bassa rapids but was even impassable for foot-travellers who had to make wide detours. As a highway to the interior the Zambesi has been all but useless and the long distance trade routes of Africa have crossed and recrossed the valley but have never moved far along its floor. The great African civilisations of the central grasslands have shunned the unhealthy, fly-ridden valley. The escarpment has been a frontier and the valley itself a no-man's land which migratory nations might cross but where they would never settle, and where dynasties fugitive from political upheaval on the high veldt could live out the twilight of their existence.

Few of the world's great rivers have so persistently failed to play the role of the 'cradle of civilisation'.

People south of the Zambesi

The Shona peoples of the Rhodesian high veldt and the different 'tribal' groups which live along the Moçambique coast and on the lower Zambesi are among the longest established of all Africa's populations. Portuguese historians of the sixteenth century spoke of the Botonga and the Mokaranga inhabiting the valley and the high lands, and Tonga and Karanga are still among the 'tribes' of this region today, although a score of different dialects and names now disguise the common linguistic and cultural origins of the peoples of this area. This diversity, however, is strong evidence of antiquity as no group who had arrived in recent times could possibly have acquired such variety.

Climate has caused a certain amount of this cultural diversity. In the dry lands of south-west Rhodesia where rainfall is little more than twenty inches a year and where drought may last for years on end, the dry grasslands and low trees best support a cattle economy. Towards the north-east rainfall increases and becomes more reliable and the northern part of the high veldt has always aided a mixed economy; cattle thrive on the grasslands but vegetables and grain are also grown and stored. The coasts and the Zambesi valley are hot and humid. All kinds of fruit and vegetables thrive but animal husbandry is hazardous, so that the inhabitants of this area are almost wholly tillers of the soil.

The first iron users lived south of the Zambesi as early as A.D. 300 (*348*, 59). A thousand years later they, or some other immigrant group, were beginning to elaborate the timeless pattern of village agriculture. In the gold-bearing granite of the south large hill-top towns grew up. By 1300 the traditional reed fences which linked the huts in each village were being replaced by stone walls made from granite blocks prised off the smooth, bare hillside after firing. The art of building in stone grew more sophisticated. It spread throughout what is today Rhodesia and into Moçambique. The buildings became immense in size and very varied in function. Stone platforms with decorated façade supported whole villages of reed and dagga huts; circular stone enclosures surrounded settlements; covered stone passageways, towers and flights of steps helped to form immense complexes of buildings covering many acres of ground.

Three principal features of this civilisation provided the stimulus for the Shona to develop their traditionally meagre material culture and to bring the small segmented units of their society into large state systems. These features are the gold trade with the Swahili merchants of the monsoon coast of eastern Africa, the religious cults, and the dominance of the chiefly clan of the Roswi. These created a strong stream of cultural continuity which enabled the Shona to survive internal political upheavals, the invasion of the firearms, the mercenaries and missionaries of the Portuguese and even to some extent the far more devastating ravages of the Ngoni hordes of the nineteenth century (*302*).

Gold was produced throughout all the country south of the Zambesi. It was panned in the rivers and dug out of the termite hills but deeper level mining was also known and modern operations have uncovered ancient pits and galleries—some as much as 150 feet beneath the surface. The gold collected all over the country was brought to trading fairs to be taxed by the chief and to be sold to the merchants. The merchants then set off along the trade route to Sofala or across the Zambesi to one of the Swahili ports north of the delta. At the coast the agents of the Islamic trading houses of Kilwa, or one of the other northern cities, bought the gold and other local produce in exchange for cloth, metal work and exotic goods from the east which included Chinese porcelain. Before the arrival of the Portuguese, Sofala was the principal port. It was a commercial appendage of Kilwa, and was also conveniently close to the centre of the Shona power at Great Zimbabwe (*312*).

During the fifteenth century this pattern of relationships changed significantly. Building at Zimbabwe ceased and the centre of Shona power shifted northwards to the Mount Darwin region where it remained until the end of the seventeenth century. The old trade route to Sofala declined and Kilwa itself began to feel the cold winds of change.

Perhaps this movement northwards was politically inspired because it coincided with the rise to pre-eminence among the Shona of the Roswi dynasty of the Mwene Mutapa. The Roswi were members of a system of related chiefly dynasties which maintained a dominant political position south of the Zambesi until the invasions of the Ngoni in the nineteenth century. These Roswi dynasties recognised no paramount chief, ruling now in a state of feudal anarchy, now acknowledging a *primus inter pares*. If new land was conquered by a Roswi chief, a Roswi sub-chief would be installed to found a new Roswi sub-dynasty. They may originally have been immigrants who established their supremacy by bringing with them the mystique of chieftainship; they may have owed their position to their control of the cult of Mwari with its network of mediums, and to the prestige attached to the shrines of the Roswi ancestral spirits. Whatever their origin they were a powerful force binding Shona society and upholding its civilisation (*302*).

The Roswi dynasty of Mbire began to build its power in the fourteenth century. In the middle of the fifteenth century the fifth in line of the dynasty, Nyatsimba Mutota, emerged as the dominant military figure south of the Zambesi. He established his power in the high veldt and successfully invaded the Zambesi valley and the Moçambique lowlands. His prowess won him paramountcy over all the Shona peoples and their immediate neighbours. He received the praise name Mwene Mutapa which became the dynastic title of all his successors. It was he who moved the centre of the Roswi power north from Great Zimbabwe (*292*, 62-3).

The rise of a new dynasty, however, does not by itself explain the drastic change in the patterns of trade and political life which resulted from the movement northward. More probably the explanation is economic. Centuries of exploitation had made gold costly to mine in the southern regions. In the north were fresh goldfields more easily exploited. The Roswi *mambos* moved north the better to supervise the collection and trading of gold in this new area, and at the same time to take advantage of the new trade routes which were opening up. Swahili dissidents from Kilwa had recently founded small settlements at Quelimane, Moçambique and Angoche just north of the Zambesi delta. These ports were well sited to profit from the new goldfields. Outposts of these settlements were built on the Zambesi whence a few days march led to the Mashonaland high veldt and the trading fairs. Meanwhile the Sofala trade declined, and with it the wealth and importance of the parent city of Kilwa (*397*, 162-3). The Portuguese have often been blamed for the decline of Kilwa and Sofala both of which fell into insignificance during the sixteenth century. Probably they only hastened a decline which had already begun as much as fifty years before their arrival in east Africa.

The paramountcy established by Nyatsima Mutota did not long survive his death. His grandson, Nyahuma, had already lost control of much of the south and centre of the high veldt region by the end of the fifteenth century. Thenceforward the 'empire' of Mwene Mutapa became only one among many independent states dominated by Roswi dynasties, though the fiction of the existence of an empire was maintained by the Portuguese to serve their own purposes. The pattern of chieftaincies which emerged from the fall of the short-lived Mbire paramountcy remained unchanged in its essentials until the nineteenth century. As the largest of these chieftaincies will be among the important *dramatis personae* of this history, they may be usefully introduced at this stage.

Changamire was the praise name of the Roswi *mambo* who successfully rebelled against Nyahuma (*257*, *393*). This name was assumed as the title of a powerful dynasty which came to dominate the south-west of what is today Rhodesia. The country

24

of the Changamire dynasty was called by the Portuguese Abutua —a name which appears in Antonio Fernandes' account of his journeys into the interior contained in a manuscript of 1515 or 1516 (*470*, 24). This chieftaincy flourished most vigorously after the successful war against the Portuguese in 1693. It was responsible for the construction of the last of the great stone hill-towns which exist today in Matabeleland. The chieftaincy finally collapsed under the onslaught of the *impis* of Ngwana and Zwangendaba about 1833, though the spirit cults of the dead Roswi *mambos* survived the fall of Roswi political power (*437*, ch 1).

Mwene Mutapas continued to rule in northern Mashonaland until the disastrous war of 1693 when the dynasty was dragged down in the collapse of Portuguese power on the high veldt. Thereafter the chieftaincy precariously survived in the hot, unhealthy, mountainous region round the Cabora Bassa rapids and upstream from there along the right bank of the Zambesi. The people of this truncated chieftaincy are variously called by the Portuguese, but include Tavara, Va-dema and Makorekore.

The most important of the smaller chieftaincies which grew to fill the vacuum left by the decline of the power of the Mwene Mutapa were the Makoni dynasty of Maungwe and the Mtoko chieftaincy whose independence was only finally extinguished by the British South Africa Company in the 1890s. In the mountainous regions of the east the chieftaincy of Manica, though always small, is of great antiquity. Originally ruled by the Chicanga dynasty, this kingdom passed under the Mutassa dynasty in the early nineteenth century before the whole area was partitioned in 1891 between British and Portuguese.

Between the Manica mountains and Sofala lay the chieftaincy of Quiteve. Never a very powerful political force, Quiteve fell increasingly under the sway of the Portuguese *conquistadores* in the early seventeenth century. It is nevertheless one of the best known of these chieftaincies, for there have been a number of excellent Portuguese descriptions of the customs, beliefs and institutions of the Teve people (*387, 445*).

The triangle of territory between Sena, Sofala and the Zambesi delta was the area most effectively and continuously occupied by the Portuguese. The only large chieftaincy to maintain its independence there was that of Makombe of Barue. This most historic state is mentioned in 1506 and survived until the campaign of 1902, although the old Barue aristocracy and the mediums of the ancestor cults were able to stage a most formidable rebellion against colonial rule as late as 1917 (*436*).

The peoples who inhabit the Zambesi valley are all connected by centuries of contacts and intermarriage. Nevertheless they maintain separate dialects and clearly separate identities. On the south bank from the Luenha to Sena are the Tonga. They are closely related to the Barue Tonga who in turn are closely linked with the main branches of the Shona-speaking peoples. The term 'Tonga' has the connotation of a subject people in many African languages. The Tonga of the lower Zambesi share many clan names and much common territory with the A-Sena who live in the area round the town of Sena. The A-Sena are sometimes said to be more closely linked with the Manganja of the north bank and clearly they have assimilated elements from north and south of the river and today bear the imprint of having lived for centuries alongside Christians and Muslims in the busy and almost cosmopolitan world of the lower Zambesi (*379*).

Up-river of the Tonga and beyond the Luenha are people called the Nhungue. Nhungue is the African name for Tete, and the Nhungue dialect is widely spoken on the river. The Nhungue were brought under Portuguese rule early in the seventeenth century, if not earlier. Nhungue country reaches upstream to the Cabora Bassa rapids beyond which the Va-dema and the Makorekore take the river beyond the Portuguese sphere (*446*, 104–6).

The gold trade and the historic chiefly dynasties of the Shona are two of the strands of continuity in their history—the third and perhaps most important strand is provided by the various religious cults. The importance of these lies in their permanence in a world of shifting political loyalties and extensive disruption to normal life.

The Shona peoples believe in the existence of a supreme being variously called Mwari, Mwali, Mlimo or Morimo. He may be approached either directly by means of offerings and prayers made at certain well-known shrines, or indirectly through the intercession of ancestor spirits. The spirits of the dead are directly concerned with the fate of the living, and each Shona family honours and respects its ancestors. The spirits of dead chiefs are thought to be able to communicate with the living by means of spirit mediums called *mhondoros* or *pondoros*. Among these spirit mediums a hierarchy exists based on the antiquity and veneration of the chief with whom they communicate. The oldest chiefs are almost mythological figures, like

Chaminuka, but others are well-known historical personalities. Through the mouth of the mediums (who are usually chosen from outside the tribe) a dead chief wields a powerful political influence. He will, for instance, have a lot to say about succession disputes.

The spirit mediums are, therefore, a very powerful priestly class and a focus for loyalty to which people can turn in time of need. The spirit mediums of dead Mwene Mutapas, for instance, outlived the demise of the chieftaincy itself and remain important personages today. As one of their functions is to remember and recite traditions of the dead chiefs, they are also an important factor in establishing the continuity of Shona culture.

The shrines of Mwari in the south of the country are also served by a priesthood which may be responsible for the transmission of the oracles of Mwari. This cult may have been associated with the Roswi Changamires and have developed as a powerful institution of their state in the eighteenth century.

Both cults provided strong traditional bonds for a people who were to suffer terrible disasters in the nineteenth century but were able to emerge from them politically broken but culturally vigorous. The *mhondoro* cult is perhaps the more important for this history—not only because it was based in the north and closely associated with the Mwene Mutapas, but also because it was readily adaptable and over the centuries there is evidence that a number of Europeans of great reputation acquired their own *mhondoros* and were venerated after their death by the local population.

People north of the Zambesi

The country north and north-east of the Zambesi was not generally known to the Portuguese until the eighteenth century, when the discovery of gold lured prospectors and traders into the interior. However, news of the northern hinterland did reach the Zambesi settlements and was recorded by the Portuguese chroniclers so that the history of this region acquires some depth of historical perspective.

The people who live north of the Zambesi between the Luangwa and the sea belong to two distinct cultural traditions. East of Lake Nyasa and the Shire valley are the Makua and the Yao; west of this line are the various groups of Marave origin. The Makua are almost certainly earlier arrivals than the Marave,

27

part of whose migration from the north-west took place in historic times.

The Marave may have been a whole nation who pressed the Makua steadily eastwards, or they may have been a comparatively small group of chiefly invaders whose military prowess or techniques of chieftainship enabled them to dominate the populations already settled on the land and to impose a certain cultural uniformity on them. Such a superimposition of a ruling dynasty on an established population would explain the underlying diversities which emerged when the ruling Marave paramountcies were weakened in the eighteenth century. It would also explain such curious features as the existence of two leading Cewa clans at the present—the clan of the chiefs and the clan of the rainmakers, the chiefs being descendants of the invaders and the rainmakers of an older more rooted stock (401, 378).

The Marave are first heard of in 1506 but only became well-established between the Luangwa and the Shire in the last quarter of the sixteenth century when a group under chief Rundo, probably the easternmost section of the Marave, clashed violently with the Portuguese. A fragment of this group appears to have crossed the Shire and, according to local tradition overrun the coastal Makua in the hinterland of Angoche. Makua chiefs in this area still claim descent from invading *ma-rundu* (397, 119-122). It is possible that this horde went on northwards to attack Mombassa and Melinde in 1587. In 1592 and 1593 the Portuguese made two disastrous attempts to check the rising power of Rundo in the region immediately north of their settlements. The defeats the Portuguese suffered and their fear of the Marave, which survived for at least fifty years, may well have encouraged the gruesome tales of cannibalism which the chroniclers told of these people and which were so widely believed and embellished in Europe (343, 402-10). These 'cannibals' the Portuguese called *Ma-zimba*—a name still used by a section of the Marave to the north of Tete.

At this stage there was no unity among the Marave chiefs. In the seventeenth century, however, the chroniclers refer to the establishment of a paramountcy over all the Marave chiefs by Kalonga—chief of the westernmost Marave group. The supremacy of Kalonga among the Marave was probably of the same kind as the supremacy of Mwene Mutapa south of the Zambesi, and just as fragile. It was based on a military predominance and control of the leading cults and chief trade routes with the interior. The structure of the empire, however, remained segmentary—easily built up and as easily broken down again into its component parts (*302*, 22–25).

Kalonga's paramountcy was quickly over. By the middle of the eighteenth century it was already a memory, but the acids which had eaten it away were attacking the segments also. South of the Zambesi the Portuguese had insidiously destroyed first the prestige and then the power of the Mwene Mutapas, and in the early nineteenth century the Ngoni wiped out the last of the independent Roswi states. Portuguese and Ngoni were to have the same disruptive effect north of the river among the Marave.

The break-up and dispersal of the Marave at the end of the eighteenth century are closely associated with their loss of a dominant economic position north of the Zambesi. In the early eighteenth century, Marave chiefs near the Portuguese Zambesi towns began to grant concessions of land and mining rights. During the second half of the century large tracts of land came wholly under Portuguese jurisdiction. Portuguese fairs and mining camps grew up in the interior and trade routes opened through the heart of Marave country reaching towards the Lunda kingdom of Kazembe.

The founding of Kazembe's kingdom in the early eighteenth century had consequences similar to Portuguese penetration. Kazembe and his followers were offshoots of the Lunda empire of Mwata Yamvo. In establishing themselves in what is today the northern part of Zambia, they displaced the Bisa whose subsequent wanderings turned them into a nation of itinerant or semi-itinerant traders. Before the end of the eighteenth century the Bisa had penetrated the Marave country from the interior and had established trade links with the Portuguese at Zumbo and Tete.

These developments are both symptom and cause of the break-up of the Marave state system, which may well have had some internal weakness hidden from us at this distance in time. At the end of the eighteenth century the westernmost Marave people—the Cewa—split up. Under Mwase and Mkanda two sections moved into the interior. Those who stayed behind suffered further fragmentation. The paramountcy of Undi remained established on the Kapoche river, but further to the west the Zimbas and the Pimbes gradually acquired a separate identity. Many of them came under a new chiefly dynasty descended from Portuguese Indian immigrants and became known as Macanga. Another group of Cewa settle on the

Luangwa and mixed with the local population—a union from which the present Nsenga derive their ancestry (*465*, 34–36).

This crumbling of the Marave political system was hastened by the Ngoni attack. In 1835 Zwangendaba crossed the Zambesi and harried the country north of Tete, and in 1839 or 1840 he was followed by Nqaba's Ngoni. Both groups disappeared northwards but Zwangendaba's son, Mpeseni, returned in the 1850s and settled in the region immediately to the north of the Marave chieftaincies of Macanga and Undi. These now felt the brunt of Ngoni raids and although the Macanga under their Indo-Portuguese dynasty were able to resist, Undi and his people were laid wide open to attack. The great prestige of Undi survived this onslaught and his paramountcy over the Cewa is still recognised today, but for a time in the second half of the nineteenth century this proud Marave state was reduced to a few rocky fastnesses in the mountains (*354*).

Further east the Marave were most thickly settled in the Shire valley and round the end of Lake Nyasa. The people of this region became known as Manganja and, although the chieftainship of Rundo must have been in serious decline, there were few incursions into the area until the middle of the nineteenth century (*391*). Thereafter disintegration proceeded rapidly. Portuguese adventurers pressed up the Shire hunting for slaves and ivory, and the Manganja of the lower Shire fell under the domination of another Indo-Portuguese family and became known as the Massingire. Around the Murchison cataracts dynasties of Kololo chiefs—originally porters in Livingstone's service—set themselves up over the local population, while from the rear Yao invaders, who had links with the Makua and the Swahili slaving ports of the Angoche coast, first raided and then settled in the Shire Highlands. In the 1860s the picture was completed by the reappearance of Maseko's Ngoni whose incursions into the Shire Highlands caused so much anxiety to the Scots missions.

As with the Shona, it would be wrong to stress the political chaos into which the Marave state system dissolved and forget the deeper cohesion which these societies possessed in their various segments. Villages and clans survived the major disasters because their bonds of loyalty and their whole pattern of existence were not really dependent on the larger political units. A single village, self-sufficient with its local industries and food supply might well survive when its neighbours were laid waste, and this strength of the village economy has undoubtedly been one of the

30

major sources of resilience for African people of all ages. More-over, as with the Shona, there were influential rainmaking and ancestor cults which functioned independent of politics, and which flourish today, though they still remain largely hidden from the profane gaze of white historians (*434*).

3 The Portuguese Penetration of Central Africa

The failure of the Sofala factory

East African gold and ivory purchased the Indian spices which were Portugal's main quest in the east. Without the control of this trade the Portuguese could never have competed with the Muslims in the Indian markets. This conclusion was grasped very early on by the makers of Portuguese policy, and was probably the advice which Pero da Covilhão had sent back to Portugal in the early 1490s. In 1505 Almeida's fleet, on the way to India, left Pero d'Anhaia at Sofala to establish a fort and factory to control the trade in gold. From Sofala Almeida passed to Kilwa where, after the fierce resistance of the local inhabitants, another fort was established. These two strong positions, together with the alliance that Vasco de Gama had made with the sultan of Melinde, were thought to be sufficient to control the whole East African seaboard.

Almeida intended that the annual fleets on their way to India should call at Sofala to pick up supplies and to drop off their sick. The fleet would then pass through the Moçambique channel to Kilwa and from there across to India. At Sofala supplies of cloth, beads and other European goods would be stored and any merchant, Portuguese, Muslim or African, could then buy from this depot and sell his gold to the factor (*260*). Annually a caravel would be sent from India to pick up the profits of the factory's trading activities.

For the first twenty years or so of its existence Sofala supported an excessively large and expensive garrison of over forty men. This garrison was always swelled by a motley selection of men awaiting the next ship to India, who consumed the supplies of the fort and contributed nothing to its wealth (*261, 277, 271, 282*). Frequent coasting expeditions were undertaken and ships were repaired and even built in the harbour but Sofala proved a costly failure. Its swampy coast line made it difficult of access

32

for the India fleets, which preferred to hurry northwards for fear of missing the monsoon and having to waste half a year in East Africa. In 1507 Almeida established a factory halfway between Sofala and Kilwa on Moçambique Island (*393*, vol 3, 129), which in 1508 was strengthened by a battery of guns. Moçambique soon proved to be a much more convenient stopping place and, after the building of the fort St Sebastian was started in 1552, it completely superseded Sofala which mouldered in obscurity until a gale and flood-tide early in this century finally demolished the remains of Pero d'Anhaia's fort.

The decline of Sofala had other causes, however. Civil war in the interior, the result of the movement northward of the Mwene Mutapa's government in the second half of the fifteenth century, was seriously disrupting trade. A second difficulty was the Portuguese failure to trade competitively. Cloth brought from Europe was not in demand in spite of its variety and the serious attempts the Portuguese made to suit the market. It proved to be too costly and Cambay cloth smuggled from India sold at half the price.

Further difficulties were caused by the meddling of the Portuguese in African politics. The captains and factors of Sofala were well-placed to acquire information about the interior and as early as 1506 were receiving embassies from inland chiefs, including one from the Mwene Mutapa himself.

The Portuguese soon discovered that African chiefs required presents before favours could be granted or business transacted. They also learnt that friendships formed in this way had political implications. Inhamunda, described by Silveira as the 'slave of Monomotapa' (*393*, vol 2, 82), was one of the chiefs favoured by the Portuguese. They backed his claim to one of the chieftaincies inland of Sofala and apparently supplied him with firearms, only to find that the power of their *protégé* grew until it dominated all the country behind the Portuguese town. It then pleased Inhamunda to cut all the routes from Sofala to the interior and lay the Portuguese under an economic blockade. Only occasionally was the blockade lifted, or were a few traders able to approach the fort secretly by bush paths left unguarded (*393*, vol 2, 62–3, 82, vol 3, 317–18, *272*, 103).

The rise to power of Inhamunda is the first clear indication of the impact of firearms on African politics; it also destroyed the whole premise on which the Portuguese had founded their eastern empire. A sea-power, no matter how dominant, depends on co-operation from the shore and the Portuguese were forced to use considerable ingenuity to extricate themselves from Inhamunda's grip.

As the commercial life of Sofala stagnated, that of Angoche boomed. The Angoche settlement ante-dated the arrival of the Portuguese and was already proving a threat to Sofala's trade when Pero d'Anhaia arrived. Angoche quickly grew and siphoned off Sofala's wealth so that by 1511 it was reputed to have 12,000 inhabitants (*393*, vol 2, 120) and large *zambucos* freighted there and carrying crews of up to thirty men were making the short sea-voyage to the Zambesi and trading in markets established on the lower river.

To attack and exterminate this centre of Muslim trade was beyond the capacity of the Sofala garrison, while the India fleets had neither men nor munitions to spare. In 1511 a small expedition of three ships was sent against Angoche commanded by Antonio da Saldanha. The town was burnt and some dhows were sunk, but the damage was superficial and the political consequences of the raid were disastrous. The Portuguese now found every chief along the coast set against them, and food supplies virtually impossible to obtain (*393*, vol 2, 122–3).

In 1523 a second attempt was made to try to destroy the Muslim trading network with an attack on the Querimba islands. Forty *fidalgos* and forty seamen raided the chief Muslim settlement in the islands, but, loaded with loot, they pulled away with the job unfinished and one overloaded boat sank on the return journey (*393*, vol 2, 162–3). A further blow was struck when a large Portuguese expedition sacked Mombasa in 1528 but such heavy-handed action had little long-term effect on the flexible Muslim commercial system.

In 1531 the captain of Sofala, Vicente Pegado, took a decision of great strategic moment. If anything was to come of the gold trade in East Africa, Portugal would have to become more deeply involved in the interior where the gold was produced and collected for sale. Accordingly he authorised the first Portuguese settlements up the Zambesi.

The sertanejos

The first ambassadors sent inland by the Portuguese were Christian Africans. The factory at Sofala soon owned a number of slaves who were, as a matter of routine, converted to Christianity, while other Africans and Muslims also became Christians

34

and were well rewarded for their pains (*260*, 185, 201). In 1513 the first European set off into the interior to spy out the gold-fields and the trading centres. 1769869

Antonio Fernandes was a *degredado*—a criminal taken from the Portuguese gaols and sent to the East to expiate his crimes by undertaking dangerous missions. Antonio Fernandes is a common name, but the explorer who bore it may have come out with one of the earliest India fleets. He served in Kilwa and Mombasa and was then transferred to Sofala where he practised carpentry and acted as the fort's interpreter. He was sent on a number of missions to buy food for the garrison and between 1512 and 1516 was chosen to undertake the first inland journeys of exploration. He died in Sofala sometime between 1522 and 1525, having completed his sentence by 1516 (*393*, vol 3, 219).

It is not clear whether Fernandes took two or three journeys into the interior during these four years but he appears to have travelled over the whole of the northern part of what is today Southern Rhodesia, through the Manica mountains and Barue to the Mount Darwin district, from there southwards towards Butua and the gold-fields of Matabeleland, north-eastwards to the edge of the Zambesi near Tete and then through the region round Salisbury and Hartley. The records of his journeys survive as notes made by Gaspar Veloso and João Vaz d'Almada. He told these men of the fairs attended by the Muslim traders, of the stone kraal which the Mwene Mutapa was building 'without mortar', of the bushmen with 'tails' in the far south-west and of traders from Ambar near Zumbo who brought cross-shaped copper ingots from the Congo (*261*, *470*).

The account of Fernandes' travels remained unpublished in Lisbon until this century, but the information he obtained inspired the Portuguese captains to explore further the great river to the north of Sofala.

Vasco da Gama had sailed into the *Rio dos Bons Sinais*—the Qua Qua river, which may then have communicated directly with the Zambesi—but since that time the river with its danger-ous bar had been avoided by the Portuguese. During the cap-taincy of Simão de Miranda (1512–1515), however, a caravel was sent to the southern Luabo mouth of the Zambesi and an attempt made to establish relations with the Muslims living on the island there. The captain of the vessel was lured into an ambush and killed and the caravel hurriedly put to sea as canoes from the shore came to capture it (*271*). This would have been slightly before Antonio Fernandes set off on his first journey and shows

35

that Miranda was making a systematic attempt to penetrate the secrets of the interior.

No immediate attempt was made to retrieve the disaster but information accumulated about the clandestine traders who used the Zambesi mouth. Sancho de Tovar, who was captain from 1518–1522, made another attempt to establish a Portuguese presence in the delta. He built a tower of wood and shipped it on board a caravel to transport to Luabo. He did not succeed, however, in erecting his prefabricated fortress, for one of his ships sank and he postponed the expedition (*393*, vol 2, 62–3).

In this way official action failed to fulfil the brilliant schemes thought up by official policy, and it was only in the 1530s that the Portuguese succeeded in establishing an official presence on the Zambesi.

The history of official policy is at best a one-sided sort of history, and in the story of the Zambesi it was seldom the officials and their policies which decided events. By 1530 the interior had already been successfully penetrated by numerous Portuguese renegades. Fugitives from the constriction of life in the royal forts, the victims of ship-wreck, or criminals on the run, they settled on the coral islands of the East African seaboard or traded into the interior in their hundreds. By 1530 they probably numbered more than the official garrisons on the coast.

As early as 1511 the captain, Antonio da Saldanha, had complained that the *degredados* were fraternising with the Africans and Muslims. He did his best to check the illicit trade that was the result of these exchanges (*393*, vol 2, 21), but by this time individual Portuguese were busy making fortunes by underselling the royal factors. It was the growing estrangement between the artificial discipline that the Portuguese tried to maintain in their forts and the facts of economic life that convinced so many Portuguese they would be better off freelancing in the interior.

In 1518 Antonio da Silveira wrote to the king that some Portuguese were collaborating with chief Inhamunda and clearly strengthening his resolve to defy the captain of Sofala (*262*) By 1528 it was reported that there were 'hundreds' of Portuguese living in the interior, one of them married to the daughter of a *senor da terra*. The backwoodsmen had already begun to infiltrate into Shona society (*393*, vol 3, 386).

Before long these backwoodsmen (the Portuguese word is *sertanejo*) begin to acquire names and personalities for the

36

historian. There is Gaspar de Veiga who opened up the Zambesi for Portuguese trade (*409*, 235), and Gonçalo da Araujo who was reputedly the first Portuguese to find silver in Zambesia (*409*, 235). There is Antonio Caiado who settled at the court of the Mwene Mutapa and became a skilled linguist and confidant of the chief and who, in 1561, wrote a moving account of the last days of Father Gonçalo da Silveira (*386*, 364–6).

Later there is Simão Lopes, a mulatto, who fled south to Inhambane on some accusation of heresy (*323*, a, 97), and Antonio Rodrigues who settled peaceably among the Muslim community of the Bazaruto Islands. The two best-known of the early backwoodsmen, however, are undoubtedly Francisco Brochado and Rodrigo Lobo. Brochado was a *fidalgo* from Almirante who had served the *Infante Dom* Luis and had settled on the Zambesi since the 1550s. Here he prospered as the agent for boats passing up the Qua Qua and Luabo rivers. He was given the title of *Guarda-mor* and is remembered by posterity as the befriender of passengers shipwrecked from the India carracks (*273*, 349). Rodrigo Lobo was more truly a backwoodsman. He lived on an island near Sofala which he held from the chief Quiteve. He was a friend of the Dominican João dos Santos to whom we owe the story of Lobo's diplomatic subtlety in dealing with his African master.

Many more of the *sertanejos* of these early days remain anonymous. There were ten to fifteen of them in Sena in 1561, together with some Christian Indians who between them maintained households of up to five hundred slaves and dependants. At the court of the Mwene Mutapa they were well-known for their greed for land, women, cattle and gold, but it seems they were sometimes trusted to arbitrate in law disputes, and it had been as a peacemaker that Antonio Fernandes was remembered among the peoples of the interior (*261*, 283). At times their intervention was more violent; there is the story of the anonymous *sertanejo* who led the Botonga of the Lupata mountains against a neighbouring people across the Zambesi in the 1550s and established a warlike nation astride the great waterway which terrorised and eventually wiped out the small settlement of Tete: a sixteenth-century Antonio da Cruz! (*409*, 238–9).

The backwoodsman has appeared as a romantic figure to many writers. Turner saw him as reliving on the American frontier the primitive stages of European evolution, and as the upholder of a rugged individualism without which democracy itself would die. The *coureur du bois* of French Canada has become an epic character in the hands of some historians, while Brazilians have written with undisguised admiration of the *bandeirante* pushing back the frontier of colonial Brazil and crossing the Andes, of his uninhibited indulgence which has supposedly sired the only truly multi-racial nation in the world, and of his religious messianism in the *sertão* which tragically grew into a struggle in which all settled civilisation seemed at stake.

The character of the Portuguese *sertanejos* in the interior of East Africa will emerge gradually as this story is told. Some of them were illiterate criminals, some were noblemen, but all were reacting against the discipline of fortress life and against the constraints of the royal monopoly of commerce.

Muslim trading fairs

The Portuguese did not pioneer trade on the East African coast or in the interior. The Muslims had opened all the trade routes and even established a pattern of settlement long before Vasco da Gama's first arrival in 1498. The early letters from the factors and captains of Sofala show how the Portuguese garrison, sitting idly on the swampy Sofala coast and wondering where all the fabled gold had gone to, gradually uncovered the full extent of the trading network the Muslims had built up and which they had so successfully hidden from the 'Franks'.

In 1509 the Moçambique factor, Diogo Vaz, warned the authorities that Muslim traders using the Zambesi route were evading the royal monopoly (393, vol 2, 100) and in 1511 Antonio da Saldanha gave the first detailed account of how this trade functioned. Trading dhows sailed up the Zambesi either by the Quelimane or Luabo mouths. They paid tolls to an African chief below the Lupata gorge and unshipped their cargoes at the narrows. They then travelled to the fair of Otonga some twenty leagues further on. Otonga was the name of a mountain and at the fair was 'a large settlement, where, they say, all the moorish and kaffir merchants in the land come to sell and to make their markets' (393, vol 2, 22).

The reason for holding fairs, explained the factor, Pedro Vaz Soares, in 1513, was that it was not worth the while of the African traders to bring their small quantities of gold all the way to the coast. At the inland fairs all this gold dust could be collected together to make up a reasonable quantity. Neverthe-
38

less some gold was brought directly to the coast and even in Soares' day, when trade had greatly declined, some gold was still brought directly to the fort from the interior. Perhaps the Africans wanted to cut out the Muslim middlemen at the fairs (*271*).

Portuguese knowledge of the fairs was greatly enlarged by Fernandes' journeys. He visited one chief who held a weekly fair attended by Muslim and African merchants, and in the report he made to João Vaz d'Almada he told of the trade in Congo copper which clearly indicated that these fairs served the internal trade of Africa as well as its contacts with the outside world.

The exact sites of these early fairs are unknown, but there seem to have been many of them, widely scattered south of the Zambesi. Probably every chief with any pretensions tried to hold his own fair, and Muslim traders must have penetrated Manica and Karangaland and even south into Butua. The mention of merchants from Ambar suggests that there was a fair as far north as the Zambesi at Zumbo, which would have established trading links with the iron-age cultures north of the Zambesi. It is now thought that the rich burials at Ingombe Ilede, some thirty miles below Kariba, date from the fifteenth century (*430*), and this would strengthen the supposition that there were important fairs on the Zambesi between Kariba and the Luangwa. Great Zimbabwe itself may have been a fair which, in spite of the evident decline it suffered after the fifteenth century, was still active into the middle of the sixteenth century. Vicente Pegado was captain of Sofala in 1531 and claimed to have met Muslim merchants who had been there and whose description of the great buildings, as recorded by the historian João de Barros, is remarkably accurate (*319*, 267).

Merchants who attended the fair paid taxes and probably contributed to the cost of mining operations as well (*319*, 271). Sena and Tete were not so much fairs as staging posts between the coast and the interior—a role they were to maintain under the Portuguese. It has been claimed that the Sinna mentioned by al-Masudi in the tenth century refers to Sena, while the Zambesi settlement called Onhaquoro visited by Fernandes has been identified with Tete. Beyond this there is no indication of the antiquity of these two towns—a problem on which only archaeology is likely to throw any light.

Many Muslims settled in the interior and founded families. In 1572 there was a Muslim village near Sena under its own sheikh, and across the Zambesi a wealthy Muslim had established a plantation where he employed forty Muslim servants and hundreds of slaves. At Mwene Mutapa's court the Muslim community had a leader, or *munhe*, also (*457*, vol 2, 605). Father Monclaro thought that there were twenty or thirty 'turbaned moors' in the interior in the 1570s and if one adds to this number the families and servants of these Muslim heads of families one gets a figure of two hundred or so for the total 'moorish 'population. The figure of 10,000 ventured by Saldanha in 1511 was the outcome of little more than a fit of panic on the part of that worthy captain (*393*, vol 2, 23).

The early *sertanejos* penetrated the Zambesi valley and the goldfields in order to take a share in the commerce of the fairs. At first they lived and traded alongside the Muslims at the fairs or at the court of the Mwene Mutapa. Probably these early backwoodsmen wore their Christianity as lightly as did some of their successors in later centuries. 'The Moors and Christians are as mixed as if they belonged to one creed', lamented Father Monclaro, whose counter-reformation Jesuit's instinct was as offended as if the Portuguese had been consorting with Lutherans.

Trouble between the two communities began with the arrival of the first Jesuit mission led by Gonçalo da Silveira in 1561. Silveira's personality seems greatly to have impressed the chiefs who accorded him an interview, and the Muslims must have realised that here was a man who would upset the *modus vivendi* under which affairs in the interior were regulated—that he was their implacable enemy. Silveira was murdered one night and his body thrown into a nearby river. Whether it really was Muslim influence which turned the Mwene Mutapa against the missionary shortly after he had accepted baptism is not clear, but the story went back to Europe that this was the evil deed of the Muslims.

Silveira's murder was not followed by a general attack on the Portuguese, but it must have made their situation very uneasy during the decade that passed before the real confrontation occurred. In 1569 Francisco Barreto was sent from Lisbon with a large military force to see, among other things, to the expulsion of the Muslims from central Africa. Judgement had already been passed on them in Lisbon for the murder of Silveira, and they were declared to be 'enemies of our holy faith and the instigators of all the evils and offences'. That their expulsion would also serve the commercial interests of the Portuguese was looked upon with the utmost complacency (*274*).

40

Barreto's army duly arrived in the Rivers in 1571 and was at once struck with fever. Men died and the horses began to suffer from sleeping-sickness. Progress in negotiations with the Mwene Mutapa proved slow and Barreto was weak enough to allow his captains to relieve the suspicions and frustrations of their men by a massacre of all the Muslims they could catch. For the greater glory of God some fifty of them were impaled, blown from mortars, torn apart on tree-trunks, axed or shot.

This massacre did not end the activities of the Muslims in the interior, though they never regained their former dominant position, and a decade later there was still a prosperous Muslim community near Quelimane ruled by none other than the brother of the sheikh of Angoche. The massacre may not even have been the major factor in the decline of Muslim trade up the Zambesi. The establishment of the Portuguese on Moçambique island and in Mombasa and the settlement of the Querimba Islands in the second half of the century cut off the Muslims of the Angoche coast from their northern contacts, and it is probable that the trade of Angoche fell increasingly under Portuguese control at this time.

In 1600 Muslims were forbidden to enter the Zambesi and were required to obtain licences even for coastal trade, and in 1608 it was reported that all Muslim trade with the interior by way of the Zambesi had ceased (275). This was rather an exaggeration, for Antonio Bocarro records that in the 1630s there were Muslims settled on the island of Luabo who supplied Sena with provisions and coconut products (321). Further south Muslim communities continued to flourish and the Sabi route to the interior was still used well on into the seventeenth century and Muslim traders maintained their contact in Butua in the south of the modern Rhodesia.

Portuguese trading fairs

Portuguese trade with East Africa in the second half of the sixteenth century was organised on a monopolistic basis. A ship was freighted annually on the west coast of India to take cloth, beads and luxury manufactures to East Africa. The annual voyage was granted by the king to some man he wanted to reward, or was sold to the highest bidder. The concessionnaire could license other ships to make the voyage if he wished (306, vol 2, 40–3). Once the ship arrived in East Africa the

41

monopoly passed to the captain of Moçambique and Sofala who had usually purchased it for a period of three years, during which time, it was alleged, fortunes of two hundred thousand ducats could be made. The captain could prohibit anyone whom he thought might injure his monopoly from trading in the interior; he could confiscate any goods traded without his licence; and he was free to trade in his captaincy and as far south as the Cape of Good Hope (*278*). For a short period there was an experiment in free trade in gold, from 1593 to 1595, but it did not commend itself to the mercantilist mentality of the Portuguese authorities.

On the Zambesi all trade waited on the arrival of the river boats freighted by the captain which would provide the trade goods for the interior. The Indian wares were bought from the captain's factor in Sena and were first taken across the river and sold among the people of Bororo on the northern side. There the traders obtained the cotton cloths of the Lake Nyasa region, which were called *machira* and which fetched high prices in Manica and Karangaland in the south. A shrewd investment might turn a hundred *cruzados* into three thousand (*409*, 234). Sena provided direct access to the fairs of Manicaland, but some goods were taken up the Zambesi to Tete which was the base for the rather longer journeys up the Luenha and Mazoe rivers to the fairs of Karangaland.

The trade of the Zambesi may have been a small part of the wealth of the Portuguese empire but nothing shows better the parasitic nature of Portugal's presence in the East. Whether in the Far East, the Persian Gulf, Indonesia or East Africa, the Portuguese were simply middlemen—a role filled with less violence and more flexibility by the Muslims of India and Arabia before their arrival.

The Muslims settled at the fairs and at the court of the Mwene Mutapa had chosen a man to act as their leader, or *munhe*. The Portuguese almost certainly imitated this example— very likely at the request of the African chiefs themselves who wanted some sort of discipline among the trading community. The most important of the fairs in late sixteenth century was Massapa which was located near Mount Darwin within a short distance of the *Zimbabwe* of the Mwene Mutapa. The merchants there elected one of their number as captain and then had their choice accepted by the Mwene Mutapa who granted him certain powers of jurisdiction. The appointment was then referred to the Captain of Moçambique and Sofala to be made into an

42

official appointment of the crown. The captain of Massapa was called the *capitão das portas*—the captain of the gates—because all traders entering or leaving the country had to pass through Massapa (*343*, 369, *445*, 271).

The *capitão das portas* was a busy man. He collected the dues which the merchants had to pay to the Mwene Mutapa. He settled all disputes among the Portuguese and heard cases involving Europeans and Africans and even purely African cases which came up in the fair. The captain had to reside permanently in the fair and to seek the permission of the Mwene Mutapa before leaving it, and before resigning his office. He was honoured with the title of the king's 'great wife' and carried as a staff of office a long assegai of black wood tipped with gold (*445*, 271). Among the responsibilities that the captain bore was the job of seeing that trade in the interior kept moving and that the Mwene Mutapa received the presents which were essential for the maintenance of good relations. His office was unpaid but he probably enjoyed the same privileges of selling his goods first in the market which the captain of Luanze did in the seventeenth century.

The late sixteenth century was one of peace and prosperity in the interior. Most traders, we are told, resisted the temptation to try to acquire and run the gold diggings themselves and were content with the considerable profits of trade. Community relations seem to have been harmonious and the Portuguese captains at the fairs, deriving their authority from three sources, were an acceptable means for regulating any difficulties that arose. Towards the end of the century, however, the interior became more unsettled and before long the Portuguese had embarked among the dangerous shoals of African politics.

The disorders that broke out in the interior in the last years of the sixteenth century were to last for the next hundred years and were to reduce the kingdom of the Mwene Mutapa to a fragment of its former size and prestige. During the fighting Portuguese adventurers were able to rise swiftly to wealth and power by acting as mercenaries to various chiefs or as strong-arm men protecting Portuguese interests in the interior. Gold-mining and trade, however, never entirely ceased during this period and had times of great prosperity.

The first change that the wars brought was a different status to the Portuguese settlements in the interior. From being alien communities under the protection of the African sovereign they acquired independence and sovereignty of their own. Francisco

Barreto had fortified Sena and Tete in 1572 and early in the seventeenth century the royal council decided that the fairs should also be fortified. The unsettled state of the interior was reason enough, but in 1607 the Mwene Mutapa ceded all the mines in his kingdom to the Portuguese in return for their aid, and it became imperative to organise the mining of gold and provide protection for those involved in the work. The forts were built by *Dom* Estavão de Ataide who was sent in 1609 to be general of the 'conquest of the mines'. At first only Luanze, Massapa and Bocuto were fortified but as the disorders in the interior grew, so every small fair and mining camp constructed its own fortifications (*275*).

Many of the Portuguese fortified settlements in the interior have now been located, plans drawn of them and three have been excavated. The forts were simple structures and were frequently re-built. It is quite usual for there to be two or three earthworks close together at one site. At Luanze there are two and at Dambarare as many as five have been located. A contemporary described Luanze as a 'palisade of stakes, filled up inside with earth, allowing those within to fight under cover. The stakes are of such a nature that when they have been in the ground for two or three months they take root and become trees which last many years.' (*321*, vol 2, 416). Luanze today consists of two fortified enclosures; the larger measuring roughly 120 yards by 85 and the smaller 70 yards by 53. Both were fortified with ditches and bastions. The larger of them had a bank five feet high and a ditch twelve feet wide (*364*). No trace of the palisade survives but the technique of constructing a wall of living trees to act as a defence was used during the last colonial wars at the beginning of this century and is a traditional type of fortification in this area.

At Dambarare and Maramuca there are clear indications of buildings within the enclosures and it is probable that there was permanently resident a captain who maintained a storehouse and arsenal. For the most part, however, the settlers lived outside the fortifications and gathered there only in times of danger. The church excavated at Dambarare was full of European burials, all male and many of them dead before reaching maturity. The pottery found at Dambarare was rich with imported wares from Persia, China and Europe but the African pottery was all markedly different from the local wares obtained from purely African sites (*365*). The obvious interpretation of this is that the Portuguese brought their African followers from far afield and did not recruit them from among the local population with its strong local loyalties. The foreign nature of the Portuguese mercenaries was emphasised by Bocarro who, writing in 1635, said that most of them were recruited from the delta or from north of the Zambesi (*321*, vol 2, 412).

From the wealth and size of some of the settlements it would be easy to assume that the fairs became large urban settlements, but this is probably not true. The Portuguese population of the rivers was always small. In 1633 it was reported to be about two hundred in all (*313*, 99), and if this figure is accurate it is unlikely that it ever greatly exceeded this number until the twentieth century. Even this number spread out over a dozen settlements does not represent a very successful colonising enterprise, and ten Portuguese together at a fair would be an unusually large crowd. In 1680 it was reported that there were only eight Portuguese resident in the interior and another forty-two on the River, together with some two hundred mulattos. Only four Portuguese were resident at Dambarare in 1677 (*166*). Each of the larger fairs maintained a Dominican priest and a church.

To chart the history of each individual fair is a confusing business. The wars and the spasmodic nature of the mining activities almost certainly left many of them deserted for years on end, and when they were re-built it was often with another name. Luanze, Bocuto and Massapa were the leading fairs in Karangaland at the beginning of the seventeenth century and all had been busy for at least forty years. They were situated in the basin of the Mazoe and its tributaries. They became centres of military activity during the wars at the beginning of the century, which probably had the effect of driving away the native inhabitants and putting an end to the local panning of gold on which the fairs depended for their prosperity. There were four other fairs in Karangaland in the early part of the century at Dambarare, Matafuna, Chipirivire and Urupande.

By 1635 northern Karangaland was firmly in European hands and there had been a large-scale exodus of the local population with their chiefs towards the south and west. In 1629 the Portuguese captains had acquired the sovereignty over the land in the immediate neighbourhood of Luanze and Massapa and the old gold-bearing regions were given over to the rivalries of the Portuguese *sertanejos* and their armed followers. Because of depopulation and disorder the trade frontier moved outwards. Dambarare now became the chief centre of trade and remained so until the end of the century. In 1667 the Jesuit Manuel Barreto suggested that it become the official centre of Portuguese rule in the interior. Quitamburvise—which may have been near the headwaters of the Hunyani—also rose in importance while Makaha on the edge of Manicaland and the Angwa river fair at Ongoe in the west continued to flourish.

The most striking example of the movement of the gold trade further into the interior is the Portuguese penetration of Maramuca (*293*). Maramuca is approximately the district around the modern Hartley and traders had been visiting it as early as the 1650s. Extensive workings have been found at Chivere Hill and along the Suri Suri river, a tributary of the Umfuli (*364*). The small group of traders who were active in the region were challenged by a powerful *sertanejo* called Gonçalo João who obtained a land concession and moved into the area with his followers. The house and walled enclosure discovered in 1965 may well have been João's headquarters. The rival groups fought for possession of the gold trade and João was defeated and driven away (*318*, 484–6). By 1680, all Portuguese activity in the area appears to have ceased.

The Manica mountains were another area of gold-mining and trading. Manica, in the early part of the seventeenth century, was nominally subject to the paramountcy of Quiteve. The Portuguese had been settled there since the sixteenth century and there were three fairs, Chipangura, where the captain resided and which was the chief settlement in Manica, Vumba and Mutuca. Mutuca was the private mining preserve of a Portuguese called João da Costa who had settled there and acted as the royal authority in the area (*321*, vol 2, 412). The Portuguese living in Manica were no more pacific than their compatriots in Karangaland. In the 1630s they dethroned and killed one Chicanga, placed their own nominee on the throne and used their base in Manica to interfere in the politics of Quiteve and Butua, too.

Expelled from Manica by Changamire in 1695, the Portuguese returned early in the eighteenth century, and the Manica fair at Massikesse and later at Aruangua continued to enjoy a fitful prosperity until the Ngoni invasions of the nineteenth century.

The story of the fairs in the seventeenth century is a story whose meaning is quite clear. *Sertanejos* and traders pioneered commercial contacts in the interior. Wherever they were successful permanent settlements were established under the surveillance of the local chief. A captain would be appointed and a church

46

constructed as the centre of a mission. The men who had come as traders were then superseded by fortune-hunters anxious to exploit the gold mines themselves or to dabble in African politics with their lucrative by-products in land concessions, slaves and loot. The conflict of the various interest-groups either led to the total expulsion of the Portuguese or to the collapse of the local African state and the dislocation of society. Thereafter the Portuguese might mine gold for themselves, but the supply always fell below that obtained in the days of peaceful trading. The trade frontier then moved further into the interior and the process began again.

When Karangaland was closed to the Portuguese after the wars of the 1690s, this pattern of trade and settlement began again north of the Zambesi. Fairs and mining camps established among the Marave were followed by wars and the passing of a great deal of land into Portuguese hands and a subsequent sharp decline in trade which was diverted away from the Zambesi towards Zanzibar. The last fair established was in 1827 when for two brief years a trading post existed at Marambo up the Luangwa river in an attempt to tap the ivory trade of the interior again.

4 The Foundation of the *Prazos* and the *Prazo* Dynasties

The Conquistadores

The history of the fairs showed that the lamp of urban culture burned dimly in central Africa. The Muslims from the east coast were city-dwellers, and in the days when they alone carried trade to the interior, the fairs may well have been on the way to becoming genuine urban centres. The Portuguese, however, had no great traditions of town life—unlike the Castilians—and, wherever they settled, it was not to found cities but to pioneer in the backwoods; to search for wealth, but also to escape from the tedious and unrewarding restraints of garrison life. For the system of forts and factories begun by Prince Henry, which had spread throughout the Portuguese empire in the East, may have been the simplest form of imperial organisation, but took a terrible toll of human life and proved culturally and socially sterile.

While the Mwene Mutapa remained strong, the Portuguese adventurers in central Africa had to live within the confines of the fairs and to respect the law. Towards the end of the sixteenth century, however, the power of the old Karanga kingdom was waning. The chieftaincies of Quiteve and Manica had become virtually independent and Mwene Mutapa Nogomo, before his death in 1589, had even ceded territory to the Portuguese captains on the Zambesi (*292*, 89). In 1596 a new Mwene Mutapa, a minor called Gatsi Lusere, succeeded, and from his reign the decline of the chieftaincy became precipitous.

The chronicler of Portuguese India, Antonio Bocarro, who probably derived most of his information about Central Africa from the Dominican traveller and missionary João dos Santos, records that the wars which were Gatsi Lusere's undoing began in the year 1597. In that year Karangaland was subject to a series of raids led by a chief who had come originally from north of the Zambesi and had asked leave to settle among the Karanga.

48

Gatsi Lusere asked the Portuguese at the fairs for help and, although with their aid he was successful in restoring order, he soon found that victories won for him by European mercenaries cost him heavily in prestige. It may also be that Gatsi Lusere's authority as chief and divine king of his people was weakened by the fact that he was blind in one eye and did not have the physical perfection which his role required (*448*, 104).

From this time successive Mwene Mutapas had to choose between following an all-African policy designed to limit the power of the Portuguese, and a policy of using Portuguese aid to maintain their paramountcy against pretenders and over-mighty subjects. The temptation to make use of the firearms of the Portuguese was strong, but political power in the end has to rest on consent and not coercion. Moreover the cost of Portuguese assistance was high and soon the *sertanejos* gathered like kites around the dying carcase of the Karanga empire.

Portuguese intervention in Ethiopia led to similar consequences and the parallel between the decline of the Ethiopian monarchy and that of the Mwene Mutapa is striking. Cristovão da Gama and his soldiers had helped to repel the Muslim invasion of Ethiopia in 1540 and had then buttressed the throne of the Negus against invasions of Galla tribes from the south. However, the Negus had only won this aid at the expense of cutting one by one the ties of tradition and religion which bound the king to his people. The *dénouement* came early in the seventeenth century when the Negus Susyenos was baptised a Roman Catholic and had to face a hostile coalition of provincial rulers, leaders of the Monophysite church and Galla nomads, with only the Portuguese community to depend on. His abdication and the subsequent expulsion of the Portuguese followed but this did not save the monarchy itself from two centuries of weakness and decay.

In 1606 Gatsi Lusere appealed again for Portuguese aid. The initial reluctance of the Portuguese captains who did not want to get involved in African civil wars, was overcome by the emergence of one of the leading traders of Tete as a military leader of energy and vision. Diogo Simões Madeira was a native of Evora (*371*, 183) who had settled in the Rivers and who traded gold together with other members of his family. Lourenço de Brito, the captain-general of Moçambique, in 1590 had granted two tracts of land to Madeira on condition that he assumed responsibility for their defence. Madeira had settled on this land and, surrounded by his family and African followers, he soon became the most powerful force in the Tete area. It was he who raised an army among the Portuguese and on 1 August 1607 met the Mwene Mutapa on the banks of the Mazoe where the terms of Portuguese aid were agreed upon.

This meeting was a triumph for Madeira and tempted the Portuguese to renew Francisco Barreto's plan to turn Central Africa into a new Peru. It was a major disaster, however, for the Mwene Mutapa. He had formally to cede all the mines in his territory and agree that four of his children should be educated by Madeira in the Christian faith. His eldest son was to be sent to the Portuguese capital in Goa. In return he was promised Portuguese military aid (*321*, vol 3, 367–9). Students of Central African history will readily appreciate the irony of seeing Rudd's famous deception of Lobengula in 1888 anticipated by nearly three hundred years.

Madeira's personal ascendancy is evident in the terms of the alliance. The mines were ceded to him personally and he received the custody of four of the Mwene Mutapa's children. The mines he made over to the king of Portugal. During the following two years Madeira's dominance south of the Zambesi was unquestioned. He recruited 4,000 Marave mercenaries (*371*, 183) and, adding to them his own slaves and dependents, drove Gatsi Lusere's enemies from Karangaland. The Mwene Mutapa himself, however, was defeated in Barue and Madeira had to maintain him and his court in Chidima during 1609 before he could be restored to his lands. In return for this favour Madeira was granted the chieftainship of Inhabanzo, which made him one of the most powerful vassals of the Mwene Mutapa's kingdom.

The 'conquest' of the mines so providentially won for Portugal was first entrusted in 1611 to *Dom* Estevão de Ataide, the new captain-general and a friend of the Jesuits who return to the Rivers in his retinue (*448*, 113). Madeira himself departed on a major trading expedition to Urupandi.

Ataide's incompetence and eagerness to line his own pockets, but still more his lack of any personal standing among the settlers soon threw the burden of mineral exploration back on Madeira's shoulders. In 1612 he received a full commission to this end from the king, Philip, so that to the prestige and power he had acquired in Africa were now added honours and prestige derived from Europe.

Madeira took up his official duties with vigour, but was held up for nearly a year by a chief called Chombe whose stockade on the river above Sena blocked the passage upstream. A previous Chombe had sent auxilliaries to aid Francisco Barreto in 1572 and had been rewarded with the control of the Lupata region. Now the Botonga of the Lupata mountains under their new dynasty of chiefs were once again threatening the Portuguese. Madeira avoided the disasters which had befallen Francisco Barreto and which were later to bring four Portuguese armies to grief in this very area in the nineteenth century. His troops were largely African and he used considerable ingenuity to counter the firearms which Chombe so successfully used in his defence. At last, under cover of wicker shields, Madeira and his men expelled Chombe from his stronghold and the chieftainship was made over to yet another loyal ally named Chitambo.

In April 1614 Madeira set off for Chicoa, where the silver mines were reputed to be and where Vasco Homem had come to grief forty years previously. He constructed forts on both the north and the south banks and built up friendly relations with the neighbouring Marave chiefs, who permitted a regular road along the north bank of the Zambesi to be opened for the first time. Apparently Madeira located a considerable quantity of silver in the Chicoa region, some of which was sent to Lisbon and Goa for assay, and some of which was melted down and sent to Sena to purchase supplies.

Madeira's exalted position naturally raised him up many enemies. In particular, his friendship with the Dominicans aroused the hatred of the Jesuits who had had to leave the Rivers with their disgraced patron Ataide. Suspicions appear to have been aroused about the genuineness of his silver finds. In 1616 Francisco da Fonseca Pinto—a high court judge— sailed with a commission to inquire into Madeira's activities and into the authenticity of the silver finds. Fonseca Pinto was a villain. Finding Madeira absent at Chicoa with his men and unable to exert his influence in Tete, Pinto ordered that he be stripped of all his possessions. The prospect of looting the richest man in the Rivers seems to have proved irresistible to the other Portuguese, a band of whom then fell on Madeira's estates, carrying off women and children, looting and burning. Madeira was recalled and an armed party sent to arrest him.

Madeira at first escaped pursuit by retreating to Inhabanzo but Pinto was determined to crush him and invoked the aid of the Mwene Mutapa in destroying his influence. Then, as the Karanga warriors descended on the lands of the fallen hero, Pinto left in his canoes for the coast, loaded with booty and the richer by 100,000 *cruzados*, his mission completed to his own satisfaction.

Francisco Barreto, wrote the historian Faria y Sousa,

> was undone by a divine, and now Diego Simões by a lawyer; and the king by employing such gownsmen in things which concern them not, lost the great advantages that might be expected from those mines (*349*, 43–4).

Madeira's prestige never fully recovered from this disaster. He was formally exonerated and restored to his honours by another judge, Castellobranco, in 1618 when the news of the scale of Pinto's villainy became known. He was given the habit of the Order of Christ and was once again given command of the mines. He may also have recovered some of his former power among the African population for as late as 1625 the king was still hoping to use him as a means of opening up the mines (*280*, *281*). By 1629 he had faded from the scene completely and a new generation of *conquistadores* had emerged.

Gatsi Lusere died in 1624. He had held his kingdom together towards the end by exploiting the quarrels of the Portuguese, and by baffling the Portuguese in their search for silver. But Diogo Simões had shown how fortunes could be won and the Portuguese settlers in the future would become more impatient for wealth than in the past.

The Mwene Mutapa who succeeded was Mavura and he too had to fight to hold together his kingdom against a pretender called Kaparidze. Kaparidze was half-brother of Mavura and the latter eventually attained the throne through Portuguese aid (*448*, 135–6). In 1629 he found himself forced to cede the whole of his kingdom to the Portuguese crown and to guarantee a wide variety of rights and privileges to the Portuguese fairs in the interior as the price of their aid. Such sweeping inroads into the independence of the old kingdom explains Kaparidze's success in uniting African feeling against the Portuguese, and the raids he carried out on the Portuguese settlements might have extinguished their power for ever but for the arrival in 1632 of Diogo de Sousa de Meneses with reinforcements. In only three months, this energetic governor of Moçambique fought three successful campaigns in Quelimane, Manica and Karanga, defeating Kaparidze and re-establishing the *Pax Lusitana* in a devastated land (*313*, 97–8).

This series of wars in the interior had caused a fearful blood-

52

letting. Hundreds of the *sertanejos* had lost their lives as had many thousands of their African followers and opponents. Opportunities were now open for a new generation of *conquistadores* to win and control the backlands. Sisnando Dias Bayão was the most powerful of this new generation.

Bayão had come to Africa at the age of sixteen and by the time of his death—probably in 1645—he had become one of the most knowledgeable of the backwoodsmen (*318, 504*). He settled in Sena and married into a local family called Mattos. His father-in-law, Lourenço de Mattos, had recently carried out a coup typical of the morality of the Rivers settlements. A Botonga chief called Sanapache had overrun the estates belonging to some of the Portuguese. Mattos had led out his men to drive off the invaders and when this was successfully accomplished, he refused to hand back the lands to their former owners. Bayão inherited these estates shortly before his own death (*318, 506*).

Bayão rose to be *capitão-mor dos Rios* and *juiz ordinario* in Sena, and it was probably in this capacity, as chief citizen of the Sena settlement, that he conquered the Marave stronghold of Mount Morumbala across the Zambesi and placed his own headmen to rule the African communities there (*318, 475*). The River passage was in this way secured and it may well have been at this period that Portuguese traders first pushed their way up to Lake Nyasa and began to tap the wealth of the northern interior (*371*).

Appointed to command Portuguese forces in Manica, Bayão intervened to restore the Quiteve Peranhe to his throne (*34*). Peranhe, in gratitude, took the name *Dom Sebastião* and submitted to the king of Portugal (*174*). Bayão was rewarded with the concession of a vast territory called Gobira, which stretched from the Pungue to the Zambesi and was later called Cheringoma (*318, 487*).

From Manica Bayão undertook his most famous exploit—the march into Butua in the far south-west. Butua had broken away from the Karanga empire at the end of the fifteenth century and had successfully prevented Portuguese infiltration. Trade was carried out by Muslims who had been driven from the goldfields farther north but were able to reach Butua by the southern Sabi River. Butua's isolation was broken in the 1640s by a succession dispute which may well indicate a weakening of the old Torwa dynasty of Butua which died out in the 1680s. A Muslim trader who had settled in the country and become rich, married his daughter to the younger brother of the chief of Butua. Using the unpopularity of the chief and the support of other Muslims, he was able to place his son-in-law on the throne and oust the legal occupant.

The defeated Changamire fled with his followers to the Portuguese at Manica, where Bayão agreed to lend him aid. The march was long and many of Bayão's men deserted, but with the aid of Changamire's own followers they were able to overthrow the pretender. Bayão left a guard of musketeers in Butua and built and fortified stockades in the country. He then returned to the Zambesi for supplies (*371*). It may have been while he was back in Sena in July 1644 that he wrote the letter to Belchior Teixeira in which he told of his labours in the Rivers and the plots against his life, which were apparently shortly afterwards successful, for Manuel Barreto, writing twenty years later, said that he was poisoned by his enemies.

After Bayão's death the garrisons were withdrawn from Butua, and Morumbala and the Sena district rose in rebellion against the Portuguese and had to be reconquered and tamed by Father Barreto himself, changing cassock for sword on this occasion to further the cause of the church.

No other *conquistadores* rose to the eminence that Bayão and Madeira had so precariously occupied. The pattern of society was changing and the clans of the settlers were strengthening the marriage ties which linked them to one another. In future a man would look to his kin for protection and avoid as far as possible the heroic isolation in which Bayão found himself at the end of his life.

The Portuguese acquire jurisdiction

Madeira and Bayão were men of action: they were also land-owners on a massive scale and built up vast personal domains which, for Bayão, were the origin of the wealth and power of one of the greatest of all the families of old Moçambique. However, to understand the character of these great private domains we need to delve more into the origins of the power of the *sertanejos*.

In most African societies land is not owned by anyone—even by the chief. A man acquires the use of land, for himself and his family, and sometimes for his heirs, from the chief. This use of the land may confer on him extensive rights but it does not make it his property. The land is thought of as belonging to the people, to God, or possibly to the ancestors, and the chief arbitrates over its use. In some respects this theory resembles the principles which lay behind Portuguese emphyteusis and the great Atlantic captaincies.

The *capitaes-donatários* who had attempted the colonisation of Brazil, Angola and the Atlantic Islands, had received land grants which conferred on them jurisdiction and governmental responsibilities. They had the right to arbitrate over the use of the land, to tax and receive tribute from the settlers, and to settle disputes of various kinds. The captain was not expected to exploit all the land directly himself, and sometimes he was specifically forbidden to do so.

The African chief performed just these functions for the members of his 'tribe' or for the inhabitants on the land over which he was chief. His position was, however, one of greater complexity. He was frequently bound to his people by real or mythical blood-ties, and he had ritual functions connected with sowing and harvesting and with the securing of a healthy relationship between the living and the ever-present spirits of the dead. The chief was thus very close to his people and the people through their elders helped to choose the chief and offered him advice. Although many African chieftaincies derive their authority from the great antiquity and the historic association they enjoy, others were founded in more recent times by successful adventurers who either gathered together their band of clients, or who received their office from an established paramount chief.

Local chiefs or headmen must have granted the earliest Portuguese to penetrate the interior, the use of land to build houses and cultivate gardens. There must also have been agreements over the use of land in and near the fairs, but it was not from these humble allotments that the great *prazos* were to grow. For the *prazos* were not so much lands owned or used by Portuguese as areas of jurisdiction where they acted as chiefs and *seigneurs*.

To find out how the Portuguese came to acquire jurisdiction in Africa is, therefore, the first task, and the second is to show how this jurisdiction became transformed into a regular form of land-holding.

The Portuguese captains of the coastal stations had held jurisdiction within the area of the fort and, in Sofala, within the town as well. This jurisdiction covered Portuguese nationals and other Christians. It also covered slaves, for the Portuguese,

55

like the Muslims before them, soon acquired large numbers of slaves whom they employed in the work of the fortress. This type of jurisdiction extended to the River stations and later to the inland fairs where, as described in the previous chapter, the captains derived their authority partly from the Portuguese crown and partly from the Mwene Mutapa, and the election of their fellow traders.

The jurisdiction of the Portuguese captains at the fairs was wide. The captain of Massapa had 'power to give verbal sentence in all cases, and he can even condemn the guilty to be hanged, without appeal against his sentence.' (*445*, 271.) It was not long before the Portuguese settlements began to widen the area of their authority to include the surrounding countryside. This secured vital food supplies and prevented the fairs and forts from becoming too isolated. The first acquisition of land may have been the result of Francisco Barreto's treaty with Mwene Mutapa Nogomo in 1573 (*292*). If land did change hands on this occasion it would have been in the Sena area. Shortly afterwards Tete acquired territory in its immediate neighbour-hood when the Mwene Mutapa punished the rebel chief of Inhabanzo by the loss of some of his land which was given to the captain of Tete (*273*, 352–3).

It was probably this land concession that was described by João dos Santos at the beginning of the seventeenth century when the African inhabitants had established a workable relation-ship with their Portuguese overlords. There were eleven villages, and these retained their headmen who were now subject to dismissal by the Portuguese captains. The captain had assumed some of the ceremonial functions of chieftaincy and was solemnly consulted before sowing and harvest by the villagers, who brought him gifts. In time of war the captains called on the village headmen to provide warriors, and these duly turned out

with their men armed with bows, arrows, assegais, hoes, axes and everything else that is required. Being arranged in order, each captain with his men, drums, trumpets and banners enters the town of Tete and present themselves before the captain of the fort (*445*, 290–1).

When Mwene Mutapa Mavura made a formal surrender of his whole kingdom to Portugal by the treaty of 1629 the Tete captaincy was confirmed in possession of its villages and similar concessions were made to the fairs. Later in the century this direct administration of the land by the captains of the forts and fairs was seen to have many advantages over the then prevalent system of individual control. The fairs, however, were by this time in decline and any attempt to revive their prosperity was vain. In the eighteenth century no land was directly administered by the fort captains though they retained jurisdiction over Portuguese nationals and general supervision of their activities.

The first individual Portuguese who acquired jurisdiction were probably those who were asked to arbitrate in disputes. In most societies there are causes which can best be settled by an outsider according to principles of equity and Father Monclaro S.J. painted a happy picture of Portuguese-African relations when he wrote:

> Portuguese who have been there related to me that they have often been chosen as judges in quarrels which had arisen amongst them [the local Africans], and even though they gave sentence against one, he who was condemned was quite satisfied because he thought they had acted according to reason and justice, and this did not prevent him choosing him as a judge again ... (409, 228).

This idyll did not last, for in a long plaint delivered by Mavura to the king of Portugal in 1645 the Mwene Mutapa complained that in cases involving Europeans and Africans the Portuguese judges invariably decided against the African. Mavura wanted jurisdiction in these cases returned to himself (175).

To act as judge is one thing, to obtain a permanent jurisdiction is quite another. To acquire permanent jurisdiction meant in Africa to acquire jurisdiction over a certain area of land and the people settled on it. Father Gonçalo da Silveira was offered land, cattle and women by the Mwene Mutapa when his mission arrived at the Karanga court in 1561. Would these offers have been made on that occasion if they had not previously been accepted by other Portuguese arrivals at court? Certainly there were individual Portuguese owning and working gold diggings in the 1570s (409, 233).

There were also wealthy Muslims settled on the coast and in the interior with large and permanent establishments. One of these living opposite Sena had an establishment of forty Muslims and a village with more than five hundred Africans of which he was the lord (343).

Rodrigues Correa is perhaps the first Portuguese land-owner who can be identified definitely. He owned land in the Querimba Islands and offered to build a church for the Dominicans in the 1580s. Further south was Pedro Lobo who at about the same time was lord of the island of Inhansato near Sofala which he had taken over from the Muslim who had been its previous owner. We know of this because João dos Santos visited the island and piously set fire to the Muslim shrine there which was greatly venerated and was a place of pilgrimage for local Muslims.

João dos Santos also tells the story of Rodrigo Lobo

who was lord of the greater part of this island [Maroupe, about four leagues up river from the Sofala fort], which was granted to him by Quiteve, who was a great friend of his, together with the title of his wife, a name which the king bestows upon the captains of Moçambique and Sofala, and upon all those Portuguese whom he greatly esteems; this name signifying that he loves them, and desires to show them all as much courtesy as he shows to his wife, and indeed the kaffirs have a great veneration for the Portuguese who had the title of the king's wife. In this island Rodrigo Lobo had many kaffirs as his slaves, and all the other inhabitants were his vassals (*445*, *225*).

Here already is a *prazo*, lacking only the title granted by the Portuguese crown. Land and jurisdiction over its inhabitants granted by an African paramount chief to a Portuguese is the classic model for future growth of Portuguese power. Lobo, it appears, had considerable diplomatic skill. One day he killed a lion when out hunting. As it was widely believed in this part of Africa that the spirits of departed chiefs sometimes inhabited the bodies of lions, to kill a lion was an act of *lèse-majesté*. Lobo, faced with the mortal consequence of royal displeasure, excused himself by pointing to the insult the lion had committed in daring to attack the king's wife. This insult to a living chief was clearly the more heinous of the two crimes and Lobo escaped from his predicament.

Concessions by chiefs of the kind enjoyed by Lobo were few and far between before the seventeenth century. Then, with the growing disorder and the Mwene Mutapa's reliance on Portuguese aid, the odd one or two cases became a flood. Diogo Simões Madeira, leading the Portuguese forces in Karangaland, not unnaturally became the first to acquire massive land concessions in the interior, and the story of how he acquired Inhabanzo can illustrate the many similar acquisitions by other Portuguese.

Inhabanzo was the chieftaincy which adjoined Tete and part of it had already been made over to the captain of Tete in the sixteenth century. In 1608 it was overrun by Matuzianhe, the rebel Mwene Mutapa, and Madeira raised a force of fifty musketeers and four thousand warriors and

> with these he attacked the enemy, routed him and dispossessed him of the lands of Inhabanzo . . . leaving only the natives who rendered obedience to Diogo Simões. On the spot where the battle took place Diogo Simões built a wooden fort, in which he placed twenty guns and three hundred kaffirs, thus rendering those lands secure.

And secure they were! The Mwene Mutapa duly bestowed them on Madeira who then found himself the lord of twenty-five settlements and two thousand adult male warriors (*321*, vol 3, 373, 432).

That the land obtained by concession from chiefs was the origin of most of the *prazos* is clearly true; that these concessions were always granted willingly and peacefully is not so obvious, and here as elsewhere possession was nine-tenths of the law.

The granting away of their 'birthright' by different chiefs to the Portuguese is, however, only part of the story of the *prazos*, the other part is to be found in the history of Portuguese colonial policy and the attempts made by the Portuguese crown to settle, develop and generally grow wealthy from its east African possessions.

The Portuguese government begins to grant land titles

Neither the Moçambique captains nor the Indian viceroys had been able to hinder or promote the penetration of the interior by the *sertanejos*. These men were playing a game with African rules, and Francisco Barreto's expedition had shown how disastrous an official intervention organised and run like any European enterprise could be. After the final withdrawal of Barreto's successor in 1576, official interest in central Africa was not revived for over thirty years—not in fact until the news

59

of the cession of the mines to Madeira in 1607 reached Lisbon.

There followed a period of intensive official activity in which central Africa was many times conquered, settled and developed in paper plans, though remaining much the same as ever actually on the ground. It was in pursuit of its fabled wealth that the government began to see the *sertanejos* as possible allies. If men like Madeira who had wealth and local prestige would lend their aid, then the mines could be conquered at little cost to the royal treasury. The best way of harnessing the local interests to those of the crown was seen to lie in the grant of land titles to regularise all the various properties and concessions that individuals had already acquired. If these could be brought under Portuguese law perhaps they would be more amenable to government influence.

For their part the *sertanejos* were anxious for the government to secure them in possession of their rights. A royal title might stand them in good stead if they found themselves threatened with shipwreck in the maelstrom of African politics, or if they faced deprivation by some rival faction of Portuguese.

Apparently *Dom* Pedro de Castro, when captain-general of Moçambique in the 1580s, granted some land to the Dominicans. If he did, these would be the first land grants of which there is any record (*277*). There is also a record of some land granted to Diogo Simões Madeira by Lourenço de Brito in the 1590s (*321*, vol 3, *423*). In 1609 the Dominicans received a further grant of land (*98*), and in 1612 a royal confirmation of a land grant was issued which has survived as the first clear indication of royal policy in these matters (*276*).

This confirmation was included in a letter which conferred on Madeira the 'conquest' of the mines and the habit of the Order of Christ. It ran as follows:

I am pleased to confirm it to him reserving to myself the mines of gold and silver or other metals which there may be in the said lands, or which may be discovered in the future, upon his declaration that he will always hold them subject to the orders and the commands of the generals of the conquest, or in default thereof, of the captain of Moçambique, and so long as the conquest is not completed he shall have such jurisdiction as is granted him by the Monomotapa, and when it is concluded he shall seek information from the general and the viceroy of this kingdom then in office and thereupon I will command due favour to be shown him according as he has

60

deserved in the said conquest; and I charge you that on its appearing to you that the said lands have indeed been given to him by the Monomotapa, you send him a grant in my name . . .

This confirmation recognised that the title derived from a concession made by the Mwene Mutapa, and it revealed that the motive of the crown in granting a Portuguese land title was to make use of the power of the backwoodsmen to master the interior. In 1612 the Dominicans also petitioned for the confirmation of their land titles and in 1618 the *regimento* for the new captain-general, *Dom* Nun'Alvares Pereira, ordered him to take measures to see that the settlers spread out over the land and cultivated it, and authorised him to grant privileges and exemptions to them provided that these were later confirmed by the crown (*256*).

Probably by this time unauthorised titles of a kind were being issued fairly regularly by the captains of the fairs and forts. In the 1629 treaty with the Mwene Mutapa there was a clause preventing further alienations of land to the Portuguese and in 1630 a *vedor da fazenda* was sent to the Rivers to regularise all the illegal titles (*395*, 100).

By 1634 so many land titles had been issued that the pattern of Portuguese settlement south of the Zambesi had assumed already the form it was to maintain until the end of the nineteenth century. Antonio Bocarro described the Rivers in the *Livro do Estado da India* (*321*, vol 2, 409):

The lands are all ours . . . not only along the river but thirty or forty leagues back from it, and extending more than one hundred leagues in length from the mouth at the bar of Quellimane up the stream. All these lands are given to Portuguese, some are subject to the captain of Sena and some to the captain of Tete.

It is already clear from the documents of the 1640s that the type of tenure introduced in these land titles is Portuguese emphyteusis. The point is made most explicitly, however, by Father Manuel Barreto in 1667. The lands, he says, were held for three lives in return for a quit-rent and with the obligation to bring warriors for the defence of the colony. In return the Portuguese crown acknowledged the jurisdiction that the *prazo*-holder exercised over the African inhabitants of the land (*318*, 467–8).

Land titles had been granted in the hope of exerting some sort of control over the activities of the backwoodsmen and enlisting their aid in the conquest of the mines. From the start, however there was little indication that the *sertanejos* would be amenable to control. The more powerful of them were building up large followings of slaves and clients who were supported by raiding and by the produce of the land concessions. The native Karanga and their chiefs were increasingly dispossessed and their authority flouted but it was not, as we shall see, till 1677 that an organised expedition was planned to remedy this situation. Through his Dominican interpreter Mwene Mutapa Mavura complained to the Portuguese king in 1645 of the devastation of the interior.

From their strongholds in the bush Portuguese adventurers were raiding the Karanga villages for cattle and carrying off children as slaves. The Portuguese did not confine their attentions to the children of the humble but took the sons and daughters of chiefs, luring the latter away with promises of marriage and then selling them off when they were tired of them. The villages were becoming depopulated and the gold mines were no longer worked, while the Mwene Mutapa's authority and that of the other chiefs was weakened. Mavura wanted the authority of the Portuguese captains strengthened, and in particular he wanted all the Portuguese to live within the fortified fairs where they could be controlled (*175*).

The problem was soon identified by earnest Portuguese officials. The population of Portuguese was too small and the power too concentrated in the hands of a small number of families—a situation familiar in Portugal itself and still the problem of rural Brazil in the twentieth century.

In 1644 the Jesuit Antonio Gomes had painted a touching picture of all the Portuguese and Indians in the interior forced into the unnatural state of celibacy because there were no women for them to marry, and living 'in what manner God knows' (*371*, 241). By this time, however, the shortage of population was already a familiar refrain. As early as 1619 Diogo da Cunha Castellobranco had written to the king that 'for want of population the lands are mostly uncultivated' (*279*, 161), and in 1636 *Dom* Filipe Mascarenhas declared that an equal distribution of lands should be made by a *mesa da fazenda*—treasury board—as in Ceylon (*165*).

Finally as a result of the serious news from the Rivers about the disorders and growing anarchy, the king ordered that a colonising expedition should be sent to the Rivers, from India and that a redistribution of land which had been granted by emphyteutic tenures should be carried out on the basis that the heir of an existing land-holder received a third of his inheritance and the remaining two thirds went to provide estates for the newcomers (*172*).

It was suggested in the following year, 1647, that forts should be built and garrisoned (*173*) to control the *poderosos*—the powerful ones—and in 1650 it was suggested that the great land concessions should be linked with the forts so that the latter could be maintained by the rents from the estates (*176*). In 1652 the king suggested that criminals be sent from India to people the Rivers as there was so much difficulty in persuading settlers to go there (*283*). Already there were stringent laws preventing people leaving East Africa. But this was all crying into the wind. The Portuguese empire had not the resources to combat the natural forces confronting it.

It is at this stage, in 1667, that the report of Father Manuel Barreto was written to the viceroy João Nunes da Cunha. Barreto had been active in the Rivers for many years; he knew all the leading *sertanejos* and had himself taken part in local wars and had acquired by his own account the nickname *temani*, which means valiant or courageous. The fear that a small group of *sertanejo* families was monopolising the land was, said Barreto, largely justified. The various Portuguese captains were unable to control the settlements unless they were themselves local men with authority firmly rooted in their local wealth and power. The writ of the king counted for much less than the authority of armed bands of retainers. Sisnando Dias Bayão and his son Francisco were dead by this time but their lands had passed into the hands of Antonio Lobo da Silva. He was a soldier who had served twelve years in Guinea and Brazil and had married Bayão's daughter Maria. He inherited the Bayão estates in 1655. Silva's own daughters had widened the family connections, so that in Sena all the men with any wealth or power were either his relatives or protégés. He was related also to the captain of Quelimane, who had just died, and he had twice been sent on missions to command Portuguese forces in Karangaland. Barreto suggested that he be appointed captain of Sena, as this was the senior captaincy and the nominal superior of all the others.

Barreto clearly thought—or had an interest in having the

viceroy think—that Silva was a zealous and upright man whose zeal and uprightness would be stimulated still further by the grant of a patent of nobility from the king. It was Barreto's plan that Silva should be employed by the crown to bring the other lawless *sertanejos* to heel, and that he should start by making a survey of the land and wealth each one possessed. However, to make royal authority depend on one of the backwoods clans was to admit that control of the colony had passed irretrievably out of royal hands.

Barreto's memorandum (*318*) slowly circulated in the official blood-stream of the Portuguese empire, and began to infuse ideas and energy into a body weakened after the disastrous wars with the Dutch and Spanish.

In March 1669 the prince regent wrote to India: 'There being among the residents there (eastern Africa) those who are willing to undertake the fortification at their own cost, it is advisable that you should pay extra attention to their petitions.' Probably the prince had already seen Barreto's memorandum. It was certainly before the royal council in the early 1670s when once again the whole situation in East Africa came under review and the hopes of instant wealth to be obtained by developing the mines were revived.

The plan placed before the royal council was to send from Portugal an organised expedition of settlers with their families, and a large military garrison. The great Zambesi estates were to be divided up, the land was to be populated, the royal treasury was to be filled with the wealth of a thriving colony. There had been previous settlement schemes for East Africa but they had had to compete with many other urgent imperial needs and the Spanish and Portuguese crowns in the days of their poverty had never pressed ahead seriously with them. The scheme which was eventually launched in 1677 was a serious attempt—almost the last serious attempt—to modify the type of society which had grown roots already in the land and was proving so destructive of good order and economic development (*313*, ch. 10).

The original plan was to send out six hundred soldiers, some of whom would garrison strong points throughout the country, and who would be offered land if they married and settled. There were also to be fifty married couples of child-bearing age who would be given land, and skilled men were to be chosen wherever possible. There were to be money subsidies and supplies to encourage participation in the scheme (*167*).

Probably to be associated with this settlement scheme and the

64

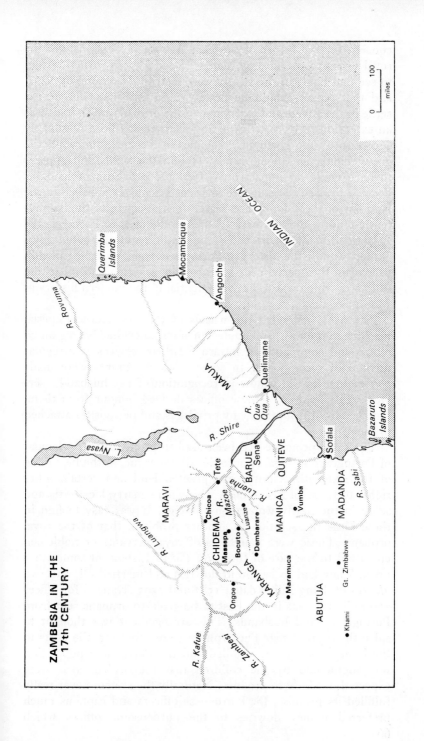

ZAMBESIA IN THE
17th CENTURY

concern for the future of the East African possessions was the royal order to the viceroy, dated March 1675, instructing him to see that lands in the Rivers were distributed among orphans, and that offices should be bestowed on any man who would settle in the Rivers and marry one of the orphans (285). This was an extension to East Africa of an idea that had been reasonably successful in the Portuguese colonies in the East, and while the great colonising scheme ran away into the sands and appears to have made no impact on Africa, the provision of lands as dowries to needy Portuguese maidens became established in the land law of the colony. The search for the origin of the emphyteutic tenures took us back to the middle ages in Portugal; the Atlantic captaincies provided the tradition of delegated royal authority; now the history of Portuguese India must be called in to explain the special provisions for the granting and inheriting of estates which was to be so influential in the modern history of Moçambique.

Patronage had oiled the wheels of the Portuguese imperial machine in the East, and noblemen and soldiers had been granted offices and commands in reward for their services as a regular method of recompense. In some cases the grants were made *post mortem* to the widow in recognition of her husband's services. The holders of these offices derived honour from them, but also profit from the many privileges and perquisites attached to them.

The same principle had been used to promote the settlement of Portuguese in Goa. Afonso de Albuquerque, at the beginning of the sixteenth century, had granted land and certain other rights to those of his soldiers who would marry local girls and settle in the newly won colony of Goa. It was easy to find in these ideas the solution to another problem, that of the royal orphans. These were daughters of royal servants or noblemen entrusted to the care of the *Casa Pia* in Lisbon, or some other town. They had to be found dowries and married off, and two *alvaras* of King Filipe dated 1583 and 1595 arranged for offices and military posts in the East to be given to orphans sent from Portugal to find husbands. This arrangement was thought to solve three problems. The orphans were cared for, the posts in the imperial service were filled and the Portuguese population was augmented by the children that the orphan girls were expected dutifully to produce. Naturally the system never really fulfilled its promise, for Portuguese officers and captains much preferred money dowries to the burdensome offices which

66

accompanied their brides (*179*, *180*). Convicts, superfluous orphans, fallen women and impoverished nobles, these are the people who have so often formed the vanguard of European civilisation in the 'backward' and 'uncivilised' parts of the world.

This system was not applied to imperial offices only. *Aldeias* were villages in Portuguese India—or more correctly fiscal units based roughly on village settlements. In the northern garrison areas of Baçaim and Damão two or three *aldeias* might be given as a dowry. The girls were expected to marry a European Portuguese, and besides paying rent to the crown they had to furnish a horseman for any military campaign in the offing. Possession of *aldeias* was by emphyteutic tenure, usually for three lives, but it did not confer ownership of the land or any obligation to cultivate it. The holder of the *aldeia* merely enjoyed fiscal and administrative rights (*395*, 108).

In Goa the same system was applied to the revenues of the *pagodas* which were either taken over directly by the Portuguese or else were made over by the Hindu inhabitants when they received baptism. These were held by three-life tenures or by perpetual emphyteusis.

In Ceylon the system appears to have been similar. Some of the four hundred odd *aldeias* controlled by the Portuguese were devoted to financing the Portuguese settlements and forts. They were administered by native tax collectors and the revenues were paid into the treasury. Others were reserved to pay the royal officers in Ceylon. The captain-general had twenty; the *capitão-mor do campo*, the *vedor da fazenda* and all the regional captains were also paid in this way. Others again were granted to worthy Portuguese or Singhalese individuals. These paid a *foro* of twelve per cent on all produce. Each grantee was liable for military service and had to provide a musketeer for every 50 *pardãos* and supporting archers and spearmen. These *aldeias* were also held by three-life tenures (*353*, 26).

In the varied correspondence of the viceroys with Lisbon can be traced the trials and errors of the system of land tenure in Portuguese India. Portuguese girls were not always marrying Portuguese men and in 1672 strict instructions were issued that the regulations should be observed (*183*). In 1623 absenteeism among the holders of the *aldeias* in Ceylon was tackled (*181*), and in 1640 the viceroys were forbidden to award *aldeias* to their own servants (*182*). In 1704 the grant of *aldeias* was removed entirely from the hands of the viceroys and vested in the king

67

(*184*). As early as 1609 a provision applicable throughout the Portuguese empire had forbidden the alienation of land to the church or religious orders.

To extend this system to East Africa was to seek fulfilment of the same three objectives, but it was also to attack a peculiarly African problem—the great private armies and jurisdictions controlled by the handful of settlers in the Rivers. Orphans had been sent to East Africa before. In 1635 King Filipe had sent orphans to the Rivers because he heard there was a shortage of women in the colony, but this was probably an isolated instance and there is no evidence that land grants to women on any scale resulted from it. From the 1670s land grants to women became frequent and it was probably early in the eighteenth century that hereditary succession to *prazos* was restricted to the female line only.

The last decades of the seventeenth century saw the problems of the Rivers as intractable as ever. The whole south bank of the Zambesi from the Zambesi delta to Cabora Bassa was in Portuguese hands, though the Lupata mountains were as uncontrollable as they had been earlier in the century (*169*). Scarcely fourteen Portuguese made up the whole of the River settlements aided by a number of Indians and half castes. Antonio Lobo da Silva's power was so vast that he could travel for a month from Sena to Sofala without leaving his land (*166, 482*). Karangaland itself was deserted by the Mwene Mutapa and only a few Portuguese and their slaves now lived there. Wild beasts inhabited the once prosperous villages, and the supply of gold had fallen off (*168, 473*).

Gold was still mined but the fairs had only a handful of merchants—Dambarare, the chief of them, had only three or four settlers. The fairs and the Zambesi towns were badly in need of arms, men and proper fortifications. More than one suggestion was made for the proper garrisoning of the fairs and the allotment of the lands for the support of the garrisons. One writer, who had witnessed the Portuguese *sertanejos* on campaign and had marvelled that eight men could dominate a vast slave army, and through it the whole of central Africa, asked why a handful of royal soldiers could not do the same (*168, 476*). This European logic was never to prove adequate to explain an African phenomenon, as Portuguese administrators were discovering even in the early years of the twentieth century. The settlers were kings in their own right and recognised no authority; they still made and unmade chiefs, and in 1676 a Portuguese band had captured

68

and killed the reigning Quiteve and replaced him by their own nominee (*166*, 482).

As for the Mwene Mutapa, his power and prestige were gone. His children were educated by the Portuguese, but the heartland of the old kingdom was ravaged and deserted. Only in the southwest did Butua retain its independence and something of its old prosperity. The *mãe de ouro*—the mother of gold—the Portuguese called it, and continued to cast greedy eyes on its legendary wealth. Probably in the 1680s the old Torwa dynasty of Butua was replaced by a new one and in 1683 a Portuguese force was badly mauled in an indecisive engagement with the Changamire in Maungwe. All the Portuguese plans to develop central Africa during the seventeenth century may have come to nothing—but salvation for the Shona peoples from the anarchy of the Portuguese conquest was close at hand.

5 Portuguese Zambesia in the Eighteenth Century

The defeat of the Portuguese in Mashonaland

During the seventeenth century the Portuguese had brought neither peace nor prosperity to the Rhodesian high veldt. Their presence had upset the elaborate balances of African society, and they and their bands of armed retainers had destroyed the political authority of the chiefs. From time to time there had arisen African leaders who, for a few years, had rallied the Shona peoples against the invader. Matuzianhe at the beginning of the century and the pretender Kaparidze in the 1630s had been leaders of power and personality, but they never won the traditional chiefs wholly to their side. For the most part the Mwene Mutapas had continued to rely on Portuguese backing with the result that the wars of the century had usually had something of the character of African civil wars, with the Portuguese lending their aid to the side of legitimate authority. It was by similar intervention that Portuguese had come to dominate Manica, Quiteve, and for a brief period Butua as well.

When a ruler has to rely on foreign military aid to maintain himself, the legitimacy of his title ceases to mean very much. This the Portuguese discovered in Ethiopia in the 1630s and when a similar disaster struck them in the interior of central Africa in the 1690s they had only their past policies and conduct to blame.

The occasion of this sudden collapse of the Portuguese was a successful rallying of the Shona peoples by the Changamire—the Roswi chief of Butua. In the 1680s a Portuguese force had been worsted in a battle fought against the Changamire in Maungwe, but there had been no follow-up of this victory, until in 1693 the Changamire joined forces with Mwene Mutapa Nhacunimbire who was trying to hold his throne against a rival called *Dom* Pedro who was nominally a Christian and was backed by the Portuguese.

In 1693 Changamire struck at the centre of Portuguese

influence in Mashonaland, the fair of Dambarare. The Portuguese were caught unprepared, for like the Rhodesian settlers in 1896, they were scattered thinly over the country and could not reach the safety of the forts in time to defend themselves. The fair was overrun and destroyed. According to the vivid account of the Jesuit chronicler, Antonio da Conceição, Changamire's warriors dug up the bones of the Portuguese in the church and burnt them, performing nameless sacrileges on the chalices and other holy objects (*337*, para. 110). Probably this account was rather highly coloured, for recent excavations have revealed no sign of any desecration of the church or of any fire (*365*).

With the fall of Dambarare the other fairs were hastily abandoned, and the residents and traders fled to the safety of the Zambesi towns. By the beginning of 1694 the Portuguese had been driven from all the high veldt, their armed retainers melting away as the reputation of Changamire's invincibility grew. In 1695 it was the turn of Manica. The Butua warriors swept over the gold workings, missions and settlements taking many Portuguese prisoners and extinguishing Portuguese power in the area. Probably Changamire intended next to descend the traders' road and attack Sena. The Portuguese waited fearfully for the onslaught, but it never came and later they heard that Changamire was dead.

Although reinforcements were rushed to the Rivers from Moçambique, the Portuguese struck only one counter-blow that had any effect, when a force raised and equipped by one of the settlers, Caterina de Faria, defeated the forces of Nhacunimbire and installed *Dom* Pedro on the Mwene Mutapa's throne. The Portuguese soon had to recognise that their once extensive conquests in central Africa were now reduced to the southern shore of the Zambesi from the Cabora Bassa to the sea, the Zambesi delta and the land lying between Sena and Sofala. Even this excessively hot and fever-ridden stretch of land gradually shrank before the encroachments of independent chiefs during the eighteenth century.

Mwene Mutapa and Changamire

The wars of the 1690s destroyed any illusions about the power of the Mwene Mutapas. This historic chieftaincy had become the plaything of the two real powers in central Africa, the Changamire and the Portuguese. The Changamire's victory and the continued weakness of the Portuguese south of the Zambesi during the eighteenth century reduced the 'emperors' of Mwene Mutapa to the status of any ordinary chief. Their effective paramountcy was gone for ever, although Portuguese writers maintained the fiction of the 'empire' of Mwene Mutapa, aware that their claims to territory in central Africa (which they were to drag out again in the 1890s) rested on the formal concessions made by the Mwene Mutapas in the seventeenth century.

For some years after 1695 the two rival lines of Mwene Mutapas struggled for the control of the chieftaincy. The Portuguese supported *Dom* Pedro and a series of chiefs who had been Christianised, and who recognised Portuguese overlordship. *Dom* Pedro even renewed the concession of the silver mines soon after winning his throne with Portuguese aid. The Changamires supported Nhacunimbire and his successors. In 1712 the war was renewed and the Portuguese Mwene Mutapa was driven from his throne and replaced with Changamire's nominee Samutumbo Nhamhandu. Although recognising the overlordship of Changamire, Samutumbo also tried to gain the friendship of the Portuguese and sought baptism—a rite which by this time had become indispensable in the coronation ceremony of any Mwene Mutapa. The Portuguese also continued to send their official garrison to the Zimbabwe and to supply the Mwene Mutapa with prestige presents and trade goods (*448*, 171–179).

However, there was no stability for the chieftaincy. João Moreira Pereira, writing in 1766, said that in the fifteen years he had been in Africa there had been six Mwene Mutapas and the country had been in a continual state of civil war (*19*). In 1760 the Portuguese formally withdrew their garrison and thereafter refrained from interfering in the politics of the chieftaincy. The confusion was great as claimant succeeded claimant to the throne, each murdering his predecessor and soon disappearing into oblivion himself, and, try as they did to keep out of this turmoil, the Portuguese found their control of the old crown lands near Tete weakened as the disorder spread among the chiefs and inhabitants of the *prazos*. In the second half of the eighteenth century most of the *prazos* on the south bank, up river of Tete, were abandoned and not reoccupied until late in the nineteenth century (*402*, 130–33).

As for the high veldt itself, just a century and thirty years separated the expulsion of the Portuguese from the first invasions of Ngoni from the south. This period was something of a golden age of prosperity for the Roswi dynasties who ruled the gold fields and rich grasslands of Rhodesia. It was during this century that the great stone towns, reviving the traditions of Great Zimbabwe, were built in Matabeleland and elaborate designs were worked into the stone faces of their terraced hillsides.

Meanwhile the paramountcy of the Roswi Changamires of Butua remained unchallenged. It was recognised in the east in Manicaland, in Maungwe and throughout the old lands of the Karanga kingdom. The Portuguese traded with Changamire in Zumbo on the Zambesi, and in Inhambane south of Sofala, some six hundred miles distant. Throughout this wide belt of territory the smaller chieftaincies remained intact, but the word of Changamire was decisive in the choice of chiefs and in the successful exclusion of the Portuguese from the goldfields (443, 220).

The fairs and goldfields south of the Zambesi

The decision to exclude the Portuguese from entering their territory was a wide decision of the Changamires. The experience of the previous century had taught the lesson that long spoons were needed to sup with the Europeans. (A similar policy of total exclusion was followed by the Ethiopians from the time of the expulsion of the Portuguese until the nineteenth century, and for a similar reason.) So strictly was this policy enforced that the Portuguese prisoners captured in Manica in 1695 remained permanent prisoners in the heart of central Africa. An attempt to ransom them in 1716 failed (394, 63), and the captives apparently settled down and married, for in the middle of the century the then Changamire asked for a priest to be sent to minister to them (481, 169). Apparently no missionary could be found for this curious assignment.

Even in the kingdom of Quiteve, which was not overshadowed in the same way by the Changamire, this policy of exclusion was applied. A Quiteve was actually dethroned and killed by his chiefs because it was believed that he was going to open the mines and allow the Portuguese into the country to work them (481, 155).

The Portuguese for their part continued to dream of re-establishing their fairs in Mashonaland. Dambarare had become for them the symbol of their past greatness and tradition had, by the middle of the eighteenth century, endowed it with extensive ruins, surrounded by orange and mango trees and with an old bell lying in the ruins of the church (428, 329). In 1769 a scheme

73

was initiated for the reoccupation of the fair. Lists of settlers were drawn up and the cost was worked out in detail (*215*); but like so many government-inspired projects it met with the silent obstruction of the settlers and the jealousy of those merchants who saw their position threatened by the revival of the Mashonaland fairs.

The Manicaland fairs were, however, re-established. About 1719 (*394*, 43) one of the leading Sena settlers undertook to re-open the fair. He sent an array of gifts to sweeten the Manica chiefs and then set off with his retainers on what appears to have been partly an embassy and partly a military expedition. A wooden fort was constructed and commerce began to move once again along the traders' road to Sena.

Until the Manica fairs were extinguished a second time by the Ngoni raids in the nineteenth century, the Portuguese maintained three trading posts. One was on the Aruangua river on the borders of Manica and Barue and was the first post reached by traders coming from Sena. It had no permanent garrison but there were two small pieces of artillery there at the end of the eighteenth century (*357*, 325). The main fair was at Massikesse and there was another post at Vumba.

The history of the Manica fairs in the eighteenth century was very different from what it had been in the previous one. Changamire was overlord of Manica and allowed the Portuguese to trade there, even granting them small areas of land for their forts, but on the strict understanding that they took no part in the mining. The Portuguese had to give an annual present to Changamire and also to the king of Manica, Chicanga. Further gifts were regularly given to the king of Barue, Macombe, through whose territory the traders had to pass, and to one of Chicanga's wives who was installed to supervise the fairs and whose demands for gifts grew steadily more importunate (*357*, 327).

At its most prosperous the Manica fair handled a wide variety of goods. The best gold available in the eighteenth century, ivory, wax, pearls, rock crystal and skins were brought to the fair from neighbouring states and trade for liquor, cloth, beads, arms and powder (*308*, 193).

Unfortunately trade never ran smoothly for long. It was a reflection of the weakness and declining prestige of the Portuguese that the traders were subjected to a continuous stream of demands for gifts and tribute, that they were arraigned for *milandos*—crimes which often amounted to little more than dis-

74

courtesy or the infringement of some local custom—and mulcted of large fines. Probably the Portuguese brought much of this on themselves. Criminals threatened with prosecution in the Rivers escaped to the fairs or were exiled there after being found guilty. The small but unruly population of Manica frequently proved too difficult for the captain to manage and there are complaints of the Portuguese returning to their old game of illicit trading outside the fairs (99).

The fair was ruled by a *Capitão-Mor* who was appointed by the viceroy, and after 1752 by the governor-general of Moçambique. He nominally commanded a garrison of ten men and acted as the administrator and judge of the community. The first governor-general of the colony, Francisco de Mello e Castro, wrote in 1755 that the captain of Manica should always be one of the settlers who had private wealth and slaves of his own which would give him more prestige and enable him to meet the numerous demands for tribute or presents without which the fort could not continue (*131*).

When the history of Manica comes to be written it will be seen that some sort of a balance was struck between potentially conflicting interests. The Portuguese grew rich from trade; the chiefs along the traders' road protected their interests by exacting presents; the kings of Manica also grew rich without suffering the dislocation which European presence so often brought. For their part the Portuguese appear not to have tried to gain political control of the region, and it may well be that Changamire's overlordship helped to preserve the peace and restrain political ambitions and excessive greed for Manica's gold.

Zumbo

To revive the Manica fairs had been a journey into the past; the founding of a fair at Zumbo was more of a pioneering venture. Portuguese traders had for many years been passing up the Zambesi beyond Tete and Cabora Bassa. Once the rapids had been circumvented there was a clear stretch of water running past Chicoa to the confluence of the Zambesi and Luangwa rivers. Here was a great parting of the ways. Southwards lay the kingdom of Butua and the gold mines of Rhodesia; northwards up the Luangwa lay the chieftaincies of the western Marave and beyond them the copper mines and the drainage basin of the Congo.

By the end of the seventeenth century traders had already pushed quite far into the interior. They had reached Anvuas which was thirty days from Chicoa and eight days' journey inland. Here they met traders who had come from the Atlantic coast of Africa. The confluence of the Zambesi and the Luangwa they called Umburuma after the chief of the district whose descent from a past Mwene Mutapa connected his state with that of the Karanga. Up the Zambesi from Umburuma lay Angoza, six or eight days' journey away, and another ten or twelve days took the traders to Mozimo. This place must have been above the Kariba gorge but apparently beyond this the Zambesi was not known. At Mozimo ivory was to be had in great abundance, which suggests that the traders had only recently begun to tap this supply. Two or three successful journeys were enough to set a trader up for life (*337*, paras 40–44).

However, in spite of these regular trade routes, there were no official fairs until, in the early eighteenth century, Zumbo was founded. The firmest date for the founding of Zumbo is 1716 (*305*, 543), though a variety of earlier years were favoured by different writers in the eighteenth century. It was founded by a Goanese called Pereira who became its first *Capitão-Mor*, and who also appears under the names of Francisco Rodrigues (*428*, 330), and Chicalea (*481*, 169). Throughout the eighteenth century it was to remain a virtual monopoly of the Goanese in the Rivers.

Sited at the confluence of the Zambesi and the Luangwa, Zumbo was ideally placed to trade north and south. From the Marave country to the north copper and ivory were brought by itinerant African traders (*308*, 204), southwards the traders looked to the lucrative markets of Butua. The fair existed very much under the shadow of the power of the Changamire who extended to it his protection, and came to its rescue when it was threatened by the chiefs more immediately its neighbours (*403*, 66).

Zumbo became the chief point of contact between the Portuguese on the Zambesi and the Changamire's kingdom in the interior. No Portuguese were allowed to penetrate the interior and the trade of Zumbo was carried on by bands of professional African traders who entered the service of the Portuguese and Indians and traded on their behalf in the Butua fairs. These professional traders, who were called *mussambazes*—a name said to derive from the verb *sambazar*, to trade, or possibly to dig for gold (*308*, 196)—were an old institution in Zambesia and probably operated on the trade routes long before the Portuguese entered the country. The Portuguese often refer to the *mussam-*

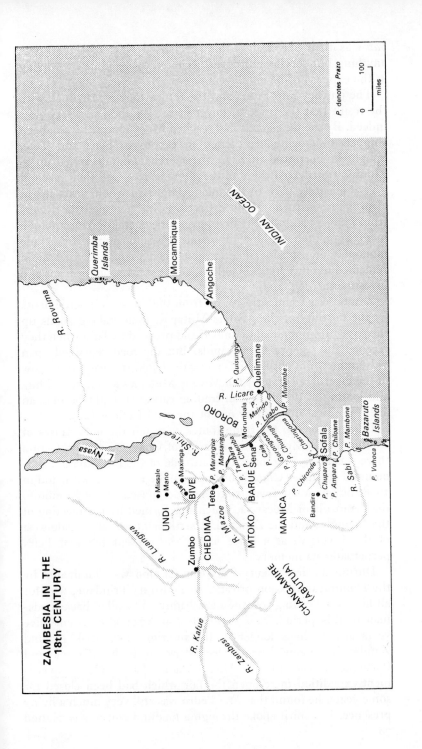

ZAMBESIA IN THE
18th CENTURY

P. denotes Prazo

0   100
miles

INDIAN OCEAN

Querimba Islands

Mocambique

Angoche

R. Rovuma

Quelimane

P. Quisungo

R. Licare

BORORO

P. Mulambe

P. Maindo

P. Luabo

L. Nyasa

Morumbala

P. Chemba

P. Tambara

R. Shire

Java

Maxinga

Missale

Mano

BIVE

P. Marangue

P. Massangano

Tete

R. Mazoe

UNDI

CHEDIMA

MTOKO

BARUE

Sena

P. Cala

Gorongosa

P. Chicanga

P. Cheringoma

Sofala

P. Chiloane

P. Ampara

MANICA

P. Chironde

Bandire

P. Chupara

P. Mambone

Bazaruto Islands

R. Sabi

P. Vuhoca

CHANGAMIRE
(ABUTUA)

Zumbo

R. Luangwa

R. Kafue

R. Zambesi

bazes as their slaves, but this specialised class of traders was anything but servile and never hesitated to make its own living at the expense of its employers.

The journey into Butua and the return took a year in all, with the result that the trade turnover in the Zambesi was very slow indeed. By the time goods had reached Moçambique by sea, been shipped to Quelimane, carried in canoes to Sena and Tete, bought or borrowed there by the merchants and carried up to Zumbo, transferred there to the *mussambazes*, and then taken at a very leisurely pace to the inland fairs two whole years might elapse. Francisco de Mello e Castro (who governed the Rivers from 1740–45 and was the first governor-general of Moçambique in 1752) pointed out how impossible it was to run the royal trade monopoly on a businesslike fashion when a single factor seldom remained in office long enough to see the returns on his loans and investments (*403*, 108).

Zumbo was frequently cut off from the other river settlements by the hostility of the Mwene Mutapas. Boats taking goods up the river to Zumbo had to unload and proceed by land when they reached the Cabora Bassa rapids. But the road remained open only at the whim of the chiefs along the bank. It is easy to see how in the disordered state of the Mwene Mutapa's kingdom, raiding and looting of the European trading caravans might become an act of political bravado by one of the rival factions (*20*).

Interruptions to the trade routes were not the only causes of trouble for the Zumbo fair. In spite of Changamire's protection there was always the mercurial attitude of the immediate neighbours of the fair—Chief Mburuma—to be reckoned with, and in 1788 the fair was moved from the old exposed site of Zumbo to the peninsula of Mocariva, which was formed by the meeting of the Luangwa and the Zambesi. A settlement was also made west of the Luangwa at a place where the present town of Feira perpetuates its memory.

During its first twenty-five years Zumbo was dominated by the Dominican mission priest, *Frei* Pedro da Trindade, who for all his sacred calling was the most canny and skilled backwoodsman of this period. *Frei* Pedro died in 1751 after twenty-five years and perhaps longer in the interior (*308*, 200). Around Zumbo his name became legendary to both Africans and Portuguese. When in 1861 Albino Manuel Pacheco led a government expedition to re-open the fair which had been closed for some years, he found that *Frei* Pedro was still very much a living presence. His spirit spoke through a medium and was consulted respectfully by the Mburuma of that day. *Frei* Pedro was not to be the only person of Portuguese origin to become after his death the centre of a spirit cult, but it was a curious and ironic sort of success for a Christian missionary to attain among those he was supposed to be converting.

Frei Pedro's history, as learnt by Pacheco, shows the friar starting work in Sofala, and setting out from there to evangelise the Dande region. Here he founded a mission and during a famine built his reputation—and his church—by offering food to starving families in return for their labour. Pacheco thought he was the first Portuguese to settle in the region and that he was the founder of Zumbo—although this was certainly not true (*423*).

Frei Pedro's power rested partly on his personality and partly on his standing as a holy man. This was not all, however, for the friar was a very wealthy man. He discovered gold-bearing rocks near Zumbo and worked these with his slaves to such good effect that when he died 100,000 *cruzados* of his estate in gold, copper and slaves were sent to Goa by the Dominicans (*308*, 201).

Frei Pedro maintained good relations with the neighbouring chiefs and particularly with Changamire, who allowed the friar's trade to pass at times when an embargo on the goods of other Portuguese had been temporarily imposed. The Portuguese authorities came increasingly to rely on the friar and he was given the official title of *Capitão-Mor* of Zumbo which he held until his death. His funeral was a major event. Thousands of Africans flocked to attend the obsequies and the Dominicans had to expend large sums on entertainment to avoid the disorder usually attendant on funerals (*308*, 200–201).

After *Frei* Pedro's death Zumbo became very disordered and conflicts grew between the Indian traders and their European captains, and between the fair and the local chiefs. As the Portuguese used Zumbo as a place of exile for convicts, the turbulent history of the fair is not really surprising, and when serious exploration of the northern interior began it was from the Tete and not the Zumbo community that the impetus came (*336*, 405).

The eighteenth-century gold rush

During the sixteenth and seventeenth centuries the Portuguese had not often ventured very far north of the Zambesi where the Marave chiefs were strong enough to keep the Portuguese at a safe distance. The awe in which the Portuguese held these north-bank potentates is reflected in the stories of cannibalism which they half believed, and half propagated to justify their reluctance to secure their northern frontier (e.g. *445, 291*).

There had always been some contact, however. In the sixteenth century the Portuguese had traded cotton cloth in Bororo, and in 1618 Gaspar Bocarro completed his famous journey overland from Tete to Kilwa (*321*, vol 3, 415–19). Diogo Simões Madeira recruited mercenaries from among the Marave and for the first time opened up a road along the north bank to skirt the Cabora Bassa rapids. He even received a concession of land from an African chief near Chicoa. In 1644 Antonio Gomes wrote of traders who frequented the Shire river and Lake Nyasa (*371*), and later in the century there are reports of a number of expeditions to subdue the chiefs round Mount Morumbala who provided asylum for slaves escaping from Portuguese control (*318*). On the whole, however, the Marave country remained closed to Portuguese infiltration.

Towards the end of the seventeenth century the Marave paramountcy was visibly crumbling. During the eighteenth century the last traces of any central authority disappeared, and the once impenetrable Marave hinterland became increasingly crossed by trade routes served by Yao and Bisa from inland and by Portuguese and Africans from Zambesia. Before the eighteenth century was out many of the historic Marave chieftaincies had disintegrated and the Portuguese presence had become as firmly established north of the Zambesi as in the previous century it had southwards in Karangaland.

The first Portuguese to prospect for precious metal north of the Zambesi was Theodosio Garcia. He had come to the Rivers in the 1640s and in 1678 was entrusted by the captain-general João de Sousa Freire, with a mission to look for the legendary silver mines. Through his personal contacts Garcia was able to reach the court of the Kalonga, chief of the western Marave. There he was shown silver ore, and brought back some to Tete (*126*).

Further discoveries were made as a direct result of the destruction of the Mashonaland fairs in 1693. A Brahmin from Goa called Domingo Carvalho fled from the workings at Ongoe, and began to trade with a chief in the neighbourhood of Chicoa who gave him silver in return for cloth. The story, as told by the Jesuit Francisco de Sousa, writing in 1710, is intricate. News of the silver reached Tete and inspired a slave in the service of

Vicencia João to search for the legendary mines. The slave ran away and obtained protection from the chief who was trading the silver. By careful watching at night he discovered where the ore was secretly mined, obtained some himself and then fled with the news to the Mwene Mutapa. The Mwene Mutapa, now deprived of his gold mines by the Changamire, sent an armed force to wrest control of the silver from this chief who fled to the Portuguese and revealed all his secrets to one of the most powerful of the Tete settlers, Manuel Pires Saro (457, 847–8).

Saro was given the office of *Capitão-mor da Guerra de Tete e Mocaranga* and told to secure the mines for the crown. In June 1696 he was able to report complete success in this mission, having located the mines at Nhacasse, five days' journey from Tete. The following year Mwene Mutapa *Dom* Pedro was persuaded formally to cede the mines to Portugal (*170*).

What happened to Saro's silver mine? No-one knows. Later in the eighteenth century there were isolated silver finds reported. *Frei* Manuel da Encarnação found some silver (*444*), and another lucky Dominican found a lump of silver ore as large as a tombstone (*308*, 199). Unable to carry it all, he took some to Moçambique, gambled it all away and died on the journey back to collect some more. And that is the last that is heard of the silver. Modern geologists know of no silver deposits in Africa—though silver in small quantities is obtained as a by-product of copper-mining. The origin of this silver, first heard of in connection with Homem's disastrous expedition in the sixteenth century and last seen adorning the houses of eighteenth-century Zambesi settlers, remains a mystery.

About gold, however, there was no mystery, and it was soon found that gold could be obtained in many parts of Marave territory. Francisco da Santa Caterina, who wrote in 1744 the first account of the eighteenth-century gold rush in Zambesia, said that gold was first discovered when the land south of the Zambesi was torn by the disorders of local wars and the Portuguese residents increasingly crossed to the comparative safety of the north bank (*444*, 3). The first gold strikes seem to have been made by *sertanejos* fleeing prosecution for debt or crime; men like Rafael Braganza whose slaves discovered the important workings of Mixonga due north of Tete, or José Pereira Velho, who had once been described as one of the most powerful of the settlers, but whom the wheel of fortune had driven as a penniless fugitive into the bush. There he had the good fortune to find the gold-bearing rocks near Mano (*406*, 280–81).

Besides Mano and Mixonga, gold diggings were opened in many other areas. Opposite Sena two Zambesi *donas* (female *prazo*-holders) sent their slaves to mine at a place called Cumbo in the eastern Marave chieftaincy of the Rundo. Opposite Tete in the lands which belonged to the chief Bive, a mine was opened which bore his name, and then a day's journey further off there were two small mines at Chicorongue and Cassunça.

Cassunça had been conquered by a military expedition into Marave territory in 1754—the first large-scale operation of its kind north of the river (*402*, 123). Towards Zumbo there were other gold diggings. At Cabora Bassa a group of Indians worked a low-yield mine for some years, and there were further workings at Mallima, Maxinga (opened 1777) (*358*, 315) and the mine of *Frei* Pedro, called also Pemba and Chipapa, which remained a Dominican preserve. In 1790 or 1791 Gonçalo Caetano Pereira began mining gold at Java (*385*, 183), and this was probably the last new goldfield to be opened up before the nineteenth century brought about the rapid decline and, for a brief period, the virtual cessation of gold-mining in southern Africa—one of the oldest of the world's industries.

The gold strikes in Marave country proved to be of much the same kind as those previously made south of the Zambesi. Geology was the determinant, for most of the veins were shallow and after initial rich rewards became increasingly unworkable. Alluvial deposits were also quickly exhausted in the first hectic days of panning. Vast fortunes could be won by those who were early on the scene, but the yield soon fell to a trickle and within two years a mine might be abandoned altogether or become the preserve of one settler assiduous enough to persevere for the tiny profits to be obtained. When Rafael Braganza began working at Mixonga it was rumoured that he was obtaining 90–110 *pastas* a day. A rush ensued and fighting broke out in which Rafael himself was killed together with four other merchants. His fortune, which had excited so much jealousy, had been hidden before his murder and was never discovered (*481*, 166). Within two weeks the workings had closed down altogether, though the mine was later reopened and became one of the most successful of all the north bank workings. Gold rushes are the same the world over and each of the north bank mines had a similar tale of violence and greed.

The extraction of the gold depended on running water, and ore mined away from a river had to be taken laboriously in baskets to the waterside to be crushed and washed. Although dry season mining was known, the early attempts to work the gold strikes seem to have taken the form of seasonal expeditions mounted by the Sena and Tete residents. Priests, Dominican or Jesuit but sometimes one of each, took charge and the expedition took its own slave labour, trade goods and supplies with it, as it was generally agreed that the local Africans could not be depended on. A rough church would be erected at the diggings, a fair opened and rough justice dealt out to miscreants among the miners (*308*, 196–7).

When the mining camps, called *Bares*, became more permanent, the two largest had an officer with the title of *Capitão-mor* appointed to supervise them, and in 1767 the post of *Capitão-mor das Terras e Bares de Tete* was created (*26*), which presumably had general supervision over all the mining operations. The post invariably went to one of the important settlers because the mines needed a good deal of supervision. In 1759 Manuel da Costa, the *Capitão-mor* of Mixonga and an Indian from Zumbo, complained that the mines were full of undesirables who had come not to dig but to make trouble (*14*). There was no need, he said, for anyone to bring his own slaves, as labour could be obtained on the spot. Nevertheless it was not uncommon for a man to work three hundred of his slaves at the mines at one time—a formidable band of retainers with which to secure the best claims.

Skilled miners had been sent from Europe to the Rivers in the seventeenth century, so it is not surprising to find those in the eighteenth who thought that a bit of European science applied to African conditions would yield better profits (*308*, 196). Skilled Brazilian miners were needed, said Antonio Pinto Miranda, one of the Zambesi settlers, and chained gangs of slaves, managed by overseers and including the sons of chiefs disobedient to the Portuguese was his recipe for a flourishing colony (*406*, 284).

More realistic was the conclusion of Manuel Galvão da Silva, who made a survey of the mines both on the north bank and in Manica, that in any other part of the world the gold would not be worth the trouble of collecting and only the peculiar conditions in the Zambesi settlements made working such poor veins at all feasible (*358*, 316).

The history of Karangaland in the seventeenth century tended to repeat itself north of the Zambesi in the eighteenth. Communal diggings and fairs gradually became the monopoly of individual backwoodsmen; the feudal structure of society, which favoured the strong and was unable to balance rival interests and claims, inevitably leading to this result. Java was the personal preserve of the Caetano Pereiras, Cassunça was mined by the Portuguese owner of the land in which it lay, and by the Dominicans (*358*, 318). Mano, in the early nineteenth century, became the private domain of Colonel Silva Botelho who lived in some state in the deep interior and was very much a law unto himself for all his Portuguese military rank (*156*, *363*, vol 1, 54).

If history were to repeat itself exactly, then one would expect to find chiefs who originally welcomed the Portuguese as traders and miners into their territory forced before long to cede territory and jurisdiction to the *sertanejos*. In 1744 Francisco da Santa Caterina was already recording the cession of land to Portuguese adventurers by the north bank chiefs in return for gifts and payments (*444*, 8). In 1754, the most important step in this direction was made when a force raised from among the river residents successfully invaded the territory of the Marave chief Bive and deprived him of his lands—in spite of attempts by the government to prevent this.

The success of this expedition and the chaos which soon developed on the north bank as the Marave chiefs battled in vain against the infiltration led to further large conquests and annexations, until by the end of the eighteenth century the Portuguese controlled the whole north bank from Lupata to Cabora Bassa.

It was the gold prospectors and *sertanejos* of the north bank who pioneered the first European thrusts into the heart of the future Zambia, just as in the previous century Sisnando Dias Bayão had marched deep into Matabeleland in the south-west.

The first exploration of the northern interior

The journey made by Lacerda in 1798 to Lake Mweru and the court of the Kazembe is the best known episode in the history of Moçambique after the Barreto expedition. Lacerda's expedition had its origins in the knowledge of the interior obtained by some Indian *sertanejos* working in the gold fields. Gonçalo Caetano Pereira had come from Goa in the 1750s and had prospered as trader and gold prospector in the northern interior. He had discovered the mine at Java and it was while he was working there in 1793 that he met some Bisa coming from the interior to trade ivory. He realised that there was an opportunity of tapping new reserves of ivory in the country beyond the Luangwa and sent his son Manuel with some slaves to accompany the Bisa on their return journey.

Manuel stayed six months in the interior and then returned bearing the first detailed account that Europeans had had of the coming of Kazembe's Lunda from the Congo, their displacement of the Bisa and their attempts to use Bisa traders to open new trade routes westwards into the decaying Marave chieftaincies.

Manuel told his story to the assembled residents in Tete in February 1798 and introduced ambassadors from the court of Kazembe. No-one can say what would have been the outcome of this embassy had it not found in Tete a newly arrived governor of the Rivers anxious to follow up all opportunities offered for exploration.

The new *tenente-geral* was Francisco Maria de Lacerda e Almeida who had sailed from Lisbon in April 1797 with orders to undertake a transcontinental journey. The idea for this had originated in the brain of the Secretary of State for Naval and Overseas Affairs, Rodrigo de Sousa Coutinho. He was concerned that British annexation of the Cape in 1795 might lead to the British driving a wedge between the Portuguese possessions on the east and west coasts of Africa. Lacerda was to prevent this by opening a route across the continent. It is interesting to see here in embryo the situation that led to the Anglo-Portuguese conflict in the late nineteenth century.

Lacerda was an academic, a lecturer in mathematics at the *Real Academia dos Guardas da Marinha* when he received his appointment, but he had already had considerable experience in field survey work. He had formed part of an expedition making a survey of the Matto Grosso region of Brazil and had served in 1777 on the frontier commission which was trying to settle the boundary between Spanish and Portuguese possessions in South America. In spite of attempts by his biographers to paint him as a paragon of virtue and nobility, he was a prickly individual who, like many academics in public life, was unable to suffer fools gladly and fatally lacked the diplomatic qualities needed for his task.

His plan was probably to make a thorough survey of the Zambesi settlements, including Manica, and then from Zumbo to strike across the continent to Angola. He arrived in Tete in January 1798, travelling slowly up the Zambesi during the wet season with his wife and two daughters, and day by day recording in his diary all his hatred and contempt of the settler community. Less than a month after his arrival Kazembe's embassy and conversations with Manuel Caetano Pereira caused him to alter his plans radically.

85

He decided to accompany the ambassadors back to Kazembe's country and hastily assembled a motley expedition made up of slaves, soldiers and a few volunteers. Struggling against illness and obstruction, Lacerda took advantage of the death of his wife to marry into one of the most powerful Zambesi families and obtain its backing for the expedition. On 30 June he set out for the interior.

Lacerda's objective was to combine an official embassy to Kazembe with his original scientific and political plan to push across the continent to Angola. It is easy to see now that he was foolishly overconfident in believing that his purpose could be achieved in face of the devious plotting of factions among the settlers and in opposition to the political objectives of Kazembe, which included regular friendly contacts with the Portuguese but not passage for the Portuguese to the west. Lacerda himself was a sick man. His expedition struggled through the dry, hilly country of Zambia, its members quarrelling, fighting amongst themselves and deserting, and the governor progressively losing control as fever and dysentery wore him down. He died near Kazembe's court on 18 October 1798.

Lacerda's expedition—or rather the pioneering journey of Manuel Caetano Pereira—began a forty-year period of regular Portuguese contacts with the Bisa and Lunda peoples of the interior. Taking place the same year as Napoleon's invasion of Egypt, it marks the beginning of the European penetration of Africa and the modern phase of imperialism. For the purposes of this chapter, it must be seen as the logical outcome of the expansion into the northern interior which had been going on throughout the eighteenth century. It marks this century not as one of decline and decadence so much as one in which a reorientation of Portuguese interests and influence took place from south of the Zambesi to north (*383, 384, 385, 298, 329, 344*).

6 The *Prazos* as a System of Land Tenure

The prazos

In the eighteenth century Portuguese Zambesia was divided into three administrative captaincies, Quelimane, Sena and Tete, and the territory of each of the captaincies was further divided into *prazos*.

The captaincy of Quelimane stretched from the town of Quelimane northwards for one hundred or so miles along the coast to the River Quissungo. It included the port of Quelimane itself and its ill-defined hinterland and it extended southwards to include all the Zambesi delta as far as the East Luabo river. There were some sixteen *prazos* in this captaincy and numerous small territories and plots of land that could be leased by the crown. Three large *prazos*—Mirambone e Maral, Licungo e Mabala, and Quissungo—occupied the whole coastline north of Quelimane. This low-lying area belonged more to the world of the coastal Islamic settlements that existed on the fringes of the Makua nation than to the world of the Zambesi. It had little contact with what was going on in the Rivers.

Mahindo e Rio Pequeno was the largest *prazo* in the delta and was estimated at three and a half days' journey across. The other *prazos* were considerably smaller, but at Boca do Rio where the Zambesi began to divide there was a flourishing settlement where the Africans held a local fair (*472*, 302). For the most part the crown estates were grouped round Quelimane itself or lay along the swampy creeks of the Qua Qua river.

The Quelimane *prazos* were alleged to have been originally founded by *Dona* Maria da Guerra at the end of the seventeenth century. Some of them had been inherited by *Dona* Caterina de Faria Leitão, who had lived to a great age, marrying for the fourth time when she was over eighty and not dying until *c.* 1777. She had never held any official titles for her lands and they had never been developed or properly controlled (*35*). During her long life

Dona Caterina had also been empire-building on her own account. At the end of the seventeenth century her father had acquired extensive lands in Bororo country which lay between the Qua Qua river and the Shire; these were a private domain and not part of the crown lands and they were not settled or exploited at all until after *Dona* Caterina's death (45). The Jesuits also acquired some properties up the river Licare in Bororo country and were granted a title to them in 1745 (266).

The largest captaincy in territorial extent was Sena. It stretched as far as the Pungue river in the south-east and north-west as far as the Lupata mountains. The Manica fairs came within its jurisdiction as did all the land north of the Zambesi and up the Shire which the Portuguese might acquire. The Sena *prazos* were mostly on the south bank of the Zambesi and included the largest and richest in the whole of Zambesia. There were approximately thirty crown estates in this jurisdiction. It is impossible to give the number more exactly because each *prazo* had a number of small territories attached to it, and these are sometimes mentioned as though they were separate *prazos*.

Luabo was an island made by the delta rivers and the sea. It was the most profitable of all the *prazos* and was very much sought after, being rich in game, sugar cane and timber. On the south bank extending up the river to Chupanga and along the coast to the mouth of the Pungue was the greatest of all the *prazos*—Cheringoma—the patrimony of Sisnando Dias Bayão. Inland, Cheringoma was divided by the river Zangwe from Gorongosa, also a *prazo* of immense size. On its north side Gorongosa bordered on the chieftaincy of Barue and the road to the Manica fairs passed through it. Both Gorongosa and Cheringoma were thousands of square miles in extent and contained tens of thousands of inhabitants.

The other *prazos* extended along the river as far as the Lupata mountains. Until the late nineteenth century the mountains were never very firmly controlled by the Portuguese, and Tambara—the *prazo* whose territory included part of the mountains—was always one of the most difficult to govern.

Across the Zambesi Portuguese authority had not advanced much since the seventeenth century. Mount Morumbala was nominally subject to the Portuguese, but its obedience was spasmodic. Had the projected move of the whole town of Sena to the cooler slopes of the mountain been effected, then all would have changed, but the settlers vetoed this move and the Morumbala and Shire chiefs continued to harbour slaves escaped from

88

the Portuguese and to threaten the river traffic. Some mining was developed across the river during the eighteenth century and a certain amount of Portuguese trade passed up the Shire (*384, 101*).

The situation in the Tete captaincy is rather difficult to discern. It was this captaincy that had the really open frontier. Northwards there was expansion across the Zambesi at the expense of the declining Marave chieftaincies and there was a certain limited penetration of Barue. West of Tete, however, the lands which the Portuguese had held since the early seventeenth century, and which included those conquered by Diogo Simões Madeira early in the seventeenth century, were increasingly abandoned as the settlers moved away from the vicinity of the disordered Mwene Mutapa kingdom and crossed to the new territories in Marave country.

A list of the *prazos* in the Tete district was drawn up for the *tenente-geral* Antonio Manuel de Mello e Castro in 1783 (*54*). There were fifteen lay *prazos* still occupied south of the river— among them Massangano, which controlled the point where the Luenha and Mazoe rivers entered the Zambesi and which was one of the most important, and certainly the most famous, of all the Zambesi *prazos*. In the seventeenth century it had controlled the main route to Mashonaland and the goldfields and had been the headquarters of Manuel Paes de Pinho, the leading *sertanejo* of his day (*318*); in the nineteenth century it was to be the centre from which the da Cruz family held the whole of Portuguese Zambesia to ransom.

A further thirty-three *prazos* were recorded as being deserted on the south bank, seventeen on the north bank had been conquered from the Marave chief Bive and sixteen from chief Sazora. There were in addition eight *prazos* which had belonged to the Jesuits, including Marangue which faced Massangano across the Luenha river and was one of the largest of the crown lands. These were all crown *prazos*, but there were in addition anything up to forty private *prazos* making the total number of estates in the Tete jurisdiction over one hundred and twenty. Once again there is a large variation in the numbers recorded and many of the Tete *prazos* were very small indeed, containing only a single village or sometimes none at all.

The *prazos* were supposed to be surveyed and marked out on the ground and a record—or *tombo*—of these details kept in the *Feitoria* in Sena. This, however, was never done. The *prazos* were traditional territorial divisions, usually coinciding with the territory of a chief or headman, which had been made over *en bloc* to the Portuguese. Their extent was usually measured in the number of villages they possessed and in the length of time it took to cross them, and they had traditional boundaries, called *miganos* (*129*), to which the Portuguese adhered. One indication of the strictness with which these traditions were preserved is that when the Portuguese enlarged a *prazo* they appear to have kept the additional territory distinct from the original *prazo* (*135*). A person would be granted a *prazo* with its *incumbes e aneixos* which were sometimes named individually. Thus an example from the *Relação das Terras da Real Coroa da Jurisdição desta Villa de Tette* compiled in 1783 (*54*) reads:

> D. *Maria Antonia Luciana de Mello a terra Nhancanga com tres incumbes, Nhamitova, Chirambane, e Songa* . . .

An *incumbe* was a large African village and appears to have been an African term taken over by the Portuguese in the seventeenth century (*371, 168*).

Towards the end of the eighteenth century a serious attempt was made to have the *prazos* surveyed. Antonio Manuel de Mello e Castro ordered a *tombo* to be compiled in 1786 (*62*) and the job of carrying out the surveys was entrusted to the town councils. There were even attempts to disallow land grants on the ground that the *prazos* in question had not been surveyed, but none of this appears to have had much effect on the way the *prazo* system was worked.

The machinery for handling prazo grants

In the seventeenth century, and up until 1752, anyone who wished to acquire a *prazo* petitioned the *tenente-geral dos Rios*, setting out his particular claim to the land. The *tenente-geral* was supposed to satisfy himself about the genuineness of the petition and was then free to issue a *provisão*—a provisional grant. After this the papers were sent to Goa where the viceroy issued a *carta de aforamento*—a deed of lease—and a confirmation of the grant (*212*).

If the *prazo* was without a *senhor* then the grant was called a *merce nova*—a new grant; if there were still one or two lives of the lease to run when a *foreiro* died then the *prazo* passed by *direito da renovação*—right of renewal—to the heir or, failing an

The *aringa* of Massangano, an engraving by A. de Castilho

The *aringa* of Massangano photographed by the author in 1964. Taken from the same place as Castilho's engraving above

3 The grave of Mrs Livingstone under the Baobab tree, near Chupanga House

4 Old-style Zambesi house in Tete, since demolished (from a photograph taken by the author in 1963)

heir, to whoever was named in the will of the deceased. In each case the grant had to be confirmed. The *foreiro* paid various dues to have his grant registered and drawn up and these were not returned if the grant was not confirmed (*42*).

In 1752 the government of East Africa was separated from that of India and at first the same procedure was followed, except that the *cartas de aforamento* and the confirmation were both issued in Moçambique by the governor-general, so that all outside check on the system was thereby removed. In answer to various queries from Moçambique, however, the crown decided that the procedures for granting *prazos* should be brought into line with Brazilian practice and that confirmation would have to be issued in Lisbon.

In the meantime a crisis had arisen in Moçambique. The newly appointed governor, João Manuel de Mello, within a few weeks of arriving in East Africa in 1758, committed suicide by falling on his sword in his palace on Moçambique Island (*468*). The government was taken over by the senior military officer, Brigadier David Marques Pereira. Pereira was deeply involved with the factions of the Zambesi settlers and proceeded to use his temporary authority to hand out patents and land grants to his friends. Later in the year another governor, Pedro da Saldanha de Albuquerque, arrived, and he at once suspended all further grants and wrote to Lisbon asking for the whole question of the *prazos* to be settled (*212*).

As a result the *Concelho Ultramarino*—overseas council—issued two decrees dated 2 and 3 April 1760 which it doubtless hoped would settle clearly all problems connected with the granting of *prazos* in East Africa (*15, 114*). It had taken the government eight years to establish an administrative procedure which should have been done at the time of the separation of Moçambique from India in 1752.

Every *prazo* falling vacant now had to be placarded in the administrative town in its district. Applications for the grant could then be made to the *tenente-geral* who had to investigate all the circumstances surrounding the vacancy. If all was in order he could then nominate the petitioner to the *prazo* and appoint arbitrators to fix the rent. One arbitrator was to represent the royal treasury and one the prospective *prazo*-holder, and if they disagreed—as was very likely—a third arbitrator was to be appointed who had to agree with one of the others. As soon as the rent was fixed the documents had to be sent to Moçambique where the *carta de aforamento* was issued by the governor-general. To be valid the grant had then to be sent to Lisbon within four years for confirmation.

These arrangements, which in Lisbon must have appeared so clear-cut, merely exacerbated the standing quarrel between Moçambique and the Rivers. The conflicting jurisdictions of *tenente-geral* and governor-general nowhere clashed more violently than over the granting of the *prazos*. The *tenentes-gerais* claimed, with some justice, that they had always made *prazo* grants and the governor or viceroy had merely confirmed their measures. They said that only the 'man on the spot' could know the best interests of the state and whenever the Moçambique government tried to interfere it made grants to pluralists, absentees and other totally unsuitable persons. The governor-generals, however, were engaged in a never-ceasing battle to assert their full jurisdiction over the church and over the powerful interest groups of the Rivers which so often controlled the *tenente-geral* and made him merely an instrument of faction.

The quarrel boiled over during the energetic governorship in the Rivers of Antonio Manuel de Mello e Castro. He was a strong supporter of the *regalia* (prerogative) of the *tenentes-gerais* and eventually secured a definite statement from Lisbon confirming the right of the *tenente-geral* to make *prazo* grants (*44, 56, 91*).

The matter was not settled quite so easily, however, and it was still being fought bitterly during the governor-generalship of Sebastião Xavier Botelho in the 1820s. Moçambique then claimed that the royal order of 1783, which had apparently settled the issue in favour of the *tenente-geral*, applied only to an isolated case and was not a general instruction (*234*). Not surprisingly immense confusion was caused by there being two officials to whom applications for *prazo* grants could be addressed.

The arbitration procedure worked well, but a lot of trouble occurred over the investigations into the circumstances in which the *prazo* came 'on the market'. Originally the job of the *tenente-geral*, this was entrusted to the *camaras* of the Zambesi towns late in the eighteenth century. Their performance of this task was usually most inefficient, and in desperation the Lisbon authorities began refusing confirmation of grants where adequate information was not presented. Naturally Moçambique resented this ill-informed, long-distance interference which apparently became serious after the removal of the royal government from Lisbon to Brazil in 1808 (*87*). In practice, of course, it was seldom possible for anyone successfully to deprive a *prazo senhor* who was actually in possession.

The confirmation procedure was also followed very irregularly. More than one governor expressed the belief that half the *prazos* were held without any confirmation or even any official title at all. Part of the trouble was undoubtedly the expense of arranging for lawyers in Lisbon to obtain confirmation of a land grant. Some governors as energetic as Antonio de Mello e Castro instituted a sort of *quo warranto* investigation and ordered all *prazo*-holders to present their titles for inspection (*38*). The authenticity and legality of a title were never totally meaningless concepts in the Rivers, but they were always a minor consideration in comparison with the task of securing actual possession and control of a *prazo*.

Renting of prazos

The crown *prazos* were held by contracts of emphyteusis; they could not be sold, mortgaged or divided up except in exceptional circumstances and with express royal permission. For purposes of economic development they were nearly useless and the state derived little from them in revenue. Many observers asked why the state did not rent out its land on a short-term basis—a much more flexible and lucrative system. This was a perennially fresh issue for reformers and many times it was tried both in the case of individual *prazos* and as a general instruction.

In 1758 when all fresh grants of *prazos* were temporarily suspended, vacant estates were rented out on an annual basis (*11*). The same was planned in the following year for the confiscated Jesuit *prazos*; they were to be rented to the highest bidder (*134*) until proper arrangements could be made for them to be leased. Sometimes *prazos* were also rented out in special circumstances— for instance when the *foreiro* failed to complete the formalities of the lease and did not obtain a *carta de aforamento* or confirmation (*76, 127*). January was the season for renting out *prazos*— presumably so that the renter would have the opportunity to sow any crop he wanted for that year (*39*).

In the 1780s a complete survey of the whole *prazo* system was carried out by the *tenente-geral* Antonio Manuel de Mello e Castro. As part of this survey a questionnaire was sent round to the most important settlers asking their opinion on the advisability of renting the *prazos* as opposed to leasing them. It was one of those bouts of democracy by referendum to which the Portuguese colonial administration was liable and which usually hid an infirmity of purpose. In their replies the settlers were unanimous in opposing the renting of the *prazos*. The reasons they gave were eminently sensible in the context of Zambesi society. A man who rented a *prazo* was under pressure to make his fortune in the short time of his contract. He would use violent and extortionate means and would drive the peaceful African peasants from the land. Moreover, no renter would ever be able to establish his control over the slaves of the *prazo*. The long emphyteutic leases, however, guaranteed a man property rights for himself and his immediate heirs, he was not under the same pressure to exploit the land and it was not in his long-term interest to do so. He would be able to control his slaves. They also pointed out that African methods of agriculture were not conducive to intensive exploitation (*41*).

The *tenente-geral* in his report fully agreed with the settlers and summarised their arguments for the benefit of Lisbon; and so the *prazo* system survived this testing and was not seriously threatened again until the 1880s. Many of the answers sent by the settlers were identical and clearly show collusion between them. It was not in the interest of the Zambesi families in 1780 to see their lands rented out and they were to resist it equally strongly in 1880. For with renting came the threat of a partition of the estates and the possibility of a plantation system which would destroy their patriarchal, and very African way of life.

The self-interest behind their arguments is quite clear when one realises that there was nothing to stop the *prazo senhors* renting out their *prazos* on their own account. And this they frequently did, retiring to enjoy their rents in Moçambique Island, Goa or even Portugal. The private renting of *prazos* thus became associated with the problem of absenteeism (*103*).

Other forms of land tenure

During the eighteenth century Portuguese Zambesia recognised two classes of land; there were the *terras da coroa*—crown lands—and the *terras em fatiota*. The crown land included all the lands acquired in the seventeenth century on the south bank of the Zambesi and any territory on the north bank which was handed over to the crown by its owners. Crown land was all leased as *prazos*. Some of the settlers, however, did not choose to hand over to the crown the lands they had bought or conquered from neighbouring chiefs and these became *terras em fatiota* (*45*).

There were about forty *fatiotas*—almost all in the Tete captaincy. The Portuguese government recognised the titles of their owners and registered them. These tenures came close to the concept of freehold property. They were perpetual and inheritance was not restricted to the female line. They could be bought and sold at public auctions or made over from one party to another by a public deed (*49*). The holders of them paid no *foro* but were liable to the tithe and to a sales tax called *ciza*. Finally, they could be jointly held by more than one person (*85*).

The most important aspect of the *fatiotas* was that they provided Zambesia with its only free market in land and thus introduced a small measure of fluidity into the economic life of the colony. Antonio Pinto Miranda, one of the most important critics of Portuguese East Africa in the eighteenth century, thought that as rich men could buy *fatiotas*, the award of *prazos* should be made to poorer families (*406*, *291*).

The distinction between *prazos* and *fatiotas* fades away in any consideration of the realities of society and politics in Zambesia.

The smallest *prazo* or *fatiota* would probably be a number of square miles in extent but, of course, there were many smaller types of property which should just be identified in passing. *Palmares* were palm groves in the coastal districts; *hortas* (gardens) or *vargens* (African gardens) were small plots of land used for growing foodstuffs; the terms *pedaço de chão* (piece of land) and *casa* (house) are also used, often for small urban properties. All these could be had from the government on long or short leases.

The contract

In discussing the contract under which *prazos* were held, Francisco de Mello e Castro (writing in 1750 but referring to the 1740s when he had been *tenente-geral dos Rios*) says that there is an

> ... obligation for them to pass always to the daughter, who will be obliged to marry with a Portuguese born in the kingdom of Portugal, excluding from order of succession male children even if they are the first born. In this way these alliances will cause the Portuguese nation to propagate and increase (*403*, *107*).

As I have suggested, the ideas underlying these provisions probably derived from Indian experience, and in India the *aldeias*—villages—had been continually modified by a stream of royal orders throughout the sixteenth and seventeenth centuries.

In the same way the land law of Moçambique was constantly being modified and altered by decrees, orders from viceroys and governors and by administrative decisions made in different cases. There was no codification of all the orders made concerning the *prazos*, and the same regulations have to be reiterated again and again, while the same disputes frequently recur. Nor is there any easy route to the discovery of what exactly was the law and the practice with regard to the *prazos*. One can take a contract—a *carta de aforamento*—and look at the terms set out there and agreed upon by the parties, but one will be no nearer understanding how these terms were interpreted in practice, nor according to what rules the original grants were made. The following sections therefore examine various aspects of the law and custom connected with the *prazos* which are seen here only as a form of land tenure in a European community.

Who could receive grants of prazos?

It was open to anyone to apply for a *prazo* grant but a successful application usually reflected the priorities of Portuguese colonial policy. The first of these priorities was linked to the traditions of the early days of the empire when personal loyalties and tradition of personal service had been strong. Grants of land or office had been intended to reward the soldiers and servants of the crown. They stood to a veteran of the fleets as a pension for his retirement, as the dowry for his daughters and as security for his widow. This same policy, which had endangered the security of the empire by making over the captaincies of fortresses to absentee widows, was still being pursued at the end of the eighteenth century with the crown estates in Zambesia. As an example one might cite the case of Francisco de Lacerda who died in central Africa in October 1798, leaving a daughter by his first wife as an orphan burdened with her father's debts. The state undertook to provide her with an income which would adequately uphold her status and give some recognition of her father's services. The new *tenente-geral dos Rios* was ordered to find her a *prazo* which would bring in an adequate income for her (*83*).

The second priority of Portuguese policy was to populate the colonies. From the Amazon to Macao the economic and social

96

ills of the empire were universally attributed to the shortage of Portuguese colonists of good character. In East Africa the population problem was more specific—it was due to the lack of white women who would beget and bring up white families. Priority in land grants then would go to maidens requiring dowries, to families without means of maintaining themselves or to widows left destitute on the death of their husbands.

Most applications for the grant of *prazos* therefore usually mentioned either the services of the applicant or the needy relatives he was unable to support.

Prazos could also be bestowed on institutions as a source of income. The religious orders, the *Camaras*, the *Misericordias* all had their *prazos*, though the last two were never important landowners (*252, 54*).

Descent in the female line

In Zambesia throughout the eighteenth and nineteenth centuries it was always women who could claim prior right to the inheritance of a *prazo*, and who were given priority by the government in the granting of vacant estates. For property to pass to female heirs when male were available must be so unusual for its existence in the Portuguese eastern empire to stand out as practically the only example in the history of European land law. It should, however, be said that in Africa it would not have appeared quite so surprising, for descent in the female line is a common feature of many African societies.

The idea almost certainly derived from Portuguese India where it was supposed to operate in the territories of the northern fortresses. It was probably instituted by *Dom* João V early in the eighteenth century (*217*) and applied to East Africa at the same time. The theory of this form of inheritance was clear enough. A girl was given a *prazo* in the first 'life' as her dowry. She married and was fruitful, and on her death the *prazo* descended automatically to her eldest daughter in the second 'life'. This daughter also married and on her death the *prazo* passed to her daughter for the third and last 'life'. When this daughter died the *prazo* reverted to the crown but could be regranted to the same family if application was made.

If a *dona* (all the European or mulatto women adopted this style) had no daughters, then her sons or her husband would be eligible to succeed her. If she had no family at all, then she was

97

free to nominate in her will whoever she pleased.

The first consequence of this law of succession was to encourage the growth of large complexes of family properties, for while women had priority in the inheritance of land, the men remained the heads of the families and saw themselves as the active and dominant members of society. Suppose a man whose wife already had a *prazo* had two daughters. He would petition for *prazos* to provide them with dowries and then marry them off. At worst he would increase his family's holdings to three *prazos*; at best he would have married his daughters into some other Zambesi clan and in this way have linked together two family groupings of *prazos*.

A second factor also contributed to the rise of powerful clans. High mortality coupled with female succession might well lead to an exceptionally healthy or long-lived *dona* inheriting a large number of *prazos* from other members of her family.

It was never very clear whether the laws of inheritance would triumph if a determined *dona* decided to leave her *prazo* to someone other than her daughter. That this often happened is undoubtedly true, for even the best Zambesi families sometimes quarrelled and these quarrels were aided and abetted by the intrigues of fortune-hunters. As Lacerda put it:

> Some people foment discord between husband and wife, brother and sister, so that these shall be offended with their relatives and shall nominate their lands to a son or daughter of the intriguer, even when he has or can expect to have another *prazo* of his own (*384*, 104).

Possession was always nine- and sometimes ten-tenths of the law in Zambesia, and the answer to this problem was always for the claimant, whoever he was, to take control of the *prazo* and worry about his title afterwards.

The Zambesi *donas* on the whole maintained their power and status until the beginning of the twentieth century, defying numerous decrees designed to put an end to the old *prazo* system. This shows the extent to which female succession had been accepted and recognised as the custom of the country and not just an administrative order of an alien government. It is not, however, possible to say how many *prazos* were in the hands of women at any one time. This is because it is never clear from the records whether a man, who is *senhor* of a *prazo*, holds the position in his own right or through his wife. As a rough guide, however, one can take the figures from a *prazo* list of 1763 which shows 43 *prazos* in female hands out of 105. If one deducts the *prazos* belonging to the church and those which were 'deserted' it is clear that women were holding rather more than half the *prazos*—and this sort of figure is borne out by other lists (*402*).

Tenure for three lives

The *prazos da coroa* were emphyteutic estates whose contracts were based on those in use in Portugal. There were no single life tenures in Africa and crown property was leased for three lives. There were, however, exceptions. The *prazos* of the religious orders were *emquanto o mundo dura*—as long as the world lasts—for the church never dies and therefore has no lives.

The *terras em fatiota* were held in perpetuity and there were isolated attempts to make the *prazos* perpetual as well. The great *prazo* of Cheringoma had been surrendered to the crown in the seventeenth century by Sisnando Dias Bayão on the understanding that it would remain always in his family. This in effect made it a perpetual tenure, although the procedure for regranting the *prazo* was always gone through after the three lives were up. (See chap. 9)

Another example is afforded by José Francisco Alves Barbosa, a tough *sertanejo* of the old school, who petitioned in 1827 that his *prazo* of Tambara should be made perpetual in his family (*232*). This petition was unsuccessful.

The general purpose of the three-life contract was to grant security of tenure to the holder while at the same time leaving some control still in government hands. With the prospect of handing on the *prazo* to his heirs or having the grant renewed, the *prazo*-holder would, it was hoped, look after his land and its inhabitants, encourage economic development in it and keep the peace. At the end of three lives the government could use its right of renewal to break up large family holdings, to increase the rent paid to the treasury, and generally to impose some sort of a check on the conduct of the *prazo senhor*.

The three-life contract, was not noticeably effective in achieving these objectives. The dynamics of society in Zambesia had set a powerful trend towards large family holdings which the three-life contract did little to counteract. The crown was seldom in a position to enforce a change of 'dynasty' if at the end of three lives the family of the last holder of the *prazo* was firmly in possession. On the other hand there were some writers who criticised the three-life contract for not providing adequate security of tenure to promote the full development of the land. The *tenente-geral*, Vilas Boas Truão, was one of the leading opponents of the emphyteutic tenures and, in 1806 when he was writing, the full flood of the successful bourgeois revolution in France had turned thinking dramatically from the paternalism of the *ancien régime* towards the pursuit of progress enshrined in private property (*471*, 9).

The length of a three-life contract could, of course, vary considerably. Cheringoma once passed through three lives within six years (see chap. 9). On the other hand, the lands of Maria da Guerra, who was active in the 1680s, descended to *Dona* Caterina de Faria Leitão who did not die until *c.* 1777 when she was described as 'being a hundred years old and having a hundred thousand *cruzados* of debt to the treasury'. Her husband died soon after her and in this case three lives lasted for almost one hundred years.

Mortmain

Alienation of land to the church or any other corporate body without express permission of the crown had been forbidden throughout the dominions of the Portuguese crown as early as 1600. In every *prazo* contract appeared the clause 'It shall not be nominated to a community of monks, friars, brothers, clerics or other persons prohibited by law'.

The purpose of this clause was quite clear. The church never died, and the lands leased to it would be lost to the crown for ever—for as long as the world lasted.

Mortmain applied to the *Misericordia*—the charitable brotherhood that had branches throughout the Portuguese world. In 1830 there was an interesting case involving an application by the Moçambique *Misericordia* for a *prazo* called Tirre. The chief justice of the colony, Joaquim Xavier Dinis Costa, was asked to report whether this grant would be against the law, whether it would harm a third party, and whether it would be to the good of the royal treasury. In his report he recommended that the *prazo* be leased to the *Misericordia* on condition that the brotherhood subleased it to the Velasco family who had a claim on it. In this way the *Misericordia* would not obtain the *dominium utile* and so would not be transgressing the law. He also suggested that the contract should be made out as though for a *prazo em vidas* and pointed out that as the property of the *Misericordia* had been taken over by the crown the purpose behind the old legislation had largely disappeared (*245*).

This case inevitably prompts the question, how effective the law had been throughout the eighteenth century in preventing the religious corporations acquiring property?

Apparently the mortmain regulations did not apply to the *terras em fatiota* and the Jesuits acquired a number of these before the dissolution of the order in 1759. In 1745, for instance, they had their title to certain lands in Bororo recognised by the crown, the royal patent stating that the acquisition of these lands was allowed because the fathers had acquired them at their own cost and they had never been part of the crown lands (*266*). When the Jesuit *prazos* were confiscated in 1759 it was found that the Sena college possessed three *prazos*; the Tete college possessed six *prazos* (one of which had been acquired as recently as 1754) and four *terras em fatiota*; the Marangue house possessed one *prazo* and four *fatiotas*; the Quelimane house held one *prazo* and three other properties. In all the Jesuits held twenty-two properties large and small, many of them acquired only shortly before the expulsion (*135*).

The Dominicans held four *prazos*—all by ancient tenures—and they did not acquire lands outside the crown *prazos* in the scramble for Marave territory in the eighteenth century. Compared with the Jesuits, therefore, it might be thought they had shown considerable restraint in breaking their vows of poverty. But this would be misleading, for the Dominicans were even more active than the Jesuits in wielding political power. One of them became *tenente-geral* and they provided a series of captains for the Zumbo fair. Moreover, they were active in gold mining and had considerable interests elsewhere in the colony—particularly in the Querimba Islands.

Marriage to a Portuguese

All girls who inherited or were granted *prazos* were supposed to marry Portuguese men from Portugal. This had been the rule which had governed the grant of fortresses and captaincies to women in the early days of the empire and the main purpose had been to make sure that trustworthy Portuguese occupied important posts in the empire. The order was probably introduced into

East Africa when the grant of *prazos* to women became common—possibly at the time of the 1677 colonising expedition. It had to be continually reiterated, for apparently the lucky damsels showed no particular inclination to marry Portuguese in preference to Indians, Africans or mulattos (*217*).

At first glance this concern that all marriages should be with European-born Portuguese appears to be a very racialist piece of legislation. This does not bear examination, however. When in 1752 the order was reiterated in Zambesia, with the strong assertion that any man contravening it would lose his *prazo*, it was made quite clear that the order referred to heiresses of all shades and hues. All girls with *prazos* had to marry Portuguese but Portuguese men were free to marry Indian, mulatto or white girls and the rights of their children would be recognised (*89, 90*). It is clear then that the government was only anxious that the great *prazos* should remain in Portuguese hands. This lack of concern for the 'purity' of Portuguese blood is emphasised by the plan of governor-general, Saldanha de Albuquerque, to import four thousand Chinese girls from Macao, where they were in substantial surplus, to provide wives for the Moçambique settlers (*11*). In 1810 another order expressly forbade any Indian man to marry a woman who held a *prazo*, and in 1831 there was even an attempt to get a marriage annulled on the basis of this instruction (*108*).

What evidence there is suggests that this aspect of *prazo* law did not work very well—and there must have been a steady darkening of the visages of the great *prazo* families as the eighteenth century wore on. Sometimes the matrimonial plans of their daughters were included in the petitions presented by hopeful fathers, but critics of the way the colony was run frequently mention the extent to which Indian men were gaining control of the *prazos* and pushing the whites into an insignificant role.

Before leaving the daughters of the Portuguese community and their marriages, a glance at the case of poor *Dona* Joanna de Sousa will show something of the lurid exploitation that could accompany the marriage market in the colony in the early nineteenth century. Virissimo Manuel de Sousa and his sister, *Dona* Pascoa, were connected with the most important families in Quelimane. When Virissimo died, his *prazo* passed to his infant daughter, Joanna, who went to live with her aunt. While still a minor she was married to Silverio Oliveira da Cunha and had the grant confirmed. Silverio died and she was married to Francisco

Geraldes da Roza who also died within a short space of time. For a third time she was contracted to marry, but at this point her *prazo* was confiscated by the governor of Moçambique and granted elsewhere. As a result, her third marriage was cancelled and her creditors at once foreclosed. She was left destitute and in 1831 was managing to survive because she was being looked after by an African, perhaps one of her former slaves (*107*).

Pluralism

Any government that resorts to the essentially feudal idea of delegating its administrative and military functions to the land-owning class faces sooner or later the prospect of having to deal with over-mighty subjects. This problem was quite familiar in East Africa from the days of Diogo Simões Madeira, and it affected the evolution of land law through the attempts of the government to regulate the size of the *prazos* and the number which could accumulate in the hands of any individual.

'Divide the lands among more settlers' had been the cry of reformers and scheme-mongers throughout the seventeenth century (*168*). In 1752 definite instructions were sent to Francisco de Mello e Castro, the governor-general, that settlers were to be sent out and that they should have divided amongst them 'some of the many lands which are there and which are in the hands of a single lord because of the lack of population'. The only grounds he was to consider as warranting a concentration of holdings were when the income from a single *prazo* was inadequate to support a single family (*89, 91*).

Twenty-eight years later it was the same story. Antonio de Mello e Castro, the *tenente-geral*, wrote to Lisbon of the failure of this order, which he attributed to the fact that *prazo* grants were being made by the Moçambique governors who knew nothing of local circumstances and often little about the applicants. Accordingly in 1783 a *provisão* of the Overseas Council ordered that the measures against pluralism should be enforced (*91*).

In 1801, however, it was the same story for a royal order of that year stated:

A larger population and the good distribution of it, which is a principle from which stems the riches of states, is not fostered in Moçambique, because, whereas there are 112 *prazos da coroa* in the country, these are in the power of only 14 or 15 persons (*92*).

It was probably an exaggeration to say that there were only fourteen or fifteen holders of *prazos* in 1801, but there may well have been only that number resident in Zambesia at the time. Complete figures for 1765 show that 34 people held a single *prazo* each, 15 held two, 2 held three, 1 held four, 1 held five and 2 held six. Twenty-one *prazos*—slightly under a quarter of the total—were in the hands of 4 individuals. In all there were 55 different owners of *prazos* in 1765. The *terras em fatiota* are not included in these figures (*377*, 26–27).

Pluralism was one of the problems which the Portuguese government continually hoped to check by tighter administrative control, and there were always isolated cases of *prazo* grants being refused because of pluralism, while a prospective grantee of a *prazo* always tried to stress his poverty and his lack of other lands if he possibly could.

Limitation on size

The size, wealth and population of a *prazo* were clearly of as much concern to the government as the number held by a single person. That vast territories like Cheringoma or Gorongosa should exist as single *prazos* was a far greater evil than the multiple holding of many little *prazos*. The *prazos* had of course always seemed too big to anyone studying them with the pre-conceptions of European landownership; they were certainly too big if the obligation to cultivate the land, which had been the main objective of the *Lei das Sesmarias*, was to be taken seriously.

In 1695 there had been legislation for Brazil aimed at limiting the size of *sesmarias* (*324*, 227–9, 309–10) and in the royal decree of 3 April 1760 similar rules were laid down for Moçambique (*15*). *Prazos* were not to exceed three leagues by one in size and, if they had mineral deposits or had a river or sea frontage, they were not to exceed one square league. Three square leagues—roughly twenty-seven square miles—was still very extensive and very much too large for a plantation. Even so a large number of the *prazos* exceeded it and continued to exceed it, for from the start these laws were totally ineffective.

As the crown must have been aware, the *prazos* were not, and never could be, simply large landed estates on the European or American model. They were chieftaincies, areas of tribute collection and jurisdiction, surrendered by the different African monarchies and with traditional boundaries which had never

104

been surveyed or marked out. Without a complete land survey it would not have been possible even to begin to carry out the law of 1760 and there was no one to carry out this immense task.

Early in the nineteenth century the Overseas Council made a number of attempts to enforce the proper survey of *prazos* before new grants were made, for they were aware that no progress had been made towards breaking up the large holdings. However, apart from a few isolated cases, they were unable to force this on the inadequate and partly illiterate administration in the Zambesi settlements—an administration which, to put it mildly, was usually in collusion with the local families.

Once again the issue lay between two totally different ideas about the nature of the *prazos*. Physiocrats, like *tenente-geral* Vilas Boas Truão, saw the *prazo* as a potential plantation and called for the subdivision of land holdings which were far too large for economic development. The *prazo*-holders countered by pointing out that large areas of land were necessary if adequate tribute was to be collected for them to maintain the slaves who kept 'order' on the *prazo* and defended the colony. Small land-holdings and high capital investment would not give them adequate reserves to survive when flood or famine or drought laid waste the valley and brought ruin to the small man.

Cultivation

Should those who held crown *prazos* be obliged to cultivate them? The answer one gave to this question depended very much on whether one saw the *prazos* as plantations or chieftaincies. The old captaincy system had certainly not envisaged that the *donatário* would personally cultivate his grant. In fact there was usually a clause in his charter which prevented his acquiring more than a certain amount of land for himself. *Sesmarias*, on the other hand, carried with them an automatic duty to cultivate the land within a prescribed space of time on pain of forfeiture. The *prazos* were looked upon as *sesmarias* and to 'better and improve them is of the very nature of these emphyteutic contracts', as one writer put it (*40*). On the other hand they were also units of fiscal and military government—in other words captaincies.

And so theory and practice, as ever, pulled against one another. Throughout the eighteenth century a chorus of complaint arose from all sides about the lack of any cultivation in

Zambesia. Zambesia, it was pointed out, could become a major exporter of the tropical products which sold so well in European markets but, as things were, the state of agriculture was so decayed that frequently the Zambesi settlements had themselves to import food from the coastal areas to meet their everyday needs.

Official opinion of Moçambique Island was firmly of the belief that the Rivers should supply food for the whole colony and make the island garrison independent of the friendship of the Islamic communities that surrounded it (see chap. 9). Mercantilist governments, however, always had a rather equivocal attitude towards the economic development of colonies. Cotton cloth, for instance, had always been locally produced in the Zambesi region. The *Junta do Commercio* in Moçambique thought that this local industry was threatening the royal monopoly of imported cotton cloth and tried—unavailingly—to prevent its further manufacture (*403*, para 24).

In his long report on the *prazos* dated 1781, Antonio de Mello e Castro pointed to the chief obstacle to the agricultural development of Zambesia—the difficulty of transport. Only the coastal *prazos* could ever dispose of any agricultural surplus and, as Lacerda was to point out, the shortage of ships made even this difficult. It would be easy to deduce from these Jeremiahs that there was no cultivation, apart from African gardens, of any kind on the *prazos*. This is not so. The eighteenth century saw the growth of a small sugar industry in the delta and the construction of half a dozen mills to process it. There was also careful cultivation of fruit trees and palms along the coast and in the gardens attached to the residences of the *prazo senhors* (*384*, 81–2, *43*).

The establishment of the post of *tanador-mor* in 1759—a post for the inspection of agriculture which had been borrowed from Portuguese India—appears at first sight to show that the government was intent on seeing that the Rivers prospered. However, it is not clear that this post ever had the official sanction of the Lisbon government or that it had any jurisdiction (*250*). Certainly the *tanador-mor* made no progress, and his chief function seems to have been seeing that *foros* were paid and the *prazos* not left unoccupied. This is perhaps symbolic, for in the nineteenth century so many well-intentioned development schemes were to end simply as new devices for tax collecting (*12*).

The *cartas de aforamento* do not specifically mention any obligation to cultivate the *prazo*, though an intention to do so is often expressed in a petition for the grant. There are cases where failure to cultivate is alleged as the reason for a *prazo* falling vacant, but it is never clear whether all these references to cultivation do not mean simply cultivation by African *colonos*. Each *prazo*-holder found, however, that his *carta* obliged him to allow any immigrant Portuguese family to settle on his land, and the government continued happily to dream of the stream of industrious colonists who would one day turn Moçambique into a new Brazil—or a Portuguese Martinique.

Absenteeism

'He shall not depart without always handing over to a single person who will collect the fruits, rents, and customary payments which it gives.' So say the *cartas de aforamento*, and implicitly it was quite legal for a *prazo*-holder not to live on his *prazo* or to have anything directly to do with it. He could hand it over to a man of business—a *procurador*—or he could rent it out to another settler. If successful arrangements of this sort could be made, there was little incentive for a *senhor* to stay in eastern Africa when he could live off his rents in Goa or even in Portugal.

Absenteeism was obviously anathema to the government and went against all its declared and undeclared objectives. An absentee *prazo*-holder was adding nothing to the security, wealth or population of the colony.

Absenteeism and the general propensity of the Portuguese to go off on their own had always worried the imperial authorities in the East. Originally all Portuguese who went out on the fleets lived under military discipline, which enabled the authorities to control their movements even when they were not actually doing garrison duty. Special leave had to be obtained from the viceroy before a man could return home. This provision had been strictly applied in eastern Africa where the chronic shortage of manpower made these licences very hard to obtain.

Implicit in the whole concept of the *sesmarias* was the obligation to reside on the land, and on occasions absenteeism was used as a plea to invalidate an existing grant or to refuse a petition. In 1759, and again in 1779, there were orders issued in the Rivers requiring the *prazo*-holders to reside on their *prazos*, but these instructions had no more chance of success than any of the other bureaucratic regulations that hung round the *prazo* system like cobwebs.

Early in the nineteenth century the issuing of licences to

people anxious to leave the Rivers was revived and numerous petitions were filed containing agonising tales designed to melt the steely heart of the governor (e.g. *104*). Absenteeism, however, like all the other ills from which the *prazo* system suffered, did not arise from loop-holes in the law but from the social and economic conditions of Africa which, in the early nineteenth century, increasingly drove people from the River colony. During 1828, when the Ngoni raids had not yet begun but when famine and disorder were at their height, Francisco Henriques Ferrão reported that there were now only three Portuguese in Sena: the priest, the factor and himself—and he was a man of Indian not Portuguese origin (*240*). The flight of the Portuguese population and the desertion of the *prazos* together form the prelude to the tragedy of the Zambesi Wars.

Taxes and rents

Every year the *prazo*-holder paid two classes of tax to the government: the *foros* and the *dizimos*. The *foros* were the quit-rents payable on all crown lands, and their payment was an essential part of the land contracts. The *dizimos* were the ecclesiastical tithes. These had been granted to the crusading Order of Christ in the fifteenth century and when the property of the Order was taken over by the crown the tithes became little more than a royal tax. The *foros* were agreed between the *prazo*-holder and the crown by arbitration when the initial grant was made, and after three lives they were re-negotiated.

The *foros* were collected by the local *juiz ordinario*—lay judge—and forwarded by him to the *feitor dos quintos e foros*. This official was supposed to keep the *tombo foral*—the register containing all the information about the *prazos*. He then forwarded the money to the *provedor da real fazenda* in Moçambique.

The *foro* was not a rent seriously related to the income of the particular *prazo*. It was more the symbol of the crown's sovereignty and to refuse to pay it was as much an act of rebellion as a simple default on tax payment. In the year 1759 the total income from the prazos was put at 4,140:000 *reis* out of an income for the whole colony of 120,726:300 *reis* (*377*, 98). It did not, therefore, provide the crown with very much of its income, most of which came from customs receipts. It was, however, the second largest single item of treasury receipts. The following table shows the income from the *prazos* for a number of selected years.

108

1759	4,140:000 *reis* (377, 98)
1786	2,242:456 „ (63)
1793	3,184:712 „ (68)
1814	3,005:776 „ (88)
1820	4,305:242 „ (93)
1822	3,465:480 „ (96)

The *foro* represented only a tiny percentage of the income of the *prazo* and in theory very much more could have been collected without anyone being very much the worse off. Any tax, however, was difficult to collect in Zambesia. All *prazo*-holders lived off their debts and debts to the government never took priority over debts to the merchants and suppliers of trade goods. Some *prazo*-holders would go as long as sixteen years without making any payment of *foros* (22). Moreover, they claimed exemption if their *prazo* was overrun or if any other disaster struck at their annual revenues. It is doubtful if any increase of a general kind would have produced better returns and the government had to be content with forcing up the *foro*—usually by a third—on the renewal of a contract (235).

Dizimos were another matter. Nominally they were a tenth of the produce of the land, but in practice they were compounded for a lump sum. Even this lump sum was not paid in full and Antonio Manuel de Mello e Castro, in his report on the payment of the tithe (58), said that when he became *tenente-geral* in 1780, the recognised custom was for half the sum due to be actually paid. In 1783 he instituted a general survey of the wealth and income of the *prazos*, requiring each *senhor* to submit an account of his wealth and property holdings, and on the basis of these he reassessed the *dizimos* (51). Writing to Martinho de Mello e Castro in 1785 he could claim that treasury receipts had already been doubled. Where the inventories of the wealth of the *prazos* have survived they are invaluable documents for anyone trying to understand the nature of the 'feudal' lordships in Portuguese Zambesia.

The tithes were paid at Easter when the settlers were expected to assemble with their slaves at one or other of the churches to receive the sacrament. Many *prazo*-holders were reluctant to fulfil this assignment because they knew that not only the royal tax collector but all their other creditors would be waiting for them as well. Mello e Castro therefore issued a proclamation that during the week of Easter there was to be no collection of debts (48). Presumably it was hoped that if the *prazo senhors* were thus protected from their private creditors they would be more willing to meet their debts to the government.

There were three sorts of dues which the *prazo*-holders were liable to pay when negotiating business concerning their estates. There were the *novos direitos* and the *direitos da chancellaria* which covered the official handling of the *prazo* grants; and there was the *ciza*, a tax of ten per cent payable on all sales of land.

Termination of tenure

Not surprisingly the *prazo* contracts could be annulled if the contract was broken. Much the same thing occurred if at the end of three lives the *prazo* was not regranted to the heir of the previous owner because it was held that he had not fulfilled his contract. In either of these cases the *prazo* was declared *em commisso*—under penalty. This meant that it was now open for new applications to be made for it.

A breach of any of the items in the contract might lead, in theory, to an annulment of the grant; thus if the *senhor* granted it to a religious order, if he failed to pay the *foros*, if he failed to get confirmation of his title, if he failed to have the survey carried out, if he failed to receive settlers onto his land, if he failed in his obligation to maintain access to his land, if he divided up his land or if he alienated it without licence, if he left it without appointing a deputy to collect the dues, in any of these cases the grant could be declared null and void.

A *prazo* could also be declared vacant if there was any fault in the original legal procedures. This was the commonest form of forfeiture, especially when there was a rival claimant who could take advantage of gaps in legal procedure. In 1793 the governor-general tried to have all *prazos* declared *em commisso* whose owners had not presented their *cartas de aforamento* for inspection (67). Failure to secure confirmation in Lisbon was sometimes penalised by forfeiture (235), though usually it was treated more leniently and the new grantee was allowed to rent the *prazo* until the confirmation was obtained.

The law also considered it faulty procedure if a *prazo* were granted to a stranger when there was a legal heir (29, 82), when it had been granted to illegitimate offspring or when the will had been made by word of mouth and not in true legal format (216). Sometimes the Overseas Council, which vetted all grants sent to Lisbon for confirmation, declared a grant null if there had not been a proper inquiry carried out into the circumstances of the vacancy or if the documents of the case were incomplete and there was inadequate proof of possession.

Finally, any contract of emphyteusis could be annulled if it was considered that the land had been destroyed or ruined in any way. This was a formal part of all Roman Law contracts of this kind. In Zambesia this might occur if the *prazo*-holder deserted the land and allowed it to be overrun by neighbouring tribes or if it was deserted by the African peasants and so depopulated. Thus a list of the Tete *prazos* for 1783 groups the names of no less than thirty-three *prazos* with the words 'Lands which are legitimately *em commisso* being totally deserted and without any cultivation.' *(54)*.

Once again much of this legislation was theoretical. *Prazo* grants were annulled for the reasons listed above, but here as elsewhere what mattered was the strength of the particular *prazo* family involved. The government had little chance of depriving a family in possession unless it could find a more powerful rival to do the work for it. There are numerous cases of a *prazo* being legally granted to a man who subsequently finds that the slaves of the previous holder are firmly in possession and running the whole *prazo* in the interest of another family *(59)*.

The value of examining the *prazo* grants in this way is that it shows the *prazo* system as in a photographic negative. The endless regulations, *provisões, relações, cartas regias, alvaras, leis, instruções, bandos, pareceres* and other documents laying down the law about the *prazos* show, not how the system worked, but how it did not work. Decrees ordering *prazo* heiresses to marry Portuguese men tell us most certainly, not that they were marrying Portuguese men, but that they were not doing so. Likewise decrees ordering the residence of *prazo*-holders are a sure indication that they were not resident.

As in all communities, society and politics in Zambesia were an elaborate game of chess in which the legal instructions of the Lisbon government or the Moçambique governor-general were only pawns—but even pawns can sometimes take queens and a student of the game cannot afford to neglect them.

7 The Government and the *Prazo*-Holders

The royal administration in Zambesia

Moçambique was administered as a captaincy of the viceroyalty of Goa until the year 1752 when the whirlwind activity of Portugal's Pombaline era first made its impact on the colony. In that year, a report from a judge of the high court in Goa Duarte Salter de Mendonça (*4*), prompted a decision by the Lisbon administration to separate the African settlements from India.

Mendonça's report was adopted too hastily, as if the administration were afraid that its own traditional indecision would gain the upper hand if it did not act promptly. With characteristic lack of preparation and forethought, a series of decrees were promulgated in April 1752 that set up the new government and appointed Francisco de Mello e Castro to be the first governor-general. Although Moçambique was thus made independent of India in all but commercial matters, it was apparently not thought necessary to issue the governor with any administrative instructions. It was only slowly, as the problems of government revealed themselves, that detailed orders arrived from Lisbon, and not until 1761 did the colony have an adequate legal framework covering defence, land tenure, finance, customs and other matters (*394*, chap 10, *305*, 41–50).

Of the other Pombaline reforms, two in particular affected the Rivers. In 1759 the Jesuit Order was suppressed in the Portuguese colonies and six Jesuit fathers were sent as prisoners from the Rivers to Moçambique—their *prazos* and slaves becoming available for distribution among the settlers.

Then in 1763 the main settlements of the colony were promoted in status. Moçambique became a city, and Sofala, Quelimane, Sena and Tete each became a municipality electing its own town council (called in Portuguese *senado da camara*). Like so many other reforms dreamt up by the bureaucrats in Lisbon, this one had no relevance to conditions in the colony. Municipal status could not check the declining fortunes of Sofala or Sena; Sofala seldom had any white residents at all apart from the garrison, and Sena frequently could not raise sufficient men qualified to constitute its town council. In 1767 the capital of the Rivers was moved to Tete from Sena and, until the present day, Tete and Quelimane have remained the only towns of any importance in this part of Africa.

The capital city of Moçambique on its coral island some two hundred miles to the north of the Zambesi delta had only precarious communications with the Zambesi. Boats plied between Quelimane and the centre of government, but the winds and currents were dangerous and many were lost on the voyage or were wrecked on the sand bar at the mouth of the Qua Qua river which led to Quelimane. Quelimane itself had no direct connection by water with the Zambesi, except at high flood time when the swamps and creeks of the delta filled and made temporary passages all of which dried out later in the year. During the eighteenth century couriers followed an overland route which skirted the coast and only existed on sufferance of Muslim sheikhs and Makua chiefs who ruled the swampy lowlands. The route was sufficiently well-established for an important government official, Francisco Raimundo Moraes Pereira, to make the journey in 1752 rather than wait in Quelimane for the next boat (*427, 359*). Bad communications made any direct interference by Moçambique in the affairs of the Rivers a comparatively rare occurrence.

The Rivers were governed by an officer called *tenente-geral dos Rios*—lieutenant-general of the Rivers. As his title suggests he was nominally the subordinate of the captain-general of Moçambique, but the distance which separated the two, and the fact that the Rivers were a much more important part of the Portuguese possessions than Moçambique Island, meant that the *tenente-geral* occupied a rather special position. Between 1635 and 1688 the Rivers had been administered separately from Moçambique under the direct supervision of Goa. In 1688 the *tenente-geral* was placed under Moçambique's control but in 1709 a new set of standing orders once again conferred on him virtual independence. He was to make all decisions of peace and war, he was to hold military and civil courts with no appeal except to Goa and he could correspond directly with the viceroy. Only in the confirmation of military and civil patents did he have to seek the authority of the captain-general (*394, 30–32*).

In 1752 when Moçambique was separated from the government of India, the captain-general became the governor-general and the highest authority in East Africa, thus replacing the Indian viceroy as the effective superior of the *tenente-geral*. The rivalry between the two officials did not cease, however, for the habit of independence from the interference of Moçambique died hard in the Rivers and there was, anyway, a genuine confusion of function. Who had the right to nominate candidates for posts or *prazos* which fell vacant? The length of time that a message took to and from Moçambique meant that temporary appointments had to be made by the *tenente-geral*. If the governor-general later wanted to reverse these decisions, then there was a fruitful source of litigation which might drag on for five years or more and was sure to end up with appeal and counter-appeal to Lisbon.

In the nineteenth century Lisbon experimented with a division of the Rivers government. In 1817 Quelimane was made independent of the rest of the Rivers but was reunited with it again in 1829. The title of *tenente-geral* had been dropped at the end of the eighteenth century and the governor of the newly reunited captaincies of the Zambesi was called *governador de Quelimane e Rios de Senna*. In 1853 the governorship was again divided. This time the boundary was made the old division between the captaincies of Sena and Tete. Sena and Quelimane now formed one governorship and Tete formed another. This division remained until the end of the century essentially unchanged though two new governorships were created for Manica in 1884 and for Zumbo in 1889 to deal with the rapid expansion of Portuguese territory in the interior (*396*, vol 4, 59).

These experiments, however, did nothing to resolve the confusion of jurisdiction—a confusion which was often made worse by purely personal rivalries, for most of the famous *affaires* between the Rivers and Moçambique involved men of strong character and pronounced views. Two examples from the early nineteenth century show the sort of entertainment which governor and governor-general provided for the appreciative spectators among the settlers.

The governor-generalship of Sebastian Xavier Botelho from 1825–29 was notorious for the quarrels between Moçambique and the Rivers, and for the personal way in which these quarrels were conducted. Botelho thought he was faced with what amounted to rebellion in the Rivers colony. In 1825 when Brazil formally established her independence from Portugal, a plot was uncovered among Brazilian slavers in Moçambique to attach Portugal's East African possessions to the newly independent country with which it had, at this period, close economic ties. Botelho alleged that the *tenente-geral*, scenting an independent command and ample booty was implicated in this conspiracy (*106*). It was not long, however, before the other side of the story was told. Botelho had been determined to outdo all his predecessors in the agility with which he made his fortune. A highly coloured account of his governorship was published in English in 1839 (*466*) in which it was alleged that on kissing hands on his appointment as governor, the king had said to him:

'Now see I am your friend—make money and take care of yourself.' It appears that he strictly followed the king's advice, as he retired from the command with an immense fortune, which he is now enjoying in Lisbon. In Moçambique the high public functionaries, even to this day, speak in raptures of his government, saying . . . he lived and allowed others to live.

Botelho later acquired quite a reputation as an opponent of slaving so that the particular accusations that were levelled against him were not connected with that traffic. Instead it was said that he had sold the office of governor to the highest bidder and had also sold vacant *prazos*; thus lining his pocket and asserting the prerogatives of the governor at the same time. The fact that he had sold the post to an Indian and a *prazo* to the Indian's son-in-law apparently made the crime still worse (*110*).

A second example was the final flourish of independence shown by the Rivers community when in 1834 Izidro Manuel de Carrazedo was nominated governor. He arrived in the Rivers in 1835 and declared that he was armed with instructions which severed his command from that of Moçambique. He proceeded to make appointments, create new posts and to declare Quelimane a free port with its own customs system (*115, 116*).

Although the Rivers never formally won their independence again after 1688, in the everyday decisions of government and in most of the major fields of policy the *tenente-geral* could do just as he pleased—or rather just as the residents permitted him.

Beneath the *tenente-geral* was the *capitão-mor dos Rios*—the captain-major of the Rivers. This was an ancient office which goes back to the seventeenth century (*318, 440*). The *capitão-mor* was the chief executive officer of the government. He was there to deputise for the *tenente-geral* whenever necessary, and was always chosen from among the powerful local inhabitants. Very often he was already the holder of some other post and during his term he acted as captain of Sena (*403*, para 25). The post was abolished in 1843 (*161*). There was also a *capitão-mor das guerras*—captain-major of the wars—who was probably only appointed to command some military enterprise being undertaken by the government of the Rivers.

The territory which the *tenente-geral* controlled was, in the eighteenth century, divided into three administrative districts based on Quelimane, Sena and Tete. Each of these had an administrative and judicial officer appointed by the viceroy and, after 1752, by the crown. First there was the *capitão* of Quelimane who performed military, economic and judicial functions. One of his duties was to handle the harbour traffic and the imports and exports of all the Rivers settlements. He was responsible for suppressing the activities of the smugglers who continually sought to evade the royal monopolies (*403*, para 4). He was assisted by a secretary and a port factor.

Until 1767, when Sena ceased to be the capital of the Rivers, the Sena district was administered by a *capitão-juiz*—a lay judge holding court of first instance—assisted by a secretary. Also in the capital was stationed the *feitor da fazenda*—the royal factor who handled the royal monopoly in trade goods—and the *feitor dos quintos e foros*—the factor of fifths and rents. He was supposed to collect the rents paid by the *prazo*-holders and to keep a record of all transactions concerned with the great estates. Tete also had a *capitão-juiz* and a *capitão-mor* in charge of justice and defence (*403*, para 112, *308*, 195). These offices were frequently filled by local settlers.

As the century progressed a few additions were made to this small body of administrators. In 1759 the post of *tanador-mor* was created (*12*). This was an office borrowed from Portuguese India, the functions of whose holder were to supervise agricultural development and to see that regulations regarding cultivation of the land and the prompt payment of rents were carried out. The *tanador-mor* was always a leading settler and it is easy to imagine how much actual supervision took place. The office of *tanador-mor* does not appear to have continued into the nineteenth century and probably his duties were taken over by the increasingly powerful *capitaes-mores das terras da coroa*.

One of the earliest occasion when this official is heard of is 1767 when Caetano Pereira was appointed *capitão-mor das terras e bares da jurisdição de Tete* (*26*). Eventually there was a *capitão-mor das terras da coroa* in each of the three River captaincies. His main responsibilities were to try cases and hear appeals involving

Africans and African law. In particular he investigated complaints against the conduct of the *prazo*-holders. He also was chosen from among the Rivers settlers.

The only other post of importance to be set up was that of *patrão-mor*—harbourmaster—in Quelimane following the suggestion made by Francisco de Mello e Castro in his memorandum of 1750.

The weakness of the Royal Administration

From the early fifteenth century the Portuguese had had to delegate authority from the centre in order to control their scattered empire. Captains of fleets and fortresses and *donatários* of islands or continental land masses had been granted almost regal powers, and, in spite of greatly improved communications, much the same sort of independence was enjoyed by colonial officials until the late nineteenth century. The effectiveness of this authority depended largely on the local community, for after the rise of Dutch and English sea power the Portuguese colonies were frequently cut off from the mother country for long periods and had to become self-sufficient in their internal economy and in their man-power and defence. It was the Portuguese communities in Brazil, Angola and Macao, receiving little aid from metropolitan Portugal, who defeated the Dutch by their own efforts. So Portugal, who could do little to help her overseas communities in time of trouble, could hardly complain of the independent attitudes they showed in time of peace, and of their rejection of the close tutelage of the mother country.

How did the imperial machine, of ancient mark and somewhat rusted up, work or fail to work in eighteenth-century Zambesia? The government of His Most Faithful Majesty of Portugal was weak, and its weakness derived fundamentally from two things; the lack of a well-paid bureaucracy and the lack of an adequate military force. True to the almost universal habit of the *ancien régime*, the Portuguese government was reluctant to pay its officials, for it was held that any gentleman should consider his status lowered if he served the government in return for payment.

The captain-general of Moçambique had originally remunerated himself from the trade monopoly which he enjoyed, while the other captaincies of the River settlements had all been conferred on local men who were involved in trade or in mining ventures and were prepared to act as 'lay' judges and captains.

In the eighteenth century some attempt was made to establish salaries. According to the accounts of 1758 the following payments were made:

Tenente-geral dos Rios	8,916:000	*reis*
Zimbabwe garrison	8,000:000	,,
Sena garrison	11,360:000	,,
Capitão-mor dos Rios	815:000	,,
Feitor dos Foros e Quintos	750:000	,,
Feitor do Porto de Quelimane	1,375:000	,,

In addition various payments were made to the ecclesiastics who served in the Rivers (*305*, 123). The captains of the fairs and the towns together with their secretaries did not receive any pay (*402*, 128–9).

Those officers who were paid did not receive their money regularly, nor were they always compensated for the expenses they met out of their own pockets. Complaints of the failure to pay salaries are frequently encountered in the petitions for the grants of *prazos*. For example, Manuel Cabral de Abreu petitioned in 1752 for two *prazos* for his daughters and alleged that he had served fourteen years as *capitão-mor* of Manica without receiving the five bales of cloth which were annually allowed for expenses (*5*).

An unpaid bureaucrat has a number of courses of action open to him. He can accept bribes; he can acquire a private income, making use of his official position to build up business connections; or he can marry a local heiress. A government, on the other hand, which does not wish to pay its officials but wishes to maintain some sort of administration, has only one recourse—to appoint wealthy and influential local people to office. All these things happened in Zambesia, and the crown's control over its officials naturally tended to dwindle as they became increasingly involved with the different local interest groups.

The lack of any effective military force was the second reason why the government was weak. Forts had been built on the Zambesi in the seventeenth century, but these were for the most part made of timber and mud bricks and were garrisoned by the settlers. In the eighteenth century a garrison of regular soldiers was maintained, which in 1758 had an official strength of fifty men and was based on the fort at Sena. Of these, ten served in Manica and another twenty made up the detachment of the Zimbabwe garrison (*481*, 161).

The Zimbabwe garrison was commanded by a *capitão-mor*, a post which had been founded in the seventeenth century and was one of the highly coveted 'jobs' in the royal service. The soldiers, their captain and their chaplain were the main support of the alliance between the Mwene Mutapas and the Portuguese. Their role was largely a non-combatant one, but none the less important for that. The arrival of a new captain was attended by the old custom of sending expensive gifts to the Mwene Mutapa. He was expected to bring a variety of luxury products to sweeten the chief and in return received ivory or slaves. He also acted as ambassador and helped to maintain good relations and freedom of trade between Portugal and the Mwene Mutapa. The Mwene Mutapa for his part greatly benefited from the prestige which these Europeans with their firearms brought him (*337*, para 47).

During the civil wars in the middle of the eighteenth century the garrison was withdrawn since the Portuguese did not want to become involved in African politics. It was never permanently restored but the Zimbabwe establishment continued on the muster rolls well into the next century—an historic survival and a useful source of government patronage (*363*, vol 2, 176, *402*, 127).

In 1767 the military headquarters moved from Sena to Tete and the official size of the garrison was raised to eighty men.

Eighty well-equipped and disciplined soldiers would have been a very useful force, but the Portuguese Zambesi garrison usually consisted of unpaid and fever-stricken convicts who, far from guaranteeing security, were a real menace to law and order. The troops sent to Moçambique Island were usually convicts from Portugal or from India and of these the worst were sent on to the Rivers. From Sena further exile was possible to the remoter stations of Manica or Zumbo should a soldier be convicted of further crimes.

Suggestions were made that Indian or African soldiers should be recruited, and in 1769 a company was formed from the local mulattos—called *patricios* in Zambesia. This seems to have been fairly successful but the *patricios* were local men and could not constitute the independent military force which royal authority needed. Sepoys were also brought from India. One lot arrived in 1767 (*25*) and in 1781 some sixty Indian sepoys were sent from Goa. Of these only fourteen survived and reached the capital, forty-six dying off Zanzibar. Of this fiasco the governor-general, Pedro de Saldanha de Albuquerque, wrote:

The state has gained much from the loss of these men and

it is losing the pay which it gives to those who have arrived alive, for they are good for nothing and are more savage than the kaffirs of Africa (*141*).

In 1768 the *tenente-geral*, Inacio de Mello e Alvim, found the soldiers at Tete so ignorant of the use of arms that they could not even do elementary arms drill (*28*), and a year later, reporting on the military might of Portugal, he wrote: 'The powder which reaches the fort at Tete is spoiled and the shot is too large. Cartridges are needed for more efficiency.' It was Alvim who had to cashier one of the officers for having cut up the garrison flag and used the sacred *quinas* for a napkin.

Nor were the forts much more formidable than their garrison. The fort at Tete was stone-built and had bastions which had been constructed at the end of the seventeenth century when Caetano de Mello e Castro was captain-general (*169*, fol 36). The other forts were all of mud-brick and were thatched in the African style. They had to be rebuilt or repaired every year, and this job was the responsibility of the settlers who did not undertake it if any excuse suggested itself—such as a bad harvest or a flood.

The forts were used as prisons but escapes were common and Father Thoman records that the Jesuits, when imprisoned in 1759, could easily have escaped had there been anywhere to escape to. He had been told by one of the officers of a secret exit. This officer had been in charge of repairs to the fort and had built the exit in anticipation of one day finding himself in need of it (*468*).

However, although the forts were crumbling away, the soldiers unable to use their guns, the munitions faulty and the guns honeycombed with rust and without carriages, money had been found to import from Portugal a magnificent carved stone gateway, complete with inscription, which was erected at Sena. No-one who knows anything of the Portuguese empire will be in the least surprised at this order of priorities.

The reality is by now clear. The government was wholly dependent on the local settlers and their resources for defence, administration, information, supplies, and public works. The question to be examined now is whether this service to the government was formalised in any way.

The Portuguese captaincies in Brazil and the Atlantic islands had conferred great privileges on the *donatários*, and promised them great wealth; but in return they imposed obligations which were spelt out in detail—obligations to defend the land and to settle it, to build towns and conquer new territory. The *prazos* of Zambesia were in this way small captaincies. The *prazo*-holder governed his land and was responsible for its internal order, he collected taxes and administered justice. However, he also had more direct obligations to the state. He had to pay an annual quit-rent and was expected to perform certain services required by the government. Some of these were general obligations which all settlers recognised and others were specific duties written into individual contracts.

The most important of the general obligations was to assemble under arms with one's slaves to defend the colony or to attack some common enemy. This obligation is neatly spelt out in a letter from the viceroy to Manuel Gonçalves Guião, a powerful *sertanejo*, in 1720:

> Likewise you will understand that the lands are given to the residents of that conquest on the condition of their joining with all their kaffirs in the wars undertaken by the *tenente-geral* both for the increase and for the defence of the said lands (*289*).

Coupled with the general defence of the colony was the maintenance of peace in one's own *prazo*. In Zambesia, as elsewhere in the world, maintaining 'law and order' was not always quite what it seemed, but here, without asking too many questions, I shall merely concern myself with the official position. The duty of the *prazo*-holder to defend his own land is implicit in the whole system of land concessions. There is no more frequent cause of a *prazo* becoming vacant than the failure of the holder to defend it. 'Invaded' or 'deserted' are the words used laconically to describe the outlying *prazos* towards the end of the eighteenth century, and anyone who claimed he could reduce one of these to order again stood a good chance of having his petition for a *prazo* granted (e.g. *139*, *140*).

In the nineteenth century the search for powerful figures who could resist the incursions of the Ngoni raiders from the south led to large *prazos* like Massangano and Gorongosa being granted to the da Cruz and Sousa families, who did indeed protect the 'marches' against raids but were themselves almost as great a scourge as the tribes they had been placed there to check.

In addition to defending their lands, all the *prazo*-holders were expected to help maintain the forts and other government buildings. As early as 1669 a royal letter to the viceroy of India urges that particular attention shall be given to the petitions of those who are willing to undertake some fortification on their own account (*284*), and in the *Tratado dos Rios de Cuama* of 1696 Antonio da Conceição records that the fort at Tete had been built by one of the *prazo*-holders, Vicencia João (*337*, para 35).

In the eighteenth century the repair work was organised communally. Before the rains came the settlers assembled and drew up a plan showing who was responsible for the repair or reconstruction of each stretch of wall and each bastion. When the Tete settlers drew up their rota in 1782 each of the four bastions were allotted to a single individual and the four main walls to four settlers each. Two of the walls were in part paid for from the income of two *prazos* without *senhors* at the time (*47*). There was also an annual rethatching of the fort, and if any government buildings were in need of repair this work was undertaken by the settlers as well. In bad years when reserves were low and discipline among the slaves weakened there might be widespread refusal by the settlers to meet obligations which they claimed were merely customary and not part of their contract (*241*).

The *prazo*-holders were also asked to clear roads and to provide carriers for government expeditions (*363*, vol 1, 56). They might also be asked to provide boats for official river traffic (*97*), and if a military force was passing through their land they had to feed it (*31*). All these obligations were broadly summarised in the land contracts with the sentence 'and he will put the royal roads in order and grant free access to springs, bridges and harbours.'

The most onerous of these duties, however, was that which fell on the *prazo*-holders of the delta region who had to keep open channels which enabled boats to pass up river to Sena when the water began to fall at the end of the rains. It was Balthasar Manuel Pereira do Lago, who was governor-general from 1765–79, who first seriously tried to keep this water route open, intending at first that the work should be paid for by the royal treasury, and subsequently trying to get the settlers to do the work with their slaves (*66, 72*).

This enterprise seems to have been rather ambitious, but work

5 The gateway to the Fort at Sena erected by João Fernandes de Almeida in 1704

6   The Portuguese supply base at Guengue, 1888

7   The Fort at Sofala, an engraving by A. de Castilho

on the Cochissone channels was periodically and inefficiently carried out until the 1830s (253).

Sometimes individual *prazo*-holders would find specific conditions attached to their land grants. Apart from the odd reference to the granting of rights to gold prospectors and small farmers, these concern ecclesiastical matters. The Jesuit churches at Chemba and Sena had been maintained by the revenues from the Jesuit *prazos*. Tiles for the churches had been made on Chemba *prazo*, bricks came from Caia and wood from Mulambe in the delta (23). Attached to the church at Marangue and contributing to its upkeep were the territories of Machesso, Cancope, Inhampende and Domue which had been bequeathed with various smaller properties by a widow in return for Masses for her soul. The Jesuit house at Tete had ten *prazos* attached to it and the Quelimane house four.

When the Jesuit property was confiscated in 1759 the estates were administered by a body called the *Junta do Fisco e Camara Real* (135). At first an attempt was made to rent the lands and sell off the slaves by auction. However, it was soon discovered that there was nobody prepared to accept the rents that were being asked, while the slaves would not oblige the government by allowing themselves to be sold off. There was no alternative but to regrant the *prazos* by contracts of emphyteusis. The *prazos* were put up for auction and into the leases were written the obligations to continue to maintain the religious establishments of the Jesuits.

The lessee—*foreiro*—of Cancope had to maintain a chaplain with 15 *corjas* of cloth a year, the *foreiro* of Marangue became patron of the church and had to maintain it (37). The *foreiro* of Chunga had to pay for the celebrations of the feast of *Nossa Senhora da Assumpção* and to help in the repairs of Marangue. Other *foreiros* found themselves saddled with the Jesuits' contributions to *Misericordia*.

It is clear, then, that services to government and community were a recognised—indeed obligatory—part of the *prazo*-holder's contract and this service was formalised and institutionalised to a large extent in a manner suggesting very strongly a feudal society and a feudal concept of land holding. This, however, is not the whole story, for the royal authorities in practice had to rely on the *prazo*-holders for carrying out almost all the functions of government.

A wise governor in Moçambique usually tried to appoint to official positions in the Rivers a powerful local man, who would command as much obedience by virtue of his wealth and the number of his slaves as by his royal commission. The account of the Zambesi settlements written in 1667 by Father Manuel Barreto is one of the best simply because the author is so sensitive to where the realities of power lie. It was a mistake, he says, for the government to appoint as captain of Quelimane a man with no local authority, for the previous captain had been a rich man and highly respected. He goes on to refer to the proposal to make a survey of the wealth of the Zambesi settlements.

> This could not well be done by an officer coming from India for fear, interest and ignorance make them leave everything in the same state as before. If Your Excellency will entrust the matter to Antonio Lobo da Silva, appointing him overseer of the revenue in that conquest, he, being very powerful, zealous and intelligent would bring the matter to a proper conclusion (*318*, 467).

One hundred years later the *tenente-geral*, Inacio de Mello e Alvim, makes very much the same point when commenting that Manuel Gonçalves Figueira is to be recommended for the post of constable of the Sena fort since he is a resident and is married to the daughter of a powerful *prazo*-holder, Manuel Gomes Nobre. So widespread, in fact, is this point of view that during the eighteenth century the great *prazo*-holders established a strong hold over the administrative posts in the Rivers.

The office of *tenente-geral* itself is a striking example of the control of the administration by the settlers. Between 1740 and 1832 there were thirty-five different holders of the office of *tenente-geral* and of these, twenty-two are known definitely either to have been local men at the time of appointment or to have contracted marriages, or formed some other close connection, with a powerful *prazo* family during their term of office.

The other administrative posts almost invariably went to those with strong local connections, while military officers who came from Portugal on active service tended also to marry locally— even if only to find some way of staying alive when their pay inevitably fell into arrears.

A glance at the administration of the colony in action reveals that its main preoccupation was with the maintenance of 'law and order'. This it had to entrust to the armed bands of the *prazo*-holders whenever anything more formidable than police operations in the towns was concerned. Private warfare had always been difficult to distinguish from officially sanctioned expeditions, and even though the field of operations was much more restricted during the eighteenth century than it had been in the previous one, there were still plenty of opportunities to pursue private aims in royal service. A remarkable autobiographical document of the early eighteenth century describes the career of one of the most powerful of the *prazo* barons of the period. The author and even the date of the document are unknown but it was brought to Portugal attached to the memorandum of Duarte Salter de Mendonça in 1751 (6). There is something to be said for the view that the author was Manuel Gonçalves Guião whose career is discussed in the next chapter.

The author came to the Rivers originally as *tenente-geral* and, after his term was over, he appears to have settled and prospered. As *tenente-geral* he restored order in the Quelimane *prazos* and then received a plea from the chief on Mount Morumbala for help against a notorious warrior who was raiding both the Portuguese and the neighbouring Africans. With government leave he set out to conquer the mountain, beheaded the recalcitrant chief, Inhabendico, and handed the land conquered from him over to the crown. He was *tenente-geral* a second time on the death of Rafael Alvares da Silva and successfully made peace with the Changamire who sent his ambassadors to Tete. The personal expense involved in this was 600 *maticals*, but this did not deter the intrepid author from intervening, again at personal expense though on royal instructions, in Mwene Mutapa's kingdom and placing chief Gende on the throne. He then engaged in a war of attrition with Chicanga of Manica who had closed the fairs, and in the middle of this enterprise had to arrest the *tenente-geral* of the day and send him a prisoner to Tete. Chicanga then offered to make peace, and off set the author to re-establish the fair and, at his own expense, to build a new fort. Further expeditions undertaken against rebel chiefs and disorderly *prazos* were all successful and the author claimed he could command an army of fifteen thousand men who were mostly his slaves. His last exploit, when he was already old and ill, was to march again to Manica and to reconstruct the fort in a higher and more defensible place.

The warning this bombastic account contained for any royal

official is unmistakable; and as a rule the *tenente-geral* tried to balance the private army of one *prazo*-holder with that of another so that the rival interests would neutralise each other. What happened when a military enterprise was entrusted to a group of settlers is well illustrated in the campaign unleashed by *tenente-geral* David Marques Pereira against the Marave chief Bive whose lands lay across the river from Tete.

The Bive *affaire*, which dragged on for years, began when the chief rashly made land concessions to some of the Portuguese from Tete. He subsequently made difficulties about carrying out his side of the treaty and in September 1754 stopped some Portuguese on the way to the mines. Pereira then summoned a meeting of the settlers and they decided to take joint action—the government anxious for the security of the trade routes along the north bank (*129*), the settlers eager for land. Pereira at this point was taken ill and the gathering of an expedition was entrusted to the *capitão-mor* of Tete. He raised a force of some 3,100 warriors and 200 musketeers who were joined by the Sena garrison with one field gun (*9*).

The expedition was duly successful and the settlers, who had had the running of the expedition, dispossessed the chief and asked for royal titles for the lands they had conquered. Francisco de Mello e Castro, the governor-general in Moçambique, hearing about this, complained vigorously to Pereira about his indulgence in such power politics when the primary interest of the state was in keeping friendly with the north bank chiefs and ensuring an open road to the mines and the fair at Zumbo (*128*). He suggested that the settlers give up their land, but *tenente-geral* Bernardo de Sa Botelho, who was still handling the case in 1759, pointed out tactfully that this would be a ruinous blow to Portuguese prestige and thus was able to provide Moçambique with a face-saving formula which allowed it to ignore the complete independence of action of the Rivers settlers.

For the *prazo*-holders government service offered many advantages. There were new lands to conquer but, more impor-tant, there was employment for the bands of armed slaves who were unruly and dangerous during peacetime. Once the army of the settlers was on the march the lands of both friend and foe were looted and burnt with equal abandon. When in 1767 José Mascarenhas petitioned for the grant of a *prazo* called Mapan-gare, he claimed that during recent campaigns one of his other properties, Pandoe, had been completely devastated by a Portu-guese army of three thousand warriors, and he called the com-

126

mandant of the expedition, Manuel Gomes Nobre, to witness the truth of the contention (27).

Perhaps Pereira had been wise to retire from the Bive campaign with a bout of judicious fever, for the experiences of more zealous royal officers in command of expeditions in the interior were not always encouraging. In 1798 Lacerda found that his expedition was torn by the jealousies of the various settlers who accompanied him, by the independence of the slaves and by the gusto with which his 'guide', Gonçalo Pereira, in the van of the party, looted and burnt the villages through which they passed. Vilas Boas Truão's experience in 1807 was still more disastrous. Having lost some trade goods he had ventured in the interior, he tried to raise an army to punish the chief he considered responsible. This was not a quarrel in which the *prazo*-holders were concerned and, although some of them reluctantly accompanied the expedition, they found a convenient way of getting rid of an unpopular governor. Truão found himself surrounded by the enemy and cut off without ammunition, was captured and subsequently murdered.

Apart from military expeditions the *prazo*-holders were regularly employed in other matters. They went on embassies and other missions to the chiefs and the government became very dependent on them for information about the interior. It was particularly inclined to employ the religious orders in this sort of work, perhaps because the ecclesiastics were rather more amenable to discipline and control, while at the same time possessing armed slaves and retainers with the best of the lay *prazo senhors*. The Jesuits were employed as receivers for debt, and their colleges were used as repositories for official documents and letters of succession, they acted as personal advisers to the *tenentes-gerais* and they were sometimes appointed to administer vacant *prazos* for the crown. On one occasion they were even entrusted with catching lions for the emperor of China (287). The Dominicans were no less influential. They provided one *tenente-geral* during the eighteenth century and administered the fair at Zumbo for years.

In 1763 the chief Zambesi settlements became municipalities and there was an opportunity for the elected councils to form a more bureaucratic, formal and impersonal link between government and the governed. However, it was the most powerful Portuguese in the Rivers who were elected to the councils—the men who had controlled affairs long before *camaras* had been thought of for East Africa—and so things went on much as before. New institutions with new names will never change the nature of government so long as the personalities remain the same.

The *camaras*, besides being entrusted with the running of the affairs of the towns, moved reluctantly into two fields of general administration. They were thought to be the most suitable bodies to report the exact circumstances surrounding the vacancy of any *prazo*, and to help to resolve disputes over who was the legal *senhor*. They were also held to be the best authority to carry out the public works which had previously fallen to the lot of the settlers individually. For instance, the clearing of the waterways was eventually entrusted to the *camaras* after attempts to get individual *prazo*-holders to do something about the problem were found to be futile.

The real reason, however, why the *camaras* never played an important part in the life of the Rivers colony was that, even though most Portuguese lived in the towns, the wealth and the culture of Zambesi society was not urban-based. The power of the great *prazo*-holders lay in their vast seigneuries, in the tribute they received and in the slave armies they maintained on their lands. For them the towns were convenient meeting places, where arms and trade goods could be obtained and, incidentally, where the government had its headquarters and the military authorities maintained a fort. There was no urban class to play any role in politics.

A possible exception might be made of the Indian community. The so-called Banians were Hindus and with their connections with trading houses in Bombay acted as financiers for the trading expeditions into the interior, loaning money to the *prazo*-holders and, on occasion, to the government (*305*, pt. 3, chap. 1).

As financiers, and as the creditors of most of the Portuguese settlers, the Banians might appear to have been in a position to dominate the politics of the Rivers. But a money-lending class is powerless without government support, and royal government was so completely dependent on the great *prazo*-holders that there was no possibility of the Indian financiers linking up with the 'crown' against the 'feudal barons' and re-enacting the triumph of absolutism in continental Europe.

There is a second good reason why the *camaras* never became important institutions. Already the Zambesi communities had developed an institution called an *adjunto* or *reunião*. The *adjunto* probably had no legal existence but was an *ad hoc* assembly designed to reconcile the real power of the settlers with the nominal power of the government. In the eighteenth century the *adjunto* seldom met of its own accord but would be summoned by the *tenente-geral* whenever the government needed the aid of the settlers for some project. The *adjunto* might be of any size but, for it to be effective, it was essential that the most important of the settlers should all attend. Separate *adjuntos* would be called for Sena, Tete and Quelimane.

Adjuntos probably began when the first two *sertanejos* met one another in the interior in the sixteenth century. It is likely that the office of *Capitão das Portas* developed from meetings of the traders at the fairs, for originally the post was elective. Groups of traders and *sertanejos* also assembled to witness and sign treaties or concessions made with chiefs in the interior in the seventeenth century. One of the earliest references to the *adjunto* by name is in the account of the wars with Changamire at the very end of the seventeenth century when the Sena settlers met to discuss the war situation and to raise troops to defend Tete (*337*, para 119).

In the eighteenth century a wide variety of problems were discussed by the *adjuntos*. An *adjunto* was called before the invasion of Bive in 1754 and afterwards to consider the terms of peace with the luckless chief. In 1760 an *adjunto* of fifteen people met in Manuel Gomes Nobre's house in Tete to consider the request by a Marave chief to pass through one of the *prazos* and to settle his wives on Portuguese land. Two Dominicans attended this meeting but the *tenente-geral* does not appear to have done so. One of the company was elected secretary of the *adjunto* and produced at the end the *termo do adjunto*—the conclusions of the *adjunto* (*137*).

In 1769 an *adjunto* met to decide what was to be done with João Moreira Pereira who had been entrusted with an important mission by the government of the Rivers but who was summoned to Moçambique to answer charges there. The *adjunto* decided that sureties should be sent in his place. In 1752 the *tenente-geral* died and a meeting of settlers was held to decide what should be done in the absence of letters of succession. In 1797 an *adjunto* was called to meet the ambassadors of Kazembe, and again in 1822 and 1830.

This gives some idea of the scope of the *adjunto* as a delibera- tive body. However, there were times when the government sought the views of the settlers not by calling an *adjunto* but by sending round a circular letter requesting answers to certain questions. In 1637 verbal testimonies had been given by the leading *sertanejos* on whether the mines should be worked directly by the royal treasury. The unanimous testimony had been for no change (*171*). Then in 1752 the government proposed to move the town of Sena across the River to the more healthy slopes of Mount Morumbala. Again the settlers were consulted and returned a virtually unanimous verdict against any change. In 1780 a circular asked whether it would be better for the crown *prazos* to be leased or rented (*41*). Again, unanimously, the settlers voted against change. In 1827 the settlers were consulted about the public works that should be undertaken by the Rivers authorities.

It is not unreasonable to call the *adjunto* a democratic body for it clearly well represented the views of its membership. It was a recognition that in this frontier society power lay with the local 'strong-arm men' and that peace and prosperity depended on getting them to work together as far as was humanly possible.

8 *Prazo* Society

Life on the Zambesi in the eighteenth and early nineteenth centuries

It is a curious coincidence, but a fortunate one for those who like to docket history by centuries, that there exist long and detailed accounts of Portuguese Zambesia written about the turn of the sixteenth, seventeenth, and eighteenth centuries. João dos Santos' account published in 1609 is matched by Antonio da Conceição's *Tratado dos Rios de Cuama* of 1696, and at the end of the eighteenth century there is Francisco de Lacerda's diary of his journey up the Zambesi. Both dos Santos and Antonio da Conceição knew the Zambesi world and, in their different ways, had close connections and affinities with it. Lacerda was a stranger, seeing it all for the first time and recording impressions of this strange world as it appeared to a well-educated and widely travelled eighteenth-century gentleman. Lacerda hated and despised all he saw and few governors coming to take up their posts can have left for the historian such a revealing document to explain their subsequent failures. His diaries provide, however, a vivid picture of the Rivers at the end of the eighteenth century (*384*).

Lacerda left Moçambique for Quelimane on 30 October 1797 and reached the bar at the mouth of the Qua Qua river on 2 November. As the vessel approached the surf which was breaking all along the bar, Lacerda noticed that the pilot was calling out one set of directions but that an old mulatto with the lead was giving different instructions which the crew were following. This little story is an allegory of the whole Zambesi colony. The mulatto knew the Rivers, for the vessel passed the bar in safety, and Lacerda landed to record his first impression of the Zambesi world.

The town of Quelimane was made up of the houses of the settlers set down without any plan. They lay surrounded by palms, mangoes and orange trees, and by the huts of their servants on the marshy river bank. When the rains came the town was flooded, so that the Portuguese could only stir out of doors carried in palanquins—called *machillas*—held above the heads of their slaves.

He found that the settlers kept cattle in spite of the various coastal diseases. He tried to persuade them to care for their beasts by making floors in the corrals so that the cattle did not have to stand always in the mud, and by treating the leeches that sucked the blood from their bellies. The rich and well-watered soil round Quelimane could, he thought, easily produce large quantities of provisions, but there was a lack of sufficient shipping to enable produce to reach its markets without spoiling.

Not only cattle but humans suffered from the heat and humidity. Dysentery and fevers of all sorts were endemic and Lacerda rightly pointed to the shallow wells, swarming with insects, from which the water was drawn as one of the most likely causes of disease. 'During this year,' he wrote, 'fifteen people died and three were born—two at one birth—while I was in the town'. The whole Portuguese community, including the Indians, consisted of a hundred and sixty people.

Lacerda left Quelimane on 1 December to travel by boat to Sena. The flotilla consisted of seven Zambesi canoes laden with the baggage and three rowing boats in which he travelled with his family and escort. In all there were a hundred and eighty rowers, each one earning four fathoms of cloth and his keep on the journey.

During the high flood season from January to August it was sometimes possible to pass directly through the marshes between the Zambesi and the Qua Qua, but at other times boats had to take the narrow channels of the delta, thick with reeds and mud, and blocked by fallen trees. Even these were only navigable when filled by the high tides. These channels, the Cochissone *grande*, the Cochissone *pequeno* and the Maindo, gave Lacerda his first real experience of the frustrations and privileges of a governor. The channels had all been cleared two years previously on government orders—at least money had been raised for the work and one of the settlers, an Indian called Ignacio Francisco Pinto, had been placed in charge of the work. All he had done was to fell a few trees which now lay half submerged in the mud causing snags on which the boats every minute risked wrecking themselves. He had also dredged some of the mud from the bottom and left it on the banks to wash back with the next rains. All the money subscribed had disappeared. 'The most essential task will be to drag out the tree trunks,' noted Lacerda, 'and the settlers ought to order the channels to be deepened for this is their duty; but they do not care about it at all.' (*384*, 91)

The other incident occurred when Lacerda noticed his boatmen apparently drawing baskets of provisions, fowls and dried fish from the river. It was explained to him that when the Africans had the good fortune to travel in the company of the *illustrissimo senhor governador* they considered it their right to rob any other boat they encountered on the river. Lacerda ordered the stolen goods to be returned but there were boats following after, and he feared the robbery would only be repeated.

Day after day the flotilla pushed through the swamps, passing a few settlements but mostly confronted with the unbroken shoreline of reeds and undergrowth. At the end of the sixth day the governor camped on the banks of the Zambesi. Like many subsequent travellers, Lacerda was immediately struck by the beauty of the great river, eight hundred yards across where he first saw it and flowing between fifteen-foot banks. Everywhere were masses of birds and wild game, taking his mind back to similar scenes on the rivers of Brazil. From his boat he saw a herd of fifty elephant, but was not so pleased by the reception he received from the African villagers 'who turned out shouting "Our lord has come" more out of interest in the beads which it is the custom to distribute than out of concern for the good or bad qualities of the new governor.' (*384*, 95)

On the ninth day the party reached the main stream of the Zambesi at Boca do Rio and stayed at a settlement on *prazo* Chupanga—possibly near the spot where Livingstone and his companions later had their headquarters and where Mrs Livingstone died. Chupanga had always been famous for its forest timbers and boats had been built on the sandy shores of the *prazo*. Ships the size of two-masted barks had been constructed there and Lacerda saw the fifty-foot keel of a vessel that had been begun and then abandoned because of the bankruptcy of its owner.

Resting the sick at Chupanga, Lacerda was endlessly serenaded by the *marimbas*, drums and dances of the local Africans, whose music sounded cacophonously in his ears but whose antics and acrobatics gained his reluctant admiration. Here at Chupanga Lacerda enjoyed the hospitality of the *senhor*, Colonel Manuel Ribeiro dos Santos, who accorded him a great welcome and cared assiduously for the fever-stricken members of the party. As in all frontier societies, hospitality was here an obligation,

133

almost a rite, as sacred as the blood feud and every visitor, however prejudiced against the Zambesi Portuguese, always gratefully acknowledged the warmth of his welcome.

The governor continued his journey on Christmas Day 1797, past *prazos* Inhamunho and Caia, past the Zangwe river flowing from Cheringoma and past the Shire river up which Manuel dos Santos had travelled and traded as a boy. On 28 December he reached the town of Sena where he was met by a ragged church procession headed by the prior of the Dominicans, who 'having soaked me with the sprinkler, censed me, given me the crucifix to kiss and intoned the *Te Deum Laudamus* very badly, performed some exorcisms over me and recited some prayers among which he sang the versicles *Nihil proficiat inimicus in eo . . .' (384, 102)*

With time now to look around him, Lacerda found that his first impressions of Zambesi society were only too amply confirmed. The inheritance of the great *prazos* and the relationships of the great *prazo* clans were the sole interests of Zambesi society. The Portuguese community was mostly made up of former retainers of the viceroys and governors, and soldiers exiled as criminals to the colonies. Marrying into the local families and suddenly finding themselves affluent, these convicts, allowed their old habits to flourish with an unrestrained luxuriance.

The first concern of the newcomer to the Zambesi world was to show what a great person he was, by his brutality towards his slaves, by his malice to all and sundry, by his pride and disobedience to the government. According to the horrified Lacerda, these men kept their own private prisons in which they tortured and killed their prisoners, and one of them had a set of royal seals which he used to open secretly all the royal correspondence that passed through his hands for distribution in all parts of the Rivers.

Corruption was taken for granted. A *tenente-geral* was expected to net a fortune of forty or fifty thousand *cruzados* during a single year in office and Lacerda was soon offered a bribe of 5,000 *cruzados* to remit a sentence on a criminal. There was general incredulity in the Rivers that this man who had forty doors—that is a fortune of forty thousand *cruzados*—should ever be shut up for long in prison.

The corruption of manners was as bad, in the eyes of the puritanical governor, as the corruption of justice. The settlers all kept harems on their *prazos* and regularly consulted witch-doctors about their ailments and other purposes. Poison was often administered to find out the perpetrator of a crime, and Lacerda said he had heard of human sacrifices being made to ensure good crops. 'The Portuguese in this colony,' he wrote in disgust, 'are more barbarous than the kaffirs, for the latter obey the orders of their sovereign with a promptness which should serve as an example.' (*384*, 117)

Sena, Lacerda found, was healthier than Quelimane and he noticed the abundant wild growth of indigo, sugar cane and cotton. The fort, which had been painted to him in glowing colours, was only four mud and thatch walls which he refused to believe could possibly be a fortress until he saw the half dozen old guns and the tattered flag inside.

For twenty days the rains had been falling and the river was rising rapidly. The local settlers were overjoyed at the ending of a long period of famine and drought when even the wild game of the Zambesi valley had been decimated and Africans had dropped dead in the streets. The governor was advised to winter in Sena, but he left the town on 8 January 1798 and set off against the flood of the Zambesi to Tete.

Three days later, on Chemba *prazo*, he passed a hundred and fifty slaves in chains being sent to the coast and found fleeting comfort for this bleak sight in the story he was told that the slave trade was conducted at a loss by the merchants. The flotilla then sailed through the Lupata gorge on 19 and 20 January and, passing Massangano and the mouth of the Luenha, arrived in Tete on the 24th.

Tete was built of stone and mud, some of the houses thatched and some with tiled roofs—both types being equally bad, for the white ants consumed the thatch and the wind blew off the tiles. The fort was a square with one side made up of the soldiers' and officers' quarters. There were four little look-out points, which were called bastions, but three of these were in a state of collapse and only two of them had any guns. The whole fort, Lacerda thought, would disintegrate in the next rains unless repairs were carried out. Not that this would much matter, for the garrison consisted of some African soldiers who did not even understand Portuguese and could only obey an order given in the local language. There were neither arms nor ammunition and no workmen who could carry out the simplest repairs on a gun.

Lacerda returned to the same theme in the diary of his journey to Kazembe.

Tete appears an infant colony in almost everything. It cannot even tan leather and it ignores soap-boiling and sugar-making.

135

These articles we might supply to Moçambique instead of importing them from Goa. And they often fail as during this and the last year when there was no leather even for heel pieces . . . Who would have expected the sugar of Moçambique to come from Rio de Janeiro and Batavia? (*329*, 62)

Perhaps Lacerda was judging the settlement too hard for, according to his showing, it was only just recovering from the devastating famines of the previous four years when, as at Sena, man and beast had starved, slaves and servants had run away and the settlers, sitting in the dark in the evenings without even enough oil for a lamp, had expected any moment to find themselves totally deserted. The town was only saved by provisions sent by canoe from the delta.

Nevertheless Lacerda's account of the river settlements and their inhabitants differs little from that of other contemporary observers. Portuguese civilisation had progressed not at all in two hundred and fifty years—that is Portuguese civilisation as understood in the great cities of Portugal and Brazil which Lacerda knew. But why should a society in Africa be judged by American or European standards? In Zambesia the Portuguese had had to confront not only the formidable African climate but the culture and traditions of the peoples of the valley and the plateau. Their society had its own values, its own norms, its own rules and regulations, its own mechanisms and balances which Lacerda and the other commentators from Europe described without really understanding.

Social and economic judgements are not lacking among the many writers on Portuguese colonial subjects, but few even of the most acute observers stopped to record the trivial details of the passing scene. In 1823 two officers from Captain Owen's admiralty survey squadron, Messrs Browne and Forbes, with an African companion, obtained leave to travel up the Zambesi as far as Sena. They were by no means the first Europeans other than Portuguese to make the journey, for there had been German, Spanish and even English priests attached to the missions. Nor was the account of their journey the first account of Zambesia to be written by a non-Portuguese, for the German Jesuit Mauriz Thoman had published his autobiography in Augsburg in 1788. Nevertheless the record of these two English officers is of exceptional interest. It was the first record of a whole series which English travellers in the nineteenth century were to produce describing the Portuguese colony and it is one of the few records which gives some vivid detail of life on the River (*421*).

Eight miles above Quelimane the party reached the settlement of Marangane which was cultivated solely by slaves without any Portuguese supervision. Much of the food produced there went to supply the slave ships calling at Quelimane. At Boca do Rio, still without meeting any Portuguese, they were entertained by the local chief who spoke fluent Portuguese and obtained palanquins for the Englishmen. The hospitality of Zambesia soon won appreciative comments from the travellers, for at Maruro they were entertained by an Indian merchant and *senhor*, Paul Marianno Vas dos Anjos, the founder of one of the famous *prazo* families of the nineteenth century.

Marianno's house was large but built of bamboo and grass with a large enclosure round it.

> His days were spent in one unvaried, mechanical routine, and the diary of one would suffice for all the others. He rose early and amused himself in the balcony until breakfast time in smoking several *carnotes*, a sort of small cigar made of shag tobacco rolled up in the banana leaf, which gives them a peculiar, and to smokers, a pleasant flavour. At eight he breakfasted, and then busied himself among his people; slept away the noon-tide hour, and dined at two; the table groaning under a profusion of meats dressed in a variety of ways, among which port wine generally formed a principal ingredient. After this repast was ended, and he had smoked another *carnote*, the old gentleman again retired to rest, and did not rise again until the coolness of the evening drew him forth, enveloped in a cloak, to enjoy the freshness of the air. At nine he supped and shortly afterwards retired to bed. (*322*, 267–9)

Described in this way Zambesi life had something idyllic about it. From Marianno the travellers obtained some useful cautionary hints; not to bathe in the river, for the son of one of the *donas* had recently been eaten by a crocodile; and to resort to sweating and drenches of rice water to cure the Zambesi fevers. From Maruro they crossed the Zambesi to Chupanga where they were warmly welcomed by *Dona* Pascoa d'Almeida at her house—probably the same house where Lacerda had stopped twenty-five years earlier and where Livingstone was to stay twenty-five years later.

The Dona's establishment was on a much more magnificent scale than that of Marianno's, and the display at meals was in every way sumptuous, the table being covered with massive silver utensils, and wines and eatables of many descriptions cooked in a variety of ways. (*421*, 142)

From Chupanga the travellers crossed the River again and stayed with a mulatto at whose house they were entertained with the same verve that Lacerda had earlier experienced.

They found a group of strolling players, exhibiting various theatrical performances, also feats of tumbling. The chase of a man by a lion constituted one part of the entertainment. The latter character was enacted by a native dressed out most formidably in a horrid mask and skin. The plot was as follows: the man after a long run reaches a tree, ascends it and endeavours to conceal himself among the branches, while the lion, after many awkward attempts at springing up to seize him crouches down below to watch for his descent; the man loudly calls for help; a hunter cautiously approaches; the lion is killed and the scene ends with wild exultations at the monster's death. (*421*, 144)

The two British travellers met with some members of the Portuguese community whom they did not fancy. They comment on the 'laziness of a subaltern, who after having often slept eleven hours during the night, still continued to slumber in the forenoon'.
Another mulatto also offended the sailors' rather vigorous morality.

He was a wretched being of half Portuguese and half Malay extraction . . . who had scarcely a rag to cover him, yet to strike [us] with an idea of his importance he was highly solicitous to impress on our minds that he did not work but slept all day, the negros labouring for him in his occupation which was that of curing fish.

Their judgement had not been much different from that of Lacerda, and it was to be echoed in numerous accounts written during the nineteenth century. A third description of Zambesi life, this time of the interior of the country, comes from the remarkable diary that Antonio Pedroso Gamitto wrote of his journey to Kazembe in 1831—quite one of the best of all the travel books written by European explorers in the nineteenth century.

138

Gamitto had come to Africa as a young man. He was only nineteen when he arrived in Moçambique and a year later he had married one of the Zambesi *donas*, Inacia da Cruz, twenty-three years his senior. Gamitto was writing from intimate knowledge of Zambesi life and with much more sympathy for the communities of Portuguese Africa than Lacerda had shown (*297*).

June 25th . . . Over a hundred negroes were waiting here for João Pedro [Xavier de Silva Botelho]. When they saw him they broke into loud shouting and singing, and travelled on beside him, surrounding the palanquin in which he was being carried. The closer we got to habitation, the greater their numbers became so that when Botelho arrived at the *Luane*, or house of the *Bar*, there were more than six hundred people singing and dancing with drums around him. From that stream to the *Bar* we went half a league north, and camped near the *Luane*, where Botelho was received with 21 rounds fired from two one-pound pieces he has there, and with the hoisting of the Portuguese flag. (*363*, vol 1, 54)

Thus a royal salute was given for a notorious harbourer of escaped criminals and leader of one of the most blackguardly of the settler factions.

The polygamous tendencies of the Portuguese were commonly commented on and in the middle of the eighteenth century venereal disease was already appallingly widespread among the Portuguese community—no doubt accounting for the low birth rate (*468*, Chap 9). The following account by Gamitto of the daily life of the *senhors* living in the interior casts what is certainly a 'curious' light on the relations of the *senhor* and his slaves. The following passage was inspired by a visit to the *Bar* of Missale, the domain of José Luiz Rodrigues, deep in the interior.

The life of a *senhor* living on this *Bar* consists in eating, smoking and sleeping, being surrounded by young negro women and giving himself up to continual sensuality. When he sits at table to eat he is surrounded by slaves, their arms folded, awaiting orders, or busying themselves changing dishes —but not changing knives and forks because he eats by hand in the normal fashion of the natives of Portuguese East Africa and Asia; the normal fashion also of many Europeans when they are alone at table because, they say, food tastes better that way. When he finally finishes a slave appears with a basin, and

another with water . . . and another slave brings a towel. . . .
Having washed [his hands clean] another slave offers a clay
pipe with reed mouthpiece, a fathom in length; and as he
smokes, which he does lying down, a slave holds the pipe while
two or three slaves pummel him, giving light blows with both
hands or fists on his calves, thighs and buttocks until he falls
asleep. This operation continues during sleep until he awakens;
and the same happens at night, the slaves complying being of
both sexes but always young. (*363*, vol 1, 113)

At this stage we may turn from these impressions of colonial
life and look at Portuguese society in a more analytical way.

Population

How large was the Portuguese community in the eighteenth and
early nineteenth centuries? In spite of a dense undergrowth of
statistics this is rather hard to determine, because so many
different units of measurement were used. Sometimes the unit is
simply a baptism, and the number of Christians included people
of all colours and places of origin. Sometimes whites are separated
from coloureds but it is never clear how the mulatto family of a
white man is counted. Sometimes individuals are not counted at
all but households form the unit of measurement. Then there are
other refinements like the use of the terms, *filho da terra* (meaning
literally 'son of the land') or *patricio*, which probably refer to
mulattos; or *filho do reino* to distinguish European-born Portuguese from those born in the colonies.

Even when all this has been digested it is fairly clear that the
figures are all pretty inaccurate. They were based on the returns
of the parish priests, on the muster rolls of the garrisons and on
the reports of the *prazo*-holders and with few exceptions these
sources do not inspire confidence (*251*).

The following figures will therefore give only a general impression of the size of the Portuguese community throughout the
period.

1722   300 Portuguese, 178 Indians and 2,914 baptised
        Africans.
1735   113 Portuguese (without Quelimane), 200 Indians
        and a total of 2,949 Christians.
1777   172 Portuguese (without Quelimane), and 1,050
        Christians.

1782   63 Portuguese and 82 Indians.
1780–1800   Average for all Christians 2,142 (*377, 71*).
1802   Portuguese households 283 (*80*).

In 1777 a breakdown of the Portuguese community by age and sex shows the following result. These figures include Indians and mulattos (*36*).

Age 0–7 years   51 boys   54 girls
       7–15 „   66 boys   71 girls
      15–60 „   364 men   239 women (aged 14–40)
      60+   „   41 men   41 women (aged 40+)
15 births and 17 deaths were registered for that year.

Some further figures will complete the confusion. Between 1740 and 1801 there were 188 white births recorded in Sena (that is for the Sena district without Luabo) and 1,344 mulatto births. Between 1764 and 1801 there were 76 whites married and 104 mulattos and between 1775 and 1801 there were 120 deaths among whites.

One hundred and twenty deaths in twenty-five years set against 188 births in sixty years gives an idea of the adverse balance of life and death in the colony (*75*).

In 1780 the professions of the Portuguese are listed as 25 military men, 30 merchants, 44 farmers (*prazo*-holders?), 4 secretaries, 1 surgeon, 2 bleeders, 4 *muzios* (?), 7 tailors, 2 overseers, 2 carpenters, 1 smith and 97 without employment (*46*).

It has already been made clear that the 'Portuguese' community in Zambesia was very mixed in racial origin. The Portuguese themselves made fine distinctions between Portuguese born in the colonies and in Portugal; between Indians from Goa, Indians from the northern forts and Hindus; between mulattos resulting from unions of Portuguese men with Indians and negresses, and of Indian men with negresses. The African population did not make such distinctions. To them the Portuguese community were all *muzungos*—a name even used for people of African parentage who lived and dressed like Europeans and were accepted in the European community. In the nineteenth century the Portuguese used the term *muzungo* rather in the opposite sense, to apply to a man of non-African origin who had settled in Zambesia and adopted African customs.

In contrast to the general statistics for the Portuguese community, here are some figures for the leading families only. They

141

are derived from the account of Antonio Pinto Miranda, dated about 1766, and the individuals have doubtless been selected by the author on a purely subjective assessment of their importance. They certainly number among them all the most important resident *prazo*-holders.

Heads of families	—	20 Portuguese
	—	11 Indian
	—	7 mulattas (os)
	—	1 Chinese

Marriages	—	Portuguese to mulatta	13
	—	Portuguese to Indian	5
	—	Portuguese to Chinese	1
	—	Indian to mulatta	6
	—	Indian to Indian	1
	—	Chinese to Chinese	1
	—	Mulatto to Indian	1
	—	Mulatto to mulatta	1

There are no cases of all-white marriages.

Hard facts are few and far between in this quicksand of figures but it would be safe to stand on the assumption that the total Portuguese community of whites, Indians and mulattos was always under five hundred and this number was spread throughout the settlements from Quelimane to Zumbo and controlled over a hundred *prazos*. One can also be fairly sure that mortality among the whites was high, that their numbers were only maintained at all by infusions of immigrant officials and convicts, and that the Indians and mulattos probably formed the basis of Portuguese power at all times.

The origin of the Portuguese community in East Africa

The Portuguese who came to the Rivers usually came against their will. They were victims of shipwreck or criminals exiled to Portugal's most pestiferous colony. Even the soldiers who came out to serve in the garrison had very often passed through a court martial and were sent to East Africa to be forgotten. Those sent on from Moçambique to the Rivers were usually the worst offenders or those the government were most anxious to get rid of.

142

The details of the convict ships which came out in 1830 show the sort of person who was reaching the Rivers colony, though many of these may have been the rather exceptional products of the Portuguese civil wars. In that year the S. João Magnanimo sailed with thirty convicts for Moçambique, among them a priest, a farmer, a landowner, a butcher, a mason, a militia captain, and twenty-three soldiers. Their ages ranged from sixteen to fifty and their crimes from forgery and desertion to robbery, murder and political disaffection. A second ship, the Galatea, carried seventy-six convicts, four of whom were destined for the Rivers. In this cargo there were three women and half of the party were soldiers. There were nine persons sentenced for murder and twelve for political crimes. Their sentences ranged from three to twelve years (246, 247).

One degredado who made himself noticed was Manuel Joaquim Mendes de Vasconcellos e Cirne. In 1802 he had been shipwrecked off Moçambique and had later been sent from India to Sofala as a convict. For crimes committed there he was forwarded to the Rivers where his career took a turn for the better. He became governor of Quelimane and then governor of the Rivers from 1829 until his death in 1832. He wrote some of the most elaborate dispatches in the archives of the Rivers, easily recognisable by their classical allusions; he dismissed one of his many enemies on one occasion by calling him the 'Heliogabalus of the Rivers'. Vasconcellos e Cirne left behind him an interesting account of the Portuguese colonies in East Africa which was subsequently published (473).

Frederick Barnard, who landed a number of times at Quelimane from the British anti-slave squadron off the African coast, met a man who might be considered more typical of the successful convict.

[He] had originally got a passage to Quillimane at the expense of the Government, for (as he himself describes it) merely giving a man a friendly punch in the stomach when he had unfortunately, by pure accident, a small knife in his hand. He has now amassed a small fortune by slave dealing like many others here, and such are the kind of people one meets and many a murderer receives a stranger with a polite bow and shake of the hand. (317, 144)

The other Europeans who settled in the Rivers were all either officials or officers in the colonial forces. They either married heiresses or acquired *prazos* and trading interests. They were not all members of the lower class and a sprinkling of men of noble birth reached the Rivers. At least one *tenente-geral*, Marc Antonio de Montaury, came of a distinguished line and, settling in the Rivers, founded a family. As far as can be discovered most of the immigrants were men. Very few women ventured to settle in East Africa and this was commented on as one of the great obstacles to the growth of the Portuguese community, for the Portuguese men had to marry dark-skinned local girls and their children grew up with strong attachments to Africa and only a weak and flickering loyalty to Portugal. Proposals to import large numbers of Chinese women were hardly practical but do reflect the ill-balance in the Portuguese community.

There were two other important classes of immigrants. First there were the Canarins—or Catholic Goanese. These men thought of themselves as Portuguese and came to take up military or administrative posts. They were also very active in trade. There is evidence that, with their close links with India, the Canarins were a more resourceful and vigorous section of the community than the European Portuguese. Gradually they came to take over senior posts and gained control over more and more *prazos* until, by the nineteenth century, they were almost the only support that remained to the Portuguese crown in the disordered colony. The Canarins aroused a certain amount of impotent fury among the European Portuguese but, although Indians were forbidden to marry European women or to acquire *prazos*, there were few Zambesi families without Indian connections and the complaints against them carried little weight (*110*).

In a rather different position were the Banians—the Hindus from British India, who had first come to Portuguese Africa in the seventeenth century and who have survived with fluctuating fortunes to the present. Theirs was a commercial community which did not mix or marry with the Christian one. The Banians elected a chief who was granted the title of *capitão-mor* by the governor. They supplied trade goods and advanced money to needy settlers and to the government. Many governors saw the Banians as the cause of the economic stagnation of the colony. Their strong commercial position made them many enemies, and it was alleged that they all hoarded their wealth against the prospect of returning to India. The wealth which should have made East Africa great was thus lost. There were even ambitious plans to expel all the Banians from Moçambique but these were never carried out and this powerful community—whose role so

144

much resembles that of the Asians in Africa today—continued
to thrive (*115*).

Family and feud

A new settler arriving in the Rivers would very soon find that he
had little chance of surviving, let alone of making his way, if he
preserved his individual status and remained unattached. If he
were a soldier or government officer he would find that his pay
reached him either not at all or else in the form of cloth which he
needed the good offices of some merchant to dispose of profitably
(*363*, vol I, 27). If he came as a prospective trader, miner or
farmer he would be robbed, swindled and possibly murdered
unless he acquired 'protection'. He would find it impossible to
acquire or to keep any slaves to work for him, he would be unable
to obtain credit and he would scarcely be able to travel unmolested.

Survival, then, meant attachment to one of the powerful
Zambesi families, and this frequently entailed marriage with one
of the heiresses with her dowry of *prazos* and slaves. Mortality
was heavy among the Portuguese community and, contrary to
what might be supposed, men died more easily than women.
Physical stamina must have contributed quite a lot to the prestige
and power of such *donas* as Ines Gracias Cardoso who married
three times and held four *prazos*; or Ines Pessoa de Almeida
Castello branco who married four times.

Kinship was the all-important consideration. A man looked to
his kin for protection against enemies and against the law; he
looked to his kin to protect his interests if he were absent, to
discipline his slaves and to suppress trouble on his *prazos*; he
looked to his kin to help him in financial trouble and to maintain
him if he were reduced to penury. In the same way he would
recognise these duties towards other relatives. In all simple
societies a kinless or unattached man is a social monster and a
menace to the whole community.

A rather pathetic, though possibly not typical, case of the
victimisation of a kinless widow is that of the wife of *tenente-geral*
Vasconcellos e Cirne who died in 1832. The *tenente-geral* had
made many enemies and no sooner was he dead than his *prazo* of
Bororo was invaded and taken over, and his movable property
stolen and carried to the fortified stronghold maintained by
Colonel Silva Botelho deep in the northern interior. Redress

proved impossible, for Botelho's connections included many of the officials in the Rivers (*156*, *157*).

In most societies where kinship is especially important, one finds that clientage also flourishes. Clientage is a form of artificial kinship in which a man obtains the benefit of protection and maintenance without any blood ties with the family at all. In this relationship the client commits himself to the service of his protector and there is frequently some symbolic act which gives the agreement a binding and sacred character.

Clientage between members of the Portuguese community certainly existed, and most of the great *prazo*-holders had their following of 'poor whites' as well as the chaplains, men of business and merchants who ran their affairs. Very often these men were mulattos, the illegitimate by-blows of the *senhors*, without inheritance but recognised as members of the Portuguese community—as *muzungos* to use the African term. On the ladder of the social hierarchy they would be just above the *mwanamambos* and the *mocasambos*, the chief slaves of the *prazo*.

Crime was very common in Portuguese Zambesia. As the letter of instructions issued for the governor-general Calisto Rangel Pereira de Sa in 1761 put it,

> the greater part of the troops of the garrison of this station, and of the settlers of the said captaincies consist of idle and wicked men who came as convicts from the Kingdom; [it is] impractical that men of such depraved habits should live according to any rule and should preserve peace with their neighbours. (*299*, vol 1, 146)

In an attempt to contain crime in the colony all suspects were tried by a military tribunal. After 1761 this sat in Moçambique Island and the forces of law and order in the Rivers were only represented by the *juiz ordinario*—a sort of lay justice of the peace who was frequently one of the settlers. He could take depositions and prepare evidence but could not conduct serious criminal cases himself.

Antonio Manuel de Mello e Castro, *tenente-geral* from 1780–1786, condemned the remoteness of justice. He was convinced of the need for capital punishment to curb the violence of the settlers and thought that cases should be heard and sentences administered near the scene of the crime so that the sight of an execution should deter other criminals (*57*). The establishment of a separate court in Zambesia would greatly have increased the independence of the Rivers from the capital—a point which may not have escaped the *tenente-geral* when he made this proposal, for he had always been a keen advocate of the rights of the *tenentes-gerais*.

This system of justice, however, only operated as and when the great *prazo* families chose that it should. With their co-operation a man might be brought to justice but without it a criminal might go free for years. In 1759 the arrest of the Jesuits was swiftly and easily accomplished simply because the great *prazo* clans, who all owed money to the order, were delighted to see their creditors discomforted and twenty-two *prazos*, hundreds of slaves and a wealth of movable property come onto the market at favourable prices.

Of course, it would be a mistake to imagine the great *prazo* families acting in concert very often. For much of the time they were engaged in bitter feuding among themselves or in enforcing their 'frontier' justice on their neighbours or on the Africans living within the *prazos* and along their borders.

Take as an example the events of Easter 1760 in Tete. On the eighth day of the Easter festival the town was quiet and the settlers all at Mass, when ten slaves belonging to Antonio Botelho de Lemos attacked an Indonesian cook in the service of Inacio Octaviano dos Reis Moreira. The cook fled to the shelter of his master's house, pursued by his assailants to the very doors. Inacio's slaves sallied out to defend their master's property and the fight that ensued was only stopped when the two masters interfered at the request of the commandant of the town.

However, José da Silva Freire, a friend of Antonio de Lemos, had in the meantime sent his slaves to join in the fray, and their arrival caused the fighting to spring up again. Before long the slave quarters of both Inacio and João Moreira Pereira were looted and burnt and the fire had spread to involve other hitherto neutral settlers (*136*).

This incident is typical in that it arose from a quarrel over slaves. This was probably the most important single cause of feuding. The slave bands of a *prazo*-holder were little more than bands of armed retainers who would be bound to fall out with rival bands when the respective masters were together in town. To prevent this the government tried to stop slaves entering the towns armed (*95*). The masters themselves made matters worse by constantly luring away slaves belonging to each other and offering them refuge on their *prazos*. This practice was also denounced as 'vile, evil and barbarous' by the government but again without any effect (*52*).

If the authorities played their cards cleverly they could often hold the balance in a conflict between two of the *prazo* clans. Too often, however, the government would intervene to try to enforce law and order and would find its whole authority staked on bringing a particular offender to justice. A private feud thus grew into defiance of the government by one or both of the original parties. This is the chemistry by which social conflict becomes rebellion and ultimately revolution.

The case of Manuel Gonçalves Guião may serve as an example. In February 1718 a vivid and outraged letter from the king to the viceroy of India sets the scene. Manuel Gonçalves Guião's wife, *Dona* Ursula Ferreira, had been insulted by the wife of another *prazo*-holder. Guião and his friend, João de Tavora e Sampayo (son of a former *tenente-geral dos Rios*), had used this as a pretext for raiding Sena, probably some time in 1715, with a band of 'kaffirs armed with bows, arrows, and guns, destroying, burning and laying waste everything, going about with the heads of the kaffirs he killed and committing many hostile acts without fear of the law.' (*286, 218*)

Far worse, he had tried to stop the new *tenente-geral* from taking office. This, said the king, must be punished by 'expelling him from the said Rivers by whatever means you think fit, to prevent the evil which his presence may cause, especially in so serious a matter as opposing the orders of the government of India, showing in this an inexcusable disobedience contrary to the duty of a good subject . . .'

The viceroy, however, was more circumspect and less indignant. In a letter of January 1719 to the captain-general of Moçambique he wrote:

> The disorder occasioned by the kaffirs of Manuel Gonçalves Guião . . . is scandalous in the extreme but as the only punishment that is possible to inflict is what you point out to me . . . it is better to dissimulate . . . for (with João de Tavora e Sampayo) these are the two men who still have some power to serve His Majesty in the Rivers. (*287*)

It then transpired that Guião was needed to help in the re-establishment of the fair at Manica as he had friendly relations with the chief Chicanga. At the same time the viceroy wrote a letter to Guião himself in which he did scarcely less than crawl before the powerful *prazo*-holder (*288*).

The letter thanks Guião for his many services, particularly in his relations with the neighbouring tribes. The attempt to prevent the *tenente-geral* from taking office is glossed over and the viceroy humbly 'presumes that you will conduct yourself in such a way that there may be only a question of emulation for the better service of His Majesty.' The letter, however, ends with a warning:

> At present I do not inflict the punishment that this deserves as I hope for more exact information. It is a service to God and the king to rid the earth from cruel and disobedient subjects, and let not those who may be included in the number believe that distance or power will exempt them from my justice.

In August the council in Lisbon backed up these threats by a caution that all Guião's honours and grants might be withdrawn if there were any more trouble. And there, after a final letter from the viceroy in 1720 (*289*), the matter rested and Guião died in 1726 leaving his *prazo* of Luabo to his wife, without ever having been brought to justice.

Guião had emerged unruffled from his brush with the government because of his own personal standing and authority in the Rivers, but a man in trouble with authority might equally well be saved by the protections of one of the *prazo*-holders. A third and last story, which illustrates this, is taken from Lacerda's diary of his journey up the Zambesi.

José Gomes Monteiro was a soldier in the Sena garrison and was exiled to Manica for insubordination. There he contracted a liaison with one of the *donas* who resided nearby. The *dona* was married and, when her husband went to Moçambique, Monteiro left Manica and lived openly with the lady. When he realised that he was receiving protection from his mistress he returned from exile and openly lived in Sena. The commandant in Manica was ordered to fetch him back but refused to act. When Lacerda arrived he was ordered into exile up the River to Zumbo out of reach of his mistress. While in prison in Tete he offered Lacerda a bribe of 5,000 *cruzados*—the money being provided by his mistress—confident of being set free. But Lacerda was incorruptible and in this case justice took its course (*384*, 110–111).

Here is the ethos of a frontier society, where incorruptible governors were few and far between. Lacerda himself shortly afterwards married into the Moura e Meneses family and only his early death prevents one from learning whether his stiff

149

moral rectitude would have survived more than a year of life on the Zambesi.

Debts of the prazo senhors

The *senhors* and *donas* of the Zambesi *prazos* with their quarrels, their feuding slave retainers, their extravagance and their indolence were very vulnerable. Like the feudal nobles of another age, they lived constantly in a state of indebtedness. Of the causes of this indebtedness, the first must be the risks involved in trading ventures; the second, the pressures on the *prazo*-holders to vie with one another in their displays of wealth, power and largesse so that they could hold together their retinues of slaves and clients.

The peculiar risk involved in trading ventures can best be appreciated by looking once again at the way trade functioned in central Africa at the end of the eighteenth century. The staple trade goods were arms and powder, spirits, cloth and beads. These were supplied under a royal monopoly to the Zambesi merchants, though in the early nineteenth century the cloth was sold at auctions held in Moçambique Island (*363*, vol 1, 27–9). Almost all transactions were credit transactions and the merchants and *prazo senhors* obtained their goods from the royal factors. These were then either sold within the *prazos* to the African inhabitants or were sent to the fairs at Zumbo, Manica, or to Marave country where they might find African buyers waiting for them. By this time the price would have risen considerably for the cost of transport was high.

The high costs of transport arose from the dues and other payments that had to be made to chiefs along the route. The route to Zumbo lay through Chidema on the south bank and Marave country on the north. Until the conquest of Bive in 1754 both areas were frequently hostile to the Portuguese and large presents had to be made to secure a passage for traders. Even after the north bank had become comparatively secure for the Portuguese, there was trouble on the south and the numerous treaties with the Mwene Mutapas all mention the rights of traders and the necessity of punishing chiefs who robbed the trade caravans (*50*).

On the Manica journey, the petty chiefs who demanded presents were legion and the Portuguese tried to prevent their merchants from giving in to the blackmail and paying any but the recognised *madontos*—or dues (*112*). Besides gifts and payments extorted by the chiefs, there was the danger of incurring *milandos* which frequently led to long and bitter quarrels between the Portuguese and a chief leading to the complete closing of the roads (*357*).

Although it remained possible to make a 'killing' by a successful trading venture, the risks of failure were very great. Few Portuguese had any capital and after one failure the terms for further borrowing were correspondingly higher. Credit came either from the royal factor or from the Indian merchants who had the wealth of the Surat or Bombay trading houses behind them. Before their expulsion in 1759 the Jesuits had also provided credit and become the hated owners of a wide range of securities.

There is evidence that before the end of the eighteenth century Portuguese trade was already becoming uncompetitive and that the ivory and other products of central Africa were finding outlets north of Moçambique Island. There is also evidence of strain in the old monopolistic system as more and more complaints came in of illegal traders going behind the backs of the royal factors and even underselling the *prazo*-holders themselves on their *prazos* (*142*).

Failure in a commercial venture could lead very quickly to social and economic disaster. Word would soon get about of the imminence of bankruptcy, other creditors would foreclose, slaves would desert the foundering ship and the free African peasants on the *prazos* would refuse to pay tribute and become rebellious. Within a matter of months a rich and powerful *senhor* might become a penniless fugitive.

João Pereira Velho, who had once been one of the most powerful of the Tete settlers, had to flee into the bush to escape his creditors (*406*, *281*). In 1769 Manuel da Costa, described only three years earlier as the most powerful of the Zumbo Indian merchants, and Gil Bernardo Coelho de Campos, a *prazo*-holder, had to ask for a moratorium on their debts to the government for five years so that they could pay off their other creditors (*213*). The same year the *tenente-geral*, Inacio de Mello e Alvim, reported that he was staying in the house of Manuel Gomes Nobre, instead of having an official residence built so that Nobre could pay off his debts to the government.

Nobre himself was the holder of five *prazos*, according to one account, and the ramifications of his indebtedness involved many of the chief settlers of the Rivers. When he died and his property was sold up many of the settlers found themselves able once again to meet their creditors.

The chronic indebtedness of the settlers explains the competition among them to acquire more lands and to build up larger holdings of *prazos*. Credit would be maintained if it could be shown, even nominally, that assets were being increased by new grants of lands. It also explains the thoroughly mercenary approach towards the acquisition of government offices. When Manuel Dassa Castellobranco petitioned in 1755 for the post of captain of the Zimbabwe garrison, he stated in the petition that his chief reason for wanting the post was to be able to pay his debts (*8*). Sometimes *prazo* grants were made on the specific condition that debts were paid before the contract was finalised (*55*).

Debt made the *prazo*-holders more amenable to government pressure. In societies where there was a system of freehold property, the events would have led to the heavy burdening of estates with debt and their eventual transfer to a new class of financiers. This sort of change was impossible in Zambesia where the emphyteutic contracts forbade alienation.

Knowing the need of the *prazo* clans for government patronage and for fresh land grants, the *tenentes-gerais* could bid, often successfully, for their co-operation. It was also able to exert pressure through the apparently insatiable appetite of the Portuguese for titles and ranks. The Zambesi community was often only too conscious of the frailty of its links with European Portugal and the darker the skin and the more African the ancestry, the keener the individual would become for some recognition of his status within the Portuguese community.

Father Manuel Barreto recorded as early as 1669 that Bayão's son-in-law, Antonio Lobo da Silva, would require a patent of nobility and the habit of the crusading Order of Christ if he were to undertake further government enterprises. Nobility and the habit of the Order of Christ, of course, carried with them not just honour but a pension and immunity from the normal processes of law (*318*).

These points are not entirely frivolous; they show that the community of the great *prazo*-holders still thought of itself as Portuguese first and foremost and saw its ambitions as being fulfilled within the context of a European society. For all their turbulence and riotous defiance of the government, there was never any danger of the Portuguese losing control of their colony entirely.

The Portuguese have always been the most stringent critics of their own colonial enterprises, and the picture painted of the Rivers colony in the innumerable reports which have come down from the eighteenth century is one of decadence, corruption, disorder, and the stagnation of all economic activity. Yet there are virtually no suggestions that the *prazo* system should be radically altered or ended. Officials from the highest to the lowest continued to believe that there was nothing wrong with the system in principle. All that was needed was to tighten up the regulations, to break up the large estates, to increase the population etc., etc., and the system would then work for the development of the colony and the prosperity of the Portuguese crown. Unbelievably, colonial theorists of the late nineteenth century continued to believe much the same thing in spite of the terrible experiences of the Zambesi Wars which had, as much as anything else, been caused by the old system of emphyteutic contracts and the social system it had fostered.

It will be argued in a subsequent chapter that the *prazo*-holders could not have developed their estates into thriving plantations even had they wished, while the dreams of Eldorado in central Africa were totally unfounded—and were known to be unfounded ever since Vasco Homen found that the mines of Manica were only small river-side washings, and that the silver of Chicoa had no existence at all. Homem left the Zambesi in 1576, and from then until 1969 when the contracts for the building of the Cabora Bassa dam were signed, there has never been any scheme for the economic development of the Zambesi valley which has had the slightest chance of success.

If Spain has lived on the memory of her 'Golden Age', Portugal has too often lived on the dream of a golden age that never really existed; a golden age that was always just round the corner, almost within reach of the most indolent Zambesi *dona* as she was jogged along the winding, dusty paths of the Zambesi valley by her bearers, the unchanging African bush brushing against the very curtains of her palanquin.

9 Luabo and Cheringoma

Contracts of emphyteusis were founded in Roman Law and certain *a priori* assumptions that were inseparable from its operation; but land law is a very practical thing which moulds and is moulded by the people who operate it and have to live and work by it. The law with regard to the *prazos* was in part case law which was elaborated by all the numerous disputes over *prazo* grants. Luabo and Cheringoma, which form the subject of this chapter, were two large and wealthy *prazos* and their history in the eighteenth and early nineteenth centuries does a lot to explain how the *prazo* system worked in practice—what the realities were behind the legal formulae.

Luabo

The name Luabo refers both to a river and a *prazo*. The river is the southernmost branch of the Zambesi after the main stream splits to find its way to the sea through the delta. The *prazo* lay on each side of the Zambesi as it passed through the delta. The neighbouring *prazos* were Maindo to the north-east, Mulambe and Cheringoma to the south-west and Chupanga to the north-west. Luabo belonged, with these last two, to the administrative district of Sena.

The Luabo mouth of the Zambesi had early been recognised as the best point to enter the river, since it had enough water at all seasons of the year. Francisco Barreto's expedition had made use of the Luabo mouth, and in the sixteenth century there was an official resident there who received boats arriving by sea and saw to the transfer of their cargoes to smaller river boats. The official was sometimes called the *Guarda-mor* and sometimes the *Capitão dos Rios de Senna* (273, 348).

As a port of access it was known to be superior to the Qua Qua river and Quelimane. The Jesuits founded a mission on Luabo which was in operation by 1631 and *Dom* Estevão de Ataide had a fort constructed there during his captaincy from 1610–13. The building of this fort seems to have been the high-water mark of Luabo's importance for in 1617 *Frei* Francisco de Avelar suggested that the river mouth should be blocked by the sinking of two hulks and that the post of *Capitão dos Rios* should be abolished (*313*, 55).

For the remainder of the century Luabo lost ground to Quelimane and royal officials repeatedly urged that it should either be closed entirely or adequately fortified. The population had also declined; at the end of the century there were no Portuguese in Luabo at all and in 1722 only one resident there. It was widely believed in the eighteenth century that the river mouth had silted up (*428*, 326) and was unusable. In the nineteenth century it was again being used, this time by slavers, and the more likely reason for its total eclipse in the eighteenth century is to be found in the rapid decline of Sofala. The Luabo mouth was the natural port of entry for ships using Sofala as their coastal point of call, but since in the eighteenth century all goods had to go to Moçambique to pass the royal customs it was obviously more economical to send cargoes via Quelimane and cut out hundreds of miles of the journey which using the Luabo mouth would entail.

Luabo, however, early acquired an importance independent of its use as a port. By general agreement it was one of the most fertile areas of the whole Zambesi valley. Antonio Bocarro in the 1630s mentioned its wealth of provisions and wood suitable for boat building, but the most lyrical descriptions of its blessings came from a holder of the *prazo*, Manuel Antonio de Almeida, He wrote in his *Memorial* in 1763:

It is very fertile, and produces all sorts of provisions including rice and corn which are not produced elsewhere in the Rivers except Quelimane. It produces millet and *michueira,* food on which the Africans feed. It has large palm plantations which give coconuts, and *sura* from which they make vinegar and oil, and wild palms from which is taken *nipa* and which is very strong like *urraca* of Goa. There are flats of salt and cane brakes from which ... two or three hundred *faraçolas* of sugar were made. Also in the land are many thickets of timber which could be extracted in great quantity for building small boats. ... (*294*)

In the nineteenth century it would be no exaggeration to say

155

FAMILY CONNECTIONS TO ILLUSTRATE CHAPTER NINE

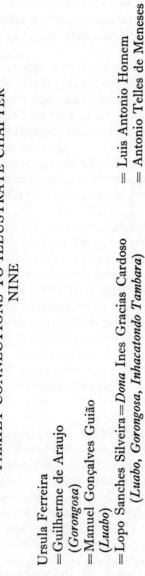
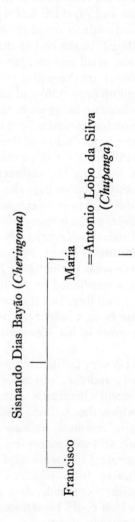

Ursula Ferreira
= Guilherme de Araujo
(*Gorongosa*)
= Manuel Gonçalves Guião
(*Luabo*)
= Lopo Sanches Silveira = *Dona* Ines Gracias Cardoso = Luis Antonio Homem
(*Luabo, Gorongosa, Inhacatondo Tambara*) = Antonio Telles de Meneses

Francisco
Maria
Sisnando Dias Bayão (*Cheringoma*)
= Antonio Lobo da Silva
(*Chupanga*)

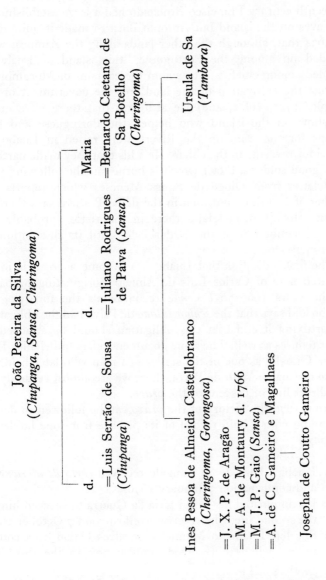

João Pereira da Silva
(*Chupanga, Sansa, Cheringoma*)

d.

Maria

d.

=Luis Serrão de Sousa
(*Chupanga*)

=Juliano Rodrigues
de Paiva (*Sansa*)

=Bernardo Caetano de
Sa Botelho
(*Cheringoma*)

Ursula de Sa
(*Tambara*)

Ines Pessoa de Almeida Castellobranco
(*Cheringoma, Gorongosa*)

=J. X. P. de Aragão
=M. A. de Montaury d. 1766
=M. J. P. Gaio (*Sansa*)
=A. de C. Gameiro e Magalhaes

Josepha de Coutto Gameiro

that Luabo became the regular source of supply for the whole of the Rivers and a place of refuge for the population in time of famine.

I do not know when Luabo first became a *prazo*. In the sixteenth century Francisco Brochado had a large establishment of slaves on the island but Antonio Bocarro made it quite clear in 1634 that, although the other lands along the Zambesi were divided up among the Portuguese, 'this island of Luabo is divided among chiefs . . . to whom the captains of Moçambique entrust the cultivation of the land and the government of the people.' (*321*, vol 2, 408) He also says that there were many Muslims on the island who helped the Portuguese and that troops for the wars up the Rivers were raised in Luabo by judicious presents to the chiefs. He adds that they made particularly good soldiers, a fact which is borne out the following year in a letter from Diogo de Sousa Meneses which reports the raising of two thousand men in the delta. Bocarro says that the Jesuits already owned land there in the 1630s—probably the Ilha Mulambe which the Order held until its dissolution in 1759.

The first indication that Luabo has become a *prazo* is in an undated note of Carlos Luis de Almeida, originating probably in the years 1660–70 (*2*). He recommends the fortifying of Luabo and says that the *senhor fulano* de Paiva had the obligation of fortifying it and that this obligation should be attached to other tenures as well. The same document refers to Belchior Dias de Sa Camello as one of the settlers—a man who later held the *prazo* of Luabo. With de Paiva, then, we are almost certainly on the direct line of descent of the *prazo*.

From 1676 the history of the *prazo* can be followed in detail, beginning with a bald record of its passage from one holder to the next.

1 Belchior Dias de Sa Camello received *carta de aforamento* and confirmation 7 January 1676.
2 He nominated his wife Maria da Guerra to succeed him in the second life. She received confirmation 7 October 1680.
3 She left Luabo to Manuel Gonçalves Guião by a codicil to her will. He received confirmation in the third life 14 June 1714.
4 Guião petitioned for the contract to be extended for two more lives but this was refused. His widow, *Dona* Ursula Ferreira, received it by right of renewal in 1726.

5 She left Luabo to her second husband Lopo Sanches Silveira in the second life in 1731.

6 He left it to his second wife *Dona* Ines Gracias Cardoso in the third life in 1746.

7 She died in March 1757 and by her will left the *prazo* to *Dom* Manuel Antonio de Almeida (*16*).

8 He left the *prazo* to his daughter *Dona* Anna de Almeida.

9 She left it to her daughter *Dona* Alexia Rita Carneiro de Sousa e Faro who married the natural son of the *Conde* de Sarzeda, the viceroy of India.

10 It passed to Francisco Carlos da Costa Lacé who received confirmation in 1822 and in 1824 a petition was lodged against this grant by Joaquim Antonio Ribeiro who wanted the *prazo* for his daughter. The *prazo* fell *em commisso* and was then rented by Caetano Camillo Vas dos Anjos (*103*).

The first remarkable thing about this list is that although the three-life rule is fairly strictly adhered to, and although the *prazo* is held by at least five women, there is no case of a daughter succeeding until *Dona* Anna de Almeida succeeded her father at the end of the eighteenth century. A clearer pattern is the descent from husband to wife and from wife to husband. This accords closely with the practical need for someone adult and well acquainted with the *prazo* and its inhabitants to take charge. A bare factual record of the descent of the *prazo*, however, tells nothing of the disputes that surrounded the succession to it.

In 1726 the new viceroy of India, João de Saldanha da Gama, stopped at Moçambique on his way to Goa and drew up plans for a granary to supply the garrison. Hoping to endow the granary with a permanent source of supply, and hearing that the *prazo* of Luabo, renowned for its fertility, was vacant following the death of Manuel Gonçalves Guião, the viceroy ordered that the lands should be handed over to the Jesuits and the rents of them sent to Moçambique to pay for the building of the granary.

The royal letter of February 1727, replying to the viceroy's announcement of his plan, set out the motives for taking over the *prazo*. Luabo would pay for the granary and help to supply it and at the same time the *prazo* would be removed from the hands of the settlers 'who, as they are few and this great dominion is divided among them, become so powerful that not only do they free themselves from the condition of subjects but on many occasions act with the tyranny of petty kings.' In this way the power of the settlers would be lessened and that of the crown increased. The *Junta do Commercio*—the council of commerce—had advised against the plan, however, and the king asked for the details of the surrender to the Jesuits (*290*).

At this stage *Dona* Ursula Ferreira enters the picture. She applied to the viceroy for the grant of the *prazo* according to the terms of her husband's will. It was granted to her pending confirmation and to avoid delay she offered an interest-free loan of 6,000 *cruzados* towards the building of the granary. The *prazo* was handed over to her procurator on 30 May 1727. However, the ship carrying her money to Moçambique was wrecked and the rector of the Jesuits asked for another loan to cover the building. The whole story is set out in her petition to the crown dated January 1728 (*3*).

The viceroy then made another offer by which *Dona* Ursula would be granted a pension of 8,000 *xerafins* a year in exchange for the land, but by this time Ursula Ferreira had married again and her new husband, Lopo Sanches Silveira, refused the offer as he thought the lands would bring in a greater profit (*294*).

For a generation the plans for the granary were dropped, but this episode is important for two reasons. In the first place it shows that the crown was unable to exercise its right of control over the *prazo* after the third life. Although technically *Dona* Ursula need not have been granted the *prazo*, the crown found it inexpedient, not to say physically impossible, to do other than renew the grant. It was, however, able to exact what was tantamount to a considerable bribe to secure the renewal. The sort of role that the Jesuits might play in the life of a colony is also well illustrated here. In the eighteenth century they were often more successful as business and financial agents than as converters of the heathen.

The serious shortage of supplies from which Moçambique suffered is the second matter to which this episode calls attention. This shortage seems to have been due to the weakening of the hold of the Portuguese authorities over the Querimba Islands and Angoche, both of them traditional supply areas for the fort. The bad relations with Angoche and their partial repair are described by Francisco Moraes Pereira in the account he wrote of the overland route between Quelimane and Moçambique in 1753. It was with knowledge of these difficulties that Manuel Antonio de Almeida revived the idea of endowing the fort permanently with Luabo.

In 1763 Almeida sent to Lisbon his *Memorial sobre as Terras de Luabo* in which he painted a glowing picture of the wealth of the *prazo*. He mentioned that he himself had spent 8,000 *cruzados* on improvements and offered to exchange Luabo for an annual payment to be fixed between his *procurador*—man of business—and the government. His reason for wanting to make this deal, he asserted, was his good will towards the government and the fact that the game on the *prazo* could only be effectively cropped by the government with its unrestricted access to firearms (*294*). Manuel Antonio had other motives, however. As he was himself resident in Goa it would obviously be much more convenient for him not to have the trouble of collecting his rents, and that he had this in mind is borne out by his request that, if the scheme came to fruition, the money should be paid to him by the government in Lisbon. Governor-general Pereira do Lago thought, however, that Almeida was faced with a declining income, that the *prazo* only brought in 900:000 *reis per annum*, so that he was anxious to negotiate a larger pension secured on the customs revenues (*33, 31*).

The Government asked for a full investigation of Almeida's assertions and received a reply in 1766. It then requested more information to which Pereira do Lago replied in a series of letters. He wanted the government to drop all idea of acquiring Luabo. He pointed out that Moçambique simply did not have adequate administrative machinery to run a great *prazo* like Luabo. A factory would have to be set up there to produce sugar, oil, and spirits, and to harvest all the crops. As for wood for boat building, it was good but too expensive to transport even to Quelimane, whereas Moçambique Island could get all it needed from ports like Quitangonha or Fernão Veloso which were much nearer. Instead he made two suggestions, one that Almeida should be deprived of Luabo and that it should be used to restore the ailing finances of the Dominican mission. The other idea was that the *prazo* should be divided into six estates which could be distributed to encourage settlers (*32*).

Pereira's reference to the suggestion that Almeida should be deprived of his title to Luabo takes the story back a few years to the lengthy dispute which had surrounded the *prazo* in the 1750s, and to another reason why Manuel Antonio de Almeida was so anxious to achieve the exchange.

Dona Ines Gracias Cardoso, who had held the *prazo* before Manuel Antonio de Almeida, was a formidable personality. She had inherited the *prazo* in 1746 in the third life, and added it to her existing territory of Gorongosa. She had then married a former governor of Macao, Antonio Telles de Meneses. Within six months she accused him of being impotent and repudiated the marriage. The ex-governor appealed to Moçambique and, apparently after medical examination, won his case and was awarded Luabo for his maintenance. On this *Dona* Ines gathered her slaves and set off at the head of them to drive her former husband from Luabo. This she achieved, expelling the hapless man half naked and wounded to seek refuge at Quelimane. However, in the process a Portuguese family and a government official were killed, and rumours circulated that *Dona* Ines had personally encouraged her slaves and had seen with approval the heads of their victims paraded on pikes. It was later established that these details were embellishments that did not entirely do justice to the *Dona* (*133*), but the crimes had nonetheless been committed and *Dona* Ines was allowed to go unpunished. She died in March 1757, leaving a will which granted Luabo to Manuel Antonio de Almeida.

Almeida was a Catholic Goanese. He was nephew of the former governor-general, Francisco de Mello e Castro, who had nominated him to the post of *tenente-geral dos Rios* in 1756. He was therefore *tenente-geral* at the time of *Dona* Ines' death. The fact that a *tenente-geral*, who had the right of nominating to vacant *prazos*, came into the possession of Luabo by agreement with the previous holder who was a wanted criminal was, to say the least, suspicious.

Almeida obtained his *carta de aforamento* for Luabo but was not able to enjoy possession for long. On 3 November 1759 a certain Antonio Correa Monteiro de Mattos filed a petition to deprive him of the *prazo*. Mattos was a soldier who had seen service in the fleets and in India and who was then resident in Moçambique Island. He had been the judge who had taken the evidence on the suicide of the governor-general, João Manuel de Mello, in the previous year. He gave three reasons for depriving Almeida of the *prazo*.

1 *Dona* Ines had held the *prazo* in the third life and the renewal should have been made after her death, not while she was still alive.
2 Almeida was Goanese and was now resident in India, both of which facts, according to royal orders, should have debarred him from the award of a land grant.
3 The renewal ought to have been made either to a female descendant of the previous holder, or to some deserving

resident of the colony, such as Antonio Correa Monteiro de Mattos who had three daughters and one step-daughter to provide for.

These charges show how seriously the legislation regarding the *prazos* could be taken, although it was unlikely that Mattos would succeed with his petition without powerful interests on the spot to back him. The crown did order an inquiry and the report that was eventually produced in 1761 by Marc Antonio Montaury—a distant connection of *Dona* Ines and the then *tenente-geral*—pointed out the real objections to Almeida's title. The issues, Montaury said, were not those of the petition but whether a *tenente-geral* could nominate himself and whether a *prazo* should be granted separately to one person while the slaves who resided on it were inherited by someone else. In her will *Dona* Ines had made over all her slaves to her god-daughter, *Dona* Ines Pessoa de Almeida Castellobranco, together with the *prazo* Gorongosa. Both these practices were highly undesirable and, after this case, were held to be illegal. Montaury, it should be said, hoped to secure the grant of Luabo to his wife, *Dona* Ines Pessoa, who owned the slaves of the *prazo* (*17*).

Mattos did not get his *prazo* and later went as *capitão-mor* to Inhambane, but the idea that Almeida's title was not quite sound persisted and enabled Pereira do Lago to propose ten years later that he be deprived of it.

Under Almeida's control the *prazo* was rented out and greatly declined. The sugar mills, which had worked in the days of Lopo Sanches, fell into disuse and in 1788 when Almeida was still alive the *prazo* was described as being 'very decadent having been badly administered since the last lordship.' (*309, 396*) However, it still produced 5,000 *alqueires* of grain every year for the *senhor*, equivalent to 65,000 litres (*64*).

Almeida and his successors were absentees living in Goa and when in 1824 a Brazilian judge inquired into the affairs of the *prazo* he roundly condemned absenteeism and the renting of *prazos* by the *senhors*,

Those who rent them care indifferently for them, attempting only to procure from them a living without performing any service except for doing violence to the slaves and freemen from which follows a great emigration to the lands of the chiefs and the *prazo* remains deprived of its African cultivators ... All this could be avoided if the proprietors who

163

possessed the *dominium utile* of the *prazos* lived in them (*103*).

In 1825 the *prazo* was finally taken over by the state and rented for an annual sum of 550 *maticals* of gold and the obligation to sell the government 1,600 *alqueires* of grain at a fixed price. When held under an emphyteutic contract the *prazo* had paid annually 36 *maticals* in *foros* (*109*). The man who rented the *prazo* was Caetano Camillo Vas dos Anjos, a member of one of the most famous of the *prazo* families of the nineteenth century, whose fortunes eventually became embroiled in the international diplomacy of the scramble for Africa (see chap. 16).

The story of Luabo covers most aspects of life in the Rivers colony, but essentially it is a tale of inertia. Little can be done to alter the *status quo*; the government cannot get rid of a *prazo*-holder it dislikes; a private petition fails although sound in law; the *prazo*-holder himself cannot achieve his aim of an exchange and a pension. The only people who achieve anything are those who have the power to act on the spot; *Dona* Ines in her feud with her husband and Manuel Antonio de Almeida extorting concessions from the old widow's death-bed.

Cheringoma

Cheringoma was the largest and richest of the *prazos*, with the single exception of Gorongosa. In 1802 it was alleged to have 2,120 African villages divided into nineteen administrative chieftaincies. It stretched from the Pungue River as far as the Zambesi delta with a sea-coast of a hundred miles including the site of the modern port of Beira. Inland it was divided from Gorongosa by the river Zangwe. To cross the *prazo* on foot entailed a march of twenty days. Originally the *prazo* had paid fifteen *maticals* a year in *foros* in 1650. In 1655 it was regranted at eighteen and a half *maticals*. In 1753 it was rated at twenty-six *maticals*. In 1829 it was paying forty-five *maticals* and a further twenty-two *maticals* in *dizimos*. The rent was thus steadily inflated but at no time exceeded two or three *per cent* of the income of the *prazo* which in the eighteenth century was thought to be 2,132 *maticals* a year (*265*).

Cheringoma had originally been conceded to Sisnando Dias Bayão by Peranhe, the king of Quiteve, 'in reward for the benefits received from him, to be held for always and to be passed on to his descendants' (*34*). Bayão made over his land to the crown on the condition that, although the grant would have to be renewed every third life, it would always descend to his family. And so, without any trouble, the succession did pass from one member of his family to the next for a hundred and twenty years.

1 Sisnando Dias Bayão died *c.* 1645 and the *prazo* passed to his son Francisco.
2 On Francisco's death Cheringoma passed to his sister Maria, married to Antonio Lobo da Silva, in 1655.
3 To Maria Pacheca de Oliveira, grand-daughter of Antonio Lobo da Silva.
4 To Antonio Lobo Pacheco, who obtained a renewal in 1695.
5 To João Pereira da Silva in 1712.
6 To *Dona* Maria Pereira da Silva, his daughter, in 1749.
7 To Bernardo Caetano de Sa Botelho, her husband, who died in 1760 (*34*).

Bernardo had a daughter Ines and the *prazo* should have passed to her, but the year 1760 saw the convergence of a whole series of circumstances that disturbed the hitherto uneventful history of the *prazo*.

To understand what followed one must look at the growth of Bayão's family connections until, by 1760, the clan was the greatest and most powerful in the whole of Zambesia. João Pereira da Silva in 1712 had held three *prazos*, Cheringoma, Sansa and Chupanga. On his death the three *prazos* were divided among his three daughters, probably in 1749. Maria, who received Cheringoma, married Bernardo de Sa Botelho who was *tenente-geral dos Rios* in 1752–3 and again in 1759. When their infant daughter was born they secured as her godmother none other than *Dona* Ines Gracias Cardoso who held Luabo, Gorongosa, Inhacatondo and Tambara. She took her godmother's family names, being known as *Dona* Ines Pessoa de Almeida Castellobranco. The two families thus controlled almost the whole of the Sena captaincy.

Ines Cardoso died, probably in 1757, having previously split up her holdings, nominating Ines Pessoa to inherit Gorongosa as well as leaving to her all the slaves which belonged to the Luabo *prazo*. As possession of the slaves was almost the equivalent of possession of the *prazo*, the little girl found herself in 1760 the heiress to half the Portuguese territory in East Africa (*16*).

Not surprisingly *Dona* Ines Pessoa was surrounded by suitors and, while still a girl, was married to João Xavier Pinheiro de Aragão. He secured on her behalf from the new *tenente-geral*, Marc Antonio Montaury, the nomination to her ancestral *prazo* of Cheringoma in 1761 (*18*). Aragão must have died soon afterwards for Ines was next married to none other than the *tenente-geral* Montaury himself. By this successful *coup* Montaury, who had only recently arrived in the Rivers, found himself the most powerful *senhor* in Zambesia as well as the chief administrative officer of the colony (*24*).

The governor-general had already in 1761 determined to use this opportunity to break up the estates of *Dona* Ines. The royal instructions to put an end to pluralism were quite explicit and Montaury's snatching of the heiress only confirmed the decision, for it was quite improper for a *tenente-geral* to acquire *prazos* while in office, as he himself had declared in the case of Luabo. Accordingly in 1763 Montaury was ordered to surrender Cheringoma to the crown (*21*), and when he refused to vacate the *prazo*, was deprived of his office. A new *tenente-geral* was appointed, but the Rivers were not used to being dictated to by Moçambique in this way and Montaury resisted his deposition by force of arms and remained in possession until his death at the end of 1766.

On Montaury's death *Dona* Ines's estates were at last broken up and Cheringoma was granted to *Dona* Maria Caetano de Mendonça Corte Real, who lived in Goa. She came across to Moçambique but died the same year (*24*), and her husband, an old soldier called João Caetano de Motta, with thirty-five years of service, petitioned for the *prazo* to be granted to him in the second life (*138*, *139*). Motta's star was in the ascendant. He was made *tenente-geral*, he received the grant of the *prazo* and married for a second time *Dona* Anna Effigenia de Almeida Barreto.

So it appeared that *Dona* Ines Pessoa had lost her *prazo*. She, meanwhile, had not been idle. The death of her second husband did not leave her too prostrate, for two days later, at midnight, she married a backwoodsman called Miguel José Pereira Gaio, a man of brutal character and unsavoury reputation who had reputedly been *Dona* Ines's lover. One of Gaio's first acts as the new head of the house of Sisnando Dias Bayão was to petition for the grant of *prazo* Sansa which had once been held by *Dona* Ines's grandfather (*140*). This he was duly granted and the sophisticated *voyeur* of bureaucratic follies is treated to the superbly illogical sight of an administration battling to break up

166

the great estates of the richest pluralist in the colony, almost succeeding in this great task and then in the same breath granting a vacant *prazo* to the same family.

In spite of the legal deprivation, however, *Dona* Ines did not give up Cheringoma. Her slaves remained firmly in control and Motta with his paltry following of sixty slaves could do nothing but accept the inevitable and rent the *prazo* to her and her husband for 600 *maticals*—a figure equivalent to about one-third of its income (*30*). Actual possession was a very much stronger card to play than legal title in this colonial game of 'beggar-my-neighbour'.

By 1773 Motta and his second wife *Dona* Anna Effigenia were dead and Gaio petitioned for the restoration of the *prazo* to its rightful holders. The whole case was extensively reviewed and the historic right of Bayão's descendants to hold Cheringoma was upheld. In February 1774 it was duly restored to *Dona* Ines.

Gaio died in 1780, unmourned, at least by the government to whom he had given endless trouble, and not mourned for long by *Dona* Ines who married for the fourth time soon afterwards. Her husband this time was Agostinho de Coutto Gameiro e Magalhães, who was at least able to secure all the family holdings, obtaining confirmation for the titles to Gorongosa, Sansa and Cheringoma in 1785 (*53*).

Dona Ines was succeeded by her daughter *Dona* Josefa de Coutto Gameiro who died in 1814 (*86*). The *prazo* then passed to *Dona* Josefa's brother, Antonio de Araujo Braganza, who married Luisa Madalena de Aragão, whom he left a widow in 1824 (*233*). The events that followed were almost a carbon copy of the previous *affaire*. There were two possible inheritors of Cheringoma, *Dona* Luisa or her daughter *Dona* Francisca, but the governor of Moçambique, Sebastião Xavier Botelho, intervened, ignorant of the facts but determined to assert the prerogative that the governors had long claimed to nominate to vacant *prazos*. He nominated *Dona* Maria Joaquina Xavier da Costa, the daughter-in-law of Francisco Henriques Ferrão, the newly appointed *tenente-geral*, who was alleged to have bought the office for himself and the *prazo* for *Dona* Maria. Quite apart from other considerations she was married to an Indian and debarred from holding *prazos* (*110*). It was five years before the *prazo* was restored to the rightful heiress, and not before the whole past history had once again been investigated and a recommendation had come from Lisbon that it should be granted on a perpetual tenure to Bayão's descendants to prevent any future difficulties.

The troubles of the family were by no means over. *Dona* Luisa Madalena was soon afterwards accused of adultery by her husband and imprisoned, while in the following year her daughter *Dona* Francisca was raped by the noble *degredado* José Joaquim de Lancastre (*160*). She inherited the *prazo* in 1843, and passed it on to her daughter who was another *Dona* Ines de Almeida Castellobranco. A decree of the *Concelho Ultramarino* had meanwhile declared Cheringoma to be held on a perpetual lease, but in 1855 the whole case was once again the subject of a legal inquiry. *Dona* Ines was still a minor and her agent petitioned for confirmation of her title. It was decided that Cheringoma must come under the provisions of the royal decree of 1854 on the *prazos* which prevented the renewal of any of the emphyteutic contracts. The *portaria* which contained this judgement said that no title could 'impose on the Portuguese government the perpetual obligation to carry out what was said to be the will of a kaffir chief . . . whose name no one knows, nor the time when he lived, nor the date of the donation.' (*459*, doc. 10)

But the impatience of a liberal government with the interminable traditions of Zambesia had little effect and there was still a Castellobranco in Cheringoma in 1875 (*439*, 373).

The case of Cheringoma mirrors all the theoretical problems and all the realities of Portuguese land holding in Zambesia. It shows the concentration of *prazos* in the hands of a single family; the opportunities eagerly seized by the *tenentes-gerais* to acquire wealth for themselves while fighting off the challenge of the Moçambique governors to control the grants of the *prazos*. It shows the realities of power which prevented a family being dispossessed of a *prazo* even when it had lost its title to the estate. It shows the difficulties that faced the government if it wished to enforce the regulations controlling the size of the *prazos* and their concentration in a few hands. It gives a preview of the struggles of the nineteenth century when the old *prazo* families fought—not this time with legal arguments—for the preservation of their world and their long traditions.

The Portuguese and
their Relations with the
African Peoples

Part One: The Colonos

Introduction

Colonial history has never been just the story of conquerors and
conquered. There has usually been a struggle of a different kind
to cut across, and partly neutralise, this stark confrontation. In
the Americas and Africa the European colonists were fighting
for their livelihood against the already existing populations, but
at the same time they were importing a slave population to work
for them and achieve the economic expansion on which their
survival would depend. As the external enemy was pressed back,
so the internal enemy was unwittingly fostered in the bosom of
the new society.

The permutations of these rivalries and conflicts are the real
stuff of colonial history, and they can produce curious and
unexpected patterns, as when the settlers in southern Brazil
recruited Indian tribes to enslave other Indians and then found
themselves opposed by the white Jesuit missionaries who had
trained the same Indians to resist and who were advocating the
use of negro slaves in the development of the Brazilian economy.

It is also in Brazil that one can first discern the pressures
caused by new waves of white immigrants on an old established
society, for this has always been a fourth element in colonial
conflicts. In many ways the problems caused by new white
immigration have been simply those of class conflict—the
immigrants coming in the wake of economic change and threatening the long-established property-owning society. This has
again produced extraordinary cross-currents of social and
political conflict; the American Civil War erupted between
white communities which were, at the same time engaging the
Indians in the west and wrestling with the slave problem at
home; the Anglo-Boer war broke out in a South Africa which

was still expanding against a black Africa in the north, which was tensed with its own internal racial strife and was at the same time importing coolie labour to feed its economic expansion.

Survival for a community in these circumstances may be achieved either by the cross-currents of conflict neutralising one another, or by the conscious or unconscious absorption of the rivals into each other—a circumstance rare in the history of modern colonisation but presumably common enough fifteen hundred years ago when the present European population was being formed.

The Portuguese claim that, alone of the European peoples in modern times, their colonies have survived because of adaptation. In the emotive language of modern politics they say that they have never had colour prejudice or imposed a colour bar, and have been willing to accept into the Portuguese community peoples of all races and colours. As a judgement on their colonial past and their colonial present this is, of course, complete nonsense. Colour prejudice and brutal racial conflict always have existed and still do today, but there seems little doubt that the Portuguese were forced to adapt themselves and their cultural values more than any other European colonists. The very weakness of Portugal in economic resources, military power and population which forced this adaptation, has thus been her real strength. The strong try to force circumstances to their will and are often defeated, the weak survive by adapting themselves to these circumstances.

When critics of the Portuguese empire in the eighteenth century pointed to the corruption, inadequacy, decadence and general decrepitude of a colony that had nevertheless been in existence for three hundred years they were pointing up a paradox that contemporaries found hard to understand but which is vitally important for the understanding of this part of Africa: that those who were the most ready to abandon European standards were often the most successful colonists.

Prazo-holders as chiefs

All the land held by the Portuguese in Zambesia had originally been acquired from more or less reluctant African chiefs. By these agreements large areas of land were transferred from African to Portuguese jurisdiction. Usually the transfer involved the territory of some traditional African chieftaincy and the change, at least at first, caused the minimum amount of disturbance to the life of the ordinary inhabitants. The reason for this is that African states were organised hierarchically in three or four tiers and the change-over took place only at the top.

At the lowest level, groups of villages were ruled by a *fumo*, or headman, who usually belonged to a local ruling lineage. The word *fumo* derives from *mfumu*, commonly used in many Bantu languages to apply to a chief. As a general term it is vague and confusing, for *mfumu* might refer to a senior member of a royal family as well as to a minor village headman, and the Portuguese also use the term in this wide and imprecise way. In the *prazos* south of the Zambesi the term *nhacuava* is also commonly used and again it is used, apparently, for chiefs of varying importance. In the Sofala district the word in use is *inhamacango* and in the Muslim area round Quelimane the term is *muene*. For the purposes of this study, however, I shall use *fumo* for the lowest in the hierarchy of African authority.

Fumos owed allegiance to a territorial chief called *mambo*. This term is used both north and south of the Zambesi but the Portuguese preferred to use their own words *regulo* or *principe* to describe these important personages. *Nkosi* (or *encosse* as the Portuguese wrote it) is also sometimes used. Commonly *mambos* acknowledged a paramount chief such as the Quiteve or the Mwene Mutapa.

'The holders of these lands [the *prazos*] have the same powers and jurisdiction as the kaffir *fumos* from whom they were conquered', wrote Manuel Barreto in 1667 (*318*)—an exaggeration, no doubt, but indicating clearly the sort of role that the *sertanejos* had adopted towards their followers and subjects early on in the history of Portuguese colonisation. The Portuguese concessionaire assumed a senior position in the African hierarchy and he came to rely greatly on this 'traditional' authority because he did not have the backing of white settlers or soldiers and was often very much on his own. On the small *prazos*—many of which had only one or two villages—the *prazo*-holder would hold the position of *mambo* but on the larger *prazos* these traditional chiefs maintained their power and the *senhor* was more remote—as a sort of paramount chief.

It can be argued that, to the African people, the Portuguese *senhor* was never more than a foreign conqueror, and that he never came to be accepted as a traditional authority in African society. This is undoubtedly true of many of the Portuguese 'settlers' who were absentees from their estates and saw the

African peasants simply as tax-paying serfs from whom an income had to be extorted. This is not the whole story, however, for it is a mistake to think that the veneration of an office necessarily implies that the holders of the office are worthy or agreeable people, or even that they are careful of the interests of those who look up to them. Moreover, veneration of an office may well survive when the office is usurped and held illegitimately by an upstart who has no right to it. To see the truth of this one only has to observe how, in Europe, honour continued to be paid to nobles and kings in the face of the irrefutable evidence of their vulgar ancestry and recent ennoblement.

In this respect African society is like any other. Chiefs may claim ancient lineages and descent from mythical ancestors, the fathers of the nation, and in some cases these ancient traditions may have some foundation. But a man may equally well rise from humble origins and become a chief venerated by his people in spite of the fact that his humble origin is common knowledge. Once he is a chief he will be accorded all the dignity and honour which the office demands.

For example, when Livingstone descended the Zambesi from Barotseland in 1856 he left some of his followers in Tete while he returned to England. These men greeted him on his return in 1858 and he took some of them back with him to Barotseland. The others, however, stayed behind and Livingstone supplied them with arms so that they might become elephant hunters. Strangers as they were to the peoples of the lower Zambesi, these 'Makololo' followers of Livingstone set themselves up as chiefs on the Shire river, attracting to themselves clients and capturing slaves who were incorporated into their followings. Before a single generation was out Livingstone's porters, who had once earned their living dancing before the Portuguese settlers, were powerful and respected chiefs, and their descendants are chiefs today. The story is even more striking for all the evidence suggests that the 'Makololo' chiefs were at first brutal and overbearing towards their subjects, carrying our frequent executions and mutilations. What the 'Makololo' accomplished was likewise accomplished by some of the Portuguese *sertanejos*.

Where African society required the figure of a chief to maintain its cohesion and to enable it to function smoothly, the *prazo*-holder might fill the role. The Portuguese *senhors* commonly performed six chiefly functions in African society. They received tribute in kind and in service; they enjoyed customary rights connected with game and exacted payments for the breaking of certain 'taboos'; they had some supervisory powers over the choice of headmen; they monopolised certain economic activities; they dispensed justice, and they performed certain ritual functions.

These six functions will be discussed in the following sections, but it is right to ask at this stage whether, granted that the *prazo*-holder in some circumstances *took the place of* a chief, it can ever be said that he was accepted by the Africans *as* a chief. In other words, did Portuguese families ever become accepted as genuine chiefly lineages?

Clearly most of them did not. Many of the 'lives' in which the *prazos* were held proved to be very short and the *prazos* therefore changed hands rapidly. There are interesting cases, however, of the slaves and members of the families of deceased *prazo*-holders remaining on a *prazo* after it had been granted to another family. This sort of situation speaks of loyalties and social ties independent of the formal land contract. There are cases of the families of former *senhors* carrying out the *muavi* poison ordeal and executing the victims and in the case of Cheringoma, a new *senhor* was forced to rent the *prazo* to the old family which had continued in actual possession.

There are also instances of the Portuguese marrying daughters of important chiefs and subsequently claiming legitimate succession to a traditional chieftaincy. At the end of the nineteenth century Manuel Antonio de Sousa tried to claim the chieftaincy of Macombe for his sons who had been born to him by a daughter of a former Macombe of Barue. There is some evidence that the Tonga chieftaincy of Motontora, which covered the *prazo* of Massangano, was acquired by the da Cruz family and that the Marave chieftaincy of Chicucuru became vested in the family of the Caetano Pereiras.

These are nineteenth-century developments, but there are earlier examples of the same sort of relationship. At least two Portuguese families obtained chiefly status within the paramountcy of Quiteve (see chap. 12), and there is the case of Antonio José da Cruz who married the sister of Mwene Mutapa Chofombo some time early in the nineteenth century and established the first ties between the da Cruz family and the African peoples on the south bank of the Zambesi.

Portuguese and African customs, beliefs and manners were interwoven in other curious ways. In the eighteenth century when a new Mwene Mutapa or a new Quiteve ascended the throne, one of his first actions would be to seek Portuguese recognition which would be sealed by an exchange of presents. The Mwene Mutapa expected the arrival of the Zimbabwe garrison with all the rich presents that accompanied it. He also expected the arrival of the priest who would formally baptise him and bestow on him a Portuguese name. This relic of the heroic days of missionary activity no longer carried with it any commitment or obligation to Christianity but had become an essential ritual without which no Mwene Mutapa would feel himself in possession of the throne (*337*, para 50). In Barue the installation of a new Macombe might be delayed for a long time until a Portuguese embassy arrived bearing the *mazia manga*— the holy water—which was used in the coronation ceremony (*362*).

These ceremonial embassies always included political discussions and frequently resulted in new treaties being drawn up between the chief and the Portuguese. Formal recognition by the Portuguese authorities was valuable to a chief because it enhanced his authority in the eyes of any doubters among his people and it strengthened his hand politically because, even if the Portuguese of the eighteenth century were unlikely to indulge in king-making as they had in the seventeenth, they might nevertheless harbour fugitives and encourage rivals to the throne (*270*).

So the Portuguese enhanced their authority by assuming some of the qualities of chieftainship and the independent chiefs strengthened their authority with the various symbols of their relations with the Portuguese. The Portuguese government and the system of *prazos* thus became increasingly involved in a series of customary relationships, which were forever evolving and developing according to need. It was clearly impossible to do what the Portuguese reformers so ardently desired and cut into this system, dividing up the *prazos* and running them as highly capitalised plantations.

The colonos

The Portuguese used the word *colono* for the free African inhabitants of the crown lands. Sometimes the word *forro*—a freeman—is used as if to emphasise the status and rights of the individual in question. In the Sena district these free peasants are often called *mussenses* from the word *mu-sendzi* meaning a peasant. In the Tete district the term *butonga*, which obviously refers to an ethnic group, is used.

The Portuguese recognised the *colono* to be a free man whose customary rights and status were in no way affected when he and his village were incorporated in a new *prazo*. He still married, begot children, died and was buried, and the rituals and practices connected with these events remained much as they had always been. His land was allotted to him and worked according to time-honoured custom and he was still ruled directly by a headman who usually belonged to an old lineage. Every year, it is true, the *colono* had to pay to the *prazo*-holder a tribute called *missonco* (or *mussocco*) or *maprere*, but he had previously paid this to an African *mambo* and, anyway, it was collected from him by his headman in the traditional way.

For most of his life the ordinary African peasant saw little of the Portuguese and would have experienced little change when he passed under European jurisdiction. There were occasions when he might be pressed into service to accompany a military expedition, to provide carriers for Portuguese service or to clear public roads. He might have to act as a guide or provide accommodation for a traveller but these were obligations to the community widely recognised in African society. The *prazo senhors* were not permitted to impose any other obligations on the free peasants—and if they did, then the peasants expressed their opposition with their feet and migrated from the *prazo*—an experience disastrous to the *senhor*'s income—as Luis de Moura found when in 1794 he tried to employ the *colonos* on his *prazo* of Maindo in clearing the Cochissone channel in the delta and found that they all fled (66).

There were circumstances when the presence of his *senhor* might be felt more immediately by the peasant. After the harvest was gathered and tribute had been paid, the *colono* might very well find that he was faced by a demand to sell some of his produce at a price dictated to him by the *senhor*. A slave of the *senhor* would appear in the village with cloth which the *colonos* had to buy. This custom was called *inhamucangamiza* and in the 1820s, when Gamitto acquired his knowledge of the Zambesi world, cloth which would normally sell for twenty-four *quitundos* of grain was sold for forty *quitundos*. At other times the *senhor* had to pay the market rate, for *inhamucangamiza* was only practised once in the year (*361*, 63).

If he got involved in some legal dispute he might also feel the presence of his *senhor*. Cases would normally be dealt with in traditional fashion by the *fumo* or the *mambo*, but there was appeal to the *senhor* as to a higher court and, in the nineteenth century, there was appeal from him to the *capitão-mor das terras da coroa.*

The strong hand of the *senhor* might also be felt if there was any disturbance in the *prazo.* If tribute was not paid, if property belonging to the *senhor* was damaged, if there was fighting between the *colonos,* then there would be a visitation from the *prazo*-holder's slave bands which were his private police force. Their methods were usually fairly drastic and the *colono* would be left in no doubt about the *senhor*'s displeasure.

Self-interest certainly dictated to the *prazo senhors* a policy of conciliation and mildness. As Antonio Manuel de Mello e Castro put it:

> The *foreiro* has the advantage of possessing and enjoying the fruits of the *prazo* all his life and on his death his son or daughter or wife or whoever the other life or the right of renewal falls to, so that he will not fail to see to its preservation, upholding his *colonos* in their practices and customs for it is they who provide the income of the land *(43).*

This was in contrast to the people who rented the *prazo,* sometimes only for a single year, and whose interest lay in obtaining the maximum amount of profit in a short time.

Unfortunately many of the *prazo*-holders did rent out their lands or installed a business agent and the short-term profit motive tended to triumph over careful, long-term husbandry.

Against oppression and extortion the *colono* had only two weapons. He could resist by force of arms and call in the aid of one of the independent chiefs who lived along the fringes of Portuguese land, or he could leave the *prazo* altogether and seek his fortune under someone else's sovereignty.

Rebellion among the *colonos* was very common. All the *prazos* between Tete and the Mwene Mutapa's country of Chidima had thrown off Portuguese control by the middle of the eighteenth century *(54)* and received protection from Mwene Mutapa's sub-chiefs, and the other Tete *prazos* on the south bank were also difficult to control. The Dominican *prazo* of Tipue was in a permanent state of revolt by the end of the eighteenth century and Tambara, the next *prazo* downstream in the Sena captaincy, was also notoriously unruly *(71).* These *prazos* were in the mountainous region of Lupata which, from the days of Francisco Barreto onwards, had always given the Portuguese the most trouble. They were supported from behind by the independent chieftaincy of Barue. This was the area which was to cause the Portuguese so much trouble in the nineteenth century, which resisted occupation until 1902 and then staged a formidable rebellion in 1917.

Desertion and flight were easier and safer remedies for oppression, however. The *colono* knew that he would always find a ready welcome in another *prazo* to which he would be bringing his tribute-paying potential. He knew that he would find a welcome for a similar reason among the surrounding chiefs. He had little in the way of property or 'household gods' to keep him in one place. Probably the accounts of the desertion of the *colonos* which the *prazo*-holders endlessly repeated were exaggerated. Like all mankind they were liable to contrast their lot at boring length with that of their predecessors in the 'golden age' which had gone before. Nevertheless the population of *colonos* was very thin throughout Zambesia and many *prazos* had no *colonos* at all and hence no income—a circumstance which made the royal decrees against pluralism particularly futile.

When João Fernandes do Rozario gave an account of his three *prazos* in 1788, he showed their population as follows. Inhacoro had no *colonos* at all but contained two villages with eighty of his slaves and their children. Through his wife he held Mulambe. This had forty *colono* families living in four villages, and sixty slaves. Impirire was his third *prazo* and this had twenty *colono* families and forty-five slaves and their children. Although it is difficult to balance numbers of households against numbers of individuals it seems that the number of *colonos* barely exceeded the number of slaves on his *prazos* taken together (65).

In 1802 the situation was much the same. A census was taken in that year of all the Sena *prazos* which listed the numbers of white, mulatto and black households. They show Gorongosa and Cheringoma with over 2,000 villages and Chupanga with over 1,000 contrasting with Pita, Gambo, Mulambe and Nhamaze with four, five, six and six villages respectively. In all some 17,000 villages and 69,000 families are estimated for the whole region. In the same year Tete was estimated to have 6,385 *colono* families and Quelimane 4,802. The total for the whole colony was put at 80,586 families (80).

Although it is impossible to estimate the accuracy of these figures, which the compiler himself warned were uncertain, it is interesting to compare them with an estimate of the population of the Tete and Sena areas made by Henri Junod in 1936. He estimated the total African population at 200,000 at a density of about three per square kilometre (379). Remembering that in 1802 they were estimating households and in 1936 individuals, it seems that the figures are not widely different. At all events it speaks of a very thin and scattered population for, as Antonio Manuel de Mello e Castro wrote:

> for the most part these lands are bush, so destitute of settlement and cultivation that frequently it is necessary to travel for a long time before one meets a house or a settlement with three or four houses together (43).

Fumos

The villages of the *colonos* were grouped in districts called *muzindas*. The term *muzinda* is still common in the languages of this area to mean the kraal of a sub-chief. In Portuguese Zambesia the term meant more than a simple village and was used to describe the administrative areas of the *prazo*. Each *muzinda* was ruled by its own *fumo*.

The *fumo* was a traditional authority and his selection and appointment depended on many factors. It is clear, however, that the *prazo*-holders claimed the right to depose a *fumo* and select his successor and that their approval had to be obtained before any *fumo* could exercise his authority. This is the way that João dos Santos describes the authority the captain of Tete had over the chiefs in his district:

> The jurisdiction of the captain of Tete is so complete over these kaffirs that he has authority even over the chiefs themselves, and can remove them from office when they do anything they should not; and when one of them dies, by his own authority he appoints another whom he thinks qualified to discharge the office, without encountering any opposition from the kaffirs who are his subordinates (445, 291).

More than two hundred years later the famous Portuguese explorer Gamitto wrote 'The *fumos* were chosen and invested by the *prazo*-holder'. (361, 62) He continues to explain how a *fumo* was selected and installed when a vacancy occurred. The *prazo*-holder inquired whether there was a *fumo* in another *prazo* who was discontented or whether there was any *colono*

178

influential enough to take the job. Having located a likely candidate, he sent a slave (*chuanga*) with twenty strings of beads. This symbolically opened the negotiations and there was then a period when the *fumo* consulted his relatives, made inquiries about the new land and the *prazo*-holder and consulted the diviners.

If he decided to accept, the *fumo* then had to choose where to establish his village. This he did by placing offerings of flour in likely places and returning after a space of time to see if the flour had been eaten. When he found it gone, he knew the spirits approved his choice. He was then taken by the same *chuanga* to greet his lord, giving him a gift of hens or a goat and receiving some cloth in return. Later he returned for the ceremony of *preca-manja* (described as clapping of the hands) and offered another gift of cloth. He was then considered to be fully invested with the office and to be symbolically 'married' to the *prazo*-holder. This symbolic marriage in no way depended on the *prazo*-holder's being a woman, but it had a lot to do with his being a chief (*361*, 62). Some of the earliest Portuguese to gain concessions from chiefs were first accepted as the chief's 'wives' for this was a traditional way of expressing the relationship of chief and subchief (*445*, 225).

Gamitto's account of the relationship of *fumo* and *prazo*-holder is deceptively simple and straightforward. The realities were more complicated. In many *prazos* the traditional *mambos* still maintained their offices and their influence over the *fumos* would be very considerable. In a similar way the position was complicated in the *prazos* on the north bank of the Zambesi where the newly acquired rights of the *prazo*-holders were frequently challenged by the dispossessed chiefs and where there was still the power of the paramount chief, the Undi, to be considered.

In 1823 an interesting case arose which illustrates this difficulty. A Marave *mambo* called Sambuze installed a *fumo* in a newly acquired *prazo* called Buze. He sent to warn the local Portuguese that the sound of drums they would hear was only the installation ceremony. The Portuguese protested that he had no right to place a *fumo* in a Portuguese *prazo*. Sambuze, however, was supported by the Marave paramount, Undi, and although the commandant of Tete had decided to send a force to sack the *fumo*'s village he eventually gave way because there were so many Portuguese in the interior who would suffer from any general war (*100*).

It is clear from this quarrel that there were at least three people with an interest in the new *fumo*; the Portuguese *prazo*-holder, the *mambo* Sambuze and the paramount Undi. In fact the choice of *fumo* would be limited by other factors as well. The *fumo* had to be acceptable to his people and therefore chosen according to traditional rules. He also had to be acceptable to the spirits—which meant in practice the spirit-mediums. Gamitto obliquely refers to this when he mentions the consultation with the spirits before a *fumo* accepted the post. However, in an area where the power of the *senhor* was well established, his choice could well be a decisive factor in the selection of the *fumos*.

The most important, and undoubtedly the most arduous, of the duties of the *fumo* was to collect and hand over the annual tribute which the *colonos* paid to the *prazo*-holders. When the harvest was nearly ripe the *fumo* and the *prazo*-holder's supervisor—the *chuanga*—listed all the households who were liable to pay the tax. This was done by a series of knots being made in a rope—an African version of the old tallies of the exchequer. When the harvest was gathered in, the collection of the tax was made in rather a novel fashion. A basket—called a *quitundo*—was placed on a mat and filled with grain. Grain was then poured onto the full basket until a mound had been made which covered the basket completely (*361, 63*).

The *fumo*'s own village did not pay the tax but the unfortunate chief was responsible for the tax of all the other households in the *muzinda*, and there were cases of *fumos* pledging their own children for the eventual payment (*406, 269*). The *fumo* may not have paid the ordinary tribute, but he was responsible for other payments. Every year he had to present the *senhor* with a specified number of *manchillas*—lengths of African cotton cloth—and he had to find more *manchillas* in payment for the ants which had been trapped and eaten by the Africans. Every two years he had to pay for all the wild game killed on the *prazo* with a slave called *mafupa*.

The *fumo*'s position could be an intolerable one. Watched over by the *chuanga* who reported his every movement to their master, he was held personally responsible for law and order and for the payment of taxes. He had to find the carriers and the fighting men, the boatmen and the workmen required by the government, and if he failed in this he was threatened with imprisonment (*242*). He had to help repair any of the *senhor*'s houses on the *prazo*. Standing always between his people and the *prazo*-holder he would have to take the brunt of their resentment when things went wrong. He might have to make difficult political judgements as well, for if the *prazo* were invaded by one of the independent chiefs, an event which was quite common in some of the outlying districts, he would have to decide whether to accept the new chief or to remain faithful to his former master. Alternatively he might be forced to take part in the political schemes of the slaves if they rebelled against a particular *senhor*. It was a difficult and responsible position.

Tribute

To receive *missonco* or *maprere* (tribute) was in itself a sign of chiefly authority. If a *prazo*-holder claimed a certain area of land or a certain village, he upheld his claim by collecting tribute there. In the same way, refusal to pay tribute was an act of rebellion.

Although sometimes described as a tithe of produce, the *missonco* was, in fact, a fixed amount. According to Gamitto it amounted to about three *alqueires* of maize for every two *colonos* (*363*, vol 2, 186), an *alqueire* being equal to thirteen litres. The Dominican convent in Sena estimated that the *colonos* on its *prazo* paid at the rate of twelve *alqueires* for each household (*73*). João Fernandes do Rozario estimated that the *colonos* on one of his *prazos* paid two *alqueires* of rice and those on another four *alqueires* of rice for each household (*65*).

Besides the *missonco*, the *prazo senhor* received fines paid for crimes or for the breaking of certain 'taboos' and he enjoyed rights over eland, wild pig and elephant killed on the *prazo*. He also received payments of various kinds from the *fumos*—regular annual payments of chickens or flasks of oil, payment for the termites and for the game consumed on the *prazo*. He could also claim a slave in compensation if the *muavi* poison ordeal was practised. In addition to these sources of income there was the commercial monopoly by which he forcibly sold cloth to the *colonos*, there was the rent paid by any white or mulatto settler on the *prazo* and there was the annual tribute paid by the slaves from their produce. The *missonco* was therefore not the only or even necessarily the most important part of the income of the *prazo*.

The Sena convent estimated its income in 1802 in this way:

1 *Missonco*, 996 *alqueires* of grain worth 99 *maticals* 4½ *tangas*
2 Payments by *fumos*, 78 small casks of oil giving 9 *maticals* and 6 *tangas*
    13 *manchillas* (cotton cloths), giving 6 maticals 4 *tangas*
3 *Milandos*, 60 *manchillas* bringing in 30 *maticals*.
    Total income 146 *maticals* 4½ *tangas* (*73*).

The Dominican *prazo* of Tipue was supposed to bring in 1,930 *alqueires* and 67 *manchillas* annually but over the years 1779–1783 it never exceeded 675 *alqueires* and the average number of *manchillas* was only 37; so clearly income was irregular and fluctuating (*84*).

Unless a *prazo* was very small and unpopulated, as many of them were, the *prazo*-holder could expect quite a variety of payments in kind. Gorongosa earned for its *senhor* gold dust, cloth, timber, honey, wax, oil, fowls, salt, grain and sugar. Its total income was estimated at 1,405 *maticals* 4 *tangas* with a value in Portuguese money of the time of 647:000 *reis*—ten times the income of the Sena convent, but not really all that large for such a vast territory (*264*). Antonio Manuel de Mello e Castro was probably right when he said that tribute alone was not enough for a family to live on.

Other customary rights and practices

When a new *prazo senhor* arrived to take up his grant he had first to be formally accepted by the chiefs. He was taken to one of the principal villages and there had to open and close the door of a hut, enter the hut and leave it, pick up a piece of the earth and break off a green branch of a tree (*10*). According to another version he had to take the green branch and the piece of earth and was made to embrace a special tree. He was then the recognised holder of the *prazo*—this ceremony apparently serving the purposes both of African custom and the Roman Law of Portugal which required a formal *traditio* or symbolic handing over (*31*).

Once installed the *prazo*-holder could be approached by the *fumos*, but only if they were introduced by one of the *senhor*'s slaves and brought a present—the indispensable preliminary to all business negotiations in Africa. The *fumo* might have a variety of business with the *prazo*-holder. He might be coming with a dispute to settle or to pay compensation for certain untoward happenings. For instance if blood had been shed on the
182

prazo, the *senhor* required compensation, or if a child had contracted leprosy or had been born deformed (*361*, 62–3).

In the case of a death where witchcraft was suspected, the *muavi* poison test might be used. According to this ritual the accused was given poison and was declared guilty if this was not vomited soon afterwards. The taking of *muavi* was forbidden by the Portuguese and the *prazo*-holder could fine anyone who administered it. However, many of the Portuguese seem to have believed in its efficacy as a means of discovering criminals and to have employed it themselves.

The *fumo* might also wish to report the killing of protected game. When an elephant was killed or found dead, the underside tusk belonged to the lord of the land. This custom Livingstone thought had been introduced by the Portuguese but almost certainly the case was the other way round—it had been adopted by the Portuguese from local practice.

There is a certain amount of evidence to show the Portuguese performing rituals in connection with the sowing or harvesting of crops. In most African societies offerings are made by the chiefs to the spirits of their ancestors to ensure a good harvest. We are told that early in the seventeenth century the captain of Tete performed these functions for the villagers under his rule (*445*, 291), and Lacerda at the end of the eighteenth century mentions rumours he had heard of sacrifices being made before the harvest by members of the Portuguese community (*384*, 115).

According to an edict of the Inquisition in Goa (*347*), the customs which surrounded birth, death and marriage in Portuguese East Africa were far from being purely Christian—although it should perhaps be said that these denunciations are very general and do not even specifically refer to the Zambesi towns. Many of the *prazo senhors*, although having only one legal wife, kept extensive harems of black slaves, following on occasions the African custom of taking the sister of one's wife as a second wife. It was, apparently, common practice for sheets to be publicly exhibited as evidence that a marriage had been consummated.

During a lying-in some twine would be placed at the head of the bed, then buried in the public highway for all the world to walk over and finally tied around the waist of the new-born infant. In case of a miscarriage the whole house would be ceremonially sprinkled to get rid of the evil. If one twin died, leaving the other still alive it was necessary to make a doll like the living twin, clothe it and deck it out with beads and bury it with the dead twin, otherwise the spirit of the dead child would come to seek the living one.

When a *senhor* died a female slave entered the grave to receive his head as he was buried. This slave then had to sleep the night in the dead *senhor*'s bed with one of the male slaves of the household, washing herself afterwards in the river to cleanse herself of the earth of the burial. Some days later she would cook a fowl and serve it to the new master of the household in which the death had taken place.

For the most part, these seem harmless enough customs, but they do show the extent to which the great *prazo senhors* and their households became absorbed into the world of Africa and shed the everyday practices of Europe. There is no need to seek some historic or mystic affinity of the Portuguese with tropical cultures and peoples to explain this. Such evidence as there is shows that in similar circumstances all Europeans have behaved in the same kind of way. Here the most important factor was the absence of European women. The Portuguese settlers had to marry African women and half-castes and it was the wives who perpetuated the customs of the nursery and the marriage bed, the lying-in and the laying-out.

In most parts of Africa it is believed that the spirits of the dead keep an intimate concern for the fortunes of the living, and the spirits of dead chiefs are frequently consulted through spirit mediums. Some of the greatest of the Portuguese *senhors* were certainly accorded this honour, and their spirit mediums (*pondoros*) continued to be consulted by their own descendants and by the local African peoples.

Much of the evidence which shows the *prazo*-holder assuming the qualities of chieftainship and their dynasties becoming dynasties of chiefs comes from the nineteenth century and is discussed in later chapters. It is difficult to judge whether this represents a genuine development in the relations of African and Portuguese *senhor* or whether the illusion of development is being produced by the more abundant evidence of the nineteenth century. My own view is that in the seventeenth century when the Portuguese penetrated deeply into the interior and when their numbers were very small, the relationship of *senhor* and peasant came close to that of chief and subject. In the eighteenth century the characteristics of Zambesi society probably moved closer to those of Europe, for the backlands were lost and the larger numbers of Portuguese residents supported a vestige at least of European culture. By the end of the eighteenth

184

century, however, another *sertão* had been opened up north of the Zambesi and this, together with the turmoil of the early nineteenth century, led to a return to conditions similar to those of the seventeenth century.

Capitão-mor das terras da coroa

The Portuguese government was clearly dissatisfied with the private jurisdiction which the *prazo*-holders had over their *colonos*. During the eighteenth century it had been argued that self-interest would always restrain the oppression of the *senhor* who would not wish to see his land depopulated and his tribute decline. This was an economic fallacy which men at the end of the eighteenth century were only too disposed to believe, even without the encouragement of Adam Smith.

However, the same self-interest which was supposed to protect the *colono* in the eighteenth century, increasingly dictated his exploitation in the early nineteenth century when the quick profits from the slave trade led to the rounding up of whole villages of *colonos* to be shipped to Brazil. It was probably this which led to the appointing of the *capitaes-mores*. The full title of these officers was *capitão-mor das terras da coroa e juiz privativo das causas cafrais*—captain-major of the crown lands and judge of African cases. Sometimes the junior rank of *sargento-mor* was used, but there was one of these officers in each of the three administrative captaincies by the 1830s.

The historian Teixeira Botelho says that the post was set up in 1820 but the title was certainly in use in the eighteenth century (74) and probably originated in the powers of the *capitaes-mores* who had been appointed to the fairs and mining camps. During the nineteenth century the system was greatly extended and there were a dozen or so *capitaes-mores* in Portuguese Zambesia by 1880.

The *capitão-mor* heard appeals from slaves or *colonos* against the *prazo*-holders. Serious cases would be heard by the *mocasambos* on the *prazos* and if appeal was made from their decisions, the *capitão-mor* would assess the case with the advice of *bazos* and *chuangas* who were experts in aspects of African law. He was particularly concerned with cases where a *colono* had been seized as a slave and had appealed to have his status protected. Inevitably this led to a large number of cases where the difference between a slave or freeman was not fully clarified. One such case

185

came before *sargento-mor* João Manuel da Silva in 1830. An African girl had strayed near the village of a certain Invielo who seized her and tried to drag her into his hut alleging that as her mother was his slave all her children were his as well. The *senhor* of the *prazo* later said that the girl and the other children had been sold to him by a cousin. The *sargento-mor* declared that they were all free (*244*).

The *capitão-mor* might also be called in to mediate in disputes involving the slaves or *colonos* of rival *prazo*-holders or in disputes between Portuguese and the independent chiefs. A proclamation in 1833 made it clear that all *milandos*—that is all cases involving infringements of African law and custom—must come before the *capitão-mor* (*153*).

One must not jump to the conclusion that the cases heard before the *capitaes-mores* constituted a sort of Portuguese version of the contemporary South African 'black circuit'. Because of their need to know the African languages, the *capitão-mor* was very often a local man and not infrequently a *prazo*-holder himself. It can be imagined how effective a restraint these men would impose on the acitvities of their fellow *senhors*. Nor was it easy to find the right man to hold the post. Vasconcellos e Cirne reported in 1830 that he had refused to give the post to a certain Felisberto de Soares because he was an uneducated mulatto without any knowledge of African customs and a drunkard (*254*).

Conclusion

There was, therefore, a wide spectrum in the relationship of the *senhor* to the free Africans inhabiting his *prazo*. Some Portuguese became very Africanised and were accepted as chiefs on their lands. Others saw the *colono* as a peasant to be exploited by direct extortion, by the more indirect methods of the commercial monopoly or by enslavement. Behaviour of the latter kind— which became all too common in the nineteenth century— tended to depopulate whole regions of Zambesia some of which became permanently lost to the Portuguese. It also swelled the bands of homeless and disordered fugitives who fled to the territory of the independent chiefs or joined the slave bands of the *prazo*-holders and sought protection at the hands of the very people who were their chief oppressors when they were free.

11 The Portuguese and their Relations with the African Peoples

Part Two: The Slaves

Slavery and clientship

In 1807 serious disorders were reported among the *colonos* of the *prazos* Tipue and Tambara in the Lupata region. The *tenente-geral*, Vilas Boas Truão, set out himself to quell them and sent urgently to the redoubtable José Francisco Alves Barbosa, the holder of *prazo* Tambara, to summon 'all the settlers able to bear arms to march at once with their slaves, selecting those who are musketeers for it is they who count for most in actions'. Axemen were to be sent ahead to break into the fortified stockades and,

> in all the enemy villages you are to have the utmost care to take the greatest number of slaves of all ages and both sexes so that we shall have in our power hostages sufficient to secure the punishment of these rebels. And you shall set fire to the villages after having looted them of all movables, livestock and food (*105*).

These are pretty instructions to be given by a governor for the maintenance of law and order in his province. But who were these slaves and why were they employed to loot and burn the villages of the *colonos*?

There are two Portuguese words used to describe the slaves, *escravo* and *captivo*. These terms suggest that the slave in Zambesia was the economic chattel which he became when transported to the Americas, and in some respects this impression is correct.

In Zambesia all forms of menial work were done by slaves. Slaves ran the households; slaves carried the litters in which all the Portuguese habitually rode; slaves paddled the canoes on the river; slaves worked in the mines; slaves hoed the gardens and fields which provided fresh food for the Portuguese; slaves took messages, and slave girls filled the harems of the *prazo senhors*. However, this is not the whole story, for we also find slaves entrusted with quite responsible tasks. Slaves administered the *prazos* and supervised the collection of taxes, slaves were sent away on trading expeditions which might last more than a year, slaves were sent on embassies to chiefs, slaves commanded military forces, and slaves were able to establish themselves in villages of their own and acquire slaves for themselves.

A *prazo*-holder valued his slaves quite apart from their productive capacity. Most of them were probably not, in fact, producing anything at all but serving as a body-guard and escort to protect the *senhor* and maintain his dignity by fair means and foul. They also acted as the police force which kept control in the *prazos*. 'The settlers', Nogueira de Andrade wrote in 1790, 'are content with the vassalage of these kaffirs who recognise them as *senhor* and who provide them with a numerous body and door guard. In this way a hundred, two hundred, three hundred and even more kaffirs are employed and exercised.' (*416*, 87–8).

To understand the real nature of Zambesi slavery, however, it is necessary to see how these slaves were acquired. Antonio Pinto de Miranda, a Zambesi settler who in the 1760s wrote one of the most informative accounts of the colony, listed six main types of slave (*406*, 269). First, there were those who were convicted of some misdeed and who sold themselves to a Portuguese, a mulatto or even another African in order to be able to pay their fines. (In the 1760s the selling price was twelve *chuabos*. equivalent to twelve fathoms of cloth.) Secondly, there were the children of the above, who were free but who entered the service of the *senhor* with their parent and after his death could stay among the slaves on payment by the lord of five yards of cloth. Thirdly, there were slaves sent as gifts from chiefs in return for some favour. These, Miranda said, are frequently guilty of petty pilfering in their own society and should not for this lose their liberty entirely.

The greatest number, however, became slaves in time of famine when selling themselves and their children was the only alternative to starvation. Fifthly, there were slaves obtained through the dubious process, much used by mulattos and Indians apparently, of kidnapping the relatives of a chief and demanding slaves as a ransom. Lastly, there were slaves obtained

188

from *fumos* as sureties for the payment of the tribute.

The German Jesuit, Mauriz Thoman, gives a somewhat similar account.

> A Moor becomes the slave of another Moor or a Portuguese, in the first place through a just war, or through an agreement made justly and freely whereby, for an agreed quantity of goods, namely cloth or glass beads, he places himself under a master; or through birth, for the slaves mostly marry and by the law of the land the children of a slave also are slaves (*468*, chap. 9).

Miranda goes out of his way to emphasise that it was not just the Portuguese who were acquiring slaves, but wealthy mulattos and Africans as well. In other words slavery was not confined to the European colony but was a common practice in the area and had been so even before the Portuguese arrived. The Portuguese were well aware that this African slavery did not carry the same significance as European slavery, for the authorities in Goa had instructed that anyone forced to enslave himself in times of famine could not lose his liberty permanently (*406*, 269). It was understood that a man selling himself in Zambesia was like a poor man in Europe entering the service of a master. Though he lost some of his liberty he did not lose his rights.

Even slaves who were captured in war and sold at slave auctions, and their daughters who were made the concubines of the syphilitic Portuguese *senhors*, found that they were part of a large establishment of slaves many of whom had entered Portuguese service voluntarily and for a good price. They found themselves part of an elaborate organisation with its own leaders; they came to expect from their masters rights and privileges, and to take them if they were not offered. Many slaves insisted that their agreement with the *senhor* precluded their being 'sent abroad' and in the early nineteenth century when the slave trade was booming one of the ways in which a *colono* could avoid being shipped as a slave was, paradoxically enough, to become the voluntary slave of a Portuguese.

The legal position of the slaves in Zambesia is set out in the preamble to a proclamation of 1835 (*159*). Slaves must only be expected to do work compatible with their physical and moral strength and their masters were only permitted the use of mild admonition and correction. They did not have powers of life and death nor were they exempt 'from the natural law which

189

cannot change'—a piece of theology which must have been very effective in curbing the brutal treatment of the slaves. A slave guilty of any serious offence was to be handed over to the authorities for trial.

In practice, however, the rights of a slave rested on custom and the determination of the other slaves to maintain the status of their class. It certainly did not preclude brutal punishment. Flogging with a *chicote*—a hippopotamus hide whip—was popular among the Portuguese *senhors* as well as the more subtle torture of the *palmatoria*—a sort of bastinado of the hands. The stocks were used and for serious offences spectacular executions were carried out, the guilty one being blown from the mouth of a cannon. But these barbarities could only be committed with the connivance of other slaves who provided the only means for carrying them out.

The most striking aspect of Zambesi slavery is the number of people who submitted themselves to enslavement because they needed protection. Refugees in time of war, fugitives from famine and pestilence, criminals on the run or simply kinless men or orphans, all saw the service of a *senhor* as the path of advancement. There is an entertaining passage from Livingstone's book on his expedition to the Zambesi which illustrates this very nicely.

A rather singular case of voluntary slavery came to our knowledge: a free black, an intelligent active young fellow, called Chibanti, who had been our pilot on the river, told us that he had sold himself into slavery. On asking why he had done this, he replied that he was all alone in the world, had neither father nor mother, nor anyone else to give him water when sick or food when hungry; so he sold himself to Major Sicard, a notoriously kind master, whose slaves had little to do but plenty to eat. 'And how much did you get for yourself?' we asked. 'Three thirty-yard pieces of cotton cloth' he replied (*390*, 49–50).

In the service of a powerful *senhor* a man who had been a wandering fugitive could expect to find a prosperous career, eventually marrying and settling down in a village and perhaps rising to hold an important position in the *senhor*'s following and even acquiring slaves of his own.

A striking example of this is given by Gamitto. On his way to the court of Mwata Kazembe in 1831 he stopped at the *Bare* of Missale, the Portuguese settlement furthest in the interior at the time. He describes how a slave company of one hundred and fifty men had been assembled there by Vicente Antonio de Quadros and how, on his death, this group had lived at the *Bare* under their *mwanamambo*, or leader. Eventually another *prazo senhor* obtained the inheritance and established control over the slaves. By this time, however, the *mwanamambo* had acquired three hundred slaves of his own. The slave was now a more powerful man than his master (*363*, 111–12).

Zambesi slavery, then, was not really the slavery known in America, but a form of clientship familiar in most other African societies. Clientship—or commendation—arises in an unsettled society when men seek the protection of the rich and powerful in return for service. It is a way of creating an artificial 'family' unit when blood kinship has proved itself an inadequate form of protection and support in times of difficulty.

Gamitto describes the ritual by which a man made himself the slave or client of another. This ritual was called 'breaking the *mitete*'.

I will now explain what it means to break a *Mitete*. In the whole of Eastern Africa it is customary to give protection to any negro, freeman or slave, who is fleeing from a persecutor, or from someone to whom he does not want to act as a slave or from some powerful man; or again if he is in danger of dying of hunger. To get this protection all he needs to do is to break some utensil, or tear a cloth, however small, belonging to the person from whom he desires help. This is done without a word being spoken. The new owner asks him why he is seeking refuge with him, whether he is a slave or free, and why he broke the *Mitete*. Then the old owner or persecutor can only get him back by paying a ransom which is usually double his value as a slave. Kaffir customs protect the new owner.

Gamitto goes on to explain that a slave made in this way could not be sold abroad (*363*, 145).

Clientship may always arise from the same sort of causes but does not always develop in the same way. It may develop into a 'feudal' system with a hierarchical society and a manorial economy; it may develop into something not very much different from plantation slavery; in conditions of continuing disorder it may give rise to roving bands of warriors living on loot—akin to the mercenary bands of the Thirty Years War or the Hundred

Years War in Europe; or, as happened in many parts of Africa, the clients may become assimilated into the kin of their protector and become members of his clan and thus be reabsorbed into the traditional structure of society.

Until the middle of the nineteenth century, the clients and slaves of the *prazo*-holder largely maintained their separate identity from the ordinary *colonos*. For the most part they formed his personal retinue or maintained his house or other establishments, but many were settled in the interior or on the frontiers of the *prazo* and supported themselves from the produce of their fields and paid tribute to the *prazo senhor*. In this way permanent villages and families grew up who established strong ties with the land and the particular *prazo* and the reabsorption of the slave into the local population could begin.

The *prazo*-holder had acquired most of his slaves originally because he was a man of power and prestige and could provide them with food and protection. He succeeded in holding together his slave bands only if he continued to be rich and successful. Any suggestion that the supplies of food were drying up, or that the opportunities for loot and riotous living were growing less would lead to the slaves deserting to a more successful rival *senhor* or continuing to live in their villages in a state of more or less active rebellion.

'The kaffir slaves,' wrote Manuel da Costa the leading merchant in Zumbo in 1769, 'live almost completely disobedient to their masters so that if these do not have any business or any goods in the house, they despise them and do not recognise their bondage . . .' (*215*).

The unruliness of the slaves was made worse for the Portuguese by the prevalent habit of 'poaching' slaves from a neighbouring *prazo*. A proclamation of 1783 specifically condemns this practice of luring someone else's slave onto one's *prazo*, and profiting by his labour and the tribute he paid while publicly denying all knowledge of his whereabouts (*52*).

The Portuguese were always anxious to claim property rights in their slaves whenever these could be effectively asserted, but in reality the bond between master and slave was a personal, not a legal, one. At its best this relationship could appear to an outsider patriarchal and benevolent. Here is Livingstone's description of the head of the Ferrão family of Sena in 1858.

The benevolence of this gentleman is unbounded. The poor black stranger passing through the town goes to him almost as a matter of course for food, and is never sent away hungry. In times of famine the starving natives are fed by his generosity; hundreds of his own people he never sees except on these occasions; and the only benefit derived from being their master is, that they lean on him as a patriarchal chief, and he has the satisfaction of saving their lives in seasons of drought and scarcity (*390*, 35).

It is not surprising to learn from other sources that Ferrão could put a large force of armed slaves into the field and that after his death his spirit was consulted through a spirit medium living near his grave (*398*, vol 2, 297).

An heir often had great difficulty establishing control over the slaves he inherited but even more difficult was the task of a *senhor*, newly granted a *prazo* and with slaves of his own, who found the territory in the possession of the slaves of his predecessor. It was not unknown for members of his predecessor's family also to be there—providing a direct challenge to his authority (*59*). Either he would have to come to terms with their leaders or reduce them to obedience by some other means.

The slaves were in a strong position to bargain with the newcomer. If they disliked him, they might intrigue with the *colonos* to resist, or they might leave and take refuge with one of the neighbouring chiefs, or they might install themselves in the fortified villages called *mussitos* and await events, living by robbery and loot.

The control a man could exert over his slaves became a major factor in government policy, for disorders among the slaves were feared by the authorities above all else. Rebellion or disobedience in one group would quickly spread to other slave groups and to the *colonos*, leaving the colony hopelessly exposed and without any defence. In 1769 an *adjunto* decided that it would be unwise to send two powerful *senhors*, João Moreira Pereira and Antonio de Araujo Bragança, to Moçambique to answer charges against them, because in their absence their slaves would desert to the local chiefs (*213*).

The greatest cause of slave disorders was the presence in the towns of groups of slaves belonging to rival settlers. The slaves arrived armed to the teeth with bows and arrows, assegais and spears, and before long the town would be in flames and the houses looted. There were the strictest orders against slaves entering the towns with arms and even against their crossing from the north bank to Tete with their arms from the Marave

193

prazos (*95*). On one occasion the slaves belonging to the Jesuit fathers in Sena attacked and burnt the house belonging to the powerful Bernardo Caetano de Sa Botelho (*132*) and in previous chapters we have already looked at the violent rampages of the slaves of *Dona* Ines Cardoso and Antonio Botelho de Lemos.

The greatest disturbances, however, usually occurred on the death of a *senhor*. His slaves then indulged in the rite known as *choriro*, the purpose of which was to make the people weep for the dead chief. It was repeatedly denounced by the authorities but was still a frequent occurrence late in the nineteenth century (*95*, *61*). Writing in 1879 of the death of Antonio Vicente da Cruz, the British consul, Henry O'Neill, said

> The death of their leader, instead of assuring peace, it is feared and expected, will cause a revival of the worst scenes of his life, and the Zambesi traders are now in fear and apprehension that his warriors will carry out their so-called custom of 'Kolira', in which they endeavour to make everyone weep for the death of their chief, a custom carried out by simple and wholesale robbery and murder from which the traders and other whites who venture within their reach will certainly not be exempt (*192*).

In this way the Portuguese and the *colonos* were made to weep for the death of a *senhor*—and they were frequently made to weep while he was alive. The leaders of the slave bands were powerful and proud men, with their own *esprit de corps*, looking down on the free peasantry and tyrannising over them, following a powerful and ruthless master but deserting a weak one and holding his *prazo* in insolent rebellion.

The ordinary slaves, who were called *chicundas* in the common parlance of the Zambesi, also developed a strong sense of identity. As son succeeded father and grandfather in the slave bands of the Portuguese, and as men of different nations were continually recruited into the company of the slaves, so a distinct language grew up—the prevalent River dialect mixed with Portuguese words and phrases—and the *chicunda* came to look upon themselves and their companions as a nation apart. Today there are tens of thousands of Africans in Zambia, Malawi and in Moçambique who call themselves A-Chikunda and who trace their origin to the slave bands of the Portuguese *senhors*. They provide another striking example of the outstanding ability of African social institutions to mould the most heterogeneous collection of people into a strong and vigorous nation (*465*).

194

Most *prazo*-holders made some distinction between the personal and household retainers they kept near their persons and the slaves who were more or less permanently installed on their *prazos*; and, of course, they made a further distinction between the slaves and the free Portuguese and mulatto servants that they might have. João Fernandes do Rozario, in the inventory of his establishments which was drawn up in 1788 and which has already been quoted, says he had three Indian and one mulatto servants, twenty-five adult male slaves and eighty females, together with a further fifty boys and thirty girls in his household. In addition he had forty-two slaves who specialised in various skills. In his smallest *prazo*, Inhacororo, he had two villages of slaves consisting of twenty men and sixty women with their children. In Mulambe, which was his wife's *prazo*, he had six slave villages with sixty slaves in all, and in his third *prazo*, Impirire, he had fifteen male slaves and thirty female with their children. A mulatto, who was a goldsmith, lived on this *prazo*, presumably as a dependent of Rozario's, and had his own slave establishment of fifty slaves and their children (*65*).

All slaves who were not the direct body servants of the Portuguese or who did not have skilled occupations were considered primarily as a military force. They were grouped in bands of ten or twelve men under the control of a *sachicunda*. Immediately above the *sachicunda* was a slave called the *bazo* (*406, 267*). When the slaves were mustered for a military expedition they were likely to be commanded by the *bazo* and would be grouped in *ensacas*, or regiments, which in the nineteenth century contained about two hundred and fifty men. The *bazos* were frequently detailed by the Portuguese *senhors* to deal with awkward legal cases that arose among the *colonos*—an abuse which the *capitaes-mores das terras da coroa* were supposed to check (*159*).

At the head of the slave establishments were the *mocasambos* and the *mwanamambos*. Many writers do not distinguish between these two, as though they were alternative titles for the same rank, but there are some distinctions that perhaps should be made. The term *mwanamambo* literally means a child-king or the son of a king. It was a title which the son of the Mwene Mutapa bore, according to João dos Santos (*445, 288*). Antonio Miranda, writing in the 1760s, tells a story which is supposed to show how the term came to be used among the slaves of the Portuguese; a story which, incidentally, shows quite clearly the difference between Portuguese clientship in Zambesia and the slavery of the Americas.

Some time in the 1740s or 1750s the son of a chief fled to the Portuguese *Dona* Ines Gracias Cardoso, seeking her protection from his father against whom he had committed some crime. This in itself was not uncommon. The *prazo*-holders habitually played at African politics, welcoming fugitives from civil wars and supporting claimants in cases of disputed succession to a chieftaincy. There had also been cases of Portuguese bringing up the sons of chiefs in their own households. *Dona* Ines propitiated the father with gifts and obtained from him agreement that the fugitive prince should remain on her *prazo* and govern it for her with the title of *mwanamambo*. *Dona* Ines' innovation in *prazo* management was copied by the Jesuits and then by the rest of the settlers. It is unlikely, however, that many of the other *mwanamambos* could claim the chiefly descent that their titles implied (*406, 267*).

The *mwanamambo* was the slave who would be left in charge of the *prazo* when the *senhor* was absent; he might be entrusted with important trading missions, embassies or military expeditions. He stood close to the *senhor* as his chief adviser and the acknowledged leader of the slaves. There would not usually be more than one *mwanamambo* on each *prazo*.

The *mocasambo* might perform many of the functions of *mwanamambo*, but it seems that his chief duty was to govern the permanent settlements of the slaves on the *prazos*. In particular he would hold the fortified villages which were placed on the frontiers of the *prazos* to prevent marauders invading the territory (*361, 62*). A large *prazo* would have many *mocasambos*; Cheringoma and Gorongosa both had twenty-eight when inventories of the slaves attached to them were drawn up in the eighteenth century (*264, 265*).

A letter written by *Frei* Fernando de Jesus Maria in 1762 gives an interesting account of the solidarity of the slaves and the commanding position the *mocasambos* might hold in the *prazo*.

> The slaves which are kept in each household as though part of the entail are called the *botaca*. These slaves have a leader who is called a *mocasambo* and another second to him called *sachicunda* who is the same as the treasurer in these *botacas* who does all the business. The *senhor* cannot give a single

negro of the *botaca* away without the others all mutinying . . .
to the *mocasambo* the negroes have such a blind obedience
that if it is necessary to execute any one of them he will
briefly consult with the eldest of the slaves and the execution
will be carried out at once without any demur (*446*, 73).

The slaves who were permanently settled on the *prazos* were
encouraged to cultivate the land, to marry and found families.
They paid tribute to the *prazo*-holder like any *colono* but they
were supposed to watch the *colonos* and maintain order in the
prazo and on the frontiers. The *senhor* would always try to see
that some at least of his slaves carried firearms and this enabled
many of them to become effective hunters as well as soldiers.
When the *prazo*-holder was summoned on an expedition by the
government he would have a body of warriors immediately at
his command.

Also stationed in the *prazo*, but employed in a rather different
way, was the *chuanga*. This slave has already been mentioned
in connection with his duties in the collection of the tribute. He
compiled the lists of those who had to pay tribute with the *fumo*
and supervised the collection. He resided in or near the *fumo*'s
village and reported back to the *prazo senhor* everything that
took place. When the *fumo* wished to speak to the *prazo*-holder
he did so through the *chuanga* (*361*, 62).

The personal body-servants and household retainers whom
the Portuguese kept close to their persons had their *sachicundas*
and *bazos* but were much more differentiated in function and
rank. The African word *butaka* refers to an inheritance and the
term was used of the personal servants of a Zambesi *dona* who
would remain with her when she married or if she changed her
place of abode. They were separate from the rest of the slaves
of the establishment. In charge of these female attendants were
the *macodas*. Male servants were called *bandazios* and the term
bicho was applied to small boys employed in the house. Two
other slave officers are mentioned by Miranda. The *mucata* who
acted for an absent *sachicunda* and the *esamacuacas* who were the
equivalent of the *bazos*. Other household slaves would be
distinguished by their particular skills. Thus there were bakers,
goldsmiths, boatmen, musicians, washerwomen, cooks, barbers
and so on (*406*, 267).

Mining was usually undertaken by women slaves only.
Gamitto explains how mining was organised on the *Bares* in the
interior—a description which shows something of the freedom

of the slaves and the contractual nature of their relations with the Portuguese *senhor*.

The slaves employed at the mine are divided into *Insakas* as usual, but each of these has six negresses, it being, as I have said, only women who mine. Each *Insaka* is under the charge of a *Nyakoda* who gives a weekly account of the work of her people. These weeks are of four days, and each woman has to account for six *tangas* a week; this satisfied, the rest is hers. It often happens that a woman gets enough on the first day to pay the quota and in this case she is not required to turn up on the following days. Owners of *Bares* usually have imported cloths, beads, etc., at them to sell to their slaves at exorbitant prices; and so these slaves buy from any passing merchant, secretly, what they need; and this was why Botelho forbade the sale of gold to members of the expedition (*363*, vol 1, 58).

Two observations may be made about the general organisation of the slaves. In the first place, it is clear that the titles and ranks were largely of African origin. The Marave chiefs employed *chuangas*, for instance, to watch over Portuguese activities at the mining camps and to collect tribute (*363*, vol 1 42), a function similar to that of the *chuanga* in the Portuguese service. The same was true of the *mwanamambo* and probably of the other titles as well.

The second point to be made is that the title and function of each office changed over the years and was often different north and south of the Zambesi. It is interesting, for instance, to compare Miranda's account of the slave hierarchy, which is broadly that given above, with the account given by Affonso de Moraes Sarmento in 1887. Sarmento lists the hierarchies of slaves and *colonos* together, distinguishing only between those officials chosen by the *colonos* and those chosen by the *senhor*. The *capitão* (captain), he says, lived in the central village of the *prazo* and was the representative of the *prazo*-holder. In the Sena *prazos* he was called the *mwanamambo*, and in the Tete *prazos*, *chuanga*. The *mocasambos* were the men who checked the collection of the tribute at the headquarters of the *fumos*.

The *fumos* and *inhacuavas* remained the choice of the *colonos* and, Sarmento says, they were usually chosen from among the ancient chiefly lineages. They did, however, receive a stipend from the *prazo senhor*. Beneath them and acting as their assistants were the *esamacuacas* (called *moenes* among the Muslims of the
198

Quelimane area) and the *sangiras* who heard cases according to African law. Both these were chosen and maintained by the *colonos*. In the eighteenth century, however, it is fairly clear that these offices were held by slaves of the *prazo*-holder called *bazos* (*447*, 64).

Although Sarmento does not mention it, the terms *capitão* and *kazembe* had almost superseded the older *mwanamambo* and *mocasámbo* by the end of the nineteenth century. They were not used with any precision, but applied to the leading followers of the *prazo senhor* who formed his council of *grandes* and commanded his troops. The term *capitão* spread widely outside the Portuguese colony and is still used throughout central Africa for the foreman of any gang of workers.

Finally, mention should perhaps be made again of the *mussambazes*. These were professional traders who travelled in the service of some master and hence were referred to by the Portuguese as slaves. They were, however, a very independent fraternity, doing much as they pleased and, according to Gamitto, using the trade goods they were supplied with to buy slaves for themselves and enhance their own status. Many writers considered, however, that they were indispensable to the prosperity of the colony as they were permitted to trade freely in the lands of chiefs who would not admit the Portuguese or mulattos. Most areas of Africa have produced their professional traders. Sometimes whole nations will take to this as a livelihood, for example, the Bisa who became traders after being displaced from their ancestral lands by the Bemba migrations about the beginning of the nineteenth century. In Angola there were the *pombeiros*—mulatto itinerant traders who penetrated deeply into Africa far beyond the areas known to contemporary Europe. In Malawi and northern Moçambique there were the Yao.

In the countries of America, where plantation slavery flourished, the slaves also had their own hierarchies and division of function, but they never achieved the independence of the slaves in Portuguese Zambesia, dictating terms alike to their masters and to the subject *colonos* under their control. A closer parallel would undoubtedly be with the type of slavery existing in many Muslim countries where the slave purchased in the slave-market might well rise to positions of high authority and responsibility, ruling over the 'free' population and enjoying a material prosperity far greater than would have been possible for a free man.

Towards the end of the eighteenth century the export of

slaves began to supersede the gold and ivory trade as the staple of the Moçambique economy, and the *prazo*-holders began to use their slaves less in mining and more on slaving expeditions. From the first the clearest possible distinction was maintained between a *senhor*'s own retainers and the slaves he had bought for export (though naturally there are some cases of confusion). It was these armed bands of slave traders and elephant hunters who, in the nineteenth century began to push deep into the interior, up the Zambesi, the Shire and the Luangwa until they met the Swahili hunters and slavers who had come from Zanzibar and whose influence was spreading throughout the region of the Lakes and into the Congo basin. It was these Portuguese slavers, and their Swahili counterparts, who did as much as anyone to bring about the diplomatic scramble for Africa after 1870.

The numbers of the slaves

Antonio Pinto Miranda attempted an estimate of the numbers of slaves held by the main families in Zambesia in the middle of the eighteenth century. He included in the figures the slaves of the Jesuits as a separate part of the calculations, although the Jesuit property had been sold up after their expulsion in 1759. He calculated that there was one family—that of *Dona* Ines Pessoa de Almeida Castellobranco—with 6,000 slaves; ten had 1,000 or more; eleven had between 500 and 1,000 and the rest under 500. Altogether his figures, which are only approximate, give 33,500 slaves as the total for the Rivers colony (*406*, 255–265).

Other calculations of slave numbers help to save Miranda's credibility. *Tenente-geral* Vilas Boas Truão, for example, in his *Estatistica da capitania dos Rios de Senna* mentions the figure of 21,827 for the total slave population (*471*, 8), and there are some enormous figures given by bombastic commanders for the size of the forces under their command on military campaigns. The anonymous hero who wrote an account of his life in the first half of the eighteenth century (see chap 7) says he campaigned with fifteen thousand men, while Antonio Lobo da Silva in the seventeenth century records that he had eight thousand men on one of his expeditions (*6*, *1*).

Figures of this kind, however, should be set against the detailed inventories that do exist. The Jesuit residence at Chemba had 70 slaves attached to it at the time of the dissolution and
200

Caia and Murassa had 105. João Fernandes do Rozario claimed to have over 500 slaves in 1788 and Nicolau Pascoal da Cruz once claimed to have 340 of whom 300 were fugitive (*267*). What of the *casa* (establishment) of *Dona* Ines Pessoa? Miranda claimed that she had 6,000 slaves but the inventories of Cheringoma and Gorongosa, which were the two largest of her estates, show a total of 1,837. The unknown factor in all these calculations, of course, is the number of wives and children a slave might possess. Including them in the calculations might well double or treble the numbers of active and effective slaves. It is also difficult to know how many of the slaves could be counted as obedient and effectively under Portuguese control at any one time.

Escaped slaves

There were many reasons why a slave might wish to escape from Portuguese service—quite as many as there were to make him enter it. He might receive brutal treatment; the master might fail to maintain him adequately or provide him with opportunities for acquiring loot and women; the death of one master might bring a hated heir to power in the *prazo* or the *prazo* might pass to a stranger who had his own slaves; there was a real fear that he might some day find himself on a ship bound for Brazil; or there might simply be the desire for a life of freedom from the essentially parasitic existence of the *prazo chicunda*.

The chiefs whose lands adjoined Portuguese territory often welcomed fugitive slaves not only because they added to the power of these chiefs, but because they were useful hostages in negotiations and bargaining with the Portuguese. The problem was an old one for the Portuguese. Father Monclaro refers in the sixteenth century to a ship-wrecked Portuguese pilot who was killed by escaped slaves (*409*, 209), and early in the seventeenth century Diogo Simões Madeira gave as one of his reasons for attacking the Tonga chief Chombe that this chief had received slaves escaped from the Portuguese (*321*, vol 3, 388).

The favourite escape route for slaves was across the Zambesi to the wooded slopes of Mount Morumbala where rival chiefs, the Inhabendico and the Massache, welcomed them. Manuel Barreto records the cynical action of one of these chiefs in luring away Portuguese slaves and then selling them back. It had been to deal with this escape route that Sisnando Dias Bayão had crossed the Zambesi and established his own *mocasambos* on Mount Morumbala to watch the activities of the chiefs (*318*).

Early in the eighteenth century the Mount was again raided and brought temporarily under Portuguese control; the Inhabendico of the day was captured and his head delivered to his rival (*6*). The trouble continued, however, and other Portuguese expeditions were sent without a permanent conquest ever being effected. In 1803 a formal embassy was sent to chief Rundo, the paramount chief of the eastern Marave who controlled the Shire River, in the hope that diplomacy could staunch the flow of slaves—but again without success. For the most part slaves moved when they liked and took service with whom they pleased (*77, 78, 79*). Most of the treaties between the Portuguese and the Mwene Mutapas and the Macombes of Barue also contain clauses providing for the return of escaped slaves (*50, 270*).

The Portuguese considered the harbouring of escaped slaves a breach of treaty and property rights (although they frequently harboured each other's escaped slaves) and they retaliated by welcoming the rival claimants to chieftaincies and other fugitives from the lands of the neighbouring African states.

Slaves escaping from the Portuguese did not always seek refuge with one of the chiefs. Sometimes they would set themselves up on their own—they had after all acquired a certain corporate identity in the service of their masters and might be strangers to their African neighbours. The fortified settlements of the escaped slaves were called by the Portuguese *mussitos*—the name given to the Tonga villages contructed from stakes that rooted in the ground and formed a living wall of trees (*318, 478*).

The judge Francisco Moraes Pereira tells something of the career of a slave who had escaped from the Portuguese on Moçambique Island. The slave was called Macambe; he was a carpenter who escaped from his master for fear of being flogged. For some years he wandered on the Makua coast gathering other fugitives and swelling his band and eventually built himself a fortified settlement in the country behind Angoche. He and his men maintained themselves by raiding the surrounding settlements and terrorising the whole coast (*427, 27*).

There were to be many instances during the Zambesi Wars of the nineteenth century when slaves and their leaders established themselves as independent communities of some strength.

Conclusion

The relations of the Portuguese *senhor* with his slaves and his free subjects were determined by African custom and the traditional social relationships of African society. The success of a *senhor* was usually related to his ability to make himself acceptable as chief by his slaves and by the *colonos*. Many of the Portuguese were predisposed to this role because the influence of their African wives and mothers in their households tended to outweigh the frail and diluted European culture of the Zambesi settlements.

However, all these cultural patterns arose from the immediate circumstances and needs of the Zambesi world; they were never the result of Portuguese official policy. Because plantation slavery was impossible in African conditions, the *prazos* could never become plantations. The Portuguese from Europe hated and despised the Africans, the mulattos and the Indians, and if they had had their way there would have been two social classes in Portuguese Africa—the masters and the slaves. But they did not have their way, and the Zambesi settlements evolved a unique set of relationships, rich in their own traditions and values, which always owed more to Africa than to Europe—and as the nineteenth century wore on became more African still.

The *Prazos* of Sofala and the
Querimba Islands

It would be easy to claim that the essential features of the
Zambesi *prazo* system were unique and so avoid the trouble of
finding and assessing parallel societies and institutions. This,
however, is not quite true and this chapter examines two other
areas of eastern Africa which the Portuguese attempted to
colonise and where the *prazo* featured fitfully as a form of land
tenure and a determinant of social and economic life.

Sofala

Sofala, the ancient port which served the goldfields of Mwene
Mutapa and was legendary in Europe for its supposed riches,
still survived as a Portuguese captaincy in the eighteenth and
nineteenth centuries. Most of its trade passed to Quelimane and
the Zambesi in the middle of the sixteenth century when the
administrative headquarters of the colony were moved to
Moçambique Island and from the 1550s it became little more
than a coastal trading port and that all-important object for the
officials of a declining empire—a symbol of past greatness. The
stone fort, proudly begun by Pero d'Anhaia in 1505, crumbled
away on the sandy shore of the Indian Ocean, already in the
eighteenth century a ruin and uninhabitable, until finally it was
swept away in a night of storms and high tides early in the
twentieth century.

In 1574 Sofala was used as the disembarkation point for Vasco
Homem's army bound for the mines of Manica, and shortly
afterwards it became the headquarters for the missionary
activities of *frei* João dos Santos. This great missionary and
ethnographer not only described for posterity the sleepy world
of the Portuguese and Muslim communities of the coast but
described in great detail the chieftaincy of Quiteve which lay
between Sofala and the Manica mountains and was the Portu-

guese' most powerful neighbour.

The chieftaincy of Quiteve once belonged to the empire of the Mwene Mutapa, but by the middle of the sixteenth century it was established as an independent paramountcy. Its territory seems at one time to have extended from the mouth of the Sabi to the mouth of the Zambesi, stretching inland as far as the Manica mountains. With this chieftaincy the Portuguese established close relations. Caravans travelled regularly to the fairs in Quiteve's country to trade in gold and ivory, and it soon became a convention that a Portuguese should be present at the coronation of a new chief. It is in the lands of the Quiteve that we first hear of Portuguese *sertanejos* acquiring grants of jurisdiction over land.

At first these grants appear to have been of small and unimportant areas and the story dos Santos tells of Rodrigo Lobo (see chap 3) is not the story of a *sertanejo* proudly and imperiously dominating a chief caught in the toils of Portuguese politics. Early in the seventeenth century, however, the tune changes for Quiteve as for the other chiefs of the interior. From being harmless traders, the Portuguese become land-hungry mercenaries, exploiting the succession problems of the chieftaincies and thrusting deeply into central Africa with their bands of slaves and their fortified stockades.

Some time in the 1630s Quiteve Peranhe was forced to call for Portuguese aid and to concede the vast territories lying between the Pungue and the Zambesi to the Portuguese captain Sisnando Dias Bayão. At one blow half his kingdom was lost, and it was not to be subsequently regained.

Had the new lands been attached to the captaincy of Sofala, which had the closest relations with Quiteve, then this captaincy would have had crown land at its disposal comparable in extent to the other captaincies, but Quiteve's concessions were incorporated in the Sena captaincy and became the *prazos* of Cheringoma and Chupanga (see chap 4). If the Sofala captaincy was now to expand it would have to do so along the twenty-five mile stretch of coast northwards from Sofala to the Pungue and on the coast stretching southwards towards the Sabi.

Even after the fairs of Manica and Karanga had been destroyed in 1694 Portuguese traders continued to send their caravans to the fairs of Quiteve and to show the talents of the successful *sertanejo*. José de Fonseca Coutinho, who had been *tenente-geral dos Rios* for a short time, moved to Sofala and at the very end of the seventeenth century indulged in one last heroic piece of king-making in the style of the earlier *conquistadores*.

From the Quiteve he purchased two territories which became the crown lands of Chuparo and Dendira, each occupying some three leagues of coast. He then organised trading caravans into the interior and used the reports of a robbery committed against one of them to organise an army against Quiteve. Coutinho was able to dethrone the chief and install his own nominee while the Portuguese gold traders moved in force into the country. His success did not last long, however, and the Portuguese pretender had to flee (*313*, 186). Coutinho had been given jurisdiction over the chiefs (*Inhamacangos*) of the territory between Sofala and the Buzi river as well as the title *May Deca* by the Quiteve and this jurisdiction was maintained by his successors. Coutinho also pioneered the extension of the Sofala captaincy southwards as I shall describe below (*350*, 375).

A somewhat similar story, which shows clearly how some Portuguese families became recognised chiefly lineages, is that of Raimundo Pereira Barros. Barros had married one of the daughters of the Quiteve and was given three villages near Sofala as a 'dowry'. He was also accorded the title of *Matire* and given chiefly jurisdiction. The descendants of *Matire* Barros had become completely Africanised by the early nineteenth century. They retained the chieftaincy, which remained a part of the Quiteve kingdom and was never incorporated into the crown lands. Barros had held the Portuguese office of *mestre do campo* and this was also retained by his successors who continued to perform ceremonial duties for the Portuguese—surely a curious piece of assimilation (*350*, 376).

Two other crown estates were acquired in the first half of the eighteenth century. João da Pinho Soares was granted the lands called Zomba in 1740 by Quiteve Bandarenhe in recompense for the losses he had suffered from a rebel chief. Soares was installed with the full ceremony of a chief into his lands (*456*, 38). Five years earlier João Pires, a merchant from Sofala, had been killed in the interior and his wife, *Dona* Maria de Maia, had raised a force to extort compensation. She had been bought off with the concession of the *Ilha* Chironde. Chironde was a valuable *prazo* and brought Portuguese territory up to the Pungue river. The Sofala captaincy now covered all twenty-five miles of the coast north of the town but never extended more than five or six leagues inland.

Probably as a result of these concessions the Quiteves began to close their lands to the Portuguese as the Changamire had already done. Ignacio Caetano Xavier, writing in 1758, reported that one Quiteve had been dethroned for wanting to reopen the gold diggings which would inevitably have attracted the Portuguese (*481*, 155). For the rest of the century this policy of isolation seems to have succeeded, for there were no further losses of territory to the Portuguese. The Catholic missions were withdrawn and even the custom of exchanging presents at the accession of a new Quiteve appears to have lapsed (*350*).

As the eighteenth century wore on, Sofala slid further into decline, although in some years a considerable trade still passed through its silted up harbour. It was not unknown for a hundred *bares* of ivory (equivalent to 64,000 lbs) to be shipped from the port together with 40,000–50,000 *cruzados* of gold dust in a year, but more often the quantities were only a third of this amount and in some years nothing at all appeared on the customs returns (*481*, 154).

In 1763 Sofala was raised to the dignity of a town and allowed to elect its own town council. The Portuguese population had, however, dwindled to no more than half a dozen persons. There was a military establishment with a sergeant, lieutenant, drummer, surgeon and chaplain commanded by a captain who combined all military, judicial and administrative functions in his own person even after the setting up of the *camara*. But the garrison was always undermanned and the soldiers considered exile to this swampy coast a worse fate even than exile up the Rivers and deserted whenever they could along the difficult overland road to Sena. Pero d'Anhaia's fort was repaired by Pereira do Lago in the 1770s (*428*, 322), but in 1795 it was an uninhabitable ruin and the small European community lived in grass huts nearby. That same year the garrison priest had to be relieved of his duties, a hopeless sufferer from *delirium tremens* (*70*).

In this twilight of European enterprise only the Indians and the Muslims flourished. Sebastião Rodrigues, a *Canarin* from Goa, became secretary of the fort in the middle of the century and acquired control of most of the crown lands attached to it. In 1755 he was refused confirmation of the grant of *Ilha* Chironde because the governor-general, Francisco de Mello e Castro, objected to the monopoly he was establishing over the crown lands and expected to be able to settle them with new immigrants from Portugal—an hallucination which apparently rose before the eyes of colonial administrators when they thought of Sofala as it did whenever they thought of the Rivers (*130*).

Chironde lay between the Buzi and Pungue rivers. It measured eight leagues by six and was low-lying, at least half of it being swamp. Herds of elephant grazed there and there was a large native African population under two chiefs. Besides the ordinary crops of Africa it produced indigo and tobacco and provided pasture for a large number of cattle.

Chironde eventually passed into the hands of Rafael Fernandes whose daughter, Antonia, succeeded in 1787. There followed a small *affaire* typical of Portuguese East Africa. Antonia was still a minor and her *prazo* was so exploited by a wicked step-father that the *colonos* all fled to the surrounding territories and the government had to intervene to protect the rights of the girl (*143*).

South of Sofala the Portuguese held the single vast *prazo* of Mambone. If the accounts of Mambone are correct then it must at one time have been almost as large as Cheringoma and Gorongosa. It extended from Chiluane, some fifty miles south of Sofala, to the Bazaruto and Benguerua islands south of the Sabi river, a coastline of over a hundred miles. Inland it extended as far as the chieftaincy of Madanda, and it included in its frontiers the ancient chieftaincy of Machanga.

Ever since the early sixteenth century the Portuguese had visited the Bazaruto islands in search of pearls and amber, which at times were traded in large quantities. They were also attracted by the Sabi valley trade route to the interior which was extensively used by the Muslims of the coast. Stragglers from the Portuguese fleets occasionally drifted south to the islands and settled there. In 1589 a Portuguese, Antonio Rodrigues, 'a native of Sofala', lived in the islands with the mainly Muslim population. He was able to obtain a vessel for the ship-wrecked survivors of the carrack *São Thomé* (*323*, a, 98–9).

In 1622 the survivors of another wrecked carrack, the *São João Baptista*, struggled as far as Chiluane where they received aid from a mulatto called Luiz Pereira, who was the most powerful man in the area, with an establishment of slaves (*323*, c, 266). In 1697 José da Fonseca Coutinho traded there and may have had a permanent establishment as well, for in that year he was asked to submit a report on the pearl fisheries to the crown.

The Bazaruto Islands and the coast opposite them, which was called Vuhoca, was ceded to the Portuguese in 1722 by a chief variously called Micissa and Inhaxinde. It was made a crown *prazo* and leased to Sebastião Rodrigues, under the name of Mambone (*396*, 238).

208

Sebastião Rodrigues paid 75 *cruzados* in *foros* for Mambone in 1762, and his heir was reputed to pay 5½ *arrobas* of ivory in *foros* and *dizimos*—the *arroba* weighing 32 lbs (*305, 122, 113*).

Towards the end of the eighteenth century the Portuguese in Sofala and the trading port of Inhambane further south began to feel the effects of the explosive changes taking place among the Ngoni clans in Zululand. In 1770 rumours were heard of the northward movement of the Thonga-Shangane peoples under pressure from the south (*388*, 24), and by the turn of the century Mambone was being invaded. The government responded by sending a detachment of troops to defend the *prazo*. For a year from 1805 to 1806 these were commanded by Sebastião Rodrigues' grandson—the last holder of the *prazo*—and then in 1806 Mambone was divided into four parts and granted to four *donas*, in an attempt to tighten up its administration (*113*).

This division of a large *prazo* is almost the only example of a land reform, which was so often urged by colonial reformers, ever being put into effect. The four new *prazos* thus created were called Mambone (which lay at the mouth of the Sabi River), Vuhoca (which included the Bazaruto islands and the mainland opposite to them), Dope and Chiluane. The reorganisation saved only Mambone and Chiluane, for the other two grants were never taken up and the land had to be abandoned.

Captain Owen's survey squadron visiting the mouth of the Sabi in 1824 found a Portuguese sergeant and six soldiers holding a little post on the south shore of the river estuary—a forlorn and marooned garrison whose communications depended on the good will of the coastal peoples (*422*, vol 1, 316). A description of Mambone in 1832 shows the little garrison still stationed at the Sabi mouth with six villages under its protection and a *senhor* who collected tribute and paid one and a half *arrobas* of ivory to the government for whom he worked as harbour-master in Sofala. These six villages were all that was left of the once vast *prazo* of Mambone and even one of these paid tribute to the Ngoni as well as to the Portuguese (*113*).

It is difficult to say how great the Portuguese control of the Mambone coast had been in the eighteenth century. Almost certainly it had been very slight and intermittent, being restricted to little more than the collection of tribute and to a coastal trade in ivory, pearls and amber. There was little or no settlement and no interruption to the continuity of African institutions in the region. The historic chieftaincy of Machanga, which lay between Chiluane and Mambone, maintained an unbroken and continuous existence (*388*, 27) and it may well have been Machanga which was the *Terra Masanga* conquered by a Portuguese force in 1812 but never occupied by them. Its chief subsequently called in Portuguese aid in a local war and the garrison of Mambone which went to his assistance was wiped out.

However, if Mambone was held in a faltering grasp, and if the invasions from the south threatened the very existence of Portuguese control, there were other signs of a vigorous revival of Portuguese activity in Sofala in the early years of the nineteenth century. Partly this is due to the weakening of the Quiteve kingdom which became hopelessly divided after the death of the paramount in 1803 (*350*, 378). The Portuguese appear to have profited by this to acquire concessions. In 1811 the lands immediately south of Sofala were conquered and incorporated into the crown lands as the new *prazo* of Ampara, whence timber and salt were soon being shipped to the town. In 1812 Masanga was briefly conquered, as we have seen, and in 1810 the Portuguese received a concession at Bandiri in the interior.

Bandiri was a gold-producing region in the foothills of the Manica mountains near the river Revue. It had probably been visited by the Portuguese traders in the days when the Quiteve kingdom was open to commerce. The story went that the site of a permanent fair had been ceded to the Portuguese in 1580 but had been lost because of the adultery of a Portuguese *sertanejo* with one of the queens of Quiteve (*458*). Whatever the truth of this, it is certain that the Portuguese obtained a new concession of a fair at Bandiri in 1810 but that they did not make anything of the opportunity through lack of any merchants rich enough and enterprising enough to mount a major expedition into the interior (*350*, 380). Instead, the concession was handed over to a local chief and it was not until 1830 that the Portuguese sent an expedition to assume control of the area and open the fair. The emissary, Luiz Felix, negotiated successfully for the formal assumption of sovereignty, but had to report that the country was being regularly raided by the Ngoni regiments from the south and any hope of opening trade must be put aside (*249*).

In 1842 the regiments of the Gaza Ngoni overran the Sofala *prazos* and laid the Portuguese town itself under tribute. The undistinguished story of Portuguese colonisation of the Sofala hinterland came to an end. Sofala itself was abandoned by the Portuguese about 1870 when the administrative headquarters was removed to Chiluane.

The Querimba Islands

The Querimba Islands are usually called by the Portuguese the *Ilhas do Cabo Delgado*. Querimba is the name of one of the islands in an archipelago which straggles from Cape Delgado southwards for a hundred and fifty miles to the Bay of Pemba where the modern town of Porto Amelia stands.

Like Zanzibar, Kilwa, Mafia and the other islands to the north, the Querimba Islands were settled by Muslim traders long before the arrival of the Portuguese in eastern Africa at the end of the fifteenth century. The islands were fertile and lay close enough to the mainland to be ideal trading bases without being too close to endanger their security. When the Portuguese began their occupation of the East African seaboard with the capture of Kilwa, Moçambique and Sofala, the Querimba Islands immediately assumed enormous importance for the Muslim traders who continued to smuggle gold and ivory through the port of Angoche and needed a base for their northern contacts.

In 1522 the Portuguese sacked some of the islands but apparently made no move to occupy them at that stage. Gradually, however, Portuguese traders and *sertanejos* must have settled in the islands for by the 1580s there was a large enough Portuguese community to encourage the Dominicans to send a mission. In 1591 João dos Santos went as its head and successfully negotiated with Andre da Cunha, the *senhor* of Querimba Island, for land to build the mission church.

The islands must have been distributed as *prazos* rather before this system of tenure spread in Zambesia. Antonio Bocarro mentions nine islands, each with its own *senhor*, in the 1630s. Querimba Island itself had a church and Ibo a fort armed with cannon. There was another fortified house on Macoloe (*219, 40–41*). The islands carried on an active trade both to the north and to the south and occasionally one of the India fleets revictualled and even wintered there. The islanders made a good living producing food for the forts and fleets of the Indian empire.

Towards the end of the seventeenth century the wars between the Portuguese and the Omani Arabs began to affect the prosperity of the Querimba Islands (*325, 344*), but when peace at last returned to eastern Africa after the fall of Mombasa in 1698 the unofficial frontier between Portuguese and Arab spheres of influence remained at Cape Delgado and the islands stayed under the Portuguese crown. This frontier, which is virtually that which today separates Moçambique and Tanzania, is thus the earliest of the frontiers of modern Africa to be fixed.

The islands came under the monopoly of the captains of Moçambique, but throughout the eighteenth century their most important contacts continued to lie northwards and out into the Indian Ocean. With the appointment of François Mahé de Bourdonnais as the governor of the French islands in the Indian Ocean, French traders became active along the East African coast. The French not only tried to obtain their share of the existing trade but with the development of plantations on Mauritius and the Île de Bourbon their demand for slave labour soon began to swell the volume of the slave trade. The French traders were welcomed as they paid a better price than the Portuguese and were more prepared to sell firearms and powder —commodities which the Portuguese government had always tried strictly to control.

The attraction of trade with the French proved increasingly to be too much for the national loyalties of the Portuguese mulatto community of the Querimba Islands. Trade between the islands and Moçambique declined and the Portuguese governors found not only that the food supplies for Moçambique Island were endangered but that Portuguese control over the islands was itself at risk. These points were all clearly set out in a report to the viceroy in 1754 (7), and in the second half of the century there were several attempts to make the Portuguese presence more of a reality.

In 1744 a detachment of twenty-four soldiers was stationed in the islands under the command of a local *senhor*, a mulatto called Antonio da Costa (*325*, a). At that time Querimba was the 'capital' of the islands which, however, were not a separate captaincy but came directly under the governor of Moçambique Island. The Moçambique authorities were represented by a *capitão-mor das Ilhas*, who was also one of the local settlers. Both the commandant and the *capitão-mor* in 1744 were resident in Querimba Island itself, but neither of them held the *prazo* of Querimba which was in the hands of a renegade Dominican priest called João de Meneses. There were thus three possible centres of authority, doubtless united in one thing only—seeing that the islands resisted outside interference and ran their own affairs.

During his governorship from 1752–1758, Francisco de Mello e Castro began the construction of a fort on the island of Ibo which from this time superseded Querimba as the centre of official activity. The fort was completed by Pereira do Lago in the 1770s and a regular garrison of fifty men was installed (*428, 337*). Pereira do Lago also had a new church erected and a government warehouse built. In 1763 Ibo achieved the status of a town and probably at this time an official governor was appointed to the islands and they became a separate captaincy. In 1786 a customs house was established and in 1791 a new fort constructed on the orders of the energetic Antonio Manuel de Mello e Castro, now governor-general (*352, 45*). This handsome star-shaped fort still graces the island.

These developments do not seem to have affected the trade of the islanders with the French, for the small, undermanned garrison was never sufficient to police a hundred and fifty miles of coast. As one writer put it, there was not even one soldier to one island. The trading activities of the French, the coming of the Yao to the coast and the gradual siphoning away to the north of the trade of the interior have all been studied in detail by other writers but all with very little attention to the seigneurial regime on the islands, although it is in the eighteenth century that the clearest picture emerges of the Querimba *prazos* (*300*).

About twenty of the islands were leased as *prazos* at different times though only a half-dozen of the larger ones were of any importance. These were Querimba, Ibo, Matemo, Macoloe, Amiza, Quisiba or Arimba, with Longo, Fumbo, Lupululy and Sito also occupied. Most of these islands had small rocks and islets attached to them and they also had rights over the sea channels through the reefs. They were also considered as having rights on the mainland opposite the island. Even as early as 1744 many of the Portuguese community actually lived on the mainland which was controlled for some distance inland by their slaves and which was of considerable economic value. The islands themselves were becoming depopulated. In 1744 the whole community consisted of eighteen Portuguese and their children, twenty-eight mulattos and their children and eight Indians. These numbers would be considerably increased if the wives were added, but there is no way of knowing the race or even the number of these. In 1777 the islands claimed to have a total Christian population of 256 (*377, 75*).

Like Zambesi *prazos*, the islands were granted on three-life tenures with specific obligations to maintain order, to cultivate the land and to make sure that the shipping channels remained open. The Dominicans and the Jesuits each held a small island but they appear to have lost control of them by the middle of the

213

century when two families had come to dominate the island communities.

The most powerful personality in the islands in the first part of the eighteenth century was *Frei* João de Meneses. He had bought the island of Querimba from its previous holder, João Valente, with what legality it is impossible to say (*325*, b), and had set himself up in the island partly as parish priest, partly as *senhor*, but in both roles as a true father to his people, for he had many sons and grandsons. In 1742 an attempt was made by the viceroy to have him recalled to Goa and the vicar-general of the Dominicans in Goa was enlisted to help, but the friar took no notice and clearly demonstrated to his supporters whose writ ran in the islands. Friar João carried on extensive trade with the French and had business contacts in India. His own private armed forces were easily sufficient to overawe the garrison whose commandant apparently lived under the friar's thumb on Querimba Island itself (*394*, 37).

Meneses died in 1749. His descendants continued to live in the islands, though the primacy among the local families moved to the Moraes. In 1744 the Moraes family had held four of the islands, the most important being the island of Quisiba, the most southerly but one of the islands. Quisiba was very fertile, had plenty of water and at one time had been the centre of a thriving community. The Moraes family, however, lived on the mainland and built up their position among the local African peoples. The centre of their power was the settlement at Arimba which eventually ousted Quisiba as the name of the *prazo*. The Moraes are another example of a Portuguese family becoming completely indigenised and successfully establishing themselves as a local chiefly dynasty. In 1781 the governor of Ibo wrote that the *mestre do campo*, João de Moraes, was the only man with an effective armed force and with authority among the Makua of the mainland (*263*, 279). In 1790 the same João Moraes and his sons are described as 'the terror of these kaffirs and the moors; they know and practise the customs and ways of the kaffirs living in the bush of one of the islands . . . there are chiefs who only sit on their thrones because Moraes has placed them there' (*416*, 123).

When João de Moraes died in 1794 two of his sons competed for the inheritance. The question of the inheritance was referred to Moçambique but meanwhile the issue was settled on the spot by the arrival of the eldest, Calisto de Moraes, in Arimba, where he was received with 'demonstrations of excessive delight', and with all the 'ceremonies practised on the accession of a new chief' (69).

In the early nineteenth century the islands were subjected to a series of raids by the Sacalava of Madagascar who appear to have crossed the Moçambique channel in vast fleets of a thousand or more canoes. In 1807 the Sacalavas surprised the Portuguese settlements and totally destroyed them, but an attack in 1816 was less successful. The invaders suffered severe losses during the sea voyage and as they landed in an exhausted state on Querimba Island they were surprised by a Portuguese detachment sent from Ibo and routed. No survivor of this expedition returned to Madagascar (422, vol 2, 12).

The military honours may have been even but the islands never recovered their prosperity. In 1817 only three of them were reported as having any inhabitants and one of these, Matemo, numbered among its residents a Meneses and a Moraes. Quisiba itself was reported to be deserted in that year, but the Moraes family later returned to it, and in 1829 Domingos Lopes de Moraes was *captão-mor* of Arimba and officially described as 'a man incapable of all and every service . . . for the settlers take no notice of his authority'; not, one may say, like the Moraes of an earlier generation. But perhaps the *sertanejo* tradition was not dead after all, for the same report goes on to say that the Muslim traders were using him as their agent to introduce trade goods into the interior (243).

This book is not primarily concerned with tracing the history of the coastal settlements of Portuguese East Africa, and I will not take the story of the Querimba Islands beyond this point. What I have written illustrates one important part of the story of Portuguese settlement. The Zambesian institution of the *prazos* and their *senhors* was not unique. It existed, recognisably the same, on the Sofala coast and among the Querimba Islands. In the Querimba Islands the Portuguese community was not cut off from the outside world as was that in Zambesia, but the tendency of the Portuguese *senhors* to 'go native' was no less marked.

The important factors determining the nature of colonial society in these areas were the lack of security, the smallness of the Portuguese population, the weakness of the colonial government and the traditional nature of the prevailing economic activities, whether fishing for pearls, slave dealing or plying coastal trade in shallow-draft, lateen-rigged dhows. However, successful as the Portuguese may have been in adapting themselves to local life, one must compare unfavourably the deserted and desolate ruins which were all that remained by 1800, after three hundred years of Portuguese control, with the thriving trading communities of Sofala and the Querimba Islands which had existed at the time of the Portuguese conquest.

13 The Nineteenth Century

The nineteenth century, tumultuous in Europe with the cross-currents of nationalism and liberalism, the emergence of new states, the building of new empires and the all-pervasive power of technology, was quite as tumultuous in Africa. It was the century of Islamic revival and holy war, of the eruption of the Ngoni people throughout the whole of southern Africa, the development of the slave trade and the arrival of the missionaries. It was also the century when modern technology first made its impact, with the spread of firearms in the interior and the appearance of the steamers and railways and telegraphs.

Portuguese Zambesia was not in any condition to withstand these revolutionary tides, which indeed threatened at any moment to inundate it, and, as if these external pressures were not enough, the Portuguese became involved in a bloody and protracted colonial war between the great *prazo* families and the government, a war which spread beyond the historic boundaries of the *prazos* and merged with wider conflicts of late nineteenth-century Africa.

The purpose of this chapter is to describe the development of the external threats to the existence of the Portuguese colony and to indicate some of the main internal developments, so that the more detailed later chapters can appear in some sort of context. The subject which is not developed at all in this book is the international diplomacy of the nineteenth century, for there exist already more than half a dozen detailed studies of the 'scramble for Africa' as it affected this area (e.g. *314, 346, 375, 376, 419, 476*).

Changing patterns of trade

The years 1800 to 1830 saw the twilight of the gold and ivory trade in Zambesia. With the decline of the Marave paramountcy and the weakening of the Marave sub-chieftaincies towards the end of the eighteenth century, three groups of people had moved in to exploit the wealth of central Africa north of the Zambesi. The Portuguese adventurers had opened up the gold workings, the Yao had extended their trading activities to include the whole of the country between Tete, Lake Nyasa and Moçambique Island, while the western interior came increasingly into the orbit of the new state ruled by Mwata Kazembe, whose commerce was carried on by itinerant Bisa traders.

The Portuguese might well have profited by this new development of the interior. Attempts were made to establish regular trade contacts with Kazembe's Lunda, beginning with the expedition of Manuel Pereira in 1796 and persisting for nearly forty years. At one stage a fair was set up on the Luangwa in an attempt to develop the ivory trade; the truth, however, was that the old machinery of the royal monopoly and the cumbersome and costly system by which their trade was organised were pricing the Portuguese out of the market. They were undersold by French and Dutch interlopers and increasingly the Yao travelled northwards to find outlets for their ivory in the region north of Cape Delgado, which was nominally subject to the sultan of Muscat and Oman (*383*).

As early as 1796 Pereira had reported that much of the ivory that had previously come to Moçambique was now being traded northwards. By 1830 the coastal Swahili merchants had already established themselves among the Lunda and the commercial star of Zanzibar was just appearing above the horizon (*363*, vol 2, 119–20). As for the Marave territory where the Portuguese influence now predominated,

> In other times there was great commerce in gold, ivory and cereals, but today there is hardly any, and this results from the same cause [the continual warfare in the area] (*363*, vol 1, 109).

South of the Zambesi trade in gold and ivory continued until the arrival of the Ngoni put an end to the fairs and the passage of the trading caravans. Some time shortly after 1830 the gold trade of central Africa, which may well have supplied ancient Egypt and the Roman empire, dwindled to nothing—though it did revive briefly at the end of the century, shortly before the partitioning of central Africa.

The Portuguese must bear a large part of the blame for the

218

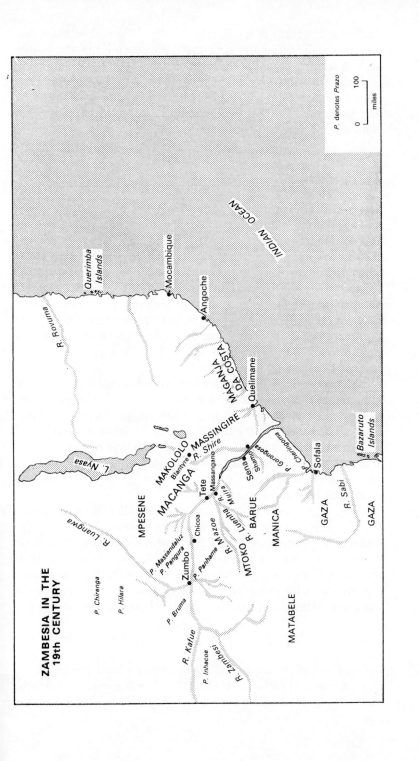

ZAMBESIA IN THE
19th CENTURY

P. denotes Prazo

0   100
  miles

INDIAN OCEAN

Querimba
Islands

Moçambique

Angoche

R. Rovuma

MAGANJA DA COSTA

Quelimane

L. Nyasa

MASSINGIRE

MAKOLOLO

Blantyre

R. Shire

MACANGA

Tete

Massangano

P. Gorongosa

Sena

Shamo

P. Cheringoma

Sofala

Bazaruto
Islands

R. Luangwa

MPESENE

P. Chirenga

P. Hilara

Chicoa

P. Massandaluz

P. Pangura

Zumbo

P. Panhame

R. Mazoe

R. Luenha

R. Muira

MTOKO

BARUE

MANICA

GAZA

R. Sabi

GAZA

R. Kafue

P. Bruma

R. Zambesi

P. Inhacoe

R. Luenpbesi

MATABELE

decline in the trade of the Zambesi valley. The violent behaviour of the Zambesi families and their slaves and the impossibly archaic trading organisation together prevented their competing with their Muslim rivals, but it should also be said that a much more lucrative source of wealth had now become available. The vast profits of the slave trade had by 1830 destroyed any will to continue the search for gold and ivory.

The slave trade

Slaves had always been exported from the Moçambique coast. They had been sold in the traditional markets of the Persian Gulf and the Hadramaut and a few had found their way to India and even to the Far East, but except for a short period in the 1640s when Brazilian plantation owners found their normal supplies of labour cut off by the Dutch occupation of Angola, scarcely one per cent of the Atlantic slave trade came from East Africa. Early in the eighteenth century, however, the French East India Company began its occupation of the Mascarene Islands which were developed as plantations and within a few years the whole scale of the slave trade was transformed.

The first cargoes left Moçambique for Mauritius probably in 1721 and in the early years of the eighteenth century exports may have totalled 1,000 slaves a year (*300*, 88–9). The slaves came from all the main ports of the colony in more or less equal quantities. The judge, Moraes Pereira, who was in the Zambesi area in 1752, recorded that in that year 300 came from Zambesia, 200 came from Sofala, 400 from Inhambane and 200 from the Querimba Islands (*308*, 216–21).

Slaves were taxed like any other commodity at the Moçambique customs house (*377*, 86), and this means that, although statistics are available for the slave trade, they are not likely to be reliable since they can take no account of the smuggling. Between 1780 and 1800 the trade reached its first peak. It appears that exports in those years ran at approximately ten thousand a year, the slaves still coming from the whole length of the coast.

On his journey up the Zambesi Lacerda passed a group of 150 slaves being taken in irons to the coast for sale and was told that the traders ran this particular commerce at a loss. The governor may or may not have believed this rather transparent untruth, but it does seem to have been a fact that the slave trade had not ousted other forms of commerce before the end of the eighteenth century.

The intensification of the war between Britain and revolutionary France led to the blockade of Mauritius by the British and its capture in 1810. Britain had already banned the slave trade and for a short time the Moçambique slave merchants found their best market closed to them.

Not for long, however, for in 1815 the island of Réunion was returned to the French and once again became a plantation colony eager to import slave labour. In the same year Portugal signed the famous 'Equator Treaty' with Britain which outlawed the Portuguese slave trade north of the equator. The Congo and Angola still remained as a source of slaves for the American plantations but, as Britain's war on the slavers intensified and the 'equipment' clauses were added to the previous treaties, enabling slavers to be arrested simply for carrying slave-trading gear, the Cuban and Brazilian slavers turned increasingly for their supplies to Eastern Africa where the British cruisers were far less active.

From 1815 to 1830 10,000 slaves left Moçambique annually for Brazil and a further 7,000 for the French Indian Ocean islands. By 1830 Quelimane had probably become the most important single slaving port in Africa. 2,550 slaves left the river annually between 1815 and 1820, and this number rose to 4,000 in the 1820s and may have reached as high as 10,000 in individual years (374, 227-8).

After 1830 the official slave trade was increasingly interrupted, and in 1836 a decree from Lisbon banned all slaving within the Portuguese dominions. The governor of Moçambique refused to enforce this decree, and it was this open defiance by the governor of one of the colonial territories, as much as anything else, which led Lord Palmerston to present to the British parliament in 1839 a bill authorising the arrest of suspected slavers even if they were flying Portuguese colours. Eventually in 1842 the Portuguese government authorised British ships to stop and search suspects and from that time one should date the official abolition of the slave trade in Moçambique.

By this time, however, the slave merchants had become a powerful group in Moçambique. There is evidence that they wanted to declare themselves independent of Portugal and throw in their lot with Brazil when she established her independence in 1825. They continued systematically to obstruct the work of the authorities in suppressing the trade and, as the demand for slaves did not fall off and their price continued to rise with the risks involved, the slave trade continued to dominate the commercial life of the colony. Slaves were still being exported from Moçambique in the late 1880s.

The effects of the official ban and the spasmodic attempts to enforce it were threefold. In the first place, slavers were driven from the official ports to the creeks and off-shore islands which abounded along the east African coast. This brought sudden and immense prosperity to the small Islamic communities which had existed there since before the Portuguese conquest. For the most part these were difficult of access for cruisers and gunboats and the sheikhs and rulers of the coast with their connections in Zanzibar and Madagascar were able to run a lucrative contraband trade. In the fifteenth century when the first rulers of Portuguese India had tried to enforce a trade monopoly, the sultanate of Angoche had grown up as the principal port of the illegal Muslim traders, and for a short time had seriously threatened the Portuguese position on the coast. However, by the seventeenth century the Portuguese blockade and the turbulance of the Makua and Marave peoples in the hinterland had reduced it to a small and insignificant village. In the eighteenth century Angoche was sacked and destroyed by the Makua and the sultanate only survived under Portuguese protection. The nineteenth-century slave trade revived dramatically the fortunes of this tiny Islamic community, and it rapidly became a considerable power on the coast and, under the leadership of a remarkable Muslim revivalist called Mussa Quantu, began to threaten Portuguese interests on the Shire and even on the lower Zambesi (*397*).

The second effect of the official ban on the slave trade was to stimulate the trading of slaves within Africa. It is probable that this internal trade would have developed anyway, for the markets which it fed were African markets and the demand arose from purely African developments. Nevertheless, there were great advantages in trading away from the hostile gaze of the British and Portuguese gunboats. It took Europeans a long time to realise the extent of this internal slave trade and when they did realise it, they were provided with an ideal excuse for intervention in African affairs and the enlargement of their empires. More than anything else it was the *mfecane*—the dispersal of Ngoni peoples and the growth of new Ngoni states—that really provided the opportunities for the Portuguese to develop their trade in slaves.

The third result of the official restrictions on the slave trade was to alter the relationship of the great *prazo*-holders with the government and with their own followers. Hitherto the Zambesi clans had had an interest in seeing the Portuguese rule maintained on the Zambesi, and the Portuguese authorities had fostered a slave-owning society. But before the nineteenth century was ended many of them had broken with their European connections and sought their salvation in fighting the expansion of European imperialism which they rightly saw as fundamentally hostile to their social order and way of life.

The Ngoni

In 1832 the captain of Manica wrote to the governor-general that two years earlier a band of warriors had appeared in the Manica highlands; they had raided cattle and departed. In May 1832 they had returned, this time in three divisions, and had sacked the Portuguese fair and had again gone away (*111*). These records of the *capitão-mor* of Manica read much like the Anglo-Saxon chronicler's record of the first Viking attacks on Holy Island, and they gave warning of events as portentous.

The dispersal of the Ngoni peoples of Natal had begun as early as 1819. In 1821 the first Ngoni appeared near Lourenço Marques; they crossed the Limpopo and in 1824 were in the neighbourhood of Inhambane. They crossed the Sabi probably in 1826 and in 1830 appeared simultaneously in Manica and in the hinterland of Sofala. These early raiders the Portuguese called *Mazitis*—a name which may have derived from the chief of the Ndwandwe, Zwide (*388*, 47).

The earliest Ngoni groups to migrate northwards were led by three Ngoni chiefs, Ngwana, Nqaba and Zwangendaba. Ngwana's *impis* were the first to push into Rhodesia and attack the Roswi kingdom of Changamire to the south. Ngwana died and his people, led by his brother Magdlela, fled eastwards before the advance of Zwangendaba, who was the second to invade Rhodesia. Nqaba meanwhile had pushed north-east from Natal into southern Moçambique, and it was his advance which was chronicled by the Portuguese coastal commanders. It was probably his *impis* which attacked Manica in 1830. Some time before 1835 Nqaba and Zwangendaba clashed and Zwangendaba's people were driven north across the Zambesi in 1835. Nqaba followed in 1839 or 1840, for his triumph had been short-lived and his generals had been defeated by a fourth Ngoni group pushing up from the south led by Soshangane—or Manicusse as he later was called. Nqaba's men appear to have skirted Portuguese territory and headed for the upper Zambesi where the group disintegrated. Magdlela's men, who had fought with Nqaba in his battles with Zwangendaba and Soshangane, crossed the Zambesi also in 1839 and headed northwards (*388*, 48–9).

By 1840 the initial storm had passed. The chieftaincies on the Portuguese borders had probably suffered more than the Portuguese themselves from the visitation. Barue had been occupied for five years by Magdlela's men, Quiteve and Quissanga had both been overrun and it is probable that the historic Manyika dynasty of Chicanga was also a casualty of these raids, for at this time it gives place to the new dynasty of Mutassa. In 1835 the Portuguese had discontinued the official fair at Manica which they were no longer able to defend. Although traders still went to the gold regions and traded, there was no *capitão-mor* and no official Portuguese garrison.

Four years' respite was all the Portuguese obtained, however, for in 1844 began the periodic visits of *impis* sent from south of the Sabi by Manicusse, king of the Gaza Ngoni. Year by year at the end of the rains they arrived in Gorongosa, split up and sent parties to Sena, Chupanga and the delta area to collect tribute. This tribute was paid both by the Portuguese and the African *colonos*, although the Portuguese tried to claim that they were only giving presents of friendship and were not recognising the overlordship of Manicusse.

The impact of the Ngoni on the Portuguese settlements of the lower Zambesi helped to accelerate the trend towards absenteeism among the settlers. Fewer and fewer Portuguese or holders of *prazos* could be found to reside in the Rivers, which in consequence became seriously depleted of population. Otherwise the impact was mostly felt by the *colonos* who lived south of the Rivers. These wretched and undefended groups were now open to the dual exploitation of the Gaza *impis* and the Portuguese slave bands. In 1827, following a plague of locusts, the Zambesi had experienced five or six years of disastrous famine, made worse by drought (*363*, vol 1, 174, *160*), so that, driven to desperation by the Ngoni raids and the fear of starvation, the *colonos* and even many of the slaves began crossing the Zambesi and taking refuge in the Quelimane *prazos* of the delta where the Zambesi protected them from Gaza warriors. This accession of population may have aided the slavers operating in the delta and to the north of it, but it also provided the basis for the economic development of the delta area which began in the second half of the century.

This disordered situation favoured the one or two powerful *senhors*, like the Ferroës of Sena or Galdino Faustino de Sousa with his base on the Shire, who were able to provide protection for the harassed population. The small man was rapidly eliminated and there took place a concentration of power such as had not existed since the seventeenth century. The fortunes of the chiefs of these few families are the subject of the following chapters.

The Portuguese had contacts of importance with other Ngoni groups. After Zwangendaba had crossed the Zambesi he led his nation northwards almost to the shores of Lake Victoria. There he died about 1845 and his people split up. One group, led by his son Mpeseni, began the return to the south, settling eventually in the Fort Jameson region of Zambia, but raiding southwards for loot and captives almost to the Zambesi.

A second group with whom the Portuguese had contacts were the Matabele. Led by Msilikatse, chief of the Khumalo, this group had halted first in the Transvaal whence they were driven by the Boer trekkers. They tried to cross Rhodesia and gain the Zambian highlands beyond the Zambesi, but eventually settled in the southern part of Rhodesia with their capital at Bulawayo. Their raiding area extended to Zumbo in the north and seems to have reached the foothills of the Manica mountains in the east. Until the 1880s their contact with the Portuguese was very friendly. Like all the Ngoni groups the Matabele increased their numbers by taking and absorbing captives from conquered peoples. The Portuguese were eager and able to sell them slaves —particularly women captured north of the Zambesi. It was Livingstone who first drew the attention of British people to the extent of this purely internal traffic which evaded the cruisers and the diplomatic sanctions so elaborately deployed to stop the sea-borne slave trade (*390*, 406).

Zumbo was also the point of meeting between the Portuguese and the Makololo. The Makololo too were casualties of the Ngoni expansion. Sotho-speaking people from the high veldt, they had been displaced by the Zulu king Shaka, and, after epic adventures under the leadership of Sebituane, they had conquered the Losi of the Barotse flood-plain and established themselves in the country as a ruling class.

Although the Makololo were overthrown in a rebellion of their subject peoples in 1868, the strong kingdom they had created survived and was another market which the Portuguese could exploit by selling slaves and firearms.

The coming of the Ngoni therefore encouraged the growth and concentration of the power of the great *prazo senhors* at the expense of legitimate trade and peaceful peasant agriculture. It provided markets for slaves and so made sure that the slave trade would survive the British blockade unimpaired. Finally, it weakened the prestige and power of the Portuguese government and reduced its authority almost to the point where this commodity, scarce at all times, vanished altogether.

The aringa system

One of the results of the disorders following the Ngoni raids was the building of the great *aringas*, the fortified strongholds of the Zambesi *senhors*. As the disorder spread and more and more of the *prazos* were deserted, so power fell into the hands of the slave bands of a very small number of men whose power ceased to depend on the holding of specific *prazos*, though these continued to be granted. Instead, the Portuguese authorities resorted to giving a local strong man the office of *capitão-mor*, investing him with judicial and administrative authority over a large area.

These men thus became the effective rulers of areas of land much larger than the old *prazos* and their slave armies were supplied with firearms by the government. Generation by generation they became darker in colour and increasingly fell under the influence of the leaders of their slave *ensacas* who came to form a council of elders—or *grandes*. Succession to the head of the family no longer bore any relation to the provisions of Portuguese law but became long drawn out struggles between close relatives of the former chief who were backed by different factions among the slaves. Once established in power, the head of the family was expected to rule in a manner congenial to the slave captains.

The heads of these dynasties still tried to obtain some sort of recognition from the Portuguese authorities—some sort of legitimacy within the framework of European society. They maintained, with an increasing lack of success, a façade of Catholic observance, donating money from time to time to the church and encouraging the visit of a priest to do some baptising among the children of their concubines. They continued to seek the title of *capitão-mor* and to wear with pride the uniforms of the Portuguese colonial militia. They still continued to speak, and in a few cases to write, Portuguese and sent some of their children for education in some centre of Portuguese civilisation. For the most part, however, they sought legitimacy in their role as chiefs and in particular in their communication with the spirits of their ancestors.

The *aringa* was the fortified base from which the *senhor* and his slaves operated. According to Antonio Porfirio Miranda, Joaquim José da Cruz was the first to build an *aringa* in Zambesia, but he cannot have started the construction of Massangano before 1849 and already in 1843 Lieutenant Frederick Barnard was able to describe the construction of an *aringa* near Quelimane (*407*, 15–16, *317*). No innovation spreads more rapidly than a military one, and by the 1850s the Zambesi valley was studded with *aringas* large and small.

Aringas were not, however, new in Zambesia; they were simply larger and more elaborate versions of a type of building that had been in existence for centuries. The Tonga and Shona peoples surrounded their villages with fences and sometimes these fences, when made of heavy wood, have very much the appearance of a fortification. As early as the seventeenth century the Portuguese had learnt that if green posts are put in when the ground is moist they will root and form living trees. The Portuguese fairs in Mashonaland were made in this way in the seventeenth century, but they were very small, with sides scarcely a hundred yards long, and most of the Portuguese lived outside them.

The *mussitos* or fortified villages of the seventeenth and eighteenth centuries were clearly an advance in the direction of the *aringa*. The technique of making a wall of living trees gave them an immunity to fire and to firearms normally lacking in African systems of defence. Portuguese expeditions against the *mussitos* contained an advance party of axemen who had to cut a breach into the stockade. There are, however, few indications of the size of the *mussitos*.

The *aringa*, which was developed in response to the disordered conditions of the nineteenth century, was a very much enlarged version of the fortified village of a chief. It might well be a mile in circumference and would contain all the huts of the *senhor*'s principal followers and their wives. An *aringa* would thus house many hundreds and even thousands of people and would attain the dimensions of a considerable town. It would usually be built on a river bank, partly out of the need for a secure supply of water, but partly also because of the possibilities of piracy on the boats passing up and down. Within the *aringa* would be a walled enclosure where the *senhor* and his family lived apart. This might be built of stone and would certainly reflect a European style of comfort.

Most *aringas* were defended by redoubts and bastions reinforced with stone-work. These were used to mount the artillery which most *senhors* seemed able to secure. In time of siege an *aringa* could hold out almost indefinitely. Livestock were stabled and even pastured inside the walls, while the stockades made of living trees easily defied such small calibre guns as could be dragged through the bush and brought to bear against them (*415*).

As the century wore on *aringas* became larger and more elaborate. The great *aringa* of Maganja da Costa, which surrendered to the Portuguese in 1897, was so large that six thousand men were able to bivouac inside it in comfort (*342*, *468*). The chief *aringa* belonging to a *senhor* was usually protected by smaller *aringas* guarding the boundaries of his territory and the approaches to his headquarters. These were supposed to hold up any hostile force but served also to keep the local population loyal to the *senhor*.

The establishment of *aringas* spread outside Portuguese territory and was adopted in Barue by the royal house and the Barue aristocracy, though there they were more usually referred to as *gutas*. When Carl Peters visited the last independent Macombe of Barue in 1900 he described what was probably the last great *aringa* still in occupation. Its ruins can still be seen by the curious traveller a few yards off the dirt road which leads from the Rhodesian border to Tambara on the banks of the Muira river. The closely-packed lines of trees grow where the green stakes of the stockade have taken root, and round the bases can be seen piles of stone rubble that once formed a strengthening to the defences. It is to be hoped that one day these historic relics, and the many other remains in the Zambesi valley will be properly explored and protected by a government which values the history and traditions of the country (*429*).

The creation of the *aringa* was an impressive response to the disorder and anarchy which had overtaken the colony; it served to concentrate economic activity in a way which must have led to considerable economic development; it contributed, as I shall describe in later chapters, to the development of interesting social and governmental forms. However, it is chiefly as a military

228

device that it deserves admiration. Students of South African history know of the failure of Zulus and Matabele to adapt their fighting techniques to the new technology of firearms; they also know how small numbers of Boers or Griquas could use the laager of waggons to protect themselves against vastly superior hostile forces. In Zambesia it was the Africans who developed the arts of defensive warfare and were able to resist the European armies sent against them.

The arrival of the Scots

As if the visitations of the Ngoni warriors were not retribution enough for the sins of the Portuguese colonials, in 1856 the invasion of Scottish missionaries began.

By this time Zambesia had already experienced nearly ten years of sporadic warfare between the government and the *prazo* interests. This sordid story of intrigue, corruption, murder and looting, regulated only by the mysterious balances and codes of conduct observed by the *muzungos* and their mercenaries, might have continued for decades unknown to the outside world. However, in 1856 Dr Livingstone arrived in the Rivers colony, a lone white man, tattered and exhausted and accompanied by a party of Africans from Barotseland who called themselves Makololo. Livingstone was hospitably received by the Portuguese who aided him on his way to England, allowing his African followers to settle at Tete to await his return. A cloud no bigger than a man's hand had gathered on the horizon of Portugal's Zambesian monopoly.

In 1858 Livingstone returned. He was equipped with letters of introduction and the rank of H.M. Consul. He brought with him a steamer and eight companions. Three of the party, Kirk, Thornton and David Livingstone, kept diaries and a fourth, Thomas Baines, painted a series of water colour sketches of river life. In 1861 the group was joined by a party of Anglican clergymen led by Bishop Mackenzie, and in 1862 a party of women arrived to join the mission, accompanied by officers and men from the cruiser H.M.S. *Gorgon*, and by James Stewart, a missionary prospector from the Free Church of Scotland. In 1863 a further church party, led by Bishop Tozer, made a brief appearance. Suddenly the Zambesi scene was illuminated by dozens of letters, diaries, memoranda, apologia and missionary tracts, aided and abetted by water colours and photographs—all the product of the vigorous minds of that energetic generation of Victorians, whose attitudes and way of life present a complete antithesis to those of the slothful and easy-going Portuguese colonials.

Of all the British who made up this minor invasion, only Richard Thornton, the young geologist who accompanied Livingstone, can be said to have been really friendly and sympathetic towards the Portuguese, for what high-minded Scots Presbyterians and university-trained Oxford Movement men must have thought of the Portuguese can easily be imagined. They wrote with horror of the slave trade, the material decadence and the sexual immorality of the colony. Kirk's diaries, only recently published, give medical information which shows well enough why the white community in Zambesia was not able to reproduce itself (*380*, *443*).

Livingstone, it is true, wrote in his published account of the expedition with a certain humour and with some of the broad tolerance and knowledge of Africa required to understand Zambesi society, but he had no reason to love the Portuguese *prazo senhors*, some of his Makololo companions having been brutally murdered by Antonio Vicente da Cruz at Massangano when they had gone there as a dancing group. But it is to Livingstone that we owe some of the most perceptive accounts of the degree to which the Portuguese had been influenced by their African environment.

Livingstone and the missionaries had all left by 1864, and for another ten years Zambesia remained unchanged and very much as if this visitation from the outside world had never taken place. It was during this decade that the Zambesi Wars reached their first grim climax in the disastrous Portuguese expeditions against Massangano in 1868–9, and that the authority of the Portuguese government came nearest to total disintegration. There were, however, now large rents in the curtain which had obscured the doings of the Zambesi *senhors* from the outside world and there were reformers of a liberal stamp in Lisbon determined to revive Portuguese imperial fortunes. The 1850s saw the first legislation designed to restructure the land law of the colony and the first measures which began to end the status of slavery in the Portuguese colonies—changing the slave into the *liberto* or freed man. Neither of these measures of reform could be enforced on the middle Zambesi, but they could be and were increasingly made effective near Quelimane and along the coast. (See chap 19)

In 1874 the Rivers came once again under international scrutiny. The British government re-established their consulate in that year, reviving Lyons McLeod's disastrous attempt to found a consulate which had been summarily ended by the slaving interests in 1858.

Consul Elton, the first man to occupy the post, was well-versed in the East African slave trade and its ways. He set about his tasks with great energy and soon revealed the extent of the slave trade which still flourished around Lake Nyasa and which found outlets on the Moçambique coast. He died while trying to track down the inland sources of the slave trade in 1878.

His successor, Henry O'Neill, also travelled widely in East Africa, arousing great anxieties among the Portuguese authorities when he visited areas nominally subject to Moçambique, but never effectively controlled by them. His reports to the Foreign Office and the Royal Geographical Society made clear the complete lack of any Portuguese presence between their coastal forts.

However, it was not the British consuls, with their notoriously tender consciences about other people's misdeeds, who most worried the Portuguese. It was the Scottish missions. These missions had been the fruits of James Stewart's preliminary survey in 1862. They had been set up after Livingstone's death as a fitting memorial to the great Scotsman and in 1875 they had established themselves in the Shire Highlands and on the shores of Lake Nyasa. The missions were supplied and assisted by the African Lakes Company—a commercial undertaking linked to the missions but with an entirely separate status. This company was the first serious threat to Portugal's trade monopoly in the Zambesi valley.

The missions were also aided by Livingstone's Makololo, some of whom had settled on the Shire river below the Murchison Cataracts and had built up chieftaincies in the same way as the Portuguese *prazo senhors*—by raiding and harrying those who did not submit to their 'protection'.

The Scots missions were not only a permanent irritation to the Portuguese, they were also a stimulant. Zambesia could now no longer be neglected. International obligations compelled the Portuguese to keep open trade routes, guarantee security of travellers, control firearms and slaving, and provide a minimum of government services—and all under the sceptical gaze of Scottish missionaries and British consuls and vice-consuls.

The Scottish missions were eventually to drag the whole future of Zambesia into the arena of international diplomacy, linking it with the future of the Congo after 1877 and with the future of the Mashonaland high veldt after the Rudd Concession in 1888, until eventually Britain and Portugal were brought to the verge of war early in 1890.

It is quite wrong, however, to see the partitioning of Zambesia and the revival of the fortunes of the Portuguese colony as entirely due to foreign pressures. In Portugal itself, after the military fiascos of the 1860s, there was a growing body of outraged opinion, ashamed of the neglect of past centuries and anxious that Portugal's empire should prove the salvation of the mother country, which had fallen so far behind the rest of Europe in industrialisation.

In 1875 the Lisbon Geographical Society was founded to bring together all those who were demanding a progressive policy in Africa, and partly under the sponsorship of this body a whole generation of energetic and able explorers, scientists and soldier-administrators went to Africa. The most important of these activists in the history of Zambesia was without doubt Joaquim Carlos Paiva de Andrada, a pioneer company promoter with a military background, ideal qualifications at this period for a budding imperialist. Andrada was the Portuguese Rhodes, without Rhodes's wealth. He had energy and vision and when his schemes came to partial fruition with the founding of the Moçambique Company in 1888 he had succeeded in forging the first substantial links between Zambesia and the forts and factories along the coast. For the first time Moçambique ceased to be a string of ports each with its hinterland and became an embryo of a modern state.

Andrada came from the outside world, from the Portuguese army and diplomatic corps and he was always a stranger in the Rivers. Zambesia, however, did at this period produce two pioneers of its own—men who can fittingly be placed alongside the other great figures of the 'heroic age' of European imperialism. The first of these was João Bonifacio Alves da Silva, who in 1862 led an expedition raised on the *prazos* to destroy the sultanate of Angoche. He died in the moment of victory, but for a short time it seemed that the coast north of the Zambesi might be conquered for Portugal by the Zambesi *senhors*. (See chap 16) The other figure was Manuel Antonio de Sousa, who came from Goa in the 1840s and made his way trading in the southern interior until he was granted the great *prazo* of Gorongosa. By 1880 he had become strong enough to conquer Barue and from then until 1890 he was the most powerful figure in Zambesia. His ambitions certainly extended to an attempted conquest of Mashonaland, and the fact that he was unable to carry out these

232

plans had little to do with Rhodes or the British government, but was simply the result of the internal politics of Zambesia at this time.

The partition of Africa and the ultimatum of 1890 which forced the Portuguese to acquiesce in a settlement dictated by Britain was partly a crisis of world events closing in on Zambesia and was partly stimulated by the direct action of outsiders like the Scottish missionaries and the company promoters in Africa, but still more it was precipitated by a crisis in the politics of Zambesia—the final stages of the Zambesi Wars which had been going on for forty years and whose roots lay deep in the early days of Portuguese empire in this region. The remaining part of this book will be concerned with the Zambesi Wars and their consequences.

14   The Pereiras of Macanga

Of all Portuguese families in nineteenth century Zambesia the Pereiras of Macanga had the most extraordinary history. Not until 1902 was Macanga 'pacified' and brought fully under Portuguese administration, after nearly seventy years of existence as a state of slave and ivory hunters ruled by its Pereira chiefs.

The power of the Pereiras had its origin in the eighteenth century when gold-prospectors and adventurers were beginning successfully to exploit the small Marave chieftaincies north of Tete. Of these gold-prospectors none was more active than Gonçalo Caetano Pereira, a man of Indian origin, who had come to eastern Africa from Goa about 1760. When the Pereiras had become legendary figures at the end of the nineteenth century numerous tales were told about them, and one of these explains something of Gonçalo's success in the goldfields.

There was a Marave chief called Nhanja who fled to the protection of chief Mocanda of the Cewa. Mocanda gave him land at Missale and Nhanja was fortunate enough soon after-wards to discover gold. He sold this to the Portuguese through the offices of a Tete merchant called Rodrigues. Gonçalo Pereira heard of the strike and claimed that Nhanja was his subject. At gunpoint he seized the gold-diggings and persuaded Rodrigues to keep his distance.

This story might equally apply to any of the first three Pereiras, for they are inextricably entangled in the folk-tales of Zambesia (*478*, [1892], 373–5).

Gonçalo never acquired a *prazo*, and it is a peculiarity of the story of the Pereiras that they never held legal title to any *prazo* even when they had come to dominate the whole north bank of the Zambesi from the Shire to Zumbo. They started as traders and gold-prospectors and, until the chieftaincy of Macanga was firmly established, this remained the principal source of their wealth.

Gonçalo was called by the Africans Dombo Dombo—the
234

terror—a name which perhaps indicates something of his methods in pushing his commercial undertakings (*383*, *384*). Legend has it that he supplied firearms to Azimba dissidents in rebellion against the declining power of the chieftaincy of Undi. This gave him an extensive following among the Azimba which he strengthened with ties of blood. Like many of the *sertanejos*, Gonçalo married widely and he seems to have established some connection with the chiefly house of Chicucuru.

Chief Chicucuru is occasionally mentioned in eighteenth-century documents and he was well known to the Portuguese. His territory lay along the Revubwe river which enters the Zambesi opposite Tete and which was known to be gold-bearing. The chieftaincy of Chicucuru was to become the heart of the future state of Macanga.

In 1790 Gonçalo opened the gold diggings at Java, five days' journey north of Tete, and it was there in 1793 that Bisa traders came to him and made the first overtures for trade between the Portuguese and Kazembe's Lunda.

Ever anxious to extend his trading empire, Gonçalo sent two expeditions carrying trade goods into the interior, and then in 1796 sent a third party, led by his son Manuel, which reached the court of Kazembe itself. It was the report of this expedition that led Francisco de Lacerda to undertake his famous journey into the interior in 1798. Gonçalo Pereira accompanied Lacerda on this journey and received the title of *capitão-mor* of Mixonga —one of the goldfields—in recognition of the power he already wielded in the interior and as a reward for his co-operation with the expedition (*385*).

Of Gonçalo Caetano Pereira's children three at least are well known; Francisca Pereira, who married a *prazo*-holder called Candido José Cardoso (*94*), Manuel and Pedro. Manuel was the eldest son and had been the pioneer of Portuguese trade with Kazembe. He inherited his father's interests in the gold-fields and his title of *capitão-mor*, and for the first three decades of the nineteenth century was the most influential man north of the Zambesi. He organised and led a number of Portuguese trading expeditions to the interior and commanded the levies on various military enterprises against those of the Marave chiefs who still tried to maintain their independence from the Portuguese. He was also asked to escort the military detachment which was sent to found the fair at Marambo on the Luangwa river in 1827 (*238*).

A letter has survived written by Manuel to his brother Pedro which explains something of the life of the *sertanejo*. The letter is dated 1824 and is an apology from Manuel for not joining his brother in a campaign against chief Bive, on which they had agreed when trading together in Bisa country. His slaves, he explains, are all ill with the small-pox and the season is far advanced and they have to see to the cultivation of their gardens to produce the food for next year (*102*).

Manuel always maintained a close contact with the Portuguese and it may be that he retired from the life of a *sertanejo*, leaving his brother to lord it in the interior, while he sought the comparative quiet of the Zambesi towns. At any rate there are letters about a certain Manuel Caetano Pereira asking leave to settle in Quelimane in 1844 and petitioning for the militia rank of major (*163*).

Manuel's brother Pedro held the rank of captain in the Tete militia but lived most of his life away from the Portuguese settlements deep in the interior. José Correa Monteiro, who commanded the expedition to Kazembe's country in 1831, described him as:

living like the kaffirs and chiefs, not only going about clothed like them but even resembling them in their customs and superstitions . . . a man who has entirely forgotten his religion and follows that of the kaffirs (*209*).

Having tried unsuccessfully to obtain his help for the expedition Gamitto, the second-in-command, describes him as an illiterate who had such a superstitious dread of letters that he would not even handle them and who lived over a hundred leagues from Tete in the interior.

Pedro, however, had not always been so unco-operative. In 1825 he had been commissioned by the authorities to negotiate for land on the Luangwa River on which to build the proposed new fair of Marambo (*236*). Once having undertaken this task Pedro found he was expected to remain and defend Marambo with his own men, although he received no pay. At one time it was proposed to make him the second-in-command and give him pay but this plan was never realised (*238*). Then, when the Portuguese detachment withdrew after their disastrous stay, Pedro was entrusted with the care of Portuguese property left behind. Perhaps it was his experiences with the Luangwa fair that made him wary of becoming involved with the Monteiro expedition to Kazembe.

Pedro Caetano Pereira was generally known as Choutama (or

Shavatama) and it was probably he who was the first of the Pereiras to hold the chieftaincy of Chicucuru in his own right. One cannot be more certain because, although nineteenth-century writers agree that it was the second Pereira who became Chicucuru, they usually confuse Pedro and his father Gonçalo when they come to the naming of the first of the Pereiras (*339, 323, 340, 515, 356, 213*). Portuguese documents often refer to Pedro and his successors as rulers of Macanga. The name Macanga was taken from a prominent range of hills north of Tete and was used to describe the state established by the Pereiras on the Revubwe river.

Raids carried out by Choutama on his enemies began the era of the Zambesi Wars. Filipe Almeida de Eça, the historian of these wars, dates the beginning of this epic story to 1840 when Choutama attacked and defeated chief Bive, driving him to seek the protection of the Portuguese in Tete. The Portuguese sent a force against Choutama in May 1841, but it was routed and a stronger force had to be assembled. This was drawn from all the Rivers settlements and was armed with light artillery. It invaded Macanga in 1843 and forced Choutama to sue for peace. Macanga was not yet strong enough to defy the government, though its time was coming.

Choutama now avoided open conflict with the Portuguese but proceeded to close the trade routes from the Zambesi to the interior, where (*299*, vol 1, 249–52), since early in the century, he and his brother Manuel had been building their trading empire. Like their counterparts on the great trade routes from Zanzibar to the African lakes they dealt in firearms, slaves and ivory both with the Portuguese on the Zambesi and the Swahili of Lake Nyasa and Kilwa. Their monopoly position in Marave country grew until all the Portuguese *prazos* and independent chieftaincies from the Shire to the Luangwa were under their sway. Chief Bive himself was eventually to become tributary to them after he had been robbed of his land by the repeated wars which the Pereiras waged against him (*339, 326*).

Choutama had not reopened hostilities when, to use Almeida de Eça's phrase, 'he gave up his soul to the devil' in 1849 (*299*, vol 1, 252). He was succeeded by his son, another Pedro, who is usually known by his African name Chissaka.

Choutama had died, so Chissaka chose to believe, after drinking gin sent to him by an Indian called Francisco Xavier who was related by marriage to the head of the rival da Cruz family. Choutama may in fact have died after a bout of gin-

237

drinking, but his son saw his death as a case of witchcraft and murder and demanded that Xavier and Joaquim da Cruz be handed over to him for punishment.

Meanwhile Choutama's slaves carried out the obsequies of the dead chief, observing the hallowed custom of *choriro*—making the people weep for the departed—and what better way of making them weep than by visiting the villages and settlements of the Tete district with fire and sword? (*334*, 30) Six or seven hundred warriors descended on the Tete *prazos*, seeking out in particular those belonging to Joaquim's aunt Eugenia Maria da Cruz. Chissaka would probably have crossed the River and raided Tete itself if a detachment of troops had not been sent to remove the canoes which had been gathered for the invasion (*299*, vol 1, 256).

In July and August 1849, at the height of the dry season, the government tried to counter-attack and drive the invaders from the north bank *prazos*. They relied heavily on help promised to them by Chief Chibisa, but during the vital engagement Chibisa's men fled the field and the Portuguese suffered another defeat, losing their field guns (*299*, vol 1, 258). Later in the year Tito Augusto de Araujo Sicard was made military commander in Tete and at the beginning of the rains he and Chissaka reached an agreement to suspend hostilities.

Three years passed before warfare flared up again. In the meantime, Chissaka publicly offered a reward of two hundred *arrobas* of ivory (about 6,400 lbs) to the man who would kill Joaquim da Cruz, but no one took up the offer. Gamitto thought that indirectly this reward helped to raise the prestige of Joaquim and contributed to the rise of his power (*297*).

During the dry season of 1853 Chissaka crossed the Zambesi below Tete and joined forces with Macombe, chief of Barue, to attack the da Cruz *aringa* at Massangano. Four thousand warriors—six hundred of them equipped with firearms—laid siege to Massangano from June to October. The Portuguese authorities maintained an uneasy neutrality, supplying firearms to neither side and expecting that at any moment the victor would avenge himself with a raid on the Tete settlements. With the beginning of the rains, however, Chissaka's and Macombe's armies disintegrated, destroyed by famine and disease. Chissaka recrossed the Zambesi and retired to the heart of Macanga. He sent a contingent to help the Portuguese expeditions against Massangano in 1854 and 1855, but never renewed the conflict with the da Cruz himself.

Instead, he threw himself wholeheartedly into exploiting the slave and ivory trades. As Livingstone descended the Zambesi in 1856 at the end of his epic journey across Africa he heard stories of the doings of Chissaka which he recorded in his journals. Having commented on the activities of the da Cruz on the right bank of the Zambesi he writes: 'Kisaka continues the same system of plundering on the side of the Maganjas, preventing all trade, as he says he has conquered that country, all belongs to him' (*392*, vol 2, 460). Further down the river he met Chissaka's men, who had crossed to Sena to sell slaves and were being regaled by João de Conceição, a relative of the Pereiras. The slaves had been three days without food and the sale was not going well. None of the merchants considered the trade immoral but Livingstone did discover that some of them had misgivings about the large quantities of arms and powder that were finding their way into Chissaka's hands (*392*, vol 2, 469–70).

Chissaka's wars cannot be simply dismissed as meaningless clashes between rival bands of mercenaries and bandits, although from Almeida de Eça's history one gets little interpretation. For Chissaka the Portuguese historian has a string of opprobrious epithets—'unrepentant highwayman', 'barbarous robber', 'confessed enemy of Portuguese authority', 'desolator of the *prazos*', 'fierce assassin', 'traitor' (*299*, vol 1, 291). The alliance between Chissaka and Macombe suggests nothing to him and the projected raid of Chissaka on Sena also appears as nothing but banditry.

However, to understand Chissaka's wars and the subsequent wars of the da Cruz and the Vas dos Anjos families—even to understand the events leading up to the British ultimatum to Portugal in 1890—one must see the pattern of political alliance and interest which united and divided the potentates of the region. The Pereiras were engaged in an extensive slave and ivory trade north of the Zambesi, supplying the caravans of the Yao and the Bisa on their way to Lake Nyasa and the Swahili coast. They controlled the whole of northern Zambesia from the Shire to the Luangwa even though the territory of Macanga itself was quite small. Any attempts by other Portuguese interests to penetrate this region were severely discouraged and traders might be robbed of their ivory on Chissaka's orders as far afield as Zumbo (*299*, vol 1, 282).

Chissaka felt himself threatened from two quarters. First the Shire route was never firmly in his grasp. Along the river there existed the remnant of the chieftaincies of the eastern Marave among whom Chibisa appears to have maintained some power.

It was Chibisa who united with the Portuguese in 1849 against Chissaka. Further down the Shire was the base of Galdino Faustino de Sousa, a powerful Portuguese slaver and the father-in-law of Paul Marianno Vas dos Anjos. When in 1853 Chissaka detached some of his men from the siege of Massangano to attack Sena, his objective was probably to strike at the growing power of Sousa in the region.

Secondly, Chissaka was threatened by Joaquim da Cruz in his stronghold at Massangano, as indeed were all the other Portuguese of Tete. The da Cruz had been established at Massangano since 1849 but through their extensive family connections they also controlled about a dozen *prazos* on the north bank. Chissaka felt that the whole Portuguese community was becoming enmeshed in the web of the da Cruz interests. The Macombe of Barue must also have felt threatened by the increasing power of the da Cruz on his very doorstep, and the military alliance of Macombe and Chissaka admirably suited the interests of both potentates.

At each stage the shifting alliances and interests of the Zambesi *senhors* must be followed before the surface turmoil of the wars of the nineteenth century will make any sense.

Chissaka died in 1858, his power still unchallenged north of the Zambesi. Livingstone records how he could make his strength felt as far distant as Kariba and how he recruited some of the Batonga from above Kariba for his army of retainers (*390*, 230), and could close the roads from Tete to the Shire at will.

Like his father and grandfather before him, Chissaka became a legend in Zambesia. The German adventurer Carl Wiese records the tradition of Chissaka's death. While on a raid against the Pimbe people near Zumbo, Chissaka found his army held up by the fortified stronghold of chief Chaguaniqueira. He built a camp and awaited reinforcements. His enemy, however, outdid him in cunning and found a witch-doctor to send a swarm of flies which routed the Macanga warriors. Chissaka died in the flight and his body was carried back to Macanga (*478* [1891], 385).

Chissaka's immediate successors are at best shadowy individuals. It is not entirely clear in which order they ruled and genealogies of the family list other still more shadowy Pereiras who may have been regents or co-rulers. The succession to Chissaka may, as Livingstone suggests, have been arranged by the Portuguese with the aid of João de Conceiçao whose influence was considerable in Macanga, for Chinkoma (or Chicomo-canhama) the new king, was deposed and exiled by his chief followers within a few years.

Chinkoma was succeeded, probably in 1863, by Kanienzi whom legend portrays as painting the walls of his house with the blood of his executed victims. Kanienzi built himself a new *aringa* in the *Serra* Macanga—a sign perhaps that Ngoni raids were now a real threat to security of the state. A further indication that Kanienzi felt his position insecure is to be found in the treaty he signed with the Portuguese authorities. By this agreement the Portuguese recognised the Pereiras as hereditary rulers of Macanga (*regentes*) and gave Kanienzi an honorary rank in the Portuguese armed forces. In return they received the nominal submission of Macanga to Portuguese sovereignty, and the assurance that settlers would be allowed into the country (*299*, vol 2, 69).

When he made this agreement Kanienzi may already have known of the plots against him and he may have hoped to secure Portuguese aid against his rivals, for it was not long before he also was deposed by his *grandes*, who replaced him with Chituzu. Later Kanienzi and his son were handed over to the Portuguese and their capture became quite a feather in the cap of the governor of Tete, Carlos Barahona e Costa, who was trying to assert Portuguese authority on the river more effectively than his predecessors had been able to do (*316*, 29).

Chituzu died as the result of an accident in November 1870. According to one account he was killed by an exploding barrel of powder; according to another a rifle barrel exploded and killed him. His successor was Chikuacha, who ruled until 1874 when he was murdered by his nephew Kankuni. This was certainly a 'time of troubles' for the Macanga monarchy and reflects a rapid decline in the power and prosperity of the state after the death of Chissaka.

Kankuni, sometimes called Saca Saca and also known by his Portuguese name Cypriano Caetano Pereira, did much to revive the fortunes of Macanga. As a boy he had been sent to Tete and educated by the Jesuits, and one of his first actions was to open negotiations with the Portuguese authorities for a new treaty (*411*, 389). This treaty was signed on 17 November 1875 in the presence of the whole Pereira family and fifty-nine of the *grandes*. By it a formal cession was made of the kingdom of Macanga to Portugal and a series of articles was drawn up to regulate relations between the chieftaincy and Tete.

There was to be free trade between the two territories and Tete was to have superior jurisdiction in all capital cases, though any Portuguese settling in Macanga would come under Macanga law. Macanga agreed to supply irregular troops for Portuguese military expeditions and Kankuni consented to pay tribute to Portugal and accept a Portuguese resident. He also agreed to consult his *grandes* in all important decisions, while the succession to the throne was to be decided by election according to the *lei cafreal*—kaffir law (*464*, 19).

Why did Kankuni sign this solemn and formal document acknowledging Portuguese sovereignty? His motives were probably much the same as those of Kanienzi who had done the same thing more than ten years earlier. By this treaty with the Portuguese he would strengthen his hand against his rivals in Macanga and would secure firearms which the Portuguese authorities were ready and willing to supply to those on whom they bestowed the rank of *capitão-mor*—for by this title even the most savage and lawless bandit was transformed into a harbinger of Portuguese civilisation in darkest Africa.

Kankuni must also have been only too well aware of the decline in the power of the Macanga state. The re-appearance of a section of Zwangendaba's Ngoni in the 1860s and the rise in the power of the Makololo chiefs on Shire at the same time, made Macanga vulnerable to attack and deprived her altogether of the rich trade of the Shire river. To make the situation worse, in 1861 the Portuguese had re-established their post at Zumbo and *sertanejos* independent of the chiefs of Macanga were building new slaving empires on the Luangwa. Macanga was surrounded by potentially hostile forces and badly needed to find allies. Two years after making this formal surrender Kankuni tried to re-establish himself on the Shire. He petitioned unsuccessfully to be granted control of *prazo* Goma which lay in the angle created by the Zambesi and the Shire, giving as his reason that he wanted to escape from Ngoni raids (*414*, 93, *146*).

By the concession of 1875 Kankuni lost nothing in real power within his kingdom and for ten years Macanga appears to have enjoyed relative stability under his strong government. Until his death in 1886 he was assiduous in cultivating the friendship of the Portuguese authorities, and his career well illustrates the ambivalence of the position of the great *muzungo* chiefs, neither wholly African nor wholly European, but a power in both worlds.

Early in 1885 Kankuni invited the famous Jesuit missionary, Victor Courtois, to visit Macanga and prepare his sons for baptism. The governor of Tete, Joaquim Vieira Braga, accompanied the expedition and the two set off early in July 1885 (*340*).

Courtois and the governor prepared themselves as for a visit to any great African potentate. Presents were exchanged and as the party approached Kankuni's *aringa* an immense crowd turned out to greet them shouting and playing on musical instruments—at its head Kankuni himself, his son Luiz and Eustachio da Costa, Kankuni's right hand man and a well-known elephant hunter. Kankuni was dressed in the uniform of a *capitão-mor* together with a plumed hat and a belt decorated with the symbols of freemasonry.

According to Courtois, the chief could speak reasonable Portuguese and could read and write with difficulty.

Kankuni's *aringa* was on the banks of the Revubwe river and was approximately five hundred yards long and three hundred wide (a mile in circumference). It was built of a living wall of trees, was surrounded by a ditch and had two bastions. The *aringa* itself was partly a seat of government and partly a residence for the chief and his family. It was divided into five enclosures. Immediately within the gate was a courtyard where the musicians played and from there a gateway to the left led to the public enclosure where a council of the *grandes* did justice and where there was a storehouse. Off this courtyard was a small private enclosure where the honoured guests of the chief were entertained. The remaining two courtyards contained the huts of Kankuni's wives where the chief himself presumably resided.

According to Courtois, Kankuni had three hundred wives altogether; the chief wife being called *Dona* Roza. The layout of his *aringa* is significantly different from that of the da Cruz at Massangano. Joaquim and Antonio da Cruz lived apart from their followers in a European-style stone-built house surrounded by a stone wall. Kankuni lived in the huts of his wives more in the style of a traditional African chief.

Courtois went to visit the burial place of the chiefs of Macanga in the *Serra* Macanga. This had originally been within the *aringa* of the Pereiras but Chituzu had moved the headquarters of the family from the *Serra* to Muchena on the banks of the Revubwe and the mausoleum was left behind in the ruins of the old *aringa*. The sepulchre consisted of a straw-covered hut with three rooms containing a variety of items of Catholic ritual and the weapons of the dead chiefs. The building was left in the charge of a *mwanamambo* called Chagundure whose job it was to remember

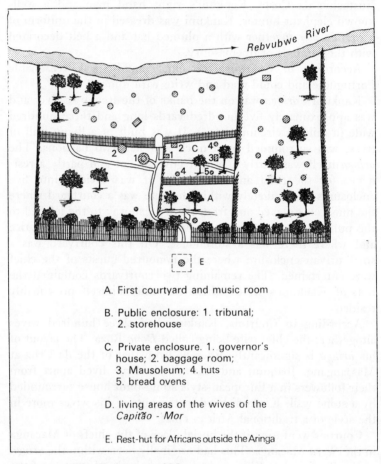

A. First courtyard and music room

B. Public enclosure: 1. tribunal;
2. storehouse

C. Private enclosure. 1. governor's
house; 2. baggage room;
3. Mausoleum; 4. huts
5. bread ovens

D. living areas of the wives of the
Capitão - Mor

E. Rest-hut for Africans outside the Aringa

The *aringa* of the *Capitão-mor* of Macanga

and recite the oral history of the Caetano Pereiras. Originally the mausoleum had been a consecrated Catholic chapel served by a priest, but in the course of time the strange gods of the Portuguese had begun to give way to the local spirit cults. When next the graves of the Pereiras were visited by a European traveller in 1891, they were in the charge of a spirit-medium who acted as the oracle of the dead chiefs—the transformation of cults was complete (*340, 354*).

Kankuni appears to have shared the government of Macanga with two of his relatives, Luis (Chaguadera) and Bernardo (Chiguate). Luis was Kankuni's brother and was described by Courtois as the 'second chief of Macanga'. He lived apart from Kankuni in his own *aringa*. Walter Montagu Kerr also met him and said that he claimed to rule part of Macanga in his own right (*410*, vol 2, 76). Chiguate was Kankuni's cousin and is cited by the French traveller Foa as one of the kings of Macanga. It is clear that, however absolute the rule of Kankuni may have appeared to outsiders, like most African states, Macanga was ruled by authority which was carefully spread among members of the royal lineage and the elders.

Two other accounts of Kankuni are of interest. Walter Montagu Kerr passed close to Macanga country in 1884. He and his companions travelled in constant fear of attacks from Macanga warriors who were raiding the surrounding country and Kerr did not meet any of the Pereiras, although he did have a long conversation with Eustachio da Costa whom he met trading ivory and slaves for firearms with Swahili merchants from the east coast. From his talks with Costa, Kerr became convinced that Kankuni's reputation was fully justified and that he ruled with 'the rod of a tyrant and the lust of a fiend . . . brandy his master and cruelty his ruling passion' (*410*, vol 2, 65).

Emile Durand, however, presented quite a different account of Kankuni. He had taken the trouble to gain the chief's confidence and had actually entered Macanga and stayed with Kankuni at Muchena while prospecting for gold in 1881. Durand commented on the military aspect of Kankuni's court but found the chief to be an intelligent young man with a smattering of Portuguese education '*mais que l'alcool et le Sérail ont privé de santé et d'energie . . .*' (*346A*, 94–95).

As for the atrocities, Durand said

il m'a été donné plusieurs fois de vivre en relations quotidiennes avec des hommes qui avaient la réputation de fair tomber les

245

*têtes avec une étrange facilité; je les ai trouvés très à leur réputa-
tion (346A, 103).*

Atrocity stories of African potentates were commonly told at this time by European travellers who wanted to enhance their own daring and explain away failures to reach their objectives. They were welcomed, indeed expected, by a public who found its imagination stimulated by horrific tales of violence. There may have been substance to some of these stories, but it must also be remembered that African chiefs tended to encourage the spread of their reputations for ferocity and violence so that concession hunters, missionaries, traders and other meddlers would keep away and leave their people in peace. It is with this in mind that one should judge the legends that attached themselves to Kankuni, Chissaka and the other Pereiras.

Kankuni died in 1886, the year following Victor Courtois' visit. The story of his death, though slightly improbable, became one of the legends of the Zambesi. According to the story, Kankuni was staying in the house of Alfred Chastaign, the renter of *prazo* Boroma. Nearby lived Luiz Gregorio, a trader who had once been robbed by Macanga warriors. During the evening's entertainment Kankuni became drunk and while he was incapacitated with gin Luiz cut his throat with a razor. The body was placed in a boat and sent to Tete while Luiz wisely disappeared into the bush, having previously distracted the attention of Kankuni's bodyguard by laying on a show of dancing girls (462, 100).

Kankuni was succeeded by Chanetta who ruled until his death in 1893. Two European travellers, Daniel Rankin and Edouard Foa, visited Macanga during Chanetta's reign. Both were well treated and entertained by the chief and both repaid this kindness by publishing accounts in which stories of atrocity were mingled with burlesque. Foa was on an official mission organised by the *Ministère d'Instruction Public* in Paris. He was under the impression that he was the first European to visit Macanga and later he wrote a rather facetious account of this African monarchy.

Chanetta, he says, was tall and thin and was carried everywhere on the back of one of his courtiers. Whenever he wished to be carried he would straddle his legs and shout *cavallo, cavallo*—horse, horse—at which someone would come running to lift him. But the burlesque is salted with the atrocious, and Foa records that Chanetta had recently thrown five of his hundred wives to the crocodiles of the Revubwe river and hung a sixth in chains because he believed them guilty of adultery.

The inhabitants of Macanga, Foa says, were called Achicunda and there was a ruling élite who were known as *muzungos* or whitemen, though these owed their status more to the clothes they wore than the colour of their skins. All children of *muzungos* were also considered to be 'white' and their wives were given the courtesy title of *dona*. In this way Foa shows how memories of their Portuguese Indian ancestry were used by the Pereiras to enhance their status—an interesting example of an aristocracy supporting its claims with stories and myths of an origin in a foreign conquering race.

The Achicunda referred to were probably the slaves and descendants of the slaves of the Pereiras and were distinct from the Azimba population of the country at large. This suggests that for all the paraphernalia of the Chicucuru chieftaincy the old social patterns of the *prazos* had not been broken in Macanga.

Chanetta had built a new *aringa* at Kamsiki and Muchena was now deserted. Outside the town was the grave of Kankuni presided over by a spirit medium. Foa himself went to commune with the spirit of the late king and asked his advice about an elephant hunt. Kankuni's spirit conveyed a suitably oracular reply and sent greetings to Foa adding that he himself was very well where he was *là-bas*. It was probably while on a visit to the oracle that Foa learnt the version of the history and genealogy of the Macanga chiefs which he later published (*354*, 262–311).

During the reign of Chanetta the period of *rapprochement* with the Portuguese authorities came to an end. In 1887 the Portuguese had tried to place a permanent resident at the Macanga court, which they were entitled to do by the terms of the 1875 treaty. Two officers were sent, but both of them were harassed and persecuted and were eventually forced to leave in 1888. The hostility of Chanetta was undoubtedly stimulated by the growing awareness of the threat posed by the European powers scrambling for African territory. News of the activities of Sousa and Andrada south of the Zambesi would have reached Macanga, as also the news of the successful attack on Massangano by the Portuguese in 1887. Forty years earlier Chissaka would have rejoiced at the discomfiture of the da Cruz, but now the fall of Massangano removed one of the strongest bastions defending the independence of Macanga.

In 1888 the da Cruz family staged their 'Hundred Days'— re-occupying Massangano and raising the country against the Portuguese for the last time. Chanetta came to their aid. The small Portuguese detachment in Macanga was surprised and massacred, and Macanga warriors swept down on the *prazos* of the north bank as they had done so often in the previous generation. When Massangano finally fell to the Portuguese in November 1888 the fugitive da Cruz were able to cross the Zambesi and take refuge with the Pereiras. Motontora, the head of the da Cruz clan, built himself a new *aringa* under the protection of the Pereiras and carried out raids on government positions and another of the da Cruz married one of the Pereira women.

Chanetta appears to have looked for other allies than the fugitive da Cruz. In 1890 he received a visit from Daniel Rankin who was touting for concessions on behalf of the Central Africa Company. On 18 December 1890 Chanetta put his chiefly signature to a document conceding broad prospecting, mineral and trading rights to the company in return for an annual rent of £200 and 1 per cent of all profits from minerals. The deed of concession, which was drawn up in English, refers to 'chikukula, Paramount Chief of the Makanga territory [that is Chanetta] . . . having sovereignty and independent rights to the district herein mentioned' (*202*). Clearly Rankin's concession would only be valid if he was dealing with an independent chief and probably it was this willingness to recognise his independent status that lured Chanetta into signing the concession which would free him from the treaty made in 1875 by Kankuni with the Portuguese.

If Chanetta had hoped to escape Portuguese control by this treaty he was soon to be disillusioned, for the final drawing of the frontiers between British and Portuguese in Central Africa left most of Macanga territory firmly in Portuguese hands. Nevertheless Macanga still had ten years of effective independence before it. So sudden had been the rising in 1888 and so completely had the Portuguese been overwhelmed that for some years no punitive expedition could be mounted against the Pereiras. One force raised for this purpose by Coutinho in 1891 was diverted to Barue and disintegrated when Coutinho himself was badly wounded in the fighting.

Chanetta died in 1893 and was succeeded by Chigaga who reigned for only three months before being supplanted by the last of the chiefs of Macanga, Chinsinga. By this time northern Zambesia had been handed over to the Zambesia Company for administration and economic development. Undercapitalised and with no immediate prospect of any profit, the Zambesia Company was not anxious to undertake a war against Macanga.

Its directors were content to let the old *muzungo* families remain in control while they concentrated their attention on the coastal plantations. In July 1895 an agreement was made with Macanga by which the country would be divided into ten *prazos* which Chinsinga would rent in the name of the company. The ten *prazos* included land that Macanga had never previously controlled and the advantage for Chinsinga lay in an extended territory and a ready supply of firearms and company stores (*355*, vol 1, 191).

In 1895 Macanga was visited by Crawford Angus, white hunter and recruiter of labour for the Nyasaland plantations. He found the slave and ivory trade flourishing and Chinsinga still able to mount regular raids on his neighbours.

The Portuguese within whose territory those districts lie favour the evil system of letting out their different districts to anyone who will pay them tribute or taxes, and they shut their eyes to anything and everything that goes on.

A typical case is Chimsinga, the great Makanga chief. He is supplied with powder and guns by the Portuguese, and is allowed to levy war whenever he wishes as long as he pays a certain yearly tribute to his patrons. Chimsinga's chief delight is in killing people who are helpless, and in slave catching, and he levies war on all around him, on everyone whom he thinks weaker than himself.

The price of slaves, Angus found, was between four and six shillings a head and the chief market for disposing of them remained Tete 'where a ready sale is found among the Portuguese police and servants, and among the officers even and other inhabitants' (*307*, 317).

Chissaka, and even his grandfather, would, one feels, have felt quite at home in Chinsinga's day.

In 1901 the Zambesi Company made a further agreement with Chinsinga by which he was to act as the chief administrator of the company's territories in the Chiuta region in return for substantial financial benefits. This agreement, however, lasted less than a year. Chinsinga was accused of embezzling company funds and a military expedition was mounted against him.

Chinsinga's position had been growing steadily weaker. In 1898 he had assisted the Portuguese in their campaign against the Ngoni along his northern border and although the campaign was victorious it left him surrounded by 'pacified' territory.

When the final confrontation with the Portuguese came, Ngoni warriors were allowed their revenge and were recruited in large numbers by the company for the attack on Macanga. Chinsinga was deserted by his followers and fled towards Nyasaland. Before he could find asylum in British territory he was captured and executed (*339*, 328–9). His followers were hunted down by the Ngoni and burnt out of the mountain caves where they tried to take refuge (*311*, 155–156).

This outline of the last days of Macanga must one day be filled in. It tells nothing of the reasons for the collapse of the chieftaincy. Was Macanga affected by the migration of its younger men to the mines and European plantations of British Africa? Was the prosperity of the state destroyed when the slave and ivory trade to the north was closed by the British? Or was there some internal weakness? Angus suggests that Chinsinga had suffered a number of military defeats which must have weakened his authority and there are indications that the *muzungos* had fallen out with the remnants of the traditional chiefly houses, for Chinsinga apparently tried to depose Bive and replace him with a nominated successor (*339*).

Whatever the reason, it cannot be the advance of European civilisation or the military prowess of the Portuguese. Until the present the northern interior has hardly been influenced at all by what European culture the Portuguese have managed to introduce into their colony, except to experience a steady depopulation as the more adventurous spirits leave for the prosperity of the surrounding countries (*339*).

15　The Da Cruz Family and the Zambesi Wars

The preceding chapter studied the fortunes of the Pereira family and its followers and touched at many points on the story of the Zambesi Wars. This chapter concerns another family—that of da Cruz—whose struggles with the Portuguese government are the central features of these wars and give coherence to what otherwise might appear to be a series of meaningless events.

The origins of da Cruz power

Nicolau Pascoal da Cruz, the first member of the family to settle in Africa, came originally from Siam. He entered Portuguese service as a soldier and formed part of the escort which accompanied the Jesuit fathers to Europe after the imprisonment of members of the Order had been decreed in 1759. In 1767 he came to Zambesia as one of a military contingent sent to reinforce the colony, and there he settled. As a Catholic coming from the Portuguese empire in the East, Nicolau was accepted as part of the Portuguese community; but as a soldier in government service he was threatened with destitution unless he followed the usual practice and established himself in Zambesi society by marrying an heiress. This he did, taking as his spouse *Dona* Luisa da Costa, a mulatta and member of a powerful Zambesi family. *Dona* Luisa received as her dowry the *prazo* of Nhabzigo and Nicolau found himself a *senhor* of slaves and *colonos*. Members of his wife's family at this time held the great *prazo* of Massangano where Nicolau's own descendents were later to establish themselves.

Nicolau da Cruz was never either very rich or very powerful. In 1809 his *prazo* of Nhabzigo had only six *colonos*, who paid eight *alqueires* of grain each in tax, and he had some forty slaves and records of a further three hundred who had escaped. Nicolau was, however, a respected member of the community and in 1807 was chosen to hold the office of *tenente-geral* in commission with José Luis de Meneses on the death of Vilas Boas Truão.

If Nicolau was poor in possessions he was rich in offspring. His wife died in 1807 having borne to him seven children, through whose marriage connections the da Cruz were to spread a network of kinship which became the great strength of the family and the great exasperation of the government.

Nicolau's eldest son was Antonio José da Cruz. He was born in 1777 and became a captain in the Tete garrison. He appears to have married, legally or illegally it is impossible to say, a daughter of the Mwene Mutapa. This was the only marriage he contracted and one son, Joaquim José da Cruz, was born of it.

Antonio José was soon to fall foul of the government. In 1807 the *tenente-geral* Vilas Boas Truão led an expedition against a chief in the Chicoa region whom he suspected of harbouring a trader who had embezzled some of the *tenente-geral*'s trade goods. While passing through the Mwene Mutapa's country the Portuguese force burnt some villages and shortly afterwards found themselves ambushed by the Mutapa's men. The government forces were defeated and Truão himself was captured and later executed. Vilas Boas Truão had been an unpopular governor and many people bore him grudges. The circumstances surrounding his defeat and death had more than the smell of treachery about them and when the investigations were all complete and arrests had been made the blame was pinned on Antonio José and his brother Agostinho.

The Portuguese historian Almeida de Eça has, rightly in my opinion, cast doubt on the guilt of Antonio and his brother, pointing out that the accusations made against them were based to a large extent on the fact of the relationship between Antonio and the Mwene Mutapa. In the end the two brothers were sacrificed to divert attention from other guilty parties. The wheels of Portuguese justice ground slowly but eventually Antonio was hanged and quartered on Moçambique Island at the end of May 1813 and his brother was sent as an exile to Inhambane.

Had the da Cruz family possessed any real power in the Rivers at that time it is impossible that some way would not have been found to save Antonio from the scaffold. However, if miscarriage of justice there were, Antonio José was to be amply avenged by his son and grandson.

The other children of Nicolau da Cruz meanwhile married

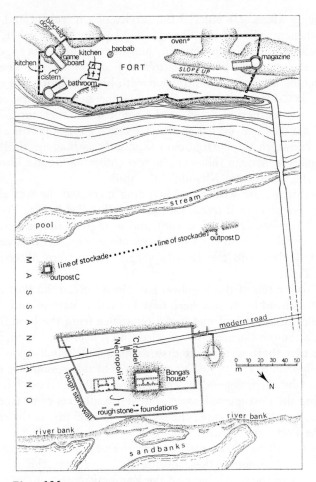

Plan of Massangano

and multiplied. *Dona* Inacia Benedita da Cruz married a distant
relative of the Count of Rio Pardo and, after his death, the young
Portuguese officer and future explorer Antonio Gamitto. Eugenia
Maria, Nicolau's eldest daughter, married Leandro José de
Aragão and lived to be over ninety years old. As the family grew
and multiplied it acquired control over a large number of *prazos*
—ten by 1840 and more as the century progressed—but always
with the centre of its power in Tete and the surrounding
areas.

Joaquim José da Cruz must have been born about the time of
his father's imprisonment and he was brought up by his aunt

Eugenia Maria. He entered the service of a merchant and back-woodsman called José Vicente de Aquino (*299*, vol 1, 184) travelling widely in his company and when Aquino was appointed official interpreter to Gamitto's expedition to the court of Kazembe in 1831, Joaquim went with him. Joaquim also served João da Costa Xavier, an Indian trader married to his first cousin, and at some period acted as the agent of another aunt, Maria Barbara da Cruz, on her *prazo* of Bamba. From that time on he was known in the Portuguese community as Joaquim da Bamba though the African followers he was gathering around him gave him the nick-name 'Nhaude'—the spider.

As his private wealth and standing increased, he was able to purchase two small *terras em fatiota* called Pandamase Pequeno and Nhaminse (*299*, vol 1, 186), and in 1849 he rented two large *prazos* which lay on the south bank of the Zambesi between the Luenha river and the Lupata gorge. These were Massangano and Tipue.

This stretch of the Zambesi had always given the Portuguese a lot of trouble. It was here that Francisco Barreto and Diogo Simões Madeira had met fierce resistance from the local Tonga and, although the area was divided into *prazos* and leased, it was here that there were most disturbances and 'rebellions' during the eighteenth century. The turbulence of this region was partly caused by the independent chieftaincy of Barue whose lands lay behind the Portuguese *prazos* and whose subjects came from the same clans and venerated the same spirit mediums as the *colonos* of the Portuguese *prazos*.

In the 1830s Barue was temporarily occupied by a group of Ngoni and although these eventually moved on, the whole of this part of the south bank of the Zambesi remained exposed to the raids of the Gaza Ngoni from southern Moçambique. It was to provide some defence against these raids that Joaquim da Cruz was granted Massangano and Tipue by the government. As the official citation put it, Joaquim da Cruz was

a well established settler, respected by the kaffirs and posses-sing the means and the strength to oppose them. In addition to this is the fact that he has performed considerable services for the state on various occasions . . . and likewise because the rent of those *prazos* will be more secure and will be punctually paid to the public treasury (*268*).

After taking possession of these territories, Joaquim at once began the construction, near the junction of the Zambesi and Luenha rivers, of the great *aringa* of Massangano which, if not quite the first of the great *aringas*, was for some years the largest and the strongest in Zambesia.

In a previous chapter I have shown how the growing power of Joaquim da Cruz at Massangano led in 1853 to the Pereiras of Macanga and Macombe of Barue banding together to crush the upstart. While this war raged the whole of the Portuguese community was split between the supporters of the Pereiras and the supporters of the da Cruz and when on the night of 15 October 1853 the besieged crept out and massacred their besiegers, it was feared that the victorious warriors of the da Cruz would descend on Tete and take their revenge on the Pereira faction.

The Portuguese authorities had had neither the means nor the inclination to interfere in this 'baronial' war, but as soon as the siege was over they sent the prestigious Gualdino José Nunes to see that relations with the victor remained friendly and that the river passage to Tete remained open (*299*, vol 1, 296). Chissaka's associates, however, were not so ready to accept Joaquim's victory.

One of Chissaka's connections was Antonio da Cruz Coimbra, a trader in slaves and firearms and brother-in-law of Paul Marianno Vas dos Anjos. After the defeat of Chissaka, Cruz Coimbra had found that his property had been rifled by a band of Joaquim da Cruz's warriors, but still worse, that Joaquim was now in control of the main stream of the Zambesi up which Cruz Coimbra was accustomed to take his boat loads of merchandise and strings of slaves.

Cruz Coimbra hastened to lay a formal complaint before the governor of the Rivers and received permission to raise an army to punish Joaquim da Cruz for his raids on the country round Tete. Cruz Coimbra turned to all his acquaintances among the slavers of the lower River for support. Slaves were sent by Galdino Faustino de Sousa, João de Jesus Maria, João Bonifacio Alves da Silva and others; arms and powder came from government stores, and in April 1854 the force, numbering about five hundred men, set off up the Zambesi.

At the same time the Portuguese government had decided to try to reimpose its authority in the Tete district. A decree dated 24 November 1853 had created a separate government in Tete, and Antonio Gamitto had been nominated as its first governor. He sailed from Lisbon on 31 December 1853, accompanied by two hundred European troops. In May 1854 the first of the new troops began to arrive on the Zambesi, but already the new governor had run into difficulties. He was ill; he found difficulty getting transport in Moçambique; he quarrelled with the governor-general. Eventually he reached his troops, who were already dying of fever and dysentery, and before he could even take up his governorship he was relieved of his post and the command of the troops was given to a local settler, Tito de Araujo Sicard (297).

It was not until October—the hottest month of the year—that Sicard at last marched up the River from Sena with the government troops. Cruz Coimbra's army had meanwhile partially disintegrated. At the end of May the motley force had reached Bandar—the towering rocky approach to the Lupata gorge. There it had come across some scouts sent out by Joaquim da Cruz and almost without a shot being fired, a panic had set in among the African auxiliaries, and a large number of them had deserted.

As Sicard advanced he was able to join forces with the remnants of Cruz Coimbra's army and the mixed force now proceeded under the joint command of the two men. This army also was rapidly and painlessly dispersed by Joaquim da Cruz. A party of his soldiers opened fire from across the Zambesi and again the African auxiliaries of Sicard's army fled, leaving the commanders no choice but to return in search of fresh carriers. On 20 December 1854 Sicard was ousted from his command by a mutiny while encamped on *prazo* Ancueza.

Both the retreat and the subsequent mutiny appear difficult to explain from the facts now available, but perhaps the explanation lies in the activities of Chissaka. At some point Sicard's and Cruz Coimbra's forces were joined by a contingent from Macanga. Shortly afterwards Joaquim da Cruz sent an ambassador to try and come to some sort of arrangement with Sicard and the Portuguese authorities, with whom he had never considered himself at war. We know that the Macanga warriors pressed for the murder of the ambassador and that Sicard refused. Probably Cruz Coimbra and Chissaka came to an agreement to get rid of Sicard and the threat of effective government control that he represented.

With Sicard gone, Cruz Coimbra led his men past Massangano and on to Tete, escorted by Chissaka's warriors but making no attacks on Joaquim da Cruz apart from murdering the ambassador who had now fallen into his hands. Apparently Cruz Coimbra and Chissaka were now satisfied that the Zambesi was open again to their trade (299, vol 1, 321–357).

Joaquim da Cruz died in 1855, much to the relief of the government and his enemies. Contemporaries did not hesitate to ascribe to him the intensification of the disorders on the Zambesi but it is by no means clear that Joaquim was not simply the victim of a series of attacks by jealous rivals. Perhaps the Portuguese should even cast him in the role of hero rather than villain, for had Chissaka and Macombe been victorious, it is highly probable that Portuguese rule on the Zambesi would have been wiped out entirely. Chissaka had vowed to destroy Tete after he had destroyed Massangano and might easily have carried out his threat.

As it was, the defeat of Chissaka greatly weakened the prestige, and hence the power, of the Pereiras, while Barue, already suffering from internal dissensions, from this time onward plunged still deeper into chaos and disorder.

From Joaquim da Cruz's death in 1855 until about 1863 the first phase of the Zambesi Wars worked itself out in a series of disjointed struggles. In 1858 the partnership of Cruz Coimbra and the Vas dos Anjos was badly mauled when government forces destroyed the Vas dos Anjos *aringa* at Shamo on the Shire. Between 1855 and 1861 there took place the series of raids and counter-raids between João Bonifacio Alves da Silva and the sultanate of Angoche which distracted the attention of this great *sertanejo* from the affairs of the Zambesi and led to his victory and death at Angoche in 1861.

Chissaka died in 1858, leaving Macanga to a succession of weak rulers and in 1863 Paul Marianno Vas dos Anjos also died and was succeeded by his son, who was too young to assume power in Massingire. All this contributed to the establishment of relative peace in the colony and to a slight revival in Portuguese authority. One sign of this revival was the appointment in 1858 of a new *capitão-mor* of Manica though Isidoro Correa Pereira, the nominated captain, never took up residence. Another was the dispatch of an expedition under the command of Albino Manuel Pacheco to restore the fair at Zumbo, a task which was successfully accomplished in 1862.

All this time the da Cruz family remained quiet. Joaquim had left at least seventeen children by a variety of wives but there was no dispute over the succession and his eldest son, Antonio Vicente da Cruz, peacefully assumed leadership of the clan.

257

Antonio da Cruz was about thirty years old at the time of his father's death and he had already made his name as a leader of his father's warriors. He was always known as Bonga—the wild cat—which name allows the unwary recorder of Zambesi history to confuse him with Paul Marianno Vas dos Anjos' brother who also bore the name Bonga. For twelve years he maintained a state of relatively peaceful co-existence with the Portuguese authorities and with his neighbours. He entertained travellers on their way up the Zambesi; he made occasional visits to Tete to have his children baptised or to conduct business and he was punctilious in paying the rent for his *prazos*. Early in 1862 he was granted the title of *sargento-mor* of Massangano and at the same time became a major in the Portuguese reserves. This made him the official representative of the Portuguese crown on his *prazos*; it enabled him to hear cases and gave him access to the government arsenals to equip his 'peace-keeping' operations. It also enabled him to wear a military uniform, which he did with considerable pride.

There is a touching story which shows how muted the rivalry of Cruz and Pereira had become in the years after Joaquim's death. In 1862 a subscription was opened to rebuild the church at Tete. The list was headed by the governor and the king of Macanga until Bonga arrived in Tete and, seeing his rival in the place of honour, immediately subscribed more and re-established the primacy of his family in this vital particular.

As late as 1863 the relations between Bonga and the Portuguese showed no signs of deterioration. In that year Bonga handed over some of the land he controlled on the left bank of the Zambesi to the Portuguese government, who made of it a *prazo* for which he now paid rent. This new *prazo* of Mahembe included the famous Bandar rock which towers over the Zambesi at the entrance to the Lupata gorge.

However, Bonga was not an easy neighbour for the Portuguese authorities in Tete. Merchants travelling up the Zambesi were frequently robbed or forced to pay protection money; the justice dealt out by Bonga in the name of the king of Portugal was frequently drastic and blood-thirsty; Massangano continued to harbour escaped slaves and other renegades; while the quarrel with the Pereiras smouldered beneath the surface and was liable to flare up any minute.

An incident recorded by David Livingstone can stand as one

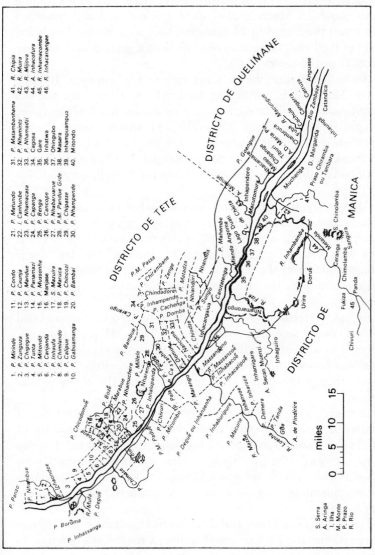

The *prazos* of Tete, Quelimane and Manica, drawn from '*Esboço de Mappa do Rio Zambeze entre Tete e Anguase*' by A. de Castilho

example among many. In 1857 the Makololo porters who had accompanied Livingstone from Barotseland and who had remained in Tete to await his return, organised a group of musicians and dancers to perform at the residences of the leading Portuguese. In Macanga they were well-received and rewarded but when they went to Massangano they were accused of being spies of the Pereiras come to bewitch Bonga, and six of them were brutally put to death (*390*).

And all this time the da Cruz empire was growing. Bonga's sister Maria settled with her husband on Marangue, the old Jesuit *prazo* which faced Massangano across the Luenha river. Bonga himself acquired Mahembe and another sister, Luisa, established herself at Guengue below the Lupata gorge on the left bank of the Zambesi, thus giving the da Cruz control over both banks of the Zambesi from below the Lupata gorge almost to Tete.

After 1863 the situation began to deteriorate and Bonga's actions became more arbitrary and damaging to Portuguese interests. There is evidence that at this time his control over his own *prazos* was being challenged by some of the traditional Tonga chiefs and the stronger line he began to take may have been dictated by the need to impose his authority in his own territory.

By 1867 relations with the Portuguese government had broken down and the governor of Tete, Miguel Gouveia, decided to send an expedition to bring Bonga to heel. Gouveia's plan was known to and approved by the authorities in Moçambique, though these later tried to avoid taking the blame for the defeat.

Gouveia's force left Tete in three columns on 1 July 1867. It contained a few European troops but was mostly made up of auxiliaries from the *prazos*. As the columns crossed the Luenha they were ambushed by Bonga's men and large numbers were killed in the ensuing confusion. Prisoners were taken, including the commandant, but these too were murdered later (*299*, vol 2, 101–126).

Gouveia's expedition had been very injudicious and it was fortunate for the Portuguese that Bonga made little attempt to exploit his victory. A truce was reached between him and the authorities through the mediation of his sister Maria. The real rewards of victory as far as Bonga was concerned came in his own territory and its environs where his authority was now unchallenged.

In the two years that followed three government expeditions

were sent against Bonga and all three ended in defeat for the Portuguese. It appeared to many contemporaries, and subsequent writers have agreed with them, that the Portuguese government got the *affaire Bonga* totally out of proportion. They staked the whole prestige of their crumbling empire on a matter which should have been a small police operation, and mismanagement of the campaigns turned small defeats into national disasters.

Up to 1867 the Zambesi Wars had consisted simply of the armed conflicts of the *prazo* factions. They caused disorder and bloodshed but there was no real danger to Portuguese rule. The da Cruz were certainly no worse than the other families and to begin with they were very much less powerful. By singling them out for attention and by mounting such large, imposing and incompetent military expeditions against them the Portuguese raised Bonga's reputation to legendary heights in his own lifetime.

The first punitive expedition assembled under the command of Oliveira Queiros in November 1867. Four hundred regular troops were included—certainly the largest military expedition sent to Zambesia since Francisco Barreto's in the sixteenth century. Queiros was joined by large contingents of slaves and auxiliaries sent from the Sena *prazos*. The largest of these was a party of six hundred men under the command of Manuel Antonio de Sousa. A smaller force was to advance on the Luenha from Tete.

Queiros' expedition had to march through the rainy season, in country where there were no supply depots or billets. It suffered considerable privation but was able to brush aside Bonga's resistance and lay siege to Massangano at the end of December 1867. Queiros, who suffered severely from malaria throughout, was the type of soldier who is anxious above all else to preserve his army intact; when he found that his small artillery could not breach the living walls of the *aringa*, that ammunition was running low, and that the auxiliaries were melting away, he resolved to retreat and led his army in good order back down the River. He had hoped to set up a base at Guengue for a renewed campaign but there was a mutiny among his men and he was forced to take them further to Quelimane. There he was relieved of his command and sent to face a court-martial in Lisbon. He was eventually acquitted.

The Moçambique authorities hastened to make good Queiros's failures and organised a fresh expedition, raising and equipping a new local regiment for the purpose. Again some four to five hundred regular troops were mustered for the march, which began from Quelimane at the beginning of the dry season in May 1868. The commander, Guilherme de Portugal e Vasconcellos, allowed his expedition to be endlessly held up by the quarrels of the Sena settlers, and it took him nearly three months to reach Massangano which he eventually succeeded in doing at the end of July.

Portugal's army met with little resistance in the *prazo* and was able to occupy the high ground behind the *aringa* and to mount guns there which fired from above into the huts and living quarters of Bonga's men. After four days of bombardment and a severe fire in the *aringa*, Bonga sued for peace and a cease-fire was arranged. According to contemporary accounts the cease-fire was treacherously broken by Portuguese soldiers who fired on the inhabitants of the *aringa* as they went down to the Zambesi to get water.

Bonga at once broke off the talks and fighting began again, but his situation was now desperate and it is inconceivable that a Portuguese commander of even moderate ability should not now have put a speedy end to the resistance of the da Cruz. On 5 August Bonga was at the end of all his resources and appears to have attempted to escape from the *aringa*. He crowded the surviving inhabitants of the *aringa* together and then in a rush they sallied out of the gates carrying their few belongings with them.

The Portuguese were totally unprepared; they thought an attack was being launched and panicked. Within a matter of minutes Bonga's men had overrun the Portuguese gun emplacements and in the ensuing confusion the Portuguese army was cut to pieces. The commander was killed as he tried to mount his horse and altogether some 260 Portuguese soldiers were killed. It was the greatest disaster suffered by European arms in southern Africa until the defeat of the British army by the Zulus at Isandlwana in 1879.

The victory had been hard-won and Bonga revelled in the spoils. The commander's horse was paraded before him and he tried unsuccessfully to ride it. The instruments of the military band were captured, as were the stores, ammunition and brandy supplies of the army. All the prisoners Bonga had taken were put to death, with the exception of two who were fortunate enough to escape, and the walls of the *aringa* were soon hung with the heads of the defeated.

The lurid accompaniment to the defeat of Portugal e Vasconcellos' army was no real evidence for Bonga's desire to continue the war. The Massangano *grandes* had in fact petitioned Bonga to re-establish peace as they needed to return to their villages for the harvest and Bonga showed himself quite ready to return to the *status quo ante* where he had acknowledged the sovereignty of Portugal but had been left with a free hand to do as he pleased in his own territories and to take tolls of the River traffic (*299*, vol 2, 302).

Emissaries now went to and from Massangano and Tete and negotiations reached the point where peace terms were put on paper. But Bonga insisted, understandably enough, that the peace should be signed by the governor-general and not by junior officials in Tete. He knew that his old rival Clementino de Sousa, at that time president of the *camara* of Tete, had been influential in drawing up the peace terms and he must have suspected that these tactics were designed to keep him quiet until another expedition could be mounted against him.

This suspicion was correct, for the metropolitan government had now decided that it must take a hand and restore the shaken prestige of the Portuguese in Africa. Troops were being raised in Lisbon and Goa, and the government had a certain success in arousing public interest in, and enthusiasm for, the expedition. Ladies in Lisbon were even found to embroider a banner to be carried by the troops.

Throughout the early months of 1869 the expedition built up unit by unit. War was officially declared in Zambesia only in May, by which time some eight hundred and fifty regular troops in addition to a battery of mountain guns had been assembled. The joint expedition was commanded by a former governor of the Rivers, Tavares de Almeida, who may have known conditions in the Zambesi well but who had little knowledge of his troops or their officers and did not succeed in welding them into a coherent force. As usual the expedition was accompanied by large numbers of slaves and auxiliaries from the *prazos*, including contingents from Macanga. Once again Bonga was isolated and surrounded—even his sister Luiza openly siding with the Portuguese.

Bonga may have had few resources and all the odds stacked against him but he had two powerful generals called 'September' and 'October', and the equally important backing of the Barue chiefs who led a diversion against Sena. As the troops struggled up the sweltering valley, finding supplies and transport inadequate, they fell ill and began to die long before any enemy was encountered. Matters were made worse by a fire in the only advanced base that had been set up at Guengue. It was not until November, seven months or more after the expedition had originally set out, that Massangano was at last reached by the decimated and half-starved army.

The rocky wastes of the Lupata region were no place for living off the country and November was the wrong season in which to do so. A relief column sent from Tete was ambushed by Bonga's men and dispersed. The army closely invested Bonga's *aringa* but it was not at all clear who were the besiegers and who the besieged, for the country swarmed with Bonga's men. Although the strategic placings had all been won and guns had been placed on the high ground behind Massangano and on the Zambesi sand banks, Tavares de Almeida was faced with the choice of immediate retreat or starvation.

After the failure of one last desperate assault, the army began to retreat. The sick were moved onto one of the islands to await River transport and the camps broken up. A night retreat is always difficult and an alarm—probably a false alarm—sounded by the rearguard threw the whole operation into total confusion. A policy of *sauve qui peut* took the place of military discipline, and boats set off down the River loaded with anyone who could scramble aboard. Other soldiers escaped on their own to attempt the toilsome overland journey to Sena. The sick were left behind on the island to be massacred next day by Bonga's warriors.

Parties of Tavares de Almeida's troops eventually re-grouped at Guengue and were ordered to set up a garrison at that point, while others were transferred to Sena. And there the troops rotted, unrelieved and unpaid, dying of fever, until by 1875 scarcely a hundred men were left of the original expedition that had numbered nearly a thousand.

For a fourth time Bonga had routed his enemies—or rather they had defeated themselves—and the taxes of Indian and Portuguese peasants thousands of miles away, and the blood of conscripts and impressed carriers, had all been poured fruitlessly away into the bush of Africa.

For some years after this fourth disaster the Portuguese planned for another expedition. Two steamers equipped with guns were ordered for the River, and they would have been a formidable problem for Bonga in any future siege. The government even received an offer from a certain William Berge to raise Boer mercenaries to put an end to the rebellion. Meanwhile Bonga and the Tete garrison skirmished and raided each other's territory. This sort of warfare was much more successful for the Portuguese and once again Bonga found his hold over his lands weakening. His sister Luiza had already broken entirely from his control and, particularly during 1874, there were large-scale desertions from Massangano. Some of the *kazembes* (commanders) left with their men for service with the Pereiras in Macanga or *Dona* Luiza da Cruz at Guengue.

In January 1875 negotiations for peace were begun and a treaty was finally concluded in June 1875. Bonga agreed to hand back to the government the stores and equipment of the expeditions and to allow the remains of the dead Portuguese soldiers and officers to be buried. Bonga himself obtained a free pardon and again acknowledged Portuguese sovereignty.

Bonga died on 8 September 1879 and, such is the irony of history, was buried with military honours provided by a detachment of troops from Tete, a requiem Mass subsequently being said for him by the French Jesuit, Victor Courtois.

The rule of the da Cruz in Massangano

Bonga's death is the right point to pause to consider the 'reigns' of the first two da Cruz in Massangano. Joaquim José da Cruz had long experience of trade and travel before he eventually settled at Massangano. His followers were thus his own personal clients and slaves who had been assembled over the years and owed a personal loyalty to him. It was usual in Zambesia for the *senhor* who first assembled a band of slaves to control them without much difficulty; it was the man who inherited a body of slaves who frequently had trouble in imposing his authority. Moreover, although Joaquim had a large number of children, he had no brothers or sisters who might have challenged his authority in his own lifetime.

Joaquim always considered himself to be a member of the Portuguese community. In 1853, when he was about fifty years old, he was described by Delfim José de Oliveira as a man of smallish stature and very thin. His skin was a dark colour but his features were rather Chinese. He was dressed in a cotton shirt and a cotton jacket striped in blue and white. Clearly his nickname of the 'spider' in part at least derived from his physical appearance, for another contemporary, Antonio Porfirio Miranda, said that he was so thin it was almost as if he was a mummy (407).

Joaquim entertained travellers in the traditional Zambesian style. When Oliveira stopped at the *aringa* in 1853 he was met on the banks of the river by the chief accompanied by all his *grandes* and by a large band of drums and *marimbas*. The evening's entertainment was provided by the slaves who danced, sang and ended with a mock attack on the *aringa* carried out with a terrifying rapidity and ferocity. One charming number was performed by an armed warrior who rushed at the guests and pretended to cut their throats. Joaquim himself got drunk on gin and wine and it was not until the morning that the celebrations subsided.

Oliveira made one interesting observation about the relationship of Joaquim and his followers. 'Inhaude, he said, lives poorly and whatever he obtains by robbery is at once divided among his wives and *cazembes*; there can be no other explanation of the fidelity with which this band serves its chief.' A *senhor* was indeed expected to provide loot for his followers; but was this just the 'shareout' of a robber band or was it, perhaps, an example of traditional 'African socialism' at work?

No reliably accurate picture of Bonga can really be drawn at all. Even in his own life-time he was the victim of a black legend that distorted every report of him and his activities. He was accused of murdering his mother; of feeding his unfaithful wives to the crocodiles; of torturing and executing his prisoners with his own hands. He is stupid, cunning, cruel, illiterate, superstitious and black; he is so feared that the mere whisper of his name can spread panic in a whole army. So his contemporaries describe him, but it is fairly safe to assume that beneath this horrific mask the real man has been totally lost to view.

Bonga appears to have had little difficulty in establishing his ascendancy over his father's warriors. He was already well known among them at the time of Joaquim's death and had made his reputation in the wars against the Pereiras. He appears to have tried to follow his father's policy of maintaining friendly relations with the Portuguese and to have wanted to be recognised as a member of the Portuguese community. He dressed in Portuguese uniforms and obtained Portuguese rank and title. He observed at least the outward forms of Catholicism and had his children christened by the *padre* at Tete.

He appears, however, to have become increasingly morose and moody, and may have been a depressive or an alcoholic. He was very much influenced by the witch-finders and the witch-doctors and many people suffered under their accusations and his credulity. He installed the remains of his father in a stone-built mausoleum next to his own house and communed frequently with him through a spirit-medium who thus acquired considerable political power in Massangano (*299*, vol 2, 246).

Bonga himself spoke little Portuguese and wrote less but he was too proud to admit this and insisted on painful conversations with his Portuguese visitors carried on without the aid of an interpreter.

Towards the end of his life Bonga's relations with his family, with his followers and with the African *colonos* were distinctly uneasy. There are reports of warfare with chiefs in the interior, there are desertions from the *aringa*, there is the exile of his brother and the independent and sometimes hostile attitude of his sister, *Dona* Luisa.

Altogether his role was an ambiguous one. Bonga was never accepted by the Portuguese and whenever he went to Tete all the settlers shunned him. On the other hand he was not accepted by the African inhabitants of the *prazos* either. Although, after his defeats of the Portuguese, his rule was never seriously challenged in Massangano, Bonga appears to have increasingly shunned the company of the *aringa* towards the end of his life and to have lived at a smaller house some distance away.

Despite his victories over the Portuguese, Bonga can hardly be considered a very able military commander. He allowed all the expeditions sent against him to reach Massangano without meeting any serious opposition and their subsequent defeat was due more to chance and the incompetence of the Portuguese commanders than to this generalship. After his death, his successors began to construct a series of fortified *aringas* along the frontiers of their territory to provide the great *aringa* with more adequate protection.

In the final estimate of Bonga one must reserve one's judgement a little. Many of the great African figures of the nineteenth century were described by contemporary European visitors in terms similar to those used to describe Bonga, and yet we know that they were great leaders and powerful personalities. Perhaps the same was true also of Antonio Vicente da Cruz.

The fall of the da Cruz dynasty

Bonga's death was followed by a struggle between different sections of the family for control of Massangano. The quarrel originally centred on the burial rites of the dead chief. Some thought he should be buried with Christian rites in the cemetery in Tete, others thought he should be interred in his father's mausoleum with all the rites of an African chief. The latter party won and perhaps one should see in this the symbolic resolution of the dilemma which Bonga had found so intractable; were the da Cruz African or European? To which world did they truly belong?

The funeral ceremonies were attended by the leaders of the

warriors, by the chiefs from inland and by the spirit mediums and it was a council of these *grandes* who elected Luis Vicente da Cruz (known as Mochenga or Muririma), the third of the sons of Joaquim José, to the throne of Massangano (*299*, vol 2, 533–539).

The following year Luis Vicente was replaced by Bonga's eldest brother Vitorino (Inhamissengo), who had been living in exile in Barue during Antonio da Cruz' last years. The reason for the change is not known, but perhaps Luis was merely 'keeping the place warm' for his brother, for he was neither exiled nor put to death and remained to take an active part in the final wars (*426*, 415). Vitorino da Cruz ruled until his death in August 1885.

During the five years of Vitorino's reign Massangano was quiet and traffic passed freely up and down the Zambesi. It seemed that the old days when the da Cruz had terrorised the whole of the colony were over, and there were even rumours that the *aringa* was falling into decay. Vitorino was no autocrat like his brother Bonga and he ruled very much under the influence of his *grandes*, though he clung to the vestiges of his Portuguese inheritance.

In July 1884 Massangano was visited by Victor Courtois, a French Jesuit missionary, who left a description of the regime he encountered there. He went at the request of Vitorino to baptise children, to say a Mass for the soul of Bonga and to investigate the possibility of establishing a mission in Cruz territory. He remained for ten days at Massangano and in his brief account shows the extent to which Massangano was now ruled by the *grandes*.

Vitorino had a council of *grandes* who acted as a court to hear criminal cases and who were consulted by the chief on such important matters as the founding of the mission. One of the questions raised concerned the Christian burial of the skulls and other remains of Portuguese soldiers which still adorned the *aringa*. Courtois was informed that as they had been placed there by Bonga, nothing could be done with them until the spirit-medium—the *mambo leão Chimuara*—who would commune with the dead chief, had been consulted. From other sources it is clear that the spirit-mediums of Joaquim and Antonio da Cruz were both powerful figures in Massangano at this time (*211*).

Although Vitorino ruled relatively peacefully at Massangano, the political scene in Zambesia was in violent turmoil. The changes which were taking place and which ushered in the third phase of the Zambesi Wars will be described in more detail later, but the most important change of all was the rise to power of

Manuel Antonio de Sousa. Sousa had aided the Portuguese government in its expeditions against Massangano and had shared in its catastrophic defeats. He had never broken this alliance with the government, and in the eyes of other Zambesi potentates he came to be almost the personification of the government and its ambitions.

In 1880 Sousa upset the whole power structure of Zambesia when he seized control of the paramount chieftaincy of Barue, occupying its territory with his men and threatening all the chiefs along its borders with similar treatment. Sousa was by now the most powerful *senhor* in the whole colony and of all the people who felt themselves threatened none had greater reason for their fears than the da Cruz of Massangano.

They reacted by strengthening their defence with a string of fortifications along their borders. It had been traditional for a *prazo*-holder to place *mocasambos* in villages along the frontiers of his *prazo* so that what the da Cruz now did was in no sense an innovation but merely an intensification of a practice of hallowed antiquity. Previously members of the da Cruz family had lived in outlying villages and in time of war had sent trusted captains to organise the defence of the *colono* settlements. Now a sort of 'Maginot line' was constructed which ran from near Tete to the confluence of the Mazoe and the Luenha and thence to the Zambesi opposite Guengue. The *aringas* encircled Massangano and were held by members of the family or by allies or trusted captains.

Sousa responded by building a parallel line of fortified posts which were often so close to those of the da Cruz that the inhabitants could hear each others' drums beating at night (*426*, *415*). This confrontation would probably have led in the end to war between the two but there is evidence that Sousa went out of his way to provoke the da Cruz, sending reports to the government of fictitious raids that the da Cruz were supposed to have been carrying out in the hope of getting government backing for a war on Massangano.

All those who felt threatened by Sousa's power now drew closer together and the da Cruz found allies among many of the Zambesi chiefs who were anxious to stem the tide of Portuguese advance. The Barue royal family, exiled after Sousa's *coup* in 1880, found a temporary refuge in Massangano and at least one of them became a captain of one of the da Cruz *aringas*. On the north bank of the Zambesi, where da Cruz *prazos* adjoined the territories of Macanga, relations between Pereira and da Cruz became closer and the foundations of an alliance were laid. The chief of Mtoko in what is today Rhodesia also sought the alliance of Massangano.

At the beginning of the critical year of 1887 it appeared that the advance of Portuguese imperialism, personified by Sousa and his associates, was to be confronted with an organised resistance movement. Aware of the existence of this system of alliances Sousa and his advisers decided to strike at Massangano, which they believed to be at the heart of the opposition. The government gave its approval and a military campaign was set in motion—an enterprise which was to prove as disastrous in the long run to Sousa as in the short run it was disastrous to the da Cruz.

The plan of campaign, worked out by Major Paiva de Andrada, was the traditional one, consisting of a three-pronged attack launched from Sena and Tete below and above Massangano, in co-operation with a force of Sousa's men operating from inland. The campaign opened in September 1887 and at once the contingents from Sena and Tete ran into stiff opposition from the outlying da Cruz *aringas*. The Sena force had made little progress when news suddenly arrived in the camp that Massangano had fallen.

Paiva de Andrada had himself accompanied Sousa's force which was operating from Manica. Meeting little resistance Andrada pushed through Barue and into da Cruz territory. When he came within sight of the great *aringa*, he found it was undefended and Andrada's soldiers were able to occupy the fortress, which had cost the Portuguese so much blood and treasure, without firing a shot. They found one old woman and eleven bodies—all that remained of the once populous town of Massangano (*426, 431, 425, 736*). What had happened?

Vitorino da Cruz had died in 1885 and had been succeeded by yet another brother who bore the same name as Bonga—Antonio Vicente—and is known as Chatara. Chatara tried to continue with the policy of friendship with the Portuguese authorities, though if Castilho's story is correct, he did this in a singularly tactless and even provocative way.

> Chatara, judging with some justification that already he was an independent chief, wrote to the governor of Tete indicating the sympathy he had for the Portuguese people with whom he desired to live in peace ... and requesting that we should nominate a consul for Massangano (*334, 37*).

In other respects Chatara's elevation to the throne (*butaca*) of Massangano had been disastrous. He had quarrelled with his family and with the *grandes*. It was even rumoured that he had had Bonga's spirit-medium murdered. The out-break of war with Sousa and the Portuguese apparently brought matters to a head and Chatara was deposed. The traditional chiefs of the Tonga *colonos* also deserted and went over to the Portuguese (*334*, 62). Shortly after Andrada had occupied Massangano Chatara was handed over to the Portuguese as a prisoner and exiled to the Cape Verde Islands.

Andrada's victory seemed to be complete. The *aringa* was looted, burnt and then abandoned. The da Cruz lands were occupied by Sousa's men under the command of two of his captains, but no attempt was made to garrison or defend the site of the *aringa* of Massangano itself.

The da Cruz wars were far from over, however. The da Cruz family had escaped across the Zambesi to the north bank *prazos*. There they chose João Sant'anna da Cruz—Motontora—as their chief. Motontora was a man of energy and resource and within weeks had engineered a dramatic revival in the fortunes of his family. The da Cruz were about to embark on their 'Hundred Days'.

In February 1888 the Portuguese authorities heard the first news of Motontora's activities. He had sent messengers to Mtoko in the south and Chikussi, king of the Ngoni, in the north, asking for their help. Members of the da Cruz family began to gather in numbers on *prazo* Mataza and brought with them powder and arms which had been bought through Muslim merchants. Messages and offers of arms also went to the chiefs of the *colonos* of Massangano, many of whom deserted the Portuguese and rejoined the da Cruz.

The rising was fixed for the period when the *mussocco* was collected on the *prazos*, when rebellion against the Portuguese would have most attractions for the average peasant. The great warrior captain Pindirire passed through the *prazos* carrying with him the *rabo da guerra*—a lion's tail stained with the blood of a disembowelled victim—as a sign for the rebels to gather round their chief, and crying out to those who would hear him that his mother had told him that the *prazos* would not be lost and that this time the Portuguese would be conquered.

Meanwhile Motontora had gone with his relatives to consult the spirit-medium of Joaquim José da Cruz on an island at the entrance to the Lupata gorge. There there took place a great *batuque* and the spirit-medium appears to have lent the weight of his authority to the rising (*334*, 38).

Two armed expeditions were now sent across the Zambesi to destroy the two captains of Manuel Antonio who were holding Massangano. One of these, Guba, was overcome by a stratagem. A band of da Cruz soldiers appeared before his *aringa* with a prisoner bound and beaten, saying they wanted to hand him over to the Portuguese. While Guba, all unsuspecting, was dealing with this situation his *aringa* was rushed and he and eight companions were killed (*334*, 59). The other expedition sent against Camba was not so successful. It was led by Mochenga—the former chief of the da Cruz—and in the fighting he was killed. Camba, however, decided to withdraw in spite of his victory and did so, burning his *aringa* as he left.

On 23 May Motontora re-occupied Massangano and his men began at once to refortify the *aringa*. All the first night, Father Hiller reported, the great war-drum, *mbiribiri*, was beaten, breaking the stillness of the night and audible many miles away 'filling the heads of the Africans with terrible visions of blood and vengeance.' (*334*, 87).

For the last time the government set on foot an expedition against the da Cruz. It was commanded in person by Augusto da Castilho, the governor-general. The campaign was organised, admittedly as told by himself, as a masterpiece of careful planning. Fortifications and supply bases were constructed. Munitions and supplies were collected and the outlying da Cruz *aringas*, like that of Chiuta on Bandar rock, were first subdued.

The Waterloo of the da Cruz was near, but before their Waterloo they were to fight their Ligny. A column of troops sent from Tete was ambushed and dispersed by da Cruz warriors on 21 June on the river Luenha just as the first expedition of Miguel Gouveia had been destroyed twenty-one years before.

The last siege of Massangano began in September and was bitterly contested. Direct attacks on the *aringa* were repulsed and it was not until the end of November that Castilho's men were able to gain possession of the heights overlooking the *aringa*. With guns placed on the hills and on the river sand-banks the *aringa* could be swept with massive fire-power, and on the morning of 29 November the Portuguese woke to find that Motontora had escaped in the night, leaving the devastated *aringa* as a prize in Portuguese hands.

For all his preparations, Castilho had only just succeeded. His men had suffered great privations and Motontora had used every inducement to get Mtoko to attack the Portuguese in the rear. Mtoko had not entered the war but the Pereiras of Macanga had been more willing and their rising on the north bank and the massacre of the Portuguese garrison in October posed a serious problem for the government. Even the final victory was not as great as Castilho's dispatch at first made out.

Motontora and the da Cruz *grandes* had escaped once more— desperately wounded as Castilho claimed—but indubitably alive (*220*). At first Motontora crossed the river to take refuge in Mataza but his following soon began to break up. The fugitives split into two groups soon after leaving Massangano, Motundu- mura leading the breakaway group (*221*). Bonga's eldest son, Moringanisa, also abandoned the party and in December 1888 surrendered to the military command at Guengue with his wife and children. He was executed (*222*).

After these set-backs, however, Motontora appears to have recovered his position of leadership. He formed a close link with the Pereiras and one of his sons, Cancune, married a Pereira woman (*342*, 251). He also constructed an *aringa* for himself in Macanga country near the border with Chikussi, from which he watched the progress of events.

The third phase of the Zambesi Wars which had begun with Andrada's attack on Massangano in 1887 was still raging. Macanga was in open rebellion and at the beginning of 1891 the whole of Barue rose at the news that Sousa had been taken prisoner by Rhodesian police in Manicaland. The da Cruz hastened to throw in their lot with the rebellion. Massangano they could not occupy because a government fort had been built on the site, but Motontora and some of his followers returned to the Muira valley and built a series of stockades—Motontora himself commanding the *aringa* of Inhacafura. Partly as a result of his action the whole of the da Cruz *prazos* joined the rebellion (*342*, 241).

The only military act Motontora is known to have led is an attack on the military post at Guengue in September 1893 which proved unsuccessful (*187*). After this the da Cruz become shadowy figures on whom the historical limelight only occasion- ally plays. Motontora lived to ally himself with Cambuemba, the mercenary captain who defied the Portuguese on the Sena *prazos* until 1897, and thereafter nothing more is heard of him. In 1894 Antonio da Cruz, Bonga's second son, was captured by the Portuguese in Gorongosa and imprisoned (*189*), and in the same year the British authorities in Nyasaland arrested Inacio

Vieira da Cruz, a wandering bandit, who since the destruction of Massangano had moved from Macanga to *prazo* Goma and finally across the border into British territory (*190*). Inacio Vieira da Cruz is not easy to identify among the known members of the family. It is clear, however, that he was one of the most important of the leaders of the 1888 rising still at large and it is just possible that he may have been Inacio Sant'anna da Cruz, Gande, who was brother of Motontora and one of those who escaped from the *aringa* on 29 November.

Conclusion

The importance of the da Cruz family had been first and foremost in the position of their *aringa* between Tete and the sea. The final destruction of Massangano by Castilho was, therefore, a military achievement as important for the Portuguese as the battle of Chaimite when the power of Gungunhana's Gaza nation was broken. But the importance of the family had also been symbolic. To the Portuguese it personified the old, corrupt regime of the *prazo senhors* which the broom of the reawakened Portuguese colonial spirit was to sweep clean. For this reason also the destruction of Massangano had great psychological value for the Portuguese.

From this distance, however, we are in a better position to realise to what extent the old *muzungo* clans, far from being swept away by a revived Portuguese imperialism, destroyed themselves. The Vas dos Anjos and the Silvas were weakened through internal dissensions until they lost control of their territory altogether. Macanga was also weakened through internal dissension and was finally destroyed by the Ngoni in 1902. Sousa was defeated and killed in a war against the Barue royal family which he had displaced in 1880, while Barue itself was ruined by its own internal strife. Even the defeat of the da Cruz was really brought about as much by the co-operation of Sousa and Inacio de Jesus Xavier with the government as by the unaided might of Portuguese arms.

When in 1902 Portugal was at last left with a pacified Zambesia, it was the reward for her tenacity. She had held on to her colony through the dark days of the Zambesi Wars, humiliated and crushed but never giving up, and in the end the 'baronial' families destroyed one another and left a power vacuum which the Portuguese were able at last to fill.

16 The Massingire and the Maganja

This chapter tells the stories of two *sertanejo* families, called Vas dos Anjos and Silva. Both families were founded by traders in ivory and slaves who pushed beyond the borders of Zambesia in the early nineteenth century and established domains for themselves outside the immediate jurisdiction of the Portuguese government. Their conquests did much to win for Portugal the country lying between the Shire, the Zambesi and the sea—the northern half of the modern administrative district of Zambesia.

Their stories differ from that of the Pereiras, however, for both the Silvas and the Vas dos Anjos lost control of the chieftaincies they created and their followers acquired their own 'tribal' identity and developed a state organisation of their own—enabling one to see that the old society of the *prazos* was something vital and living and not merely dependent on the tyranny of the Portuguese slave-owner.

The Massingire

In 1823 the two British naval officers from Captain Owen's survey squadron who were travelling on the Zambesi, were entertained at Maruro by a venerable Indian gentleman who traded in gold and ivory and ran a large plantation stretching for two or three miles behind his house. He was a militia colonel and a man of some standing in the community named Paul Marianno Vas dos Anjos (*422*, vol 2, 49).

He had two contemporaries of the same patronymic who were probably his relatives. There was *Dona* Francisca Vas dos Anjos who held *prazo* Mussembe and Caetano Camillo Vas dos Anjos, also a militia colonel and a man who had held a variety of important posts including the captaincies of Zumbo and of the Zimbabwe garrison. It was Caetano Camillo who rented *prazo* Luabo and became the only settler able to provide food and shelter for the refugees who fled from up the river during the terrible famine years at the end of the 1820s.

So far there is nothing remarkable about the family, but one of the younger members, Paul Marianno II, married the daughter of one of the most powerful *senhors* of Sena, Galdino Faustino de Sousa, a slave trader and lord of a large army of slaves. In 1852 or 1853 Sousa invaded the country round Mount Morumbala and subdued the native population, killing one of their leading chiefs. In this he was only doing what many of the Sena settlers had done in the past, for the Morumbala mountain was a notorious refuge for escaped slaves and a hideout for those who made a living by raiding the traders on the Shire and Zambesi. However, unlike Sisnando Dias Bayão and the other Portuguese who had attacked Morumbala, Sousa decided to make a permanent base there and built an *aringa* for his followers (*118*).

In 1853 the Pereiras failed to capture Massangano and the growing power of the da Cruz family was arrested. Sousa had good reason to fear the da Cruz and in 1854 he supplied a large contingent of soldiers and carriers for the government expedition against Massangano. His men were commanded on this occasion by his son-in-law, Paul Marianno II, and when Sousa died the same year his slaves, his *aringa* and his trading interests all passed into Paul Marianno's possession (*299*, vol 1, 314).

On Sousa's death his followers had set out to make the country weep for the loss of their master (*119*), but they were reassembled on the Shire by Paul Marianno, who set about making them the most formidable force on the lower Zambesi. Through his sister, Paul was related to Antonio José da Cruz Coimbra, the chief agent for supplying the French plantations with contract (*engagé*) labour. Coimbra supplied firearms and other trade goods and Paul Marianno dispatched boat-loads of slaves to the delta for shipment to the Île de Réunion.

It was not long, however, before the hot-headed Paul Marianno became involved in a feud as bitter as that between Pereira and da Cruz in the Tete area. In the Sena captaincy the dominant family had, since the beginning of the century been that of Ferrão—a family of humble origins but which was, by the 1850s, the possessors of the Bayão inheritance obtained through a judicious marriage. It was with Isidore, son-in-law to the head of the Ferrões, that Paul indulged his feud.

The slave bands of the two *senhors* were soon devastating and burning the villages and fields around Sena. Paul's men appear

276

to have got the worst of the fighting, for the authorities at Sena sided with Isidore and successfully excluded Paul from entering Sena with his followers.

As a result the young Vas dos Anjos was forced to establish a base on the other side of the Zambesi, and began to construct a formidable *aringa* at Shamo on the Shire river just below Mount Morumbala (*441*). The stockade of Shamo lay with one side on the Shire and with its back protected by a lake. It was large enough to contain a considerable town and was surrounded with a double line of stakes, strengthened by earthworks and loop-holed for musketry. Paul's own house within the *aringa* was made of brick and was comfortably furnished in the European style. The *aringa* also contained the huts of his principal followers and a store-house and arsenal where some seven thousand muskets and four brass cannon had been collected (*469*, vol 1, 70).

Sousa had co-operated closely with the Portuguese authorities; he had even wanted to hand over his conquests to the crown and have them made into *prazos da coroa* (*118*). Paul Marianno's activities, however, soon led him into a war with the Portuguese. His men, raiding for slaves, caused a turmoil on the lower Zambesi; they carried off *colonos* from the *prazos* and on one occasion were supposed to have raided the town of Sena itself. Paul's personal reputation, too, was extremely unsavoury. He earned the nickname Matakenya—the causer of trembling—because on one occasion he had personally massacred fifty of his prisoners with an assegai.

So open were Paul's slaving activities and so scandalous was his behaviour, that the authorities, who were prepared to wink at the activities of those who maintained a discreet silence, were forced to take action. While the wars between the da Cruz, the Pereiras and the government continued higher up the river, Paul Marianno and his brother—known as Bonga, the wild-cat—were quite safe, but with the peace which followed the death of Joaquim da Cruz in 1855, fortune began to turn against the Vas dos Anjos family.

In 1857 Paul Marianno was arrested while on a visit to Queli-mane. This was undoubtedly an attempt by the government to break up the slave-trading ring that operated in the Zambesi delta, but there must also have been other motives, for the arrest was followed by the mounting of a military expedition to destroy the *aringa* at Shamo and disperse Paul Marianno's followers.

Shamo was defended by Paul's brother Bonga and its defences were quite as formidable as those of Massangano. The Portuguese certainly risked another defeat similar to those they had suffered at the hands of the da Cruz. However, on 9 September 1858, after a campaign lasting five months, Shamo was taken without any serious resistance. The *aringa* was well-stocked with food and it seems probable either that there was a panic and the defenders lost heart, as John Kirk suggested, or that ammunition gave out and resistance was no longer possible (*380*, 72).

The capture of Shamo was a severe blow to the prestige of the Vas dos Anjos, and many a lesser Zambesi family would have been ruined by it. Bonga withdrew with some of his followers towards Morumbala, while other fugitives straggled down the Zambesi towards the estates of their master at Maruro (*380*, 81). For the first time in nearly twenty years the Zambesi was at peace.

With his people defeated and his property confiscated, Paul was released and lived for a short time—presumably under surveillance—near Sena. Cruz Coimbra crossed to India and lay low until the hunt for the slavers should die down. It was reported that he offered a substantial bribe for the release of his kinsman (*391*, 117), but in spite of this Paul Marianno was sent for trial to Moçambique at the very end of December 1859.

There, with his fortunes at their lowest ebb, the tide began to turn once more. Paul Marianno was fined and allowed to return to Quelimane to raise the money. Once back in the Rivers he was surrounded by his former associates anxious for the return of the good old days; he obtained trade goods and set off for the Shire. There his followers, leaderless since the war, rallied round their chief and by the middle of 1860 the Vas dos Anjos were once more raiding in the Shire valley. Cruz Coimbra also returned to Quelimane (*390*, 402).

The old family lands had been seized by the victors of the war of 1858, so Paul Marianno and his brother established themselves on Mount Morumbala whence they were only dislodged by a government expedition comprising forces from Quelimane, Sena and Tete in November of 1861 (*461*, 375). From Morumbala Paul then moved into the Shire valley looting, burning and destroying among the peaceful Manganja people. His arrival in the Shire highlands coincided with the first incursion of the Yao and with the raiding of Livingstone's Makololo porters, whose activities so much resembled his own. For a short time he settled near Mount Milanje, but later retired from the area of the cataracts and built a new *aringa* south of the Ruo river, leaving the higher reaches of the Shire to the Makololo.

278

The power and reputation of Paul Marianno attracted large numbers of followers from among the broken Manganja villages and these were welded into a new state, just as the Azimba had been reassembled under the chieftainship of the Pereiras. Marianno's people became known by the name Massingire—a name supposed to derive from *ku-txindjire* meaning to cut wood for a stockade (*446*, 10).

Paul Marianno II died late in September 1863 and was succeeded by his son Paul Marianno III, who also took the African name Matakenya. As he was only eight years old when his father died, he was frequently distinguished as Marianno *pequeno*—Marianno the little. During his long minority, power among the Massingire was shared by his mother Adriana, his aunt Maria, and one of the *capitaes* called Chagunde and nicknamed Machingachinga—perhaps after Chinga Chinga mountain (*255*, 209).

Maria may have been the old woman described so affectionately by João de Azevedo Coutinho, who knew her in the late 1880s when she was an old woman.

> In all the numerous occasions that I passed Chamuara I never failed to go to see the old Senhora Maria. She was black and easily seventy years old, looking well-fed and with her crinkly hair quite white. She was always neat and clean and dressed herself scrupulously in the Indian manner. She was relatively well-off, her house was high and tiled and it seemed partly an African and partly a European house. She had innumerable female servants and *bandazias*, negresses and house boys, who lived in the small village which was inhabited almost solely by them. She possessed other residences (*luanes*) one downstream of Vicente and another in Caia Murassa where she had a house and orchard which produced the very best green tangerines. This old lady always showed me great affection, and told me the old tales of the Zambesi, that once mysterious region, and about the personalities and events of her day, speaking in bad Portuguese (*342*, 113).

Dona Maria had a weakness for *crême de menthe* which she called green gin and Coutinho never failed to bring her some when he came to visit her. But all this was later, when the power of the Vas dos Anjos had been smashed.

After the death of Paul Marianno II the Massingire were too weak to resist the growing power of the Makololo chiefs.

Machingachinga, looking for allies to help stem their advance, called in the aid of *Dona* Luiza da Cruz, sister of the chief of the famous family of Cruz, who held *prazo* Guengue which was also threatened by the Makololo advance. The alliance proved a total disaster and the Massingire lost further ground until some time in the 1870s the frontier between the two peoples was fixed (on the left bank at least) more or less permanently on the Ruo river (*255*).

In 1875 the Scottish missions had arrived in the Shire highlands. Their arrival greatly increased the confidence of the Makololo for, in spite of all the caution of the Scots and their determination to remain aloof from compromising politics, it was assumed by everyone that they and Livingstone's former porters were natural allies and that behind the scenes they would be encouraging the Makololo in their attacks on Portuguese territory. Both the Makololo and the Massingire were now becoming known in the consulates and foreign offices of the world and they were soon to be in the eye of an international diplomatic storm (*414*).

In 1877 the Makololo carried out their most daring raid, devastating *prazo* Goma and putting Sena itself into a state of alert. At a meeting with the commandant of Sena, the Makololo chief, Chipitula, claimed that the raid had been carried out on the orders of the 'English' (*177*). Even without this information, however, the Portuguese had become convinced of the threat posed by the Scottish missions and had decided that they must strengthen their hold on the Shire valley. Who better to undertake this task than Paul Marianno III, chief of the Massingire?

In 1879 Paul accepted the office of colonel in the militia offered him by the government and the pension and supply of arms that went with it. Originally the agreement had been that, in exchange for this official guarantee of his position, he would surrender his lands to the Portuguese authorities. This part of the agreement does not appear to have been carried out, but for a short time the young Matakenya enjoyed his newfound status in the Portuguese community.

Late in 1880 Paul led some of his men to help the government suppress disturbances near Sena and it was then that he was seen by the Frenchman, Paul Guyot. Guyot described him as a man of dark complexion but with straight hair. He wore European dress, decorated with gold chains and lions' claws. He had been sent to Goa for some education but his behaviour was uncouth and on one occasion he amused himself by firing his rifle at all the Africans he could see from the door of his hut (*373, 674, 684*).

This was the Indian summer of Vas dos Anjos power. In July 1881 the Makololo raided south of the Ruo again and by the end of the year had occupied a large part of Massingire country. In despair at their chief's inability to resist these attacks, the leading *capitaes* seized Paul Marianno and handed him over to the Portuguese authorities. Deserted by his followers and answerable for many crimes, the unfortunate prisoner was sent to Sena and from there dispatched with an escort to Quelimane. He was murdered during a stop at Mopea in December 1881 (*122*).

The Scottish missionaries at Blantyre thought that Marianno's downfall was due to the fact that he was a tyrant who had committed many murders and other atrocities. He had the blood of a Portuguese officer to answer for and had threatened to kill the next Englishman he could lay his hand on, for he thought the English had been supplying the Makololo with firearms (*178*). However, no Zambesi *senhor* had previously suffered because of a reputation for murder and cruelty.

The reason for Marianno's fall was clearly his failure to defend Massingire territory and to provide his followers with the good things of life that they had come to expect from a great *senhor*. His deposition was not an unprecedented occurrence, for chiefs of the Pereira and the da Cruz families suffered similar treatment at the hands of their discontented *grandes*. The Vas dos Anjos family itself was not expelled from Massingire and Adriana remained an influential figure in the country after the death of her son (*414, 94–5*).

The Portuguese authorities were overjoyed at the death of Marianno. An inquiry into the murder was instigated but nothing was discovered, and meanwhile the policy-makers in Moçambique moved eagerly to take advantage of the situation. Having deposed Marianno, the *grandes* of the Massingire had petitioned the Portuguese authorities for protection against the Makololo. This was an ideal opportunity for the government to establish control over the Shire valley. Accordingly on 12 May 1882, the governor of Quelimane, José de Almeida d'Avila, raised the Portuguese flag at the village of Pinda on the Shire and received the formal submission of the Massingire chiefs. The cession was made by the assembled '*chefes da povações, capitaes do prazo, manamambos, mocasambos e inhacuavas* of the late Marianno Vas dos Anjos'.

If this formula means anything, it indicates that the traditional chiefs of the Manganja were as involved as the leaders of the slaves in the politics of Massingire. The cession included the land occupied by the Makololo and the governor promised peace and justice for the region if it remained loyal. At the request of the Massingire chiefs a small military detachment was to be stationed at Chironje 'as a guarantee that the government will not forget them afterwards' (*464*, no 16).

This agreement differs strikingly from that made with Macanga in 1875. The Portuguese had dealt with Macanga as with an independent state of some power and standing. It treated the Massingire as a conquered people—a great mistake for, if they were indeed conquered, it had not been by the Portuguese.

Two years separated the setting up of the Portuguese administration and the outbreak of the Massingire rebellion—for the Portuguese one of the most disastrous episodes of the Zambesi Wars. First among the causes of the rising must be placed the obvious failure of the Portuguese government to check the power of the Makololo and the threat it represented to the security of the Massingire. In 1883 the Makololo chief Chipitula demanded the return of one of his wives who had escaped to Massingire territory. This incident had occurred some years before (*207*), and the Portuguese believed it had been revived as a pretext for mounting another raid south of the Ruo. Then early in 1884 Chipitula was murdered by an English trader called Fenwick and again the whole of the Shire was in a turmoil as the Makololo closed the river to traffic and even went as far as to sink a steamer belonging to the African Lakes Company.

The second main cause of the rising was the behaviour of the Portuguese administrator in Massingire. The Massingire had not submitted to the Portuguese with any idea of seeing control of their affairs taken out of the hands of their chiefs. Half realising this, the Portuguese administrator had moved cautiously. He collected no *mussoco* (tribute) in the first year and the second year collected only half the usual amount (*208*). Then at the end of 1883 orders were issued for a census to be taken 'without which a complete collection of the *mussoco* is impossible' (*152*).

To take a census was an act of administrative efficiency which marked the new concern of the authorities that the Zambesi colony should be well-run. In 1878 a census had been ordered for the Quelimane district where the government was experimenting with direct administration of the *prazos*. It had resulted in widespread resistance by the African peasants who, like peasants in many other societies, saw in a census the beginning of the rule of the tax collector and the recruiting sergeant. Fearful

282

Macombe Chavunda, Cambuemba's son and other prisoners of the 1902 Barue war on the way to the Cape Verde Islands

An enormous Baobab tree inside the *aringa* of Missongue at Barue

10 African weaver smoking a huge
    tobacco-pipe

11 Blacksmith's forge and
    bellows of goatskin

12 A wedding procession at Tete

of causing open revolt, the government had stopped the taking of the census, but now in Massingire they tried again (*149*).

Rumours of the census soon spread in the interior. As Fred Moir, the manager of the African Lakes Company, put it, the Africans were afraid that taxes were now going to be collected 'not only from the men and women, but from boys and girls and from the very children unborn' (*208*).

The Portuguese administrator also began to replace the *capitaes* of Massingire with his own nominees and even went so far as to depose Pedro Antonio de Almeida, a *capitão* who had been one of the signatories of the 1882 agreement and who ruled in Paul Marianno's old *aringa*. Finally, the Portuguese administrator tried to prevent the administration of the *muavi* poison test which, according to Montagu Kerr, was being administered to find out who was responsible for Marianno's death. Two chiefs were arrested and sent to Quelimane. It is perhaps not reading too much into these incidents to see an organised attempt by the Portuguese to get rid of the Massingire leaders and so 'pacify' the people as a whole (*152*). However, before the two arrested chiefs, Bezingwe and Raposo, had reached Mopea they escaped their captors and raised the country against the Portuguese. George Chokobwino, vice-consul Foot's interpreter, reported:

On July 19th I crossed the river to the other side of Mpassa and I found the Portuguese there who were very kind to me. And on the next day the war came and killed them—And the war caught one of the white people called commandante. He killed one of the war people. Then I heard calling from the other side of the river saying, 'Tamandu, what is that, what is that?' Then Tamandu said 'The war is come'. Then they said 'Where is the war come from?' Then Tamandu said 'From Machinjera.' (*196*)

This was the first information the British community in the Shire Highlands received of the rising, which was totally unexpected.

The rising broke out at two widely separate places. On 20 July the Portuguese contingents at Chironje and Mpassa were attacked and killed—only two individuals being spared, a lieutenant who had married one of Marianno's daughters, and one son of the commandant. All the other settlements and trading depots on the Shire fell quickly to the rebels. Shamo and

Chimuara were looted, a number of Portuguese were killed and French, Dutch and British traders lost their goods.

At the same time a rising began on the *prazo* of Maganja behind the plantations of the Opium Company at Mopea. A group of these rebels attacked a Dutch trading station at Mutu on 3 August. To those on the spot it appeared that the whole of the lower Zambesi had erupted in rebellion, and it was not until later that it was realised that there were two separate risings. Refugees crowded the small fort at Sena and in Quelimane an extraordinary panic ensued with the Portuguese governor of the town taking refuge on a boat anchored out in the river and sending urgent messages to the *prazos* up country asking for irregular troops to defend the port (*414*, 99).

The defence of Quelimane was organised by Fred Moir of the African Lakes Company, who raised a force of fifteen Europeans armed with modern rifles and a number of slaves, boatmen and carriers. On 11 August this tiny army met the advance guard of the rebels. They were besieging the Opium Company's warehouse which was being defended by a band of three Europeans and a dozen or so Indian clerks and their families.

In the short and sharp encounter that followed, the leader of the besieging force, Chief Pandidya, was killed and his followers retreated towards the Shire (*414*, 100). It seems quite probable that the men who besieged Mopea were not Massingire at all but rebels from the *prazo* of Maganja. Part of this *prazo* had been granted as a concession to the Opium Company and the man who had at one time been the *senhor* of the region, João Coelho Barata, resented the loss of his influence among the *colonos*. It is fairly clear that he, his wife Ines and *Dona* Captiva Alves who rented *prazo* Absinta, all sent their slaves and clients to join in the rising—partly because loot and rapine were the staples of the old Zambesian way of life, and partly to stem the advance of the commercial companies and of ordered government which were slowly circumscribing the activities of the Zambesi *senhors*.

Major Caldas Xavier, at that time manager of the Opium Company, put most of the blame for the violence on João Barata. Pandidya, the chief killed in the attack on the Opium Company's warehouses at Mopea, appears to have been one of Barata's *capitaes* and it may even be that the Massingire themselves never left the Shire valley (*330*).

Having destroyed the Portuguese on the Shire swiftly and effectively, the leaders of the Massingire hoped they could obtain British protection. Apart from their resentment at the

284

attacks of the Makololo, which they believed were instigated by the British, the Massingire had always sought British friendship —even as early as 1858 when Livingstone had visited the camp of the rebel Bonga, and had considered mediating between him and the government. Later Livingstone had been fêted by Bonga in his house and on the death of Paul Marianno II in 1863, the Massingire chiefs had come to the Universities Mission to seek formal British protection. The Reverend Horace Waller had even thought at one time of placing himself at the head of Marianno's warriors (*335, 228*). Now Chief Bezingwe came humbly to Fred Moir to apologise for any loss the British might have suffered, while an embassy of Massingire visited the Makololo to ask for their aid against the Portuguese (*408*, ch 20, *197*).

The British, however, kept aloof from any official involvement in the rising and before September was out a Portuguese army of black mercenaries, commanded by the redoubtable Manuel Antonio de Sousa, arrived on the Shire to exact retribution. The Massingire made three stands against Sousa and held out in Marianno's old *aringa* for some time, but Sousa had crushed their opposition by the end of November—the rebels being either fugitives in the hills or dead in the burnt-out villages.

Massingire country was made part of the new district of Manica which was set up in 1884, but no official Portuguese resident returned until 1887. From that year until 1892 the area was once again administered by a military commandant at Chironje. As Portuguese and Makololo struggled for control of the Shire in 1888 and 1889 (the struggle which ended abruptly with the British ultimatum of 11 January 1890) the Massingire continually threatened once more to rise in rebellion. Had they done so the international repercussions would have been disconcerting for the Portuguese. The reason that they did not rise, according to the British naval officer, Lieutenant-Commander Keane, was that they hoped for British protection when the dispute between the two countries was finally settled, for 'they have always considered themselves as belonging to the English' (*201*).

When the frontier between Moçambique and Nyasaland was finally drawn in 1891, most of Massingire territory remained in Portuguese hands, though some of it on the right bank of the Shire came under British control and the British concluded a series of agreements with their chiefs.

Massingire territory which fell within the Portuguese sphere of influence was handed over by the government to private enterprise in 1892 when it was rented by the German adventurer Carl Wiese. Wiese was only interested in the strip of land along the river and the hinterland remained 'unpacified' until 1898 when Maganja da Costa was finally occupied by a Portuguese expeditionary force under the command of old *Dona* Maria's friend João de Azevedo Coutinho (*188*).

The Massingire rising can stand as good illustration of the strength and cohesion which the followers and subjects of one of the great Zambesi families might attain and which could survive when the *senhor* himself had ceased to rule.

Maganja da Costa

Of all the great *senhors* of nineteenth-century Zambesia, only the Silvas had an indubitably European origin; indubitably, that is, if one accepts João de Azevedo Coutinho's account of their origin. According to this account, the founder of the family was a Portuguese from the province of Beira called Antonio Alves da Silva, who settled in Zambesia as a trader at the beginning of the nineteenth century. He travelled to all the fairs north and south of the Zambesi and in particular frequented the fair of Ingode on the Licare river near Quelimane, where ivory and slaves from Lake Nyasa were traded to the Portuguese. His main trading partner was João de Jesus Maria, father of another famous *sertanejo*, Romão de Jesus Maria. Antonio Alves da Silva had two sons, João Bonifacio and Vitorino, and one daughter who married a *prazo*-holder called Azevedo and was the mother-in-law of Livingstone's friend Nunes (*342, 467*).

João Bonifacio prospered in the manner traditional among the Zambesi *sertanejos*, trading and fighting and gradually assembling a band of loyal followers. In 1853 he and his brother, Vitorino, went on a trading expedition deep into the interior. From Quelimane they journeyed to the Shire and then west to the Luangwa valley in search of ivory. From the Luangwa they crossed Bemba country and reached Lake Mweru. The journey did not pass off without the two brothers having to fight their way home with their commercial gains.

The following year João Bonifacio and his father's old associate, João de Jesus Maria, accompanied Antonio da Cruz Coimbra's expedition against Massangano (*334*, 83), and João Bonifacio must have held his men together after the rout of the army at the end of May, for he later joined Tito de Araujo Sicard, the new governor, and remained loyal to him when mutineers deprived Sicard of his command (*299*, vol 1, 363).

João Bonifacio's mother was *Dona* Teodora Temporaria de Matos, a legendary figure who died in 1898 reputedly aged 110 years. She had held the *prazo* of Quelimane do Sal since 1829 and it was probably from a base on her land that her son was able to expand his trading interests up the Moçambique coast (*368*, 61). When the opportunity offered, João Bonifacio rented the *prazo* of Licungo on the coast and settled his slaves there. Gradually he extended his control as far as the river Moniga, which was the traditional boundary between the lands of the Quelimane captaincy and those of the Sultan of Angoche. Then in the heart of his *prazo* work was begun on the great *aringa* of Maganja da Costa, the largest ever to be constructed in Portuguese East Africa. His men also built an *aringa* at Bajone to protect the anchorage at the mouth of the Moniga river (*342*, 468).

Here João Bonifacio was on the frontiers of the Zambesi world. Further north the *senhors* had never looked—though the couriers going overland to Moçambique had sometimes travelled the road leading through the heart of the Makua country. In the normal course of events João Bonifacio would probably have been content with his vast dominions and the ample opportunities for trade that these afforded him. However, he soon discovered that he was confronted by a resourceful and determined opponent in Mussa Quanto, the half-brother of the Sultan of Angoche.

In 1855 Mussa Quanto raised a large raiding party from his brother's dominions and from the Makua chiefs subject to Angoche and, according to the tradition, struck deep into the hinterland. He overran the Milanje district and reached the Shire river where he was repulsed by some of Marianno Vas dos Anjos's men. His advance thus checked, Mussa Quanto retreated south-east and devastated the *prazos* around Quelimane, including João Bonifacio's *prazo* of Licungo, before leading the remnants of his vast disintegrating army back to Angoche. If this account be true, a single raid carried out in a single season covered every bit of seven hundred miles. This seems hardly credible and it is probably the case that the oral traditions of Zambesia have telescoped a number of separate raids into one epic adventure (*397*, 185).

João Bonifacio had already suffered from raiding parties with their base in the Sultanate of Angoche and had had to watch his *colonos* escape across the border from his tax-gatherers. He had been too weak to resist Mussa Quanto and had had to watch his stockades being looted and burnt, his men enslaved or killed and his women raped. As soon as the storm had subsided he planned his revenge.

When João Bonifacio eventually crossed the Moniga at the height of the dry season in August 1861 he led an army of 2,000 specially recruited black mercenaries and was accompanied by eighteen European soldiers and three field guns. From the start he had been encouraged by the government in his enterprise, and he had received large consignments of muskets which enabled him to arm half his men with guns. João Bonifacio's army had been assembled and trained at his *aringa*, which became known as M'Passue (supposed to be a corruption of Bonifacio), a name which was used as a title by the Silvas themselves. His men were divided into twelve *ensacas* of two hundred and fifty men each, and Coutinho thinks that this organisation later determined the pattern of development of the independent state of Maganja (*342*, 476).

Living off the country as it marched, João Bonifacio's army took nearly a month to cross the territory of Angoche, coming face to face with the enemy on 25 September outside the capital town of the Sultanate. The trenches and fortifications were stormed, the defenders slaughtered and two days given over to loot, but Mussa Quanto himself escaped and João Bonifacio was struck down by a bullet in one of the last skirmishes of the war.

Under the vigorous command of Mateus, one of the first of the black mercenary leaders of whom we hear in the Zambesi Wars, raiding parties of Zambesi warriors reached as far north as the bay of Mocambo, almost within sight of Moçambique Island, but João Bonifacio's brother and heir, Vitorino, had no intention of trying to add Angoche to his dominions and gradually the Zambesi mercenaries were withdrawn and Angoche was handed over to the government. By 1863 the last of João Bonifacio's men had left.

Vitorino continued to rule in Maganja until his death in or near 1874. In 1867 he was asked to accompany the expedition against the da Cruz at Massangano and in 1872 he married José Nunes's aunt and tied his family and the Nunes still closer together.

Vitorino's death marked the end of the direct line of the Silvas but the various connections of the family continued to form a controlling interest in the Quelimane area. *Dona* Teodora de Matos continued in possession of Quelimane do Sal, but Licungo had passed by 1875 into the hands of the Albuquerque family, one of whom, José Bernardo, married *Dona* Ursula da Silva, João Bonifacio's grand-niece (*342*, 214). João de Jesus Maria was still alive and the holder of *prazo* Pepino. The main inheritance of Silva's, however, fell to Marianno Henrique de Nazareth, and his *éminence grise*, always known as the '*muzungo* Aurelio'.

Aurelio was a mulatto, son of a Goanese and an African woman, and he had apparently been adopted by João Bonifacio and had inherited some of the great leader's charisma (*342*, 184). Marianno Henrique, however, probably owed his connection with the Silvas to marriage, for he seems to have been the son of Joaquim Henrique de Nazareth, a *prazo*-holder, who died about 1874. Marianno Henrique inherited the Silva title of M'Passue and the Silva *prazo* of Licungo—by 1881 he had become the most powerful man in the Quelimane area.

Of all the *sertanejos* of the late nineteenth century none played a more clever political game than Marianno Henrique. He was always ready to provide men for government service, whether on military expeditions or on public works. For his co-operation he received hand-outs of firearms, which somehow never found their way back to the government arsenals. At the same time he carried on an extensive trade in ivory and slaves from his private port of Bajone on the Moniga river. In 1881 José Nunes, the British vice-consul, wrote

> It is well known that Umpasso's [Marianno Henrique's] men are respected all over the country, as far as near Lake Nyasa, to which place they go now and then to purchase natives and steal them in small skirmishes (*193*).

Rumours of the marauding activities of Marianno Henrique's men continually filtered through to Quelimane. In 1879 he was taken to task by the government for fighting which had occurred between his men and those of Balthasar Farinha in Boror (*150*), and as late as 1894 the British consul in Moçambique carried out an investigation into allegations that the slave trade was still smouldering on along the Maganja coast.

Although Marianno Henrique's authority on the *prazos* may have been extensive it is by no means clear that the descendants of João Bonifacio's men were subservient to him. These warriors, whose reputations stood high after the conquest of Angoche, had formed what amounted to an independent military republic based on the great *aringa* of Maganja da Costa.

The organisation of this republic filled João de Azevedo Coutinho with admiration. The twelve *ensacas* or regiments which had originally been raised by João Bonifacio for his campaign against Angoche were retained. They were, however, greatly increased in size as new recruits were attracted to join them, and eventually each *ensaca* numbered 1,000 to 1,200 men.

The head of each of the *ensacas* was called *kazembe* and he was elected by the regiment's 'non-commissioned officers' (*mucatas*). The *kazembe* was always chosen from among the veteran warriors of the *ensaca* but the choice had to be approved by a council of the *kazembes* presided over by the chief captain of the *aringa*. Each *kazembe* was entrusted with the collection of tribute in different parts of the country, and the sums collected went towards the maintenance of the great *aringa*.

The *kazembes* elected one of their number as chief captain and he held supreme military and political power. He had two deputies who were also elected by the *kazembes*—a second-in-command with the title of *bazo* and a third called *canhongo* (*342, 477*).

Although this state organisation derived from the traditions of the old Zambesi *prazos*, there appear to be no parallels to it in the history of Moçambique. Comparisons might be made with the regiments of the Ngoni or the self-perpetuating military élite of the Mamelukes in Egypt. Coutinho is probably right, however, to call it unique in the history of Africa.

In this republic the power of the Silva family was weak and ill-defined. *Muzungo* Aurelio lived in Maganja and was the close adviser of the *kazembes*. The Portuguese authorities thought that he was responsible for hostile attitudes adopted by Maganja towards the Portuguese. Marianno Henrique probably maintained close contacts with the *kazembes*, but he did not live in Maganja and his influence there cannot have been very decisive. *Dona* Ursula da Silva was called the 'Queen of Maganja' by the Portuguese and her husband, Bernardo de Albuquerque, was used as an intermediary between the Portuguese authorities and the Maganja *kazembes*. Coutinho is probably right when he says that the family, after the death of Vitorino, became councillors but nothing more.

Not surprisingly, the Portuguese government found the existence of this military republic on its flank a considerable embarrassment. It was, however, no greater embarrassment for them than the presence of the independent *senhors* of the Zambesi who openly defied Portuguese authority within the walls of the townships themselves. The regiments of Maganja da Costa were only too ready to be hired for service with any government punitive expedition which would offer them opportunities for loot, and supply them with firearms and ammunition.

In 1884 a contingent was raised to help suppress the Massingire rising (*187*) and another regiment accompanied Serpa Pinto's march up the Shire in 1889. In 1891 João de Azevedo Coutinho hired four hundred Maganja soldiers for his projected expedition against Macanga—the expedition that was subsequently diverted to the invasion of Barue.

This contingent had been negotiated for Coutinho by Bernardo de Albuquerque and arrived under the command of the captain of the *aringa*, Mateus. Each soldier brought with him his own servants and they formed the *corps d'élite* of Coutinho's force.

> These uncontrolled and undisciplined expeditions are a source of much evil. Disorder, drunkenness, and robbery prevail wherever they pass. The acts of these expeditions do not impress the natives with the dominion and dignity of an European State; on the contrary they occasion nothing but ridicule (*204*).

These words were written by William Churchill, acting British consul, in 1892 when the full fiasco of Coutinho's expedition was known. After marauding at will in the Zambesi valley, the army had eventually invaded Barue and laid siege to the *aringa* of Inhachirondo. A casual shot from the defenders exploded the ammunition dump, killing or wounding all the European officers in the besieging army. Coutinho himself was desperately wounded and his Maganja soldiers, unpaid and defeated, set off to fight their way home like any other mercenary army robbed of the spoils of victory.

As they marched they devastated the *prazos* round Quelimane, attracting other supporters as they went, and finally descended on Villa Formosa, the chief settlement of Boror *prazo*, on 20 February 1892. This they occupied for six days and totally destroyed. An attack on the fair at Ingode was beaten off and the soldiers then passed on into Maganja territory. Two weeks later they returned in force, probably with the object of taking Quelimane itself. The town was put into a state of alert and earthworks thrown up outside it. This time, however, a gunboat arrived in time to stop them crossing the Macuse river (*203*).

291

Vice-Consul Ross thought he could detect the hand of Marianno Henrique and Bernardo de Albuquerque in the attack on Boror but this remains conjectural (205).

In spite of this lawless behaviour and the official expressions of outrage, the government was again considering hiring Maganja soldiers when it looked as though trouble might break out on the Zambesi in 1893 (187). It was this year too that the Portuguese made the first tentative efforts to control Maganja. The partition of south-east Africa had placed the region firmly in the Portuguese sphere but the omens for the future of Portuguese sovereignty were not auspicious. In 1887 an officer had been sent to investigate charges of slaving and piracy in the Tejungo river. He and all his companions had been murdered—or they were presumed to be murdered—for the officer, Simão de Oliveira, had travelled disguised as an Indian merchant in a trading dhow and had probably met the fate usually meted out to spies.

The Portuguese government now tried to place a resident in Maganja and in 1893 a young officer called Feijo Teixeira set out for the *aringa*, having first received permission through the Silva family in Quelimane in the usual way. Teixeira was much liked in Maganja. He had got on well with the contingent which had been sent on the expedition to Barue and he was admired for his dexterity on the bicycle, which had just made its appearance in the colony. The captain of the *aringa* had only agreed to his presence as representative of Portugal provided he was the sole European in the party, and so Teixeira was accompanied only by twenty Angolan troops. He was granted quarters in one corner of the great *aringa*.

The arrival of Feijo Teixeira made little practical difference to the government of Maganja. He was virtually a prisoner in the *aringa* and, of course, could not collect *mussoco* or carry out any of the functions of administration. He was forced to leave in 1895 after disagreements with the *capitão* and, although the Maganja were then favoured with a visit from the governor of Quelimane and agreed to receive another resident, they remained for all practical purposes sovereign in their vast territory.

In 1897 João de Azevedo Coutinho became governor of Zambesia and decided to take a strong line with all the *capitaes* and mercenary leaders who still survived from the era of the Zambesi Wars. He decided to try to replace the resident in Maganja with a full detachment of troops.

Events now moved swiftly towards the climax that Coutinho intended. An independent fighting chieftaincy could not be tolerated alongside a European colony either in Natal, in Rhodesia or in Moçambique. Zulu mercenaries were sent under two European officers and installed themselves without resistance in the *aringa*, only to find that their supplies and mails were intercepted by Maganja warriors on the road. Fighting now became general along the borders of the Quelimane *prazos* and Maganja, and a column was dispatched with supplies for the Zulus in the *aringa* but with orders also to build a fortified camp on the edge of Maganja country. This was the usual Zambesi army made up of Portuguese residents and *senhors*, their slaves and carriers, professional mercenaries and a few regular troops. The force, commanded by Vieira de Rocha, met resistance at the Maballa river and although it forced the passage, it was hemmed in by Maganja warriors and was forced to dig itself in. Soon Rocha lost control even of the hard-won river crossing and was virtually besieged. He was burdened with a large force to feed and maintain. He decided to divest himself of the sick and other supernumeraries and a hundred and twenty Africans duly left the *aringa* to try to get back to their villages. Seventy of them died in an ambush laid for them by the Maganja.

Coutinho then set out to raise yet another force on the *prazos* of the lower Zambesi and was able to dispatch Massano de Amorim to relieve both the force besieged in Maballa and that in the *aringa*. Amorim marched swiftly and without any opposition was able to occupy the great *aringa*. Coutinho himself followed but the great final battle with the warriors of the Maganja never came. One night in his encampment Coutinho was called to a secret meeting by one of his followers. He was told that some of the Maganja *grandes* wanted to speak with him in private. So, without telling a soul, Coutinho set out at two in the morning to a secret rendez-vous armed only with his pistol and without an escort. The risk was calculated and successful. He guaranteed peace terms if the *grandes* would come to the *aringa* in three days time and surrender.

The next day Coutinho formally entered the great *aringa* and on 22 June received eighty of the *grandes* of Maganja. A tribunal was set up to try those suspected of war crimes and in the end six were executed, the rest receiving pardons.

Why had the Maganja at the very last collapsed without a fight? Coutinho more than hinted that it was the awe inspired by his reputation that had put unwonted courage into his men and had caused a collapse in the morale of the enemy. One naturally suspects this explanation, coming as it does from Coutinho's own pen, but at any other suggestion one can only guess. Only two of the *grandes* of Maganja refused to surrender; the *kazembe* Siza and Aurelio, who fled northwards and took refuge in the district of Moçambique where Coutinho's writ did not run.

Coutinho sent a flying column northwards across the whole of Maganja but was prevented by a peremptory order of the governor-general from pursuing the Maganja fugitives into the province of Moçambique itself. Other columns travelled inland receiving the surrender of the arms of outlying detachments of Maganja soldiers, and the area remained 'pacified'. Soon afterwards Aurelio returned secretly to Maganja but was seen and shot by Portuguese soldiers. By the end of 1898 the final chapters of the history of the Vas dos Anjos of Massingire and the Silvas of Maganja had been written (*342*, 463–528).

17　The Portuguese on the Middle Zambesi

While the great struggles of the Zambesi Wars were revolving round the rivalries of the *prazo* dynasties on the lower river, the Zambesi above Tete had passed largely into obscurity and totally out of Portuguese control. The *prazo* system had never been extended beyond the Cabora Bassa rapids, and the interests of the Portuguese beyond this point had been entirely commercial, interspersed from time to time with mining ventures. Until the eighteenth century any settlement had always been frustrated by the cunning of the chiefs who held the territory along the north and south banks, but after 1700 a fair had been established at the confluence of the Luangwa and the Zambesi and seasonal and permanent mining camps had grown up in the interior.

By the early nineteenth century most of the mining *bares* had fallen into private hands and existed as oases of Portuguese rule, often deep in the interior and almost always unrelated to any *prazo* contract. These *bares* served as centres for trade as well as mining and it was from them that the Portuguese tried to tap the wealth of north central Africa.

The fair at Zumbo had, meanwhile, been slipping into anarchy. It was frequently attacked by neighbouring chiefs, its communications with Tete were not secure, and it was torn by internal rivalries among the traders. Then in the 1830s the area was hit by the invasion of the Ngoni. The fair at Zumbo was closed in 1836 and most of the Portuguese *bares* in the interior must have disappeared about this time as well. Only the Caetano Pereiras were able to hold onto anything substantial during those turbulent years and, as a result, by the 1840s they commanded what was virtually a monopoly of the trade in ivory and slaves reaching the Zambesi from the north.

The Pereiras, of course, could not operate alone and besides their slaves, they had many mulattos and even European Portuguese in their service. So considerable was the trade that passed through their hands that Gualdino José Nunes could write in

1853 that more trade was done at their headquarters than at Tete itself (*299*, vol 1, 276).

The Pereiras remained on the watch to prevent any rivals from invading their trading preserves, and they were assisted in this by the hostility which the chiefs of the middle Zambesi showed towards the Portuguese in general (*389*, chap 29). Nevertheless there were always some traders willing to follow the old route to Zumbo and the Luangwa and consequently many clashes took place in the bush—at least one of which was still being talked about when Livingstone descended the Zambesi for the first time in 1856. The event had occurred some time before 1853, when Chissaka had waylaid a merchant called Pedro do Rosario Gama and robbed him of more than a hundred tusks. Another trader, Simões, had been robbed and murdered by his father-in-law (according to Livingstone) but almost certainly on Chissaka's orders. And there were other victims of Chissaka's raids as well (*299*, vol 1, 276, *392*, *371*).

In 1856 Chissaka's was still a name to be feared but, after his defeat by Joaquim da Cruz in 1853, his hold was relaxing. Livingstone found that a number of Portuguese traders were operating near Zumbo, although memories of the fate of Simões were still very much alive and the chiefs Mpende and Kaimbwa on the north bank of the Zambesi were doing their best to keep the slavers at a distance. At Mozimkwa's village Livingstone met two Portuguese traders, David da Costa and José Anselmo Santanna (*392*, *384*).

When Livingstone and Santanna first met, the latter was only beginning his career as a trader in the interior, but when they met again during Livingstone's second expedition to the Zambesi, Santanna was becoming a power in the land. He had recently returned from an expedition to the interior with 25,000 lb. of ivory and he and his hunters had killed 210 elephants; he had also established contacts with Ngoni who were settled north of Chissaka's sphere of influence (*390*, *327*, *339*).

In 1860 Santanna attacked and murdered chief Mburuma, whose land included the site of the old fair of Zumbo, and installed a rival of Mburuma on the throne, receiving in exchange a concession of land. The historical sequences which had led to the foundation of the *prazos*, first in Mashonaland and then Marave country, were now being repeated in the region of Zumbo.

In 1861 Albino Manuel Pacheco was sent with an official expedition to take advantage of Santanna's concession and reopen the fair at Zumbo. This was a clear indication of the decline in the power of the Pereiras and Pacheco's mission was a success. Negotiations took place with the Mburuma and the spirit of *frei* Pedro da Trindade was consulted. Eventually on 25 March 1862 the fair was formally re-established. Among those who witnessed the raising of the flag were two Zumbo residents, João de Abreu and Manuel do Rosario Andrade. The latter was probably the founder of the notorious bandit family of the Rosario Andrades which was to dominate the Zumbo area until the twentieth century (*423*, *464*, 13).

During the years immediately after the re-establishment of Zumbo, Portuguese influence spread rapidly on the middle Zambesi. The decline of the Pereiras has already been indicated as one reason for this. Another was the rapid disintegration of the chieftaincies of the western Marave. The Marave chieftaincies north of Tete had broken up earlier, during the eighteenth century, and largely as a result of Portuguese penetration of the area. The western Marave chieftaincies, however, acquired a further lease of life when many of them had migrated to the Luangwa valley and beyond. They were now devastated first by the Ngoni and then by the slavers from Zanzibar and the Zambesi.

The raids of Mpeseni's Ngoni, who were now established in what later became the Fort Jameson region, were both a threat and an opportunity for the Portuguese. Whereas Mpeseni would sometimes raid as far as Zumbo itself, his attacks on the Marave chief provided the Portuguese with the sort of opportunity that vultures find in the depredations of lions. The broken Marave peoples were left defenceless against the exploitation of the Zambesi *muzungos*.

There was, however, a third reason for the rapid advance of the *muzungos* after 1860. In the eighteenth century the Portuguese government had always tried to restrain the settlers from acquiring territory in the hope that the colony would prosper through peaceful trade with neighbouring chiefs. In the nineteenth century, however, the authorities encouraged openly the acquisition of new land. By fair means or foul chiefs were to be persuaded to surrender their lands to the Portuguese *muzungos* and, if they refused, they were to have their lands seized. The formal cessions of territory—vassalages the Portuguese called them—which were sometimes not even signed by the chief at all (*464*, 17), were duly published in the *Boletim do Governo* and broadcast to the world as evidence of Portugal's control of the interior—a question which was now assuming international importance.

The lands acquired in this way by the *muzungos* and their armed followers were sooner or later handed over to the government. They were then formally declared to be crown land and were made into *prazos*. As emphyteutic tenures had been abolished by this time they were auctioned off to the highest bidder willing to rent them. Almost invariably they went to the *muzungo* who had originally conquered them. In this way new and extremely powerful seigneurial families were created whose influence was cemented by the grant of patents of *capitão-mor* or *sargento-mor*, which carried with them the right of jurisdiction over the Africans of a large area, access to supplies of firearms from government arsenals and the right to raise armed levies to keep the 'peace'.

By 1890 the *prazo* regime had been extended to the country between the Luangwa and the Kafue, to the Luangwa valley itself for much of its length and to all the country between Zumbo and Tete (see map). The following pages will briefly describe something of the career of these last black *conquistadores* of the Portuguese empire—men whose like had conquered Mashonaland for the Portuguese in the seventeenth centuries and whose Muslim contemporaries were carving out chieftaincies in the Manyema and the Bahr al Ghazal.

The Muzungo clans of the middle Zambesi

Among the legendary figures of the Zambesi, none had a more fearsome reputation than José do Rosario Andrade—Kanyemba. His family came from Tete and set up as traders in the Zumbo region in the 1850s. Gabriel do Rosario Andrade accompanied Pacheco's expedition to Zumbo in 1861 (*464*, 13) and settled there. In 1869 he was appointed judge in African cases (*404*, 277). Another relative, Manuel, was already resident in Zumbo when Pacheco arrived.

Kanyemba is first heard of in 1873 when two crown lands put up for auction in Zumbo found no bidders. Kanyemba, we are told, had been accustomed to hold them for nothing and there was no one 'who would resolve to have questions with Canhemba and receive insults and God knows what more'. (*404*, 281). From this time Kanyemba and his associates carried all before them in the Zumbo region and José himself became, in the words of

Zumbo's chronicler, 'one of the chronic calamities suffered by that region'.

In 1876 Kanyemba and his *Chikunda* followers established a base at Inhacoe on the Zambesi beyond the confluence with the Kafue. There he assembled a band of six hundred armed men and raided up the Zambesi beyond Kariba scattering the Batonga villagers, burning, looting and carrying off slaves. Frederick Courtenay Selous visited the area towards the end of 1877 and saw something of the havoc that Kanyemba had spread on both sides of the river. Some of Kanyemba's Portuguese and half-caste agents and gunmen were still operating there; some slaves were being traded for ivory and others were chained together by the neck or cultivated the fields round Kanyemba's settlements. An old soldier, Manuel Diego, arrived leading two African girls he had bought from Kanyemba. When these two tried to escape they were lashed with the hippopotamus hide whip which Selous said hung at the ready from the verandah of the house (*449*, chap 15).

Kanyemba took care that his raids were done with the full knowledge of the Portuguese authorities and from his houses flew the Portuguese flag. He never paid any rent for his lands or allowed them to be put up for auction but the Portuguese recognised his usefulness by making him *sargento-mor*, and subsequently *capitão-mor*, of Inhacoe (*404*, 322, 340). Had he chosen to reside permanently near Kariba he might well have replaced the Batonga peoples whom he enslaved with a new nation of *Chikunda* with himself as chief. But Inhacoe was only an outpost of Kanyemba's interests and his main *aringa* he built near Zumbo on his *prazo* of Chipera.

Kanyemba's reputation for savagery surpassed even that of Bonga or Paul Marianno II. Punitive expeditions led by him in the interior resulted in the rounding up of large numbers of slaves, in the seizure for Kanyemba's harem of as many women as he fancied and in the castration of their husbands. He also practised the castration of boys for use in guarding his women (*404*, 324). His conduct caused the wretched African *colonos* to rise repeatedly in rebellion and to petition the authorities to have him removed. But he was far too useful for the Portuguese, and although Castilho dismissed him from his office of *capitão-mor* in 1889 he was reinstated the following year (*404*, 355, 386). With his allegedly 10,000 men he was the mainstay of Portuguese authority on the middle Zambesi and the foundation of Portugal's claim to control the territory as far as Kariba. Bishop

Knight-Bruce, who met Kanyemba in 1888 and was sumptuously entertained by him, thought that he alone was protecting Zumbo from attacks of the Matabele and that without him the Matabele power would be planted on the Zambesi at Zumbo (*382*, 46, 126). Kanyemba was still alive in 1899, though a paralytic invalid and unable to worry the Portuguese authorities.

Kanyemba's son-in-law and a man whose power became, if anything, greater even than his, was José de Araujo Lobo—Matakenya—not to be confused with Paul Marianno Vas dos Anjos who was also called Matakenya. Lobo we first hear of in 1869 in similar circumstances to Kanyemba. He had been plundering the Senga country of chiefs Mpende and Pangura and had conquered two large *prazos* which he did not hand over to the Portuguese crown until 1884 (*404*, 278). He was later to acquire Pangura's other territories and also the *prazo* of Panhame on the opposite bank, where he built an *aringa* at the mouth of the Hunyani river. His position astride the Zambesi below Zumbo was thus very like that of the da Cruz astride the river below Tete.

In 1878 Lobo became *capitão-mor* of Zumbo and chief executive officer of the government in the whole area. During the 1880s Lobo's power extended still further. A brother of his, José Miguel Lobo, conquered the *prazos* of Chuambo and Pimbe of which he was made *capitão-mor*, and this extended the family lands down the Zambesi as far as Macanga. Lobo was also empire-building on the Luangwa.

The serious penetration of the Luangwa valley probably only began in the middle of the 1880s but it proceeded very fast. In 1885 Chief Cancoma was forced to cede the vast territories of Hilara on the right bank of the Luangwa and Francisco Lubrinho became *sargento-mor*. Lubrinho may well have been Lobo's agent for the Luangwa soon became his preserve and in 1890 Xavier de Araujo Lobo, another of Matakenya's brothers, was made *capitão-mor* of Hilara (*404*, 386).

A vivid picture of the rule of Lobo on the Luangwa can be found in the long dispatch sent by Alfred Sharpe to the British Consul, Harry Johnson, in July 1890 (*200*). Sharpe had been trying to make treaties with the chiefs between Lake Nyasa and the Kafue on behalf of the British South Africa Company and he was soon astonished at the vast operations of the Portuguese *muzungos* in the interior.

Sharpe reached the capital of the Ngoni chief, Mpeseni, on 28 March 1890. There he found a Portuguese officer in residence and the influence of the German adventurer Carl Wiese dominant. Sharpe had ideas of buying Wiese but he came to appreciate that the German had invested his future with the *muzungos* of the Zambesi. He had rented *prazos*, he had property, he had married and had a large capital in trade goods, all in the Portuguese sphere.

Six days' journey from Mpeseni's capital brought Sharpe into contact with the first Portuguese *sertanejo*, a man called José Pacheco. There he suffered the chagrin of being overtaken by messengers of Mpeseni warning chiefs throughout the Luangwa valley of his approach.

On 18 April Sharpe reached the Luangwa at a point by his own estimate, 13° 45′ south, some hundred and fifty miles within the present frontier of Zambia. Four days later he reached the first of Lobo's settlements at Pakalimapua, a point where the trade caravans for the interior crossed the river. The day before, Lobo's brother *Pedulo* had crossed accompanied by a number of *muzungos* and with 700–800 men. Sharpe wrote:

> They are going presumably for elephant hunting, but doubtless it means like all Matakenya's other raids, making war of extermination against all weaker tribes they come across, robbery, murder, etc. and I fancy, from the large amount of stores they are said to have with them, that they must intend making a permanent settlement on the Luapula River, where elephants are said to be plentiful.

Sharpe soon saw the results of Lobo's rule in the valley. When entering a village he found the Senga headman imprisoned in a slave-stick by three *chikunda*, who were following *Pedulo's* party and had decided to take three girls from the village with them. The whole country east of the Kafue was in Lobo's hands and the population had been driven out and replaced by scattered villages of *chikunda*.

Recrossing the Luangwa and heading north again, Sharpe found himself in country entirely controlled by Lobo. All the villages had a headman who acted directly for Lobo in his area and who made their villages into staging posts for the larger caravans for the interior. The original inhabitants had all either been killed or had fled westwards.

No one in this country owns anything, everything a man becomes possessed of is 'Matakenya's'. In trying to buy canoes

301

and food the same answer was invariably given, 'It belongs to Matakenya'. There was never a more complete despot and I was never more tired of hearing anyone's name.

And so, in despair, Sharpe headed back for Lake Nyasa, convinced in spite of himself of the reality of Portuguese power as far west as the Kafue and as far north as the thirteenth parallel.

If the black Muzungo influence is to be considered as Portuguese influence, then truly Portugal has the whole of Loangwa and Ilala, Kafwe, etc. completely under control; but if it is not to be so considered, then Portugal has no influence in the Loangwa valley nor up the Zambesi beyond Zumbo.

The treaty of 1891 between Britain and Portugal took little account of the full extent of Portuguese penetration. It did, however, cut short Lobo's career in the interior, for Sharpe is probably right in thinking that within a few years the Zambesi *muzungos* would have spread their influence as far as the Congo.

Even shorn of his Luangwa empire, Matakenya was a formidable force in Zambesia. He continued to control Pangura and Panhame and resisted the attempt of the Jesuits to set up a mission on Pangura in 1892. He died in 1894 leaving a brother and twelve sons to carry on the family name (*404*, 438).

His immediate heir, and the guardian of his sons, was Pedro (*Pedulo*), his brother. Pedro refused to hand over his brother's property to the authorities who wished to protect the rights of the sons, many of whom were absent in Lisbon being educated. But in 1895 Pedro died—allegedly of poison—and the *aringa* of Panhame, together with the legendary wealth which Matakenya had hoarded there, was taken over by Caetano and Romão de Araujo Lobo, sons of Matakenya. They also defied the government and Romão went as far as to accuse his mother (Kanyemba's daughter) of murdering *Pedulo*.

These family quarrels were reminiscent of the story of the da Cruz, and the Portuguese were soon to see other parallels in the situation. Romão de Araujo Lobo continued to defy the government and in 1896 an expedition under Trindade dos Santos was sent to capture the *aringa*. The siege nearly ended in disaster for the Portuguese. Romão and his *grandes* decided to resist, and fortune played into their hands. A boat carrying a piece of government artillery ran aground and was captured by their men. This loss forced Santos to retreat, leaving the Lobos triumphant (*404*, 444–450).

Panhame, however, does not rival Massangano in the hall of fame of the Zambesi Wars, for in 1897 another of Lobo's sons appeared on the scene. Joaquim had been in Lisbon receiving an education and, when he reached the Zambesi, he went to the Portuguese authorities to try to gain their help in retrieving his patrimony. The *grandes* of Panhame had already shown signs of wanting to become friends with Portugal once again and apparently they welcomed the return of another Lobo. Joaquim was received in Panhame in 1897 and the property of his dead father, or what was left of it, was handed over to him.

Joaquim continued in peaceful possession of Panhame well on into the twentieth century. This 'intellectual' among the *prazo senhors* was met by Major Gibbons in 1898.

He insisted on us repairing to his residence, which was a large, well-built house, approached by some eight stone steps, on either side of which was a stuffed lion fixed to the balustrade. Senhor Loba, though very black, had regular, well-cut European features. He had been educated in Lisbon, spoke a little English, and assured us that he could read it as well as he could read Portuguese. His spacious sitting-room contained a very presentable library, containing among others, several English books of travel (*369, 50*).

We must now turn to the story of some of the other *muzungo* leaders. A glance at the modern map of Africa shows that, just where the Zambesi turns from flowing due east to south east, the Portuguese acquired large tracts of the northern interior. To a certain extent this was due to the conquests of the Pereiras, but to a still greater extent it was a tribute to the careers of two highly successful freebooters, Firmino Luis Germano and Vicente José Ribeiro.

Germano was a sergeant in the Portuguese army but of African parentage. In 1863, he witnessed the formal cession of Mahembe to Portugal by Bonga (*464, 17*), and in 1869 came with a military contingent to Zumbo (*404, 277*). Shortly after this he must have entered the service of Kanyemba, for Carl Wiese says that he learnt to castrate his prisoners from this master of the art (*478, 265*).

Working on his own, Germano carved out a domain for himself between Chicoa and Zumbo, founding the captaincy of Cachombo. From his base at Cachombo he soon became one of the most feared of all the slavers in the interior. He came to dominate much of the country between the Zambesi and Mpeseni's country and struck up an association with the Ngoni chief which made Portuguese influence paramount at the chief's court.

A close associate of Germano's was Vicente José Ribeiro—Chimbango—who in 1885 occupied the territory of Mandoruze. This name was corrupted by the Portuguese into Mussanda Luz. It was made into a captaincy with Chimbango as *capitão-mor*. Carl Wiese, on his way to the court of Mpeseni in 1890, described the devastation of the country after a visitation by Chimbango who had driven the last remnants of the independent Marave peoples to take refuge under the rule of Mpesesni's Ngoni (*478*, 388). The raids of Chimbango and the other *muzungos* had reduced all the country east of the Luangwa to virtual desert.

This account has by no means exhausted the list of prominent Zumbo *muzungos*. There was, for instance, Sebastio Moraes de Almeida—Perizengi—who held the *prazo* and captaincy of Mussenguez at the mouth of the river of that name. There were the Guarinho brothers, the Santannas and many more.

The dominance of the middle Zambesi by these *senhors* and their *chikunda* soldiers was not a very edifying story. The evidence of their methods is too plentiful to be at all ambiguous. Encouraged by the Portuguese government, who supplied them with firearms and readily took credit for their conquests, they attacked chief after chief, wearing down even the most determined resistance, enslaving villagers, raping, castrating and sending swarms of fugitives across the Luangwa towards Katanga. A hapless African once reported to the authorities that a *muzungo* had cut off his ear. This, said the chronicler of Zumbo, was a *ninharia*, a trifle, for scores of ears were cut off, from Europeans as well as Africans.

Some of the most detailed evidence of the conduct of the *muzungos* comes from the writings of Carl Wiese—himself by no means the least influential of the traders of the middle Zambesi. He describes, for instance, the ceremony by which *rabo da guerra* (the tail of war) was prepared before a campaign. The *rabo* was the tail of a zebra or some other animal which was used to ensure victory in the forthcoming campaign. An old slave, said Wiese, was seized and disembowelled and the *rabo* dipped in his entrails. He was then left on the ground to die in his agony (*478*, 250).

Even when the *muzungos* had established themselves in the land in the place of the chiefs, the rapine did not cease. All those who did not submit to them and enter their service as *chikunda* werc liable to constant harrying. Fail to pay tribute, get into debt, and a party of *chikunda* would raid your village and kill or enslave every living thing. Chiefs who had ceded their lands to Portugal in return for protection ended by becoming virtually the slaves of the *muzungo capitaes* who represented the government in their area (*478*, 342–3).

The Portuguese authorities were powerless to intervene. Their small detachment of troops at Zumbo usually took part in the activities of the *muzungos*; the *capitaes-mores* were drawn from the local *muzungo* families and the judges to whom the Africans were supposed to bring their complaints were frequently the most notorious of the bandits. No governor of Tete ever visited Zumbo before the very last years of the century and when an African on the *prazos* was given a royal order, he would reply, 'I do not know the king, I only know my lord and that is enough' (*478*, 347).

On the north bank the Portuguese were merely the anvil on which the *impis* of Mpeseni hammered the wretched Marave peoples. Even so, many of these fled to Mpeseni for protection, preferring his rule to that of Germano or Lobo. 'It is better to die at the hands of the Ngoni than to live with the Chikunda' was, according to Wiese, a local saying (*478*, 247). South of the Zambesi the position was the same, for just beyond the valley, on the high veldt, were to be found the Matabele, a Ngoni people more to be feared even than the subjects of Mpeseni.

It is, therefore, remarkable that African resistance was as determined as it was. Chief Mburuma was the man who rallied the north bank peoples against the Portuguese; between 1887 and 1890 he and a number of chiefs allied to him kept up a continued and successful guerrilla war against the Portuguese. In 1888, so daring did he become, he was able to lay siege to Zumbo itself (*404*, 351). In 1890, however, he agreed to make peace with the government and in 1891 the bulk of the old Mburuma chieftaincy was incorporated into the British South Africa Company's territories.

It is too easy to dismiss the activities of the *muzungos* as entirely destructive, as it is to dismiss their Arab and Swahili counterparts further north simply as slavers. The armed followers of the *muzungos*, with their wives and children, soon acquired a 'tribal' identity of their own. They proudly called themselves *A-Chikunda* and wherever they burnt, destroyed and enslaved they also planted colonies. *Chikunda* villages spread along the Luangwa and north and south of the Zambesi. In many

305

areas they entirely superseded the original population and acquired a territorial identity of their own. Probably this process is not dissimilar to that by which most African peoples at one time established their identity and found a homeland.

If there had been no 'partition', Central Africa would probably have been settled by a series of *chikunda* 'tribes' under chiefly families with Portuguese names. But this historical process was rudely cut short by the coming of European rule.

The Zumbo Portuguese and the Zambesi Wars

The wars of Kanyemba and Matakenya had little or no connection with the wars on the lower Zambesi, but the quarrel between the da Cruz and the Portuguese government was too all-pervasive not to affect the Zumbo area in some way. The link was formed by the ancient, but now decadent, chieftaincy of the Mwene Mutapa which now for the last time was to influence the fortunes of the Portuguese.

The sovereignty of the Mwene Mutapas was by this time limited to the Chidema country on the south bank of the Zambesi above Tete, but the chiefs remained independent of the Portuguese until the late 1860s when Kataruza died (*291*). He was succeeded by his eldest son Kandeya, who appears to have tried to form some sort of alliance with the da Cruz of Massangano on the basis of their common descent from Mwene Mutapa Changara.

Miguel Gouveia, the governor of Tete, feared that Bonga's power might soon encircle Tete and reacted to this alliance by annexing part of Chidema and turning it into two *prazos* called Degoe and Broma. There followed Gouveia's disastrous war against Bonga but, after this was over, a force set out from Tete to deal with the threat posed by Kandeya. One of the soldiers who accompanied this expedition was Ignacio de Jesus Xavier, who as a young boy had gone with Livingstone on his first visit to the Cabora Bassa rapids (*425, 726*).

Kandeya was defeated and driven from the vicinity of Tete and soon thereafter died or lost his throne to Dzuda. Dzuda was able to restore some of the lost Chidema territories, probably with Bonga's assistance, until some time after 1876 when Ignacio returned from Quelimane, where he had been living, and rented *prazo* Degoe from the government. Bonga protested against this and tried to occupy the country. He did not succeed,

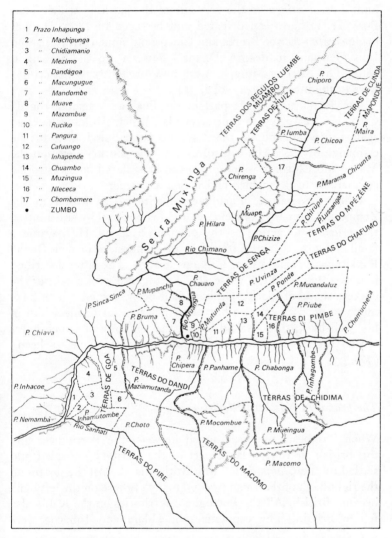

The *prazos* of Zumbo, drawn from '*Mappa dos Prazos do Districto do Zumbo*', *Sociedade de Geografia de Lisboa*

however, and Ignacio began to construct a series of *aringas* from the Mazoe to the Zambesi protecting Tete to the south-west (*425, 728*).

From this time onward Ignacio's power grew rapidly. He conquered Inhautere and Broma and finally occupied Chicoa and built a great *aringa* on the very site of the battle in which Vilas Boas Truão had been defeated and betrayed in 1807. He was made *capitão-mor* of Broma and Chicoa and joined with Firmino Luis Germano to destroy Dzuda's power once and for all in 1884. The Mwene Mutapas were now driven as pathetic fugitives to the interior (*332*, vol 2, 321).

Ignacio played a large part in the final wars against the da Cruz. He was privy to the secret plan which Andrada hatched against Massangano in 1887 and he contributed men to the campaign of 1888. His control over all the country between the Mazoe and Chicoa was complete, and he suffered no catastrophe comparable to that which ended Sousa's career.

When this part of Portuguese territory was leased to the Zambesia Company, Ignacio secured his position by sub-renting the *prazos* and acting as the company's agent. He became a familiar figure to many travellers in Zambesia. He met Daniel Rankin in 1893 and Major Gibbons in 1898. The latter described him as a 'tall, slight, "half-caste" Portuguese with a skin of the darkest shade of black'. Gibbons had been warned not to have much to do with Ignacio but nevertheless went to meet him in his 'well-built, thick-walled house, the windows of which overlooked the River from a height of forty feet above its level'. (*369*, 33)

The prazos in Northern Rhodesia

When Zambesia was partitioned between the Portuguese and the British in 1891 a large part of the territory occupied and settled by the *Chikunda* fell into British hands. All the *prazos* on the right bank of the Luangwa and many of those on the left bank became British. All the Portuguese territories on the Kafue also fell to Britain. The captaincies of Hilara and Inhacoe were entirely lost to Portugal.

With this territory the British South Africa Company inherited a large *Chikunda* population and a number of *muzungo* chiefs, who included among their number Caetano Anselmo Santanna (descendant of José Anselmo Santanna) and Caetano Francisco

Lubrinho—Chimtanda. What was the fate of these *prazos* thus cut off from Portuguese Zambesia?

When the British South Africa Company was first allotted these vast territories, it had no means either of occupying or even controlling its northern province. It was not until 1902 that any attempt was made to set up an administration in the Luangwa valley, so that for ten years the area existed in a sort of power vacuum. In this vacuum flourished the prowess and personality of John Harrison Clark.

Clark, who died in 1927, became an object of legend and almost of veneration, embodying, as he did, so much that the early prospectors and miners in Rhodesia admired. Tales about him are legion, and are about as true as most tales of their kind. They are informative, not about the facts of Northern Rhodesian history but about the values of settler society. But Clark also found his way into government confidential prints and diplomatic papers, so that it becomes quite respectable for an historian to take notice of him (*327*).

Like so many of the backwoodsmen in Portuguese Zambesia, he came as a fugitive from the law. He was the son of a hardware dealer in the Cape and one day his gun had gone off, quite accidentally, when it happened to be pointing at an African. Clark did not have powerful enough friends and so had to go north to seek his fortune.

He arrived on the Zambesi about the year 1887, while still in his twenties, and began operations as ivory trader, hunter, slaver and anything else that came his way. There is no mention of him in Alfred Sharpe's long account of the Luangwa valley in 1890, so it is fair to assume that for a number of years Clark lived in comparative obscurity, only coming into his own when the frontier lines of 1891 cut off the *Chikunda* communities in British territory.

As the power of Kanyemba and Matakenya disappeared, Clark stepped into their shoes. He recruited a large armed band of Senga and Ila peoples and soon established his authority over the *Chikunda* who challenged him. The story which sums up this process, and which delighted the Rhodesian settlers, tells how Clark was one day attacked by a band of *Chikunda* led by a *muzungo capitão*. As they approached his house, Clark put down his drink and shouted 'Footsack you bloody nigger!' at which his attackers fled.

Wearing the shoes of the great *muzungos* involved adopting their methods. 'Whenever Clark sees a girl he fancies, he takes her as his mistress for a few days, and when tired of her sends her home,' complained Caetano Francisco Lubrinho. Lubrinho travelled all the way to Salisbury in 1899 to lodge a formal complaint against Clark and in his sworn statement can be seen something of Clark's ways.

Clark sent his agents through the villages to collect hut tax and head tax. A large box of grain had to be paid for each hut and a goat or fowls by its owner. When an elephant was killed, Clark (like the Zambesi *senhors* as far back as the seventeenth century) claimed one of the tusks. Cattle and women were seized at will and Lubrinho claimed that he had had to send some of his wives and cattle to Portuguese territory to be out of Clark's way.

Clark waged a ceaseless war on the slavers who still operated along the old trails after 1891, and when he had captured and 'freed' slaves from a caravan he made a large profit selling them where he could get the best price. The Jesuit mission at Miruru was, apparently, an eager buyer of these potential converts. Clark also supplied contract labourers to the Rhodesian mines.

Clark did not confine his activities to the strong-arm methods of the old *senhors*; like them he tried to reinforce his position by formal land concessions. Eventually he hoped that the British government would recognise his claims and that the loot of the bandit would thus be changed into the landed property of the country gentleman.

Clark secured treaties with most of the chiefs whose lands lay between the lower reaches of the Luangwa and the Kafue and one of those who was forced to sign away his land was Caetano Francisco Lubrinho himself.

Lubrinho's land lay on the Lusemfwa river where Clark eventually built his *aringa* of Algoa. The treaty runs as follows.

I, Caetano Lubrinho (Chimtanda) concede to John Harrison Clark, the *mineral rights* in my country known as Chimtanda . . . I also agree to supply him with labour for all mining purposes, and also for building, carrying or other work. I also agree to supply him with hunters and carriers for any part he may wish to explore or hunt, and also to accompany him on all his trips.

I also grant him the right to locate lands in my territory for either farming, building, or any other purpose, but not to interfere or locate lands cultivated by the natives. In the event of hostilities with any outlying native tribe or tribes, I shall assist him with my subjects if called upon by him. In consideration of his paying me £12 per month when on service for him. (*327, 23*).

These were sweeping powers which could be used by Clark to impose his will as and when he chose. Just such treaties had been dictated by the *conquistadores* to the Karanga chiefs in the seventeenth century.

Clark's relations with the Portuguese authorities were bad. Each side tells stories which interpret the situation to suit its own pride. The Rhodesian tradition was that Clark had, on one occasion, attacked Zumbo and chased the Portuguese away, raising the British flag in the town. Another story shows Clark captured by the Portuguese and escorted across the frontier by Portuguese black soldiers. Having reached his home, the soldiers were frightened to return alone through the bush, and so Clark had to escort them back to Zumbo.

According to the Portuguese, Clark was captured by Trindade dos Santos and imprisoned in a granary on which Santos trained a piece of artillery. This thoroughly cowed Clark and he was eventually released (*404, 455*). A more likely story tells that in the year 1899 Clark, and his agent Law, were 'recruiting' contract labour for Southern Rhodesia. They had got together four hundred men to be sent to Salisbury and Clark then raided Portuguese territory to get supplies on the cheap to keep the men while on the march.

The wheels of British colonial governments ground slowly, but eventually they caught Harrison Clark and ground him exceeding small. With the arrival of the official administration in Feira in 1902 Clark found that his treaties were disregarded. He was allowed three farms to retire to and eventually he built a house and went to live on a tiny five acre estate at Fiperere, abandoning his old stronghold at Algoa. For some years Clark was hounded by the administration as one by one his misdeeds came to light, and he died in 1927 aged about 67.

1902 was the year of Coutinho's conquest of Barue and of the defeat and death of the last Pereira king of Macanga. It is the year that really closes the era of the Zambesi Wars.

18 Manuel Antonio de Sousa, the Kingdom of Barue and International Politics

With the single exception of the Fashoda crisis of 1898, the British ultimatum to Portugal on 11 January 1890 was the most dramatic confrontation between rival European powers in the period of the 'scramble for Africa'. For Portugal the ultimatum came as a profound shock to national pride and self-esteem. The Portuguese had fed themselves—as they still do today—on a largely, and sometimes wholly, fictitious view of their colonial glory and their civilising mission. The ultimatum deprived them at one blow of the dream of an empire stretching from the Atlantic to the Indian Ocean. In the long run it weakened the prestige of the monarchy and contributed to the fall of the throne in 1910. It was an experience for Portugal almost as devastating as the Spanish-American war of 1898 was for Spain.

The British have always considered their case a just one. Portugal received, by the eventual settlement, only as much territory as she had effectively occupied (Britain, of course, had not effectively occupied any of her territory but that did not matter); the godly Scottish missionaries were saved from Catholic bigotry; the natives of central Africa were saved from ruthless Portuguese exploitation; and the rich plateau lands of the Rhodesias were in the hands of a power with the will and the capital to develop them.

Many people in Britain thought, in fact, that the Portuguese had had an exceptionally favourable deal. Lord Salisbury's intervention had stopped the British South Africa Company from seizing by force a corridor to the sea for their territory—a thing they could easily have done—and Portugal was left with the major ports of the Indian Ocean in her hands as well as the sea terminals of the Pretoria and Rhodesian railways.

The history of the ultimatum and the events leading up to it has been frequently written, but without exception these studies have concentrated on the diplomatic activity of the years 1875 to 1891; on the growing awareness in Britain and Portugal of the wealth and potentialities of Central Africa; on the Scottish missions; the freedom of navigation on the Zambesi; the 'rose-coloured' map; the British consuls and vice-consuls and the activities of British concession hunters. But were the African people themselves supine and passive during these years? Did they play no role in the events of the 'scramble'? These questions are not really asked, let alone answered, by the majority of writers.

In fact the great decisions of these years were not being made in Europe but in Africa. Under the inspiration of Joaquim Carlos Paiva de Andrada—a freelance concession hunter—the Zambesi Portuguese were to make a serious bid for the control of what is today Southern Rhodesia. Andrada had neither money nor official backing when he started out at the end of the 1870s, so he hitched the wagon of his ambitions to that of Manuel Antonio de Sousa, incontestably the most powerful of the Zambesi *senhors*, with whom he was involved in the third phase of the Zambesi Wars.

Together these two occupied Barue and the Pungue valley and in 1886 began the invasion of Rhodesia. They were confronted by an alliance of independent African chieftaincies and in 1887 received a temporary check from Chief Mtoko. Andrada and Sousa then turned aside to destroy what they considered to be the centre of the alliance against them, the da Cruz stronghold at Massangano. When they were again prepared to resume their advance into the high veldt it was too late, for the British South Africa Company had its treaties of concession and its 'pioneer column' already on the way.

The fact that a large part of Mashonaland fell to Britain and not to Portugal at the time of the 'scramble' has therefore less to do with Cecil Rhodes and Lord Salisbury than with the African politics of Mtoko, Barue, Sousa and the da Cruz.

The rise of Manuel Antonio de Sousa

Manuel Antonio came from a catholic Goanese family. He was born at Mapuça in the province of Bardez in Portuguese India on 10 November 1835. He was sent to study at the seminary at Rachol in the province of Salsete—perhaps with the idea of his becoming a priest—a fantastic thought in the light of his later career. In 1852 or 1853, before he was twenty, he was sent to eastern Africa to administer the estate of an uncle who had been a trader in the Rivers. The uncle's name was Felix Mascarenhas and on arrival Manuel Antonio married his orphaned first cousin, Maria Anastasia (*341*, 11–12, *440*, 20).

His inheritance was 30,000 rupees—presumably in trade goods—and Manuel Antonio used it to make a career for himself as a trader. Basing himself on the now dwindling town of Sena, he traded throughout the Sena district, down-stream of the da Cruz *prazos*, and in 1854 or 1855 built himself a permanent base in the interior on Mount Gorongosa. There he constructed a fortified settlement high among the granite outcrops and gained a measure of fame by defeating an *impi* of Gaza warriors sent by Umzila to dislodge him.

He now began to gather round him a formidable body of elephant hunters and slaves, who made their first appearance on the Zambesi in the wars against the Vas dos Anjos in 1858. In that year also the government had tried to revive the official Portuguese presence in Manica and had appointed Isidoro Correia Pereira as *capitão-mor* of Manica and Quiteve. Probably this was not an attempt to revive the old fair of Manica so much as to create an administrative authority in the various Portuguese possessions existing, or about to exist, in the interior. In 1863 Pereira died and the government appointed Manuel Antonio de Sousa to succeed him (*210*).

So far Sousa's career had been one of continuous success, but it was to receive severe set-backs. During his absence in Sena to receive his appointment as *capitão-mor*, Gaza *impis* sacked his base at Gorongosa and, in the years immediately following, Sousa and the Sena settlers suffered a whole series of raids when the Ngoni mercenaries in the service of Anselmo Ferrão took the opportunity of their master's death to make the Portuguese *prazos* 'weep' for the sad event (*341*, 14).

During the 1860s Sousa began to construct a line of *aringas* to link his base in the Gorongosa mountains with the Pungue and the upper waters of the Luenha. As a result of this strategic line of defence the whole of this north-western region was closed to the Gaza *impis* which were forced to take the southern route through Cheringoma to reach the delta *prazos*.

The growth of Sousa's power in the interior thus thrust a wedge between the vast empire of the Gaza in the south and the independent chieftaincy of Barue in the north, and both of them began to feel threatened by the new, successful and aggressive chieftaincy.

3 Part of Tete looking up the Zambesi river

Manufacture of sugar at Latimo: making the panellas or pots to contain it

15 Manuel Antonio de Sousa

16 João José de Oliveira Queirós

17 Captain A. de Portugal Durão

18 Guilherme Frederico de Portugal e Vasconcelos

The years 1867 to 1869 saw the four disastrous attempts of the Portuguese to suppress the da Cruz, and Sousa took part in all the expeditions. He provided large contingents of soldiers and bore much of the brunt of the fighting for possession of the *serra* Bancampembzue above Massangano. He formed the rearguard during the retreat of Oliveira Queiros's army and he personally acted as mediator in the negotiations between Bonga and Vasconcellos e Portugal. Although there were murmurs that Sousa had betrayed the army (*299*, vol 2, 249), the overall result of his efforts was that he acquired the reputation of a loyal servant of Portuguese interests. Until his death Sousa remained convinced that there was always much to be gained by remaining friends with the Portuguese and pursuing his ambitions while nominally in their service.

Neither Sousa nor the Portuguese were yet strong enough to crush the da Cruz but there were other directions where expansion was possible. 1874 saw a cholera epidemic in Zambesia and in that year Mutassa, king of Manica, was attacked by his neighbours Makoni and Macombe of Barue. He appealed to the Gaza king for protection as he was nominally a subject of Umzila's empire. A Gaza *impi* was sent to his aid, but was defeated. Mutassa then consulted the spirit-mediums and they advised that he should seek the help of Manuel Antonio de Sousa. Messengers were sent to Sousa at Chemba on the Zambesi, and Sousa agreed to help if Mutassa would accept him as overlord.

The invaders were driven out of Manica territory by a force of Sousa's soldiers and on their return his captains presented him with a gift of earth taken from the hut of the spirit-medium Mazina as a token of the surrender of Mutassa's sovereignty. From this time Sousa claimed to be the lord of Manica.

It is fair to say that, despite the circumstantial detail of this account, there is a lot of doubt attached to it. The sovereignty of Sousa over Manica was not continuously exercised and Sousa never had any of his soldiers stationed there on a permanent basis. It is even doubtful if he collected tribute there. The story was published to substantiate Portuguese claims at the time of the conflict between the British South Africa Company and the Portuguese for the control of Manica (*223*).

On the Zambesi Sousa entered into formal contracts with the government to rent a block of *prazos* stretching from the Lupata mountains to Sena. These included Chemba, Gorongosa, Tambara, Inhacaimbe, Santa Manga and Sansa and made him the greatest land-holder in Zambesia, although he held the lands by short terms of rental and not by emphyteutic leases.

Meanwhile the situation in the chieftaincy of Barue was fast reaching a point when it would be ripe for Sousa's intervention. The chieftaincy lay due south of Tete, separated from the Zambesi by the *prazos* of Massangano, Tipue and Tambara. Its western frontier lay roughly along the line of the modern frontier of Rhodesia and Moçambique and in the south it reached the Pungue; it extended approximately 370 kilometres at its longest point and 150 at its widest.

Barue lay so close to the Portuguese *prazos* and to Tete that each could not help being involved in the affairs of the other. The Portuguese had dominated Barue in the seventeenth century and had established missions in the country, but in the eighteenth century the chieftaincy became independent and exacted tolls from caravans passing to the Manica fairs; sometimes closing the roads completely. One relic of Portuguese domination did survive and that was the bringing of the *mazia-manga*—the holy water for the coronation of the Barue kings (*453, 270*). This rite was similar to others recorded for the coronations of the Mwene Mutapas and the Quiteves. Whether it was a Christian baptismal rite adopted into pagan ritual or whether it was a pagan ritual exploited by cunning missionaries to steal another soul from hell, one cannot now tell.

For four years, between 1826 and 1830, Barue was without a king and it may be from this time that the split in the royal house of the Macombes of Barue can be dated (*248*). Shortly after this Barue was overrun by Ngoni warriors and endured a five-year occupation before the Ngoni crossed the Zambesi and left the region. By the 1840s the split in the ruling house was plain. Portuguese settlers were backing Chibudo the pretender to the throne of Macombe in 1846 and in 1854 we hear of an *impi* of Gaza warriors being sent by Umzila in an unsuccessful attempt to support Chibudo's claims against those of Chipatata (*164, 120*).

Meanwhile Barue had become involved in the Zambesi Wars. In 1853 the Macombe had joined with the Pereiras in their attempt to destroy Joaquim da Cruz and suffered in the catastrophic defeat that da Cruz inflicted on his attackers. The Macombe joined the expeditions of Cruz Coimbra, which were equally unsuccessful, but thereafter a change seems to have set in. The chief now saw himself threatened more by the power of Sousa in Gorongosa and by the extension of Sousa's power towards Manica, than by the da Cruz. Sousa invested heavily

in the four expeditions against Bonga and had they been successful Barue would have been surrounded on three sides by territory
controlled by Sousa. Not surprisingly the Macombes now threw
their support behind Massangano and led diversions against Sena
in 1868 (269) to threaten the communications of the armies sent
against Massangano. At some time during these years Macombe
went so far as to attack Manuel Antonio in Gorongosa and
suffered a severe defeat.

Sousa now planned the absorption of the ancient kingdom, and
as a first step secured marriage, in about 1874, between himself
and a daughter of the reigning Macombe. Sousa had many other
wives and Macombe had many sons to succeed him, but Sousa
was determined that this marriage should be the basis of his
own claim to the chieftaincy of Macombe (341, 24–5).

He set out to build himself a party by bribing some of the most
important of Macombe's advisers, and not long afterwards the
right occasion offered itself. One of Sousa's captains was assaulted
and robbed by Barue warriors, and Sousa demanded satisfaction.
Macombe's advisers begged the chief to give way to Sousa.
Accordingly a tusk filled with earth was sent to Manuel Antonio
as an act of submission and, in exchange, Sousa gave some sort
of assurance against any attempt by Chibudo's party to acquire
the throne (341, 24–5).

In 1880 the old Macombe Chipatata died and Sousa at once
moved in to occupy the whole chieftaincy. His plan was to have
his eldest son by *nhanha* Adriana, the daughter of Chipatata,
declared chief. But young João Francisco Xavier de Sousa, as the
little boy was called, was barely six at the time and Sousa
arranged to have him educated in Lisbon while he himself acted
as regent in Barue (122, 124).

Sousa's occupation of Barue was ruthless and systematic.
Between thirty and forty *aringas* were built throughout the
country, in each of which Sousa placed one of his captains and
one of his wives. The wives, all daughters of important local
figures, were supposed to be an extension of the leader's own
presence and reported back to Sousa how his captains behaved
(342, 202). The free inhabitants of Barue were regrouped in
settlements near the *aringas* and new chiefs were chosen under
Sousa's supervision and had to reside where the captains could
keep an eye on them. According to Paiva de Andrada this
arrangement led to peace and quiet throughout the whole vast
territory (424, 18–20).

The members of the royal family of Chipatata fled into exile

317

or, if they fell into Sousa's hands, were killed. Some of them fled to the da Cruz at Massangano, others to Manica.

Sousa's territory now stretched unbroken from the Pungue to the Zambesi, and it was by no means clear to the Portuguese authorities that he considered Barue as territory belonging to Portugal at all.

At this stage the ambitions of another individual became involved with those of Sousa. Joaquim Carlos Paiva de Andrada was an artillery officer attached to the Paris embassy. He was greatly influenced by the revival of interest in the empire which had taken place in the previous decade and which had led to the founding in 1875 of the Lisbon Geographical Society as a political pressure group and a centre for promoting imperial enterprises.

Andrada had political friends in Lisbon and in 1878 he obtained a vast concession of mineral and timber rights extending in a thirty-six league radius from Zumbo to Tete. The concession took in a large part of the present Rhodesia and Zambia as well as most of Portuguese Zambesia. 'Paiva de Andrada Concessions' was launched on 26 December 1878—a paper enterprise un-backed by finance, unacceptable in international law and bearing no relation to the area of land actually occupied by the Portuguese. The 'giddy dance of paper empires' was just beginning in Africa.

Andrada had all the vision of a Cecil Rhodes, but unfortunately none of Rhodes' money. For the next ten years his career was devoted to a constant search for capital and a constant battle with sceptical European financiers who were reluctant to venture their money in Zambesia and unreasonably expected Portugal actually to control the areas of the concession and guarantee some sort of security.

Andrada's first reconnaissance in 1879 resulted in a confirmation of his concession and enabled him to launch the *Société Générale de Zambésia* in Paris. The Paris consortium took the trouble to send out a team of experts to make a survey of the Zambesi country in 1881 and as a result of their report the Paris capital was withdrawn. The folly of speculative investment in Africa was just at this moment being impressed on the French by events in Egypt and it is not surprising that the world of the da Cruz and the Pereiras seemed less safe even than the Cairo of Khedive Tewfik. The expedition did, however, have one favourable outcome for Andrada, for he was able to gain the promise of aid from Manuel Antonio de Sousa who met the party at Chemba and supplied them with provisions and carriers (*346A*, 75).

Next Andrada formed the Ophir Company and went to London to get financial backing (*314*, 123). Sir William Mackinnon showed interest and agreed to take up shares to the value of £15,000, provided Andrada himself put up £5,000. The Ophir Company was duly launched in February 1884—but £5,000 did not easily come Andrada's way, Sir William showed signs of wavering and the Ophir Company appeared as still-born as the others, which 'are all, my Lord, now historic proofs of Major Andrada's energy and persistency as well as of his enthusiasm and faith in the resources and future of the country in question . . .' (*198*), as the British Consul, O'Neill, wrote to Lord Salisbury with a certain amount of intentional irony.

In an earlier comment of Andrada's concession O'Neill had pointed out Andrada's real difficulty. The Gaza Ngoni, the Makololo and the da Cruz would never allow the economic exploitation of land under their control (*192*). By 1884 Andrada had himself realised this, and had decided to pursue his objectives through direct action on the spot.

He had already had some success in stimulating the Portuguese authorities in Moçambique into action. During his stay in Moçambique in 1881, when he still hoped that his French backers would support him, Andrada had convinced the governor-general, the *visconde* Paço d'Arcos, that the only hope of ever controlling Zambesia, with its turbulent *senhors* and their private armies, was to secure an alliance with Manuel Antonio de Sousa. It was well-known, Andrada had argued, that Sousa could put ten or twelve thousand armed men in the field and that with this force Zambesia could be secured for Portugal. It was believed that Sousa would welcome the alliance. He wished to have his sons educated in Lisbon at the expense of the government and he needed supplies of firearms and, of course, money (*122*).

At the end of 1881 the governor-general cabled for advice to Lisbon and the following year the deal was arranged. The two little de Sousa boys were established in the *Escola Academica* in Lisbon at government expense and Sousa began to receive his arms and money.

The next step was to create a new administrative district. Since the seventeenth century there had been administrations in Sofala, in Zambesia, and in Moçambique. Now the district of Manica and Quiteve was to be created out of Sousa's territories, to establish Portugal's rights in this area against any foreign rival and to try and seal off the southern route through Cheringoma, which the warriors of the Gaza still followed on their annual forays to Chupanga and the delta to collect tribute. The new district was set up in July 1884—another major achievement for Paiva de Andrada, who could now tell his European associates that Portugal 'administered' this part of his concession.

In the same year and the same month Sousa's alliance with the government bore real fruit. On 19 July there broke out on the Shire the Massingire rising, which has been described in a previous chapter. It showed the world how powerless Portuguese authority was when seriously challenged by the old settlers and their slaves. The Portuguese turned to Sousa as the man alone able to restore control, and this he proceeded to do.

Collecting two thousand five hundred of his own men and a further one thousand five hundred from other settlers, Sousa set off for the Shire in September 1884. The Massingire made two or three attempts to resist but by the end of the year the last resistance had been crushed and Sousa had reached the Ruo. There he faced an anxious British vice-consul and a band of Scottish missionaries who expected any minute to see him cross the Ruo and annex the Shire Highlands to Portugal. However, Manuel Antonio had no interest in the Shire. Two years before, when he had gone with Governor Avila to receive the submission of the Massingire chiefs, he had toyed with the idea of occupying the country. Elephant were becoming scarce in Gorongosa and his hunters could find new herds in the Shire marshes, but now he was more interested in the highlands of Manica and Inyanga. He therefore welcomed his recall by the governor-general who was terrified of sparking off an international incident by invading the area of Scottish missionary activity (*194*).

So Sousa returned with his victorious army and it was on the leisurely march back to Manica that he met and entertained the British traveller Walter Montagu Kerr. Kerr and his party were greeted profusely by Sousa at his camp and given a good meal. They were then seated in the shade while Sousa insisted on displaying to them his treasure chest full of gold medals and chains. His most prized possessions were an English gold watch and a silver-plated Winchester rifle which he asked Kerr to have repaired in Cape Town. He gave Kerr an account of the Massingire war and in answer to the question 'Are you paid by the Government, and also armed by the Government?' he replied 'Oh yes. Before a regular Portuguese army could reach the Shire river half of them would be dead.' Memories of the Bonga wars perhaps! (*410*, vol 2, 277).

It was during this campaign that Sousa and Andrada reached agreement on a common course of action south of the Zambesi (*195*).

For a long time Sousa had wanted to control the lands which lay along the frontiers of Barue, endangering his security. Due west lay the vast escarpment of the Inyanga mountains where a few small chieftaincies maintained their independence on the cold granite uplands and preserved the last vestiges of the tradition of stone building that had once been common throughout all the country between the Zambesi and the Limpopo. Then on the Zambesi itself was the stronghold of the da Cruz at Massangano and Sousa made no secret of his desire to see the end of their power. Moreover Massangano controlled the mouth of the Luenha river, the gateway to Mashonaland and the valley of the Mazoe. It was known that the da Cruz were extending their control up the valley and also that this was the easiest way to reach the promised land of the Mashona goldfields on which Andrada also had his eye.

According to the private informant of the British ambassador in Lisbon, the agreement between Andrada and Sousa was to the effect that Sousa would help Andrada to occupy Manica and in return Andrada would assist in the crushing of the da Cruz (*199*). Probably against Sousa's better judgement, the decision was reached to leave the da Cruz in Massangano alone for the time being and to try and advance into the country along the western border of Barue.

Manica, ruled by Chief Mutassa, was one objective and Andrada sent presents in order to establish friendly relations with the chief. However, although Sousa had a rather shadowy claim to the overlordship of Manica, the chieftaincy really fell within the sphere of influence of the Gaza king. In October 1884 the old king, Umzila, had died and his successor, Gungunhana, was as yet an unknown quantity. Embassies were sent to ask him for leave to prospect in his territories and to establish treaty relations with him and while these plans were maturing Andrada turned his attention further north.

The frontier of Barue ran approximately along the Luenha river. Beyond the Luenha to the west lay a number of smaller chieftaincies stretching westwards to the Mazoe and south-west to Manica. In August 1885 Andrada set off to visit this region, where the Portuguese had once traded from their fairs at Luanze and Makaha but which had not been visited in recent years by any European except the German Carl Mauch. He found the chiefs suspicious of his intentions, for word soon spread that he was closely associated with Manuel Antonio de Sousa and the chiefs of this region lived in continual fear of depredations from Sousa's mercenaries. The area was also full of refugees from Barue who had fled from Sousa's reprisals and there were members of the Barue royal house there to stiffen resistance.

Although ostensibly travelling to seek friendship with the chiefs, Andrada had all the time been spying out the land, seeing where gold was washed, examining the strength of the stockades and planning where settlements and command posts could be placed. When some of the loads carried by his porters disappeared, he assigned the blame to chief Rupire and hastened back to Gorongosa to obtain troops from Manuel Antonio (*424*).

In the account which he subsequently published of his travels in this region, Andrada was at pains to explain why he had not gone to obtain aid from Tete or from Inacio de Jesus Xavier whose *aringas* were nearer than Sousa's, but there is little doubt that all along Andrada had intended that Sousa should occupy the region by force. Permission for a punitive campaign was obtained from the governor-general, and early in 1886 Sousa assembled his forces. Two raiding parties were dispatched across the Luenha, one commanded by Macaningomba and the other by Cambuemba, the greatest of all the mercenary captains of his time. The expedition was nominally under the command of the governor of Manica, whose presence gave it a certain official respectability.

Only two chiefs, Rupire and Massaoa, had been implicated by Andrada in the robbery and it was against these that the attack was launched—the governor-general, Castilho, vainly advising moderation in the instructions he issued for the commander (*186*). The battle was short and bloody, and victory was complete. Eighteen hundred Africans were burnt to death inside the *aringas* and Sousa took the opportunity to receive the submission of twenty other chiefs between the Mazoe and the Luenha (*425, 723, 372*).

Sousa now proceeded to occupy the whole of the country as previously he had occupied Barue. Cambuemba was stationed in the north on the Mazoe, and Macaningomba to the south in Rupire. Together they commanded a garrison of four hundred men and across the Mazoe faced the captains of a friend and ally, Inacio de Jesus Xavier the *capitão-mor* of Chicoa. The encirclement of the da Cruz in Massangano was now complete and Sousa was in control of the main highway to the gold fields of Rhodesia. The date was May 1886 and Cecil Rhodes had scarcely yet turned his attention to the lands north of Bechuanaland.

Between the lands of Rupire just occupied by Sousa and the Rhodesian high veldt lay the ancient powerful chieftaincy of Mtoko. Mtoko was harried on his southern and western side by Matabele raids but he had been accustomed himself to dominate the chiefs of the lower Mazoe. He was connected by marriage with some of them and the trade of his kingdom descended the Luenha to the Zambesi through their land. The growth of the power of Sousa and Xavier was a severe blow to the security and economic prosperity of his people.

The political nature of this threat was clear and was not long in manifesting itself. Throughout the latter part of 1886, while Andrada was away in the south, Sousa's captains were consolidating their hold on the conquered territory and were preparing for the attack on Mtoko as soon as the rains should be finished.

In March the invasion began—unusually early for campaigning in Zambesia—and at first all went well. Sousa's soldiers overran the approaches to Mtoko and threatened the chief's capital. There two pitched battles were fought in which Sousa himself was hotly engaged. Mtoko's men were beaten back and Sousa subsequently told Andrada that he had fired 613 rounds himself.

One night, however, Sousa's hopes were shattered by one of the inexplicable chances of war. For no apparent reason alarm and panic spread among the soldiers and Sousa was deserted by all but two hundred of his followers. He was forced to fall back on his fortified positions in Rupire and summon reinforcements from Barue (425, 725).

This account of the Mtoko expedition was given by Andrada to the Lisbon Geographical Society at the end of 1887 when negotiations for the launching of the Moçambique Company were still being conducted. Sousa had not been defeated, Andrada suggested, but had been the victim of the devilment of the spirit-medium Inhamavio of Mtoko. No serious doubt was, therefore, cast on Sousa's military reputation.

But to the African peoples of Mtoko, the defeat of Sousa became one of the epic traditions of their chief. The traditional account of Sousa's defeat is also much more credible than Andrada's written record. According to the oral tradition Sousa armed the levies of the Luenha chiefs with firearms and himself accompanied the invasion carried in a litter and taking with him his great war drum *Chiuzingu*. *Chiuzingu* was more than a symbol of Sousa's military might, it was a fearsome object in itself. After a successful battle Sousa would take one of the captives, cut his throat over the drum and then beat a tattoo on the blood-soaked instrument to summon the people to do homage.

One understands what F. C. Selous meant when he said that the methods of the *muzungo* chiefs of the Zambesi would not commend themselves to the Aborigines' Protection Society (*290A*).

Having driven off two of Mtoko's headmen, Sousa built himself a fortified camp and waited for the appearance of Mtoko's soldiers. Mtoko, who was an old man, entrusted the defence of the kingdom to his son, Gurupira, who had inspired the hostility towards Andrada in 1885.

Gurupira surrounded Sousa on all sides and blockaded the camp, keeping his men well-hidden in the rocks. Sousa was cut off from any water supply and sallied out the following day to drive off the besiegers. The skirmish was indecisive but as his men withdrew towards the camp, Sousa's *capitão* was struck down. Sixty or more years after the event, one of Sousa's old soldiers recorded:

> As I ran I happened to glance at the man who was running beside me, and I saw that he was Gouveia's (Sousa's) captain who had led us out against Gurupira. As I looked at him I saw an assagai pierce the back of his neck and the blade come out through his mouth. I did not wait. The death of this man made us lose heart and we decided to return to our homes. That night we slipped away, taking Gouveia with us but we were harried on our journey and many of us did not see our kraals again (*327A*).

So the desertion of Sousa's men followed the death of his *capitão*—a much more satisfactory explanation of the defeat than Andrada's attribution of it to the machinations of the spirit-medium—though, as I shall show, the spirit-medium probably played an important role in these events.

In the haste of Sousa's retreat, *Chiuzingu* was left behind as a trophy for Mtoko.

Back in Rupire, Sousa received word from the commander of his rearguard, Cambuemba, of an alliance that was being constructed against him. Eager for allies to help him fight the Portuguese, Mtoko had sent messengers to the da Cruz in Massangano with the result that Chatara agreed to provide active help. Pindirire, the most redoubtable of the *capitaes* of Massangano, was dispatched with a thousand men to take Sousa in the rear but on 13 May this force had been surprised and dispersed by Cambuemba (*425, 729*).

The defeat of Sousa and his withdrawal from Mtoko's country, removed the immediate need for the alliance but attempts were made by the da Cruz to revive it early the following year when Motontora was planning his reoccupation of the *aringa* at Massangano. On this occasion messengers were sent to Mtoko and later, during the siege, Motontora sent his niece Eugenia (Bonga's daughter) as a wife to stimulate Mtoko into a more active involvement in the struggle. According to one account, Mtoko kept the bride but provided no help; according to another Motontora sent two of his daughters who were intercepted by Mutassa Chifumbasio of Manica and added to his harem, thus preventing their reaching Mtoko (*299*, vol 1, 70).

The alliance was reactivated for a third time during the successful Barue rising against Sousa in 1891–2.

It is easy to see the political interest which bound the allies together but it is probable that the spirit-medium Inhamavio of Mtoko played an important part in organising the resistance to Sousa. Andrada says that the messengers who were sent to Massangano in 1887 were commanded to bring back the flesh of Sousa's men for the *pondoro* and, as we have seen, Andrada also thought that Inhamavio was responsible for the desertion of Sousa's men. In a previous chapter I have shown the importance of the spirit-mediums in Massangano and their role in Barue politics and in the politics of the Mashona rebellion of 1896–7 is already well-established (*436, 437*). It is a reasonable inference that the spirit-mediums were as active in building the alliance against the Portuguese in 1887 as they were in building the alliance against the Rhodesians in 1896.

When they realised the full extent of this alliance against them, Sousa and Andrada took a decision which was to be critical in determining the whole future of central Africa. Had they chosen to regroup their forces and renew the attack on Mtoko, the odds are that they would have been victorious and would have been able to occupy a large part of northern Mashonaland. They decided, however, to strike first at Massangano and eliminate what they considered to be the moving spirit of the alliance.

Conferences were held with the governor-general, the governor of Manica and with Ignacio de Jesus Xavier. In September the attack against Massangano was launched and once again Sousa provided the bulk of the forces. Four thousand of his men formed the main army which marched from Gorongosa to take Massangano. He was accompanied by Andrada in person and by the governor of Manica, Fereira Simões, who was nominally in command.

As already recorded in the previous chapter the resistance of the da Cruz collapsed and Massangano was captured without opposition on 14 September 1887. It seems, however, that this rapid and successful campaign may have witnessed one of the darkest deeds of Moçambique history which is, perhaps, worth recording.

Andrada had accompanied Sousa's men on their last forced march to the *aringa*, but Governor Simões, ill with fever, had stayed behind. He had been housed in an *aringa* commanded by Sousa's captain, Bastião. There, according to Andrada, he had been seized with delirium and had shot himself and one or two bystanders with his rifle. Andrada had been only a short, half-day's march from the scene of the tragedy but he had not returned to bury his compatriot or to investigate the story of the death. In a pamphlet published in 1888 Alfredo Cesar Brandão drew attention to these facts and suggested that Simões' death may have been arranged by Sousa, and that Andrada may have been aware of the plan to dispose of the governor.

The suggested motive for the crime has a direct bearing on the history of these times. Andrada was at this time trying desperately to found the Moçambique Company—his latest attempt to make good his concession. Rumours were reaching Europe that the district of Manica was simply an area controlled by Sousa's captains without any sort of effective administration. The continuous disorders in the Manica area and the failure to reach any agreement with Gungunhana were making life very difficult for Andrada. Among the few people who knew the real fragility of Portugal's rule was Governor Simões. He had already quarrelled with Sousa and Andrada and his death during the campaign was the most convenient thing that could have happened (*326*).

With Massangano destroyed and Chatara a prisoner in Portuguese hands, Andrada might have been forgiven for assuming that the African alliance against the Portuguese was broken, and that at last he would be able to establish Portuguese control over the gold reefs of Manica and Mashonaland. What now seemed necessary was not action on the spot but the maximum parade of public opinion at home in favour of his imperial schemes.

So to Lisbon he went, and there followed papers to the Lisbon Geographical Society and a round of social and political meetings in Lisbon which resulted in March 1888 in the launching of the 'Moçambique Company' to amalgamate Andrada's own interests with those of other concession holders in Manica and the Sabi valley. Later the Moçambique Company was to receive a charter and become endowed with sovereign powers over the territory between the Zambesi and the Sabi, but at this stage it was still a small affair with £40,000 of capital subscribed in London and Lisbon; its only apparent assets were the Portuguese claims to the goldfields of Manica; its liabilities included the fact that Manuel Antonio and his men were firmly in control of the largest part of the company's concession.

Andrada persuaded Manuel Antonio to accompany him to Lisbon and thither the last and greatest of the Zambesi *senhors* travelled. He was fêted in Lisbon, becoming *commendador* of the Order of Avis and a colonel in the Portuguese army. He was introduced to the king and the prime minister and the Portuguese aristocracy—and, of course, the Lisbon Geographical Society. He was greeted as one of the greatest of Portuguese imperial pioneers—though it was nothing but the chance of Zambesi politics which prevented the da Cruz being hailed as the heroes and Sousa being dismissed as a blood-thirsty bandit (*341*, 20).

His visit lasted until July 1888. Can it be that the energy and determination of the old warrior was at last beginning to decline? He was fifty-three and life in the interior, the continual marches and raids and being married to about ninety wives must have begun to take their toll. While he and Andrada were feasting and entertaining in Lisbon, their prize was rapidly slipping from their hands. The South African concession hunters were gathering at Lobengula's court and in August Charles Rudd set out for Bulawayo armed with discretionary powers from Cecil Rhodes.

Even so Andrada and the Portuguese had a long start over Rhodes and the South Africans. Andrada's company was incorporated in March 1888 and Rhodes' British South Africa Company was not granted its charter until October 1889. The Portuguese plan of advance was well thought out and should have achieved its objective. Three expeditions were equipped, one under Cordon destined for the upper Zambesi, one under Andrada for Manica and one under Serpa Pinto for the Shire.

The careful plans of the Lisbon imperialists, however, soon ran among the shoals of Zambesi politics. The turbulent valley which Andrada had left pacified the previous December had again boiled up in disorder. In May the da Cruz returned to Massangano and in October the Pereiras of Macanga also rose in rebellion. The governor-general arrived to take command but the war dragged on until the end of November, and even when Massangano fell on 29 November large areas of the Zambesi remained disturbed. It was not until well on into 1889 that the expeditions were able at last to leave to assert Portuguese power in central Africa.

The events that now took place are among the best chronicled of the scramble for Africa. Cordon reached his destination, but returned after setting up a few command posts. Andrada busied himself with the founding of the port of Beira and with establishing Portuguese control on the Sabi while Serpa Pinto charged like a bull into the diplomatic china shop of the Shire valley. On 11 January Lord Salisbury, in bed with 'flu in Hatfield, delivered his ultimatum ordering the Portuguese to halt on all frontiers pending a general settlement.

Portugal had in fact lost Mashonaland, which four years before had seemed almost in her grasp, and the only reason she lost it was the embroilment in the Massangano wars, and the desperate resistance of Motontora to the destruction of his clan.

The fall of Manuel Antonio de Sousa

It remains to chronicle the fall of Manuel Antonio. Since the destruction of the da Cruz, Sousa's empire had expanded so that it now included not only his own *prazos* and the kingdom of Barue but the da Cruz *prazos* of the right bank and the chieftaincies lying between the Mazoe and the Luenha. Everywhere throughout this territory were stationed Sousa's captains with *aringas* garrisoned with Zambesi sepoys and well supplied with government firearms, and every year Sousa drew tribute from this vast territory.

Both he and Andrada assumed that the Manica mountains were part of the territory of the Moçambique Company. The Company set up a command post at Massekesse, near where the old Portuguese fair had been, and in October 1890 Andrada sent a message to Mutassa of Manica to secure his allegiance to the Company. He was shortly joined by Manuel Antonio who made the journey to the Manica mountains accompanied by *Dona* Rosa Fernandes of Chemba and a large cortège of *machilla* bearers, armed guards, porters and female attendants. By this time Rhodes' pioneers had occupied Mashonaland and had perceived that the passes through the Manica mountains were the only access their territory could expect to the sea. Rhodes' men sent messages to try to discourage Portuguese activity but in vain, for on 14 November Sousa and Andrada arrived at Mutassa's kraal to confirm the Moçambique Company's occupation of the mining districts under Mutassa's sovereignty.

There they were surrounded and taken prisoner by Forbes of the British South Africa Company's police. Not one of Sousa's body-guard offered any resistance and he and Andrada were sent as prisoners down the long overland route to the Cape (*476*).

This so-called 'Manica Incident' has frequently been described as an important landmark in the history of Rhodesia and of Anglo-Portuguese relations. Its full significance for the history of Moçambique has never, however, been pointed out. Portugal's control over the land between the Zambesi and the Sabi rested wholly on the power of Manuel Antonio. A number of British observers had commented on this with a view to disparaging Portuguese imperial claims, but as long as Sousa worked in close co-operation with the Portuguese government this fact had little significance. However, the power of a Zambesi *senhor* lay entirely in his personal hold over his followers and on the mystique of success and invincibility he was able to radiate. It has been suggested that among the reasons for the successful return of Motontora in 1888 had been the rumour that Sousa was dead (*310*). Now Sousa *was* dead—if not literally so, at least for all political purposes.

Sousa's disappearance in November 1890 precipitated the collapse of his personal empire and with it the collapse of Portuguese control in the district of Manica. It was fortunate for Portugal that the full extent of this collapse was hidden from the diplomats in London, otherwise she might have lost in the final settlement much more than she actually did of the territory she claimed.

As soon as it was known that Sousa had really disappeared, Motontora, head of the da Cruz clan, crossed the Zambesi from Macanga with his brothers. They could not return to Massangano, which was garrisoned with government troops, so they moved to the Muira valley and began to construct new *aringas* there. They sent messengers to Mtoko, Rupire and the other Botonga chiefs to renew the alliance of 1887. The *pax lusitana*, which Castilho had established with such a flourish in 1888, now crumbled away like a sandcastle in a tide of African rebellion (*342*, *225*).

Canga, son of the last Macombe of Barue, had been a refugee since 1880, first in Massangano and then in Manica. Now he appeared with his followers in Rupire which was still garrisoned by two of Sousa's captains, Cambuemba and Capovo, though their position was one of total isolation now that Sousa had gone. After brief negotiations they agreed to hand over the stores and fortified posts under their command to the Barue rebels.

Without a shot being fired, Canga reoccupied Massanga and advanced on the *aringa* of Magaço, another of Sousa's captains. Magaço defended himself half-heartedly for seven days and then withdrew, enabling Canga to take possession of almost all of Barue for the ancient line of the Macombes.

Throughout Gorongosa and the Sena *prazos* where Manuel Antonio had ruled undisputed for thirty years, the disappearance of the *senhor* left power in the hands of the captains of his *aringas*. Sousa had placed one of his wives at each *aringa* but these were a poor focus for loyalty to their vanished lord and only in Chemba, where Sousa's daughter *Dona* Victoria was living, was there a member of the Sousa family able to maintain Manuel Antonio's interest. In each *aringa* the captains now took control and awaited the passage of events. Like all soldiers of fortune they were not men of sentiment and determined to hold their positions until they could sell their swords to another.

This was the situation when, at the beginning of the dry season in 1891, Sousa was released by the British. In May he was back on the Zambesi determined to regain his position. However, he was joined by only a few of his former captains, and turned for help to the Portuguese officer João de Azevedo Coutinho who was busy raising a mercenary army to fight the rebellion in Macanga. Together they agreed to attempt the reconquest of Barue—Sousa invading from the direction of Gorongosa, Coutinho from the Zambesi.

Sousa now hurried to his headquarters in Gorongosa and set about raising an army of reconquest. At first he was held up when supplies of arms failed to reach him but having eventually assembled an army, he took the initiative and stormed Inhangona, the chief fortified *aringa* in central Barue. The Barue army was forced back into the north-western part of the country and it looked as though Sousa might win a swift and decisive victory. At this stage, however, the rains set in and, either because he thought the battle won or because he lacked the energy and drive to conduct a campaign during the rains, Sousa dallied. It was not in fact until January 1892 that he eventually moved against the *aringa* of Missongue on the upper Muira river.

The *aringa* was grimly defended and Sousa's forces were weak and in bad condition. It appears that they did not even establish an effective blockade of the place and allowed supplies to be brought to the defenders. The defence was stiffened by the presence of white mercenaries and one sortie led by the defenders succeeded in taking Sousa's men by surprise. The guns were captured and Sousa himself was wounded in the fighting. As the news of his injury spread through the army, the soldiers panicked and fled. Sousa himself tried to get away alone into the bush but he could not go far and was eventually found by a boy who killed the old warrior rather than risk taking him wounded to the *aringa* (*342*, 277).

Sousa's defeat and death had been preceded by the destruction of Azevedo Coutinho's expedition. Coutinho had opened his campaign on 6 November and had been joined by Sousa's captain, Camba, and his soldiers, bringing the total of his forces up to nearly four thousand men. The *aringa* of Mitondo at the mouth of the Muira was taken and Coutinho's army then marched up the valley along the route taken by Francisco Barreto over three hundred years earlier. Ahead of him lay the *aringa* of Mafunda, heavily fortified and well supplied with food and ammunition.

The attack on Mafunda took place on 19 November and, for a Zambesi battle, the casualties were high, over eighty soldiers of Coutinho's force being killed. While the battle raged Coutinho and his European staff stood in the shade near the ammunition dump. A stray shot from the defenders suddenly set off an immense explosion which blew the group of European officers to pieces. Only Coutinho and one or two others were carried, desperately burnt, back to the Zambesi. This disaster was not the only one of the day, for among the dead was Camba (*342*, 238–58). With Camba and Coutinho *hors de combat*, the motley force of irregulars broke up. A few contingents stayed with Coutinho but the rest dispersed to their homes.

Portuguese authority on the lower Zambesi had for so long rested on the personal authority of Sousa that the administration had no resources on which to fall back. Throughout 1892 and 1893 the situation became ever more confused. Barue warriors raided Gorongosa and bands of soldiers from Gorongosa raided the river-side *prazos*. Sousa's captains encouraged the local chiefs not to pay *mussoco* and began to intercept river traffic passing up the Zambesi from the delta to Tete. The small detachments of loyal troops were confined to their forts in Sena and Chupanga (*224, 225*).

However, with their extraordinary capacity for survival, the Portuguese clung on. The international sky was now clearing and the agreement with Britain was completed by the end of 1891. The Moçambique Company had been granted its charter as a sovereign company and was beginning to construct the port of Beira and the railway to Rhodesia. White rule in Mashonaland also aided the Portuguese. Mtoko, swallowed up in Rhodes' empire, was no longer to be feared and the western side of Barue was ringed by British territory.

Still, the Portuguese position would have been virtually untenable if the da Cruz, the Barue royal family and Sousa's former captains had been able to combine effectively. Such a combination never occurred and the rivalries of the captains and the various branches of the Barue royal house and the personal animosities among the old *muzungo* clans enabled the Portuguese to divide and rule as they had always done. This was the twilight of the power of the *senhors*, the captains and the slaves and we must conclude by following this final stage of the Zambesi Wars to its close.

Along the right bank of the Zambesi in the area of the Sena *prazos*—the oldest area of Portuguese settlement—Sousa's heirs clung to a diminished heritage. *Dona* Victoria, married to a Corsican adventurer called Lemagna, ruled in Chemba and in spite of heroic postures and complicity in some disturbances in 1892, co-operated increasingly with the government in eradicating other rebel and bandit chiefs. She enabled the government to run Chapananga to earth (*228*), and in 1894 provided labour for the construction of a company fort (*227*).

At Inhaparapara Sousa's captain Magaço continued to occupy an *aringa* and maintain friendly relations with the Portuguese, but his great days were over. He had rejoined Sousa on his last campaign, but slowly and with reluctance, and much suspicion of treason had attached itself to him. Near Magaço another captain of Sousa's had an *aringa*. This was Gizi, son of an Indian called Azevedo Cangreme who had been one of Sousa's colleagues. On Sousa's death Gizi had married his wife, *nhanha* Muanga, and continued to occupy the houses and the *aringa* that Sousa had built for himself (*227, 420*, vol 2, 323).

Most important of all, however, was Cambuemba. Coutinho describes how, as he lay recovering from his wounds received at Mafunda, he was told that a party of thirty men had arrived at the camp led by

a negro with olive-coloured skin, small and dried out, dressed in the cap of an artillery captain, his face in a perpetual grin and with a notable vivacity in his eyes and his movements. He stationed himself before me, gave an imitation of a military salute and shouted, as if he ought to be known to everyone— 'Cambuemba' (*342*, 278–9).

Cambuemba was the son of an Angolan soldier who had come to the Rivers. He had quarrelled with Manuel Antonio during the last campaign against Massangano and had been instrumental in handing over the *aringa* of Massanga to Macombe. For a short time he had gone to Macanga and now, with Manuel Antonio dead, he presented himself to the Portuguese because 'the lands of the king did not have a *capitão grande*'.

Cambuemba's reputation still stood high and his adhesion to Portugal was important. Coutinho placed him in control of the Sena *prazos* where for two years he ruled much as he pleased, maintaining good relations with the Portuguese all the while. He established contacts with Macombe, with the da Cruz and with other Tonga chiefs, and saw himself increasingly recognised as a chief by the free inhabitants who began to filter back into the area under the protection that Cambuemba offered them.

However, Cambuemba was not satisfied with the role he was required to play. He saw that the chiefs and *capitaes* of the interior who remained in open rebellion lived in virtual independence, while loyalty to the Portuguese meant for him that he had to pay the *mussoco* for his people and that he had continually to find carriers and labourers for the government. He saw also the successful game that other chiefs played when they refused to pay *mussoco* and entered into a state of rebellion and then allowed themselves to be reconciled to the Portuguese on the receipt of a large present. In 1897 he refused to pay *mussoco* himself and began to defy the Portuguese on his *prazos*.

Cambuemba probably thought he could depend on the support of the other former captains of Manuel Antonio in Gorongosa and on the backing of the Tonga chiefs of the Lupata region. He also put faith in a piece of artillery he had succeeded in capturing together with the two soldiers to work it. He was disconcerted by the speed with which an expedition was mounted against him.

It was the first major Portuguese expedition in Zambesia since 1892 and it was led by João de Azevedo Coutinho, who had recently been appointed governor, and was mustering men for the final war with Maganja da Costa. Coutinho's column made a lightning raid on the Sena *prazos* in July of 1897. Cambuemba tried to make a stand with his piece of artillery, but he found that it made no impression on Coutinho and in a fit of anger he murdered the two white soldiers and retreated with his men into the interior. Coutinho was able to capture eighteen *aringas* and pacify the whole of the right bank from the Lupata gorge to Sena (*342, 433–462*).

However, even after this success the Moçambique Company was in no position to establish its authority. 'The Company is a woman and does not know how to make war' became a local saying, for having been rescued from one *muzungo capitão* they proceeded to rent the Sena *prazos* to another, Eusebio Ferrão.

The power of the Ferrões was based, like that of the other Zambesi families, on their slaves and clients. In the middle of the century they acquired Cheringoma through marriage with Ines Castellobranco but they lost control of the *prazo* subsequently (*459*). They made up for this reverse by establishing close relations with the Gaza warriors who raided the Sena area and even recruited their own body-guard of Gaza Ngoni. With the defeat of both the da Cruz and Sousa, the Ferrões became once again the leading Sena family.

The conquest of Barue

Following the defeat of Cambuemba in 1897, Coutinho prepared for his campaign against Maganja da Costa. Cambuemba, meanwhile, had fled to Barue and taken refuge in that last bastion of African independence in central Africa. It was a tragedy for the African cause that in the decade following Sousa's death the Barue Tonga were unable to find any great leader. Instead of a vigorous national unity they were torn by strife and civil war which laid them open to the exploitation of white adventurers and eventually to conquest by the Portuguese in 1902.

The events of this last decade of Barue history are very con-

334

fused, and the existing accounts are impossible to reconcile. That which follows is derived from the story told by Coutinho, who commanded the campaign of conquest in 1902 and who obtained his information from Sousa's captains.

The rebellion against Sousa in 1891 had been led by Canga, younger son of the last Macombe Chipatata. After Sousa's defeat and death Canga was ousted by his elder brother Samacande who, as an exile, had visited a number of European settlements and had acquired a following of white adventurers.

Samacande's two or three years of power were marked by the dominance of George Taylor over Barue and Rupire. Taylor was an American (English in one account) who had come to Africa as an employee of the Beningfeld syndicate. He had ingratiated himself with Mutassa Chifumbasio, chief of Manica, and married the daughter of one of the Manyika *indunas* called M'jojo—a name which Taylor himself then assumed. When the British South Africa Company took over in Manica, Taylor was exiled and went to join Samacande. He organised the defence of Inhachirondo (Missongue) against Sousa in 1892 and secured the defeat of Samacande's rival, Canga, at the same place.

Taylor's ascendancy in Barue during 1893 and 1894 was complete. He visited the chiefs between the Mazoe and the Luenha and imposed his authority on them—threatening them with the return of the days of Manuel Antonio if they caused any trouble. Meanwhile the Moçambique Company was supposed to be ruling Barue and with fox-like cunning appointed Taylor to be its representative in the country.

The British South Africa Company appears also to have made approaches to Taylor. This was the period when Rhodes was still trying to bully and bluff a way to the sea for his infant colony and Taylor may well have been an instrument of this policy. He began to be absent in Rhodesia for increasingly long periods, leaving his affairs in Barue in the hands of a crony called Newman and the Portuguese all believed that he was paying the taxes he collected to the British South Africa Company. But if Rhodes was planning a 'Barue incident' as he had planned the various Beira and Manica 'incidents' his plans never came to fruition, for Taylor disappeared from the Barue scene—possibly at the time of the overthrow of Samacande by Canga.

It is easier to explain Canga's return to power than it is to date it. Samacande was unpopular, he was cruel, he had let in white adventurers and he himself dressed like a white and had adopted many European habits. His overthrow, however, coincided with the re-appearance of a pretender to the throne of the Macombes and at least one writer (*420*) attributes his overthrow directly to the newcomer.

The pretender was a member of the rival Macombe royal dynasty of Chibudo. His name was Chipitura and there are indications that he had originally joined Sousa in 1891 and had come to occupy part of Barue in the wake of Sousa's invasion. He was certainly the candidate favoured by the Portuguese. In March 1896 the Moçambique Company's administrator in Africa was able to report that 'the Barue question appears to be nearing a solution favourable to the interests of the Company' and he went on to describe Chipitura as a man 'who lived for many years in the Sena district in contact with white people and who is more civilised than the natives of the interior' (*230*).

Samacande's unpopularity and the rivalry between him and Canga undoubtedly led to Chipitura's gaining a lot of support. He was able—probably in 1895—to seize control of much of the country, pushing Canga north to the Muira valley but never finally defeating him.

From now until the end of the century the kingdom of Barue remained permanently split between the Chibudo/Chipitura line, holding the larger part of the country and ruling from Mungari and the Chipatata/Canga line, based on Inhachirondo and the Muira valley. Chipitura eventually died and was succeeded by his son, Cassiche, who tried to bargain with the Portuguese for help against his rival. This led, in 1900, to his being deposed by his *grandes*, who placed Chavunda on the throne. Chavunda ruled until captured by Coutinho in Inhangone in 1902.

All this time Canga continued to rule his small domain in the Muira valley—recognised as the true Macombe but controlling only a tiny fragment of the former kingdom. Canga's capital was the powerful and much disputed *aringa* of Inhachirondo (or Missongue) and shortly before independent Barue was finally snuffed out by Coutinho, we can see a portrait of Inhachirondo and its ruler, Macombe Canga, reflected in the distorting mirror of Dr Carl Peters' account of his journey in search of Ophir.

For the connoisseur of the theatrical fantasies into which the tradition of African exploration had degenerated by the end of the nineteenth century, Carl Peters' *Im Goldland des Altertums* is a precious specimen. Once the hero of the colonial party in Germany, Peters had acquired the all too rare distinction of being expelled from the German colonial service for the savage brutality of his conduct towards the Africans of Tanganyika. In

1900 he organised an expedition to prospect for gold in Portuguese Zambesia and to clear up a few mysteries of African prehistory on the way.

In July he set off up the Muira valley, and reached Inhachirondo on 18 July, having incidentally found the Queen of Sheba's palace and a centre of phallic Baal worship on the way.

The entrance of Inhachirondo he described as crowned with two skulls and once installed within the walls took up his pen to give an account of the town.

> Hard the sun burnt down upon our tents in the centre of dusty Misongwe with its indescribable smells. The town has from four to five thousand inhabitants, who live closely together within a narrow palisade; the streets are narrow and winding, and in the centre is the 'palace' of Macombe, which consists of a number of large huts around a wide open square; all these buildings are surrounded by a special wall of palisades. The fortifications round Misongwe have several bullet-proof bastions from which the glacis around can be commanded ... it lies—from a nigger's point of view—like an impregnable stronghold on the margin of the valley of the Muira, about thirty feet above the bottom of the river (*429*, 105–106).

Canga he describes as 'a strongly made man of middle size, with intelligent eyes, a rather soft mouth and a curled beard (*429*, 108). The expression on his face is decidedly pleasing, his behaviour modest but full of dignity, and I had involuntarily the feeling that I was in the presence of no common man.'

During his visit Peters liberally dispensed champagne and brandy until he discovered that, having created the demand, he was expected to supply drink to all on the slightest pretext, and saw his treasured prophylactic against the black-water fever disappearing. Hastily he packed bags, assembled his porters and food supplies and set off for Inyanga. Peters had found a warm reception on Missongue but had had it made quite clear to him that the Portuguese were unwelcome and would not be admitted to Macombe's dominions.

In 1902 the Portuguese government took vigorous action to end the continuous disorders in the Moçambique Company's territory. This was the year of the campaigns against Macanga on the middle Zambesi, of the Bailundo campaign in Angola and it marked a real determination to crush the remnants of African independence. Coutinho was appointed to command the

337

army and he toured all his old associates on the Zambesi, calling
the retired mercenary captains to the colours, again with prospects of loot and rapine in Barue. From Goma and Guengue,
from Sena and the delta, and from as far afield as Angonia and
Maganja da Costa the mercenaries gathered under their captains. And then Coutinho struck with the speed and vigour
which distinguished his campaigns.

Canga had persuaded the rival Macombe Chavunda to join
him in the defence of Inhachirondo and they had called Cambuemba to their aid. The three gathered their forces about the
great *aringa* to give battle and there they were destroyed by
Coutinho's army on 28 August 1902.

Those of the Barue royal family who were not killed or taken
prisoner escaped across the border into Rhodesia—some of them
to live to fight again in 1917.

The campaign against Barue had been short and decisive but
there had been a very real risk of the Portuguese finding themselves involved in a very much larger war. Across the border in
Rhodesia, M'Pondera was causing the Rhodesian police a lot of
difficulty in the Zambesi valley. He had contacts in Barue and
might have caused the war to spread up the River as the Barue
rising of 1917 was to do. In Gorongosa the last of Sousa's captains, Luis Santiago, still maintained his independence and
might also have joined with the Macombes to defeat Coutinho.
Indeed he was approached for an alliance but delayed and
hesitated until too late.

On Sousa's death, his *aringas* in Gorongosa had been seized
by two of his *capitaes*, Chitengo and Luis Santiago. They refused
to hand over to the Moçambique Company the stores in the
Gorongosa *aringas* and reputedly shared out eight hundred
barrels of powder. It was not long, however, before Luis and
Chitengo fell out and the defeated Chitengo fled to the Portuguese (*342, 552*).

For ten years Luis Santiago ruled in Gorongosa. He did not
absolutely exclude the officials of the Moçambique Company
nor those of the sub-contracting Gorongosa Company, but he
remained in undisputed control over the inhabitants and almost
every year the Portuguese authorities recorded Luis' infringements of the *pax lusitana*. In 1894 the Moçambique Company
thought it would try to break his hold on Gorongosa by importing
one of Sousa's sons from Portugal. Young Caetano de Sousa was
brought out to east Africa but it was at once realised that his
presence would merely add to the turmoil and he was sent south

338

to the Company's station at Chiluane (*226*).

Another device was to employ Luis as the agent of the company. This move was a well-tried gambit of Portuguese colonialism. Grant a title and an office to the chief bandit and call him 'saviour of the fatherland' and, at the stroke of the pen, a rebellious colony has become a loyal province of the fatherland. Luis accepted his monthly salary, the uniform of corporal and a sword that he was offered, but continued to collect tribute on his own account (*452*, 14–15), and maintained conspiratorial contacts with Barue (*231*).

Luis Santiago was only able to defy the Moçambique Company because he was protected by the powerful Barue chiefs to the north. No one was hoodwinked by his amateurish political manoeuvres and with the fall of Barue his power was at an end. A column hastily dispatched against him succeeded in capturing his *aringa* and when Luis himself fell into Portuguese hands he was summarily shot.

The Zambesi Wars were at last over.

Conclusion

How important historically is this story of bandits and mercenaries, raid and siege?

Contemporary Portuguese could talk with exaggeration of the national disasters at Massangano, and the great triumphs of the Lusitanian military spirit in the marauding expeditions of Coutinho and the depredations of Zambesi mercenaries enlisted in Portuguese service. But how far did this approximate to the truth?

Without doubt the Zambesi Wars account for the fact that Portugal was unable to claim more substantial areas of central Africa in the final carve-up of the area. Lord Salisbury justified the final settlement that was reached in 1891 by saying that it gave Portugal the historic lands of the Zambesi *prazos* and a bit more. But how much more would its share have been had Sousa and Andrada not turned aside in 1887 to fight the da Cruz?

One must also try to fit the Zambesi Wars into the general pattern of African resistance movements. This is a difficult and complex business. The Zambesi Wars began long before Livingstone had crossed Africa and long before European partition of Africa was even a cloud on the horizon. The early phases of the Zambesi Wars have their place in African politics but cannot be reduced to any formula of resistance to colonialism. Only in the Massingire rebellion of 1884 and the other disturbances related to it can one find an easily recognisable element of resistance by the old *prazo* interests to the new, stricter regime on the Quelimane and delta *prazos* which had come in in the 1870s.

In the final phase of the Zambesi Wars, which begin with the attack on Massangano in 1887, there are clear indications of an African alliance against the advance of European influence. Mtoko, Barue, Rupire, the da Cruz and the Mwene Mutapa found themselves in alliance against Sousa, Xavier and the Portuguese. But in this confrontation there were *muzungos* of old Zambesi *prazo* families fighting on both sides. Even in the final stages of the wars in 1902, old captains of Sousa, like Magaço and Azevedo, fought for the Portuguese against Cambuemba and Luis Santiago who were in alliance with the Barue chiefs.

This picture of confusion is not, however, unique, as most areas of Africa show the same diversity of reaction to the coming of Europeans. Some African leaders welcomed Europeans as allies against traditional enemies, while others opposed the Europeans in bitter wars, often just because of the European alliance with their traditional African foes. In every case what was decisive was the local political situation and not any national consciousness that might be burgeoning.

19 The *Prazo* System in the Nineteenth and Twentieth Centuries—1

On 13 August 1832 José Xavier Mousinho da Silveira, Minister of Finance and Justice, published a decree in Lisbon putting an end to all residual rights of the crown in private property throughout Portugal. What had once been crown property now became the property of private individuals. It was assumed that this legislation would apply to the Portuguese colonies as well as to metropolitan Portugal.

This decree was not, however, enforced in East Africa and *prazo* grants continued to be made and the confirmation of titles sought in Lisbon. For six years no lead was given to indicate the direction in which *prazo* law would change, and then in June 1838 came an order to stop all further grants of *prazos*. This was shortly followed by a decree of extreme brevity drawn up by the marquis de Sa da Bandeira suspending further land grants pending a thorough revision of the law. The decree was followed by an administrative order instructing the governor-general to rent out vacant lands and to submit a plan for the redistribution of land in the colony to be based on the principle that no grant should exceed one league square—the size originally proposed in the decree of 1760 for all riverain and mineral bearing lands (*438*, 12).

No reform of land law followed. In 1841 Moçambique received instructions to see that the decree of 1838 was carried out but the old objections to the renting of land remained. In a petition dated 1841, *Dona* Rosa Saramago claimed that 'when *prazos* are rented to the settlers of the Rivers of Senna, they do them no good and treat them so as to ruin them. They look after their interests and do not care if the *prazo* is ruined' (*117*). In a letter to the Secretary of State for the Colonies in 1843 the governor of Quelimane tentatively suggested that the provisions of the 1838 decree should be relaxed in cases where the *prazos* could be granted to people who were resident (*162*). In short, the debate on the *prazos* ran still in the grooves that had been cut so deeply in the eighteenth century.

One reason for this was the extraordinary shortage of information about Portuguese Africa available for any sort of public discussion. Before 1854 there was no printing press in Moçambique and no official government gazette was issued. Registers of administrative orders and decrees were kept but there was always great difficulty in finding relevant documents and there was no way of informing the settlers of what was being ordered and what was being done, except by the posting of a proclamation.

In Lisbon the government received a large number of reports on the state of the colonies both from officials and from private individuals and there had been an attempt to assemble a reliable body of geographical and ethnographical information about East Africa at the end of the eighteenth century (387). There were also the occasional pamphlets and articles referring to conditions in East Africa and Zambesia, but it would probably be fair to say that until the publication of Sebastião Xavier Botelho's *Memoria Estatistica sobre os Dominios Portuguezes na Africa Oriental* in 1835 there was no source of information available to the general public about Portuguese East Africa more recent than João dos Santos' famous account of 1609 or Francisco de Sousa's *Oriente Conquistado* of 1710. Unfortunately the publication of Botelho's book did not help public debate very much, for it was very ill-informed and quite unbelievably inaccurate. It was pulverised in the *Edinburgh Review* in 1837 with a destructive sarcasm unusual even for that journal.

In the 1850s the situation began to improve. In 1854 the *Annaes do Concelho Ultramarino* began to be published and, in its 'unofficial' section, it contained a wide variety of different accounts of the colonies. In 1854 Gamitto's *Mwata Kazembe* appeared and in 1857 the illustrated journal *Arquivo Pitoresco* began to publish a series of articles by Gamitto about conditions in Zambesia. Then in 1859 appeared the six volumes of Francisco Maria Bordallo's *Ensaios sobre a Estatistica das Possessões Portuguesas no Ultramar*. From this time a lot was published about the Portuguese colonies both in Portugal and abroad, but until the 1890s the debate on the *prazos* largely hinged on information contained in the writings of Botelho, Gamitto and Bordallo, while for English readers Livingstone's books provided all the information that was readily available.

Sa da Bandeira's decree of 1838 had given reasons for putting

342

an end to the emphyteutic contracts. The *prazos* had always been awarded to people who had no capital to develop them agriculturally and, as a result, the territories were depopulated and uncultivated. Many previous writers had stressed the need for cultivation and the failure of the *prazos* as a system of plantation agriculture, but in Sa de Bandeira's decree there appeared for the first time the official recognition that what was at the root of the problems in the Portuguese empire was lack of capital. It was this idea that was to run through all the confusing legislation on the *prazos* that appeared in the next ninety years.

In 1854 Sa da Bandeira at last produced his comprehensive land law on the *prazos*. All *prazos* were to be abolished and the *senhors* compensated with awards of land according to the length of time their lease still had to run and the amount of land they had held before the decree. The compensation was to conform to the provisions of the decree of 1760: that *prazos* should not exceed three leagues by one in size. The free African peasants were to receive fifty hectares of land as private property and were to pay a hut-tax (*palhota*) directly to the state. They were no longer to be liable for any other dues or service obligations. The *senhors* were bound to cultivate their land within five years and were to pay a tax of ten per cent of their income to the state.

In 1855 detailed instructions were published for the carrying out of this decree but, as the preamble to another law of 1880 said, 'its execution has been in a state of suspension for twenty-six years for reasons of *force majeure*, one of these being the repeated and prolonged wars in Zambesia.'

The decree of 1854 may have been virtually a dead letter but circumstances in the middle of the nineteenth century were such that the old *prazo* regime was anyway fast disappearing. The Zambesi had been subject to continual invasion and disorder since early in the 1830s, as horde after horde of Ngoni migrants appeared south of the Zambesi, settled for a time and then moved on. In the dark days of the 1830s and early 1840s most of the *prazos* were abandoned and those areas which were not paying direct tribute to the Ngoni fell into the hands of the few Portuguese *senhors* who had survived.

Towards the end of the 1840s the situation began to stabilise. The Sena *prazos* were annually visited by an *impi* from the Gaza capital and the Portuguese settlers paid tribute to the Gaza king. The Tete district was torn by the wars of da Cruz and Pereira and only in Quelimane was any sort of ordered and continuous life possible. In these conditions large numbers of the *prazos* fell *em commisso* and reverted to the crown. They were not re-granted. Instead they were left unoccupied unless someone could be found to rent them. Probably no emphyteutic contracts were made out after the middle of the 1840s, although there are a few cases of contracts which still had one or two lives to run being renewed right up to the 1880s.

When Francisco Maria Bordallo compiled his statistics on the *prazos* for the year 1856 he was able to show the extent to which the three-life contracts had already disappeared. In Quelimane, relatively unaffected by the disorders, all but three of the sixteen *prazos* were still held by contracts of emphyteusis. Of the seventy-two *prazos* in the Tete district only three were still held by emphyteusis, fifteen were rented and the rest were recorded as being invaded by the Africans—in other words they had no holder. The Sena district had thirty-one *prazos*, sixteen of which were still held by contracts of emphyteusis, seven were rented, and the rest were empty (*438*, 38–44).

Over the next twenty years this process of change slowly continued. As three-life tenures came to an end, they were not renewed and the *prazo* in question was rented out. Figures for 1875 show the situation twenty years after Bordallo's account. In that year Quelimane had only five out of twenty estates still held as *prazos*, the rest were rented. Of the thirty-two Sena *prazos* on the list sixteen were rented, eight held by emphyteusis and eight were empty. In the Tete district all *prazos* were either rented or without holders at all. It should be noticed at this point that the *terras em fatiota* were not included in these considerations as their tenure was looked upon virtually as private property (*439*).

In other words, the number of estates held by three-life tenures had fallen from thirty-two in 1856 to thirteen in 1875.

When the *prazos* were rented, it was only for a period of three years and all the renter acquired was the right to collect the *mussoco* or the hut-tax which had been substituted for it. This, in theory, gave the government very much more control over the system and in areas where its writ ran it began a series of experiments in the direct administration of some of the *prazos*. Before this experiment is discussed, however, we must consider another set of legal provisions affecting the *prazos*—the laws on slavery.

Between 1850 and 1880 various legal enactments issued forth from Lisbon on the subject of slaves in the Portuguese empire. Their general tenour is well-known. In 1854 all government slaves were freed and the status of *liberto* was introduced—a

344

status midway between being slave and free. A *liberto* was free but had to work for his former master for a fixed period. In 1858 it was decreed that slavery would end in the Portuguese empire in twenty years' time and in 1869 all slaves were freed but were to remain *libertos* until 1878. Meanwhile the slave trade was outlawed and all slaves had to be registered in the colony (375, 59).

These regulations applied to the whole Portuguese empire; they had no particular reference to Zambesia, and no particular relevance to it either, for most of the slavery in Zambesia was really a form of clientship and the personal relation between slave and master was not a property relationship. The laws had, however, more relevance in the coastal settlements where slavery had always been much more a matter of the purchase and sale of slaves brought from the interior and where there were plantations and estates run by slaves.

These laws are usually described as emanating from the sentimental and liberal politics of nineteenth-century Europe, but this is to forget that regulations on slavery in the Portuguese empire had been issued ever since the sixteenth century. Even in Zambesia there had been attempts to protect the *colonos* from enslavement, to forbid various practices which led to the enslavement of freemen and to control the powers of *senhors* over their slaves. The decree of 1854 on the *prazos* had also been concerned with the rights and status of the *colonos*. It had outlawed the illegal enslavement of *colonos* and had tried to entrench their economic security in large peasant holdings of land— although admittedly these ideas had little reference to African conditions or to the realities of African society.

However, nominal acceptance of the abolition of slavery meant that all debate on the future of the *prazos* and the agricultural development of the colony had to concern itself with the question of supplying labour on a free or semi-free basis.

The attack on slavery and the according of full civil rights to the African was also implicitly a blow at the power of the old Zambesi families. It was rightly perceived that these families with their bands of armed retainers, their slaving activities and the tribute they extorted from the *colonos* were the source of much of the disorder in the colony and hence the major obstacle to any development. The formal abolition of emphyteutic contracts and of slavery, however, had no effect on the political and social realities of Zambesia. The great *senhors* and their armies had existed before the *prazos* were instituted and continued to exist long after the *prazos* were legally abolished.

345

Here then were the new factors in the colonial debate that began in the 1870s and led to the attempts to transform land law and society in Zambesia between 1888 and 1892.

In considering the changes attempted in these years, one must remember that the Portuguese authorities controlled only a very small area of land indeed. The whole of the Tete district, the whole of the southern bank of the Zambesi as far as its mouth and the north bank from the Shire river to the Lupata gorge were all controlled by the great Zambesi clans. It was only in the old district of Quelimane that Portuguese authority was obeyed and then only fitfully, for along the coast the power of the da Silva family in Maganja was as great and as independent as that of the da Cruz or the Pereira. There were also numerous lesser *senhors* and *senhoras*, like *Dona* Ines Barata or *Dona* Captiva Alves who were as independent as they dared to be.

In the middle of the 1870s the Quelimane authorities began to experiment with the direct administration of some *prazos* that fell vacant. Broadly speaking, this was an attempt to carry through some part of the legislation of 1854. The old tribute (*missonco* or *mussoco*) which had traditionally been collected from the *colonos* had been abolished and replaced by a hut tax (*palhota*) in 1854 and this was now collected directly as a government tax.

Obviously direct administration by the government severely limited the power of the old *muzungo* families on the *prazos* and its introduction, coinciding with the formal abolition of slavery and the coming of the first commercial companies to Zambesia, brought about considerable changes in the delta region. Something of these changes and the unrest that accompanied them can be seen in the register of correspondence of the Quelimane government for the years 1876 to 1882 (A.H.U. Moç. Codice 1460).

In November 1876 the governor, in a letter to the military commandant of Sena, explained the advantages of direct administration. The tax, he said, was collected without 'the intervention of the *muenes* or *fumos* or *samacoas* which would have left the *colonos* in dependence of those authorities'. He went on: 'I do not consider it profitable to exact manual labour from the *colonos* without payment on all occasions but only for the clearing of the roads, rivers and channels' (*144*).

The *colonos* were experiencing for the first time a direct relationship with the state which would in time sap their communal institutions and make capitalistic development easier. This direct relationship enabled the *colonos* to complain much more easily about the oppression to which they were subjected from the *muzungos*, and the various cases recorded in this correspondence throw an extraordinary vivid light on life on the *prazos*.

For example, there is the simple accusation levelled against Francisco Vidigal that his armed bands have been attacking villages and carrying off female slaves (*145*). Then in October 1877 Isobel Caetana da Costa was arraigned because 'barbarously and according to the old ways she had whipped her maid servant with a whip with two tails, having first taken care to tie her firmly to a stake. The complainant bears on her body vividly the marks of the whip which was administered cruelly and hurt her badly' (*147*).

In December the same year Caetano Piedade de Sousa, the renter of *prazo* Inhassunge, was accused by one of the *colonos* of having carried off his wife, children and belongings after he had paid the *mussoco* which he had owed (*148*). Similar complaints were not uncommon, which suggests that allegations of failure to pay tribute had, in the past, led to raids and the kidnapping of slaves by the *senhors*.

In 1878 the government undertook a census of the Quelimane *prazos* in order to make the collection of tax more effective. The taking of a census appeared to the peasants the ultimate weapon of tyranny as it equipped the government with information which could be used to impose its control over the peasant communities.

As soon as the census began to be taken, disturbances broke out through the whole delta region led by the chiefs and headmen of the *colonos*.

The government was worried and issued orders for the census to be discontinued (*149*) distributing arms to the *muzungos*, who must secretly have been delighted at this opportunity to resume their traditional role as the guardians of 'law and order' on the *prazos*. In the months that followed, arrests were made and the troubles gradually died down.

They recurred in 1884 when the Massingire of the Shire valley rose against the Portuguese administration which again was trying its hand at taking a census. This rising spread from the Shire along the whole of the north bank as far as Quelimane and appears to have been actively fomented by the old *muzungo* families who again took the opportunity of the disturbances to demand arms from the government.

In spite of these troubles, the government persisted with direct administration of the *prazos*, and in 1880 a new *prazo* law was drawn up. This law repeated the provisions of the 1854 decree almost word for word but it was followed by a number of detailed regulations indicating how the tax was to be collected.

In 1881 proposals were submitted for the extension of direct administration to the Tete *prazos*, but the governor-general in passing the idea on to Lisbon poured cold water on it.

> But will the renters of the *prazos*, who today are still real feudal *senhors*—and more than feudal *senhors* for they virtually never render homage and fealty to the sovereign power, will these who are absolute and dominant in their so-called *prazos* or captaincies be willing to allow themselves to become simple proprietors of small estates subordinated to the common law in an area where all the Africans recognize them as *senhor*? (*121*)

Direct administration was clearly impossible in the Tete district as long as the *senhors* ruled the land, and it was discredited by the disasters that followed the direct administration of Massingire, but it found an ardent advocate in Augusto de Castilho, the conqueror of Massangano.

In March 1886 Castilho issued a set of instructions for the collection of the *mussoco* in the Quelimane district. The *prazos* were to be rented out and the renter could farm any empty land on his concession but he was to hand over the *mussoco* to the government. For the first time, however, the collection of the *mussoco* was related to the labour needs of the colony and the *colono* was granted the option of paying the tax in money or commuting it for labour (*438*, 24–26).

Later Castilho was to urge still more direct control of the *prazos* by the government and he later attributed his dismissal from the post of governor-general to his too ardent advocacy of this policy. In the instructions which he drew up in 1887 for the new governor of Manica, Ferreira Simões, he wrote:

> Experience has shown that administering the *prazos* on behalf of the government has more advantages than the public auction of the right to collect the *mussoco*. Up till now lack of statistics and the fierce opposition of the settlers has prevented it from spreading. It has taken much persistence on my part to have light thrown on this subject but now a regime of morality and order has been inaugurated in place of public penury and scandalous private wealth. Wherever possible the governor

348

should take over the *prazos* if he has suitable men to administer them, and adequate statistics. This will not only increase the wealth of the government but will give it a force of loyal soldiers and the people will be preserved from spoliation (*125*).

But was Castilho right? What had been the relative success of renting out the collection of the *mussoco* and collecting it directly through government officials? A pamphlet published in Goa in 1883 had little doubt. By simple arithmetic, its author, Joaquim Correa de Noronha, demonstrated to his own satisfaction how disastrous was the policy of renting out the collection of the *mussoco* when compared with the financial allurements of direct administration. His whole argument hinged on his assessment of the African population of the Quelimane district. He rightly pointed out that the renters of the *prazos* tended to understate the numbers of the *colonos* in order to reduce the value of the *prazo* in government eyes and so keep down the rent. According to his estimate there were a quarter of a million households in the area and if each of these paid 1:600 *reis mussoco*, 0:500 *reis* in hut tax and 0:200 *reis* for public works from each man, then the income derived by the government from the *prazos* would amount to 876,000:000 *reis*. This he compared with the income of 25,762:000 *reis* paid in 1881 by the Quelimane *prazos* (*417*).

These were hypothetical figures, but the real figures were impressive enough. Since the late 1870s the annual income derived from the *prazos* had been rapidly rising. Averaging only 6,000:000 *reis* a year between 1868 and 1879, the income rose sharply in the financial year 1880–1 to 26,458:000 *reis* and continued to rise rapidly thereafter (see appendix 2). Although the income from the Tete district showed a modest improvement, this dramatic increase was almost wholly due to the rise in the revenues of the Quelimane district.

In a report which was placed before the *prazo* commission in 1888, the governor of Quelimane, Guerreiro de Amorim, gave evidence of the overwhelming success of direct collection of the *mussoco*. His figures were the most recent available and covered the year 1887–8 when fifteen *prazos* were being administered directly. He estimated their income at 54,618:000 *reis* compared to the 15,464:636 *reis* which they had produced when the collection of the tax was put up for auction. Ten *prazos* were still rented out and he estimated their income at half what they would bring if directly administered.

These conclusions were clear and unambiguous but, as the

prazo commission emphasised, they said nothing about the economic and social development of the colony (*438*, 64).

What was the economic condition of the colony in 1888? While the government had experimented with different methods of tax collection, had there been any change in the traditional economy of subsistence agriculture and trade caravans connecting the coast to the inland fairs?

Commercial companies

There had been a few attempts to exploit the Portuguese colonies in East Africa by means of joint stock companies; one such attempt being made in the seventeenth century. The nineteenth century had already, by the 1880s, seen its crop of abortive commercial ventures. There had been the *Compagnie Commerciale de Lourenço Marques* of 1824 and the *Compagnie d'Agriculture et de Commerce* in 1838. In 1853 there had been the *Compagnie Luso-Africaine de l'Afrique Orientale*, and there were others as well. But Portugal lacked capital to invest overseas, and, what was more important, she lacked the capitalist mentality which could create large enterprises even where capital was lacking (*413*, 68).

The laws against alienation and mortmain had always proved effective in preventing the Zambesi estates passing into the hands of commercial companies or corporate bodies of any kind. So official policy had discouraged company operations by Portuguese while any thought of using foreign capital to develop east Africa was even more severely discouraged.

By the 1870s the scene was changing in many ways. The wave of minor speculation in Africa was beginning among European commercial houses; international pressure to open up Africa to the free trade of all nations was growing, and the Christian missions were busy carrying out part of Livingstone's missionary programme and were organising economic activities on a considerable scale.

In 1875 the Portuguese government granted a monopoly of shipping rights on the Zambesi to a concern called *Companhia da Empressa Mineira e da Navegação a Vapor da Zambesi* (*185*). This monopoly not only offended the free trade scruples of the British but was totally unacceptable in international politics as it would confirm Portugal's sovereignty in parts of Africa which she had never occupied and which Britain, for one, had no intention of admitting her right to occupy. The monopoly perished in 1878, having never been exploited by the concessionaires (*314*, 20–22).

This episode led, in 1877, to the fixing of a recognised customs tariff for foreign traders using the Zambesi and a recognition that, within the terms of this agreement, the Zambesi was open to international commerce. Already a Scottish company had established itself in Zambesia. The Scottish missions had set out for the Shire Highlands and Lake Nyasa in 1875 and the following year they had been joined by the African Lakes Company which was to supply the missions and open the Nyasa to 'legitimate' commerce. This company did modestly well and commerce on the Zambesi began to quicken.

French and Dutch firms also established themselves. *Fabre* and *Régis*, both of Marseilles, and the Dutch *Oost-Afrikaansche* company began to trade. They built warehouses and a regular steamer service was running on the lower river by the early 1880s. When the middle reaches of the Zambesi were pacified, these companies also established branches in Tete but they were not able to play any important part in the development of Zambesia, for the new *prazo* legislation of 1890 had the effect of bringing down a new curtain of commercial monopoly throughout the whole region (*191*).

While the foreign trading houses established themselves in Zambesia there were signs of a revival in Portuguese enterprise. In 1873 João Correa, a member of an old Zambesi family and related to Isidoro Correa Pereira the former *capitão-mor* of Manica, rented the large *prazo* of Maindo in the Quelimane district. He went into partnership with Carlos de Carvalho and together they founded the company of *Correa e Carvalho* which developed plantations on the *prazo* with a reasonable degree of success (*338*). The prosperity of the company, however, really depended on the production of sugar-cane spirit which was sold in large quantities in the coastal settlements.

They were soon followed by other purveyors of rotgut spirit. Another entrepreneur born in Zambesia was Caetano Piedade Sousa who operated a still at Inhassunge, while yet a third was in operation at Macuse under the direction of Balthasar Farinha (*461*, 480). A small factory was started on *prazo* Anguaze for the manufacture of peanut oil while bricks and tiles continued to be made at a variety of sites, and boats of various kinds were constructed from local timber for the Zambesi traffic.

The most important development, however, was the launching

at Mopea in 1874 of the Opium Company. Paiva Raposo, the concessionaire of the *prazo* Maganja aquem Shire, imported skilled Indian poppy-growers and the prospects for the success of the enterprise seemed so good that the government of British India became quite alarmed and asked Henry O'Neill, the British consul in Moçambique, for a report. O'Neill himself was also impressed, and reported in 1880 that the company had seventy-four acres sown with poppies and had already shipped the first cargo of opium from Quelimane.

The Opium Company, however, suffered from a serious shortage of labour. Quite simply, there was no tradition in Zambesia of Africans taking regular paid employment and the *muzungos* and their armed followers certainly did not want to see the company rival their own authority, and so discouraged the *colonos* from coming forward to offer their services.

At first the company had to resort to the traditional methods of obtaining labour. The military authorities at Mopea were asked for a contingent of troops to help recruit labour and their manner of operation was subsequently described by Caldas Xavier, the manager of the company. The soldiers would set off through the *prazo* stopping in villages at random and demanding labourers. Those who would not come were fined or flogged with a hippopotamus hide whip. At night the soldiers demanded to be fed and housed free of charge in the villages and usually helped themselves to any girls they fancied (*331*, a, 35).

This method produced a labour force inadequate in numbers and useless for work. As a result Caldas Xavier in 1882 began an experiment which was to have a far greater importance than merely providing the solution to one company's labour problems. He informed the African *colonos* on the *prazo* that they might pay their tax by commuting it for two weeks' labour on the company's plantations.

The results, Xavier claimed, were astonishingly successful. A labour force of nearly two thousand was soon in existence at Mopea, the Africans coming voluntarily to discharge their tax debt. Children were employed at half the adult rate, and if the *colonos* agreed to an extra day's work they were given food, water, and wood free by the company. Soon the company's *prazo* was attracting immigrants from miles around and its population rose steeply.

Caldas Xavier himself explained why the Africans found work preferable to the payment of taxes. Money was scarce in Zambesia and payment in kind laid the *colono* open to every form of

352

extortion. Tax collection became a regular war between the African and the agent of the *prazo*-holder. Every device of tax evasion known to an oppressed peasantry was employed. Unmarried men and women claimed to be minors and exempt from tax; married men passed their wives off as the 'second' wife of another man and claimed to be single; sometimes whole families hid in the bush leaving an aged relative to pose as the sole occupant of the hut. Labour for the company at least ended this war and saved the *colonos* from the arbitrary depredations of the black mercenaries of the *prazo senhors* (*331*, a, 25–27).

The very success of Xavier's system brought about the downfall of the Opium Company. The old *muzungo* interests in Maganja were represented by João Coelho Barata and his wife Ines. When the government's direct collection of the *mussoco* in Massingire threatened to cause a serious revolt on the lower Zambesi, they called their former retainers in Maganja to arm. Barata kept his options open. He could either help the government to suppress the Massingire with his mercenaries, or join the Massingire and benefit from the generous opportunities for loot that the rising offered. Either way the Opium Company would be destroyed.

About half of the Maganja *prazo* joined Barata and it was probably for the most part his men who attacked the Opium Company's buildings early in August 1884. The attack was beaten off but all the company's property was destroyed and its crops ruined. It never recovered from this blow and a few years later sold out to a sugar company.

However, Xavier's scheme for the recruitment of labour did not pass unnoticed. As a result of his epic, almost single-handed, defence of Mopea in 1884 he became a national hero, so that when he took to propaganda on behalf of the Zambesi colony he was eagerly listened to. His account of the Massingire rising was published in 1886 and two years later he published a pamphlet called *A Zambezia*, urging the adoption of a plan for the development of the Zambesi valley as a plantation colony.

The prazo commission

Caldas Xavier's pamphlet appeared in time to be one of the most influential documents laid before the Royal Commission on the *prazos* which was set up in November 1888. Chaired by the great writer and historian J. P. Oliveira Martins, the commission produced its report in February 1889 (*438*, 28–85).

The fifty-two pages of the report represent the first attempt to analyse the *prazos de coroa* in detail from both the historical and contemporary points of view. The historical account of the *prazos* has not stood the test of time (*395*), but the analysis of the social, political and economic nature of the property regime in Zambesia as it appeared in 1888 is masterly.

The commission began its analysis by dividing the Zambesi *prazos* into three categories. First were the *prazos* in the interior, which were threatened with invasion by hostile tribes. These were rented to 'feudal' *senhors* who ruled them with their slave armies and maintained a patriarchal absolutism within their boundaries. These *prazos* did little for the finances of the State and still less for the economy of the colony but they did defend the frontiers and provide protection for the other areas.

The second category consisted of the 'fiscal' *prazos* where the renter was content simply to collect the tax through his agents. This category had always existed, even under the regime of the old emphyteutic tenures, but it had increased with the slow implementation of the abolition decree. This system neither created order, nor provided good returns for the government, nor helped to develop the country. The abuses to which it gave rise were considered to be one of the major causes of the disturbances on the *prazos*, and hence one of the major reasons why the commission had been called.

The third and last category consisted of those *prazos* which were being developed economically by individuals or commercial companies.

The commission then isolated the two prevailing views on the future of the *prazos*. The first considered that the *prazos* should be directly administered by the government because in this way the state derived the maximum income from the tax. The figures produced showed incontrovertibly that this was the case, though it is doubtful if any account were taken of the cost of collection. It was, however, pointed out that this system did nothing to encourage the economic development of the *prazos*.

The second main body of opinion wanted to see the proceeds of native tax used for the economic development of the colony. Portugal lacked capital to invest in the *prazos* and labour was scarce for any entrepreneur daring enough to set up shop on the Zambesi. Yet the commission agreed that Zambesia only had a future as a plantation colony. It could never thrive as a home for white settlers or as a centre of commerce. Was the priority then

354

to increase the income of the colonial government at the cost of leaving Zambesia undeveloped and with the risk of more rebellions like the Massingire rising of 1884; or was the priority the establishment of plantations. The commission opted for the setting up of plantations.

With an intellectual acumen that does it credit, it was persuaded that the centuries of tradition in Zambesia made it impossible to dispense with the personal relationship between *prazo senhor* and African peasant altogether. The fate of the decrees of 1832 and 1854 had shown this, as had the many earlier and more modest attempts at reforming the *prazo* system. What was needed, therefore, was to adapt the traditional system to meet the requirements of the modern world. It was Caldas Xavier's experiment in Mopea which showed the commission how this could be done.

The commission's main recommendations were simple and clear. The *prazos* should be rented for periods of thirty years; the renter should have the obligation to cultivate a certain proportion of the *prazo*; he should collect part of the *mussoco* in labour; he should raise armed police to maintain public order and he should be responsible for providing food in times of famine. Above all there was to be set up an inspectorate over the *prazos* to see that the terms were carried out and the *colonos* were not oppressed.

Few commissions have had their ideas realised with quite such speed. Portugal's position in central Africa was certainly in need of drastic measures. The Zambesi Wars had reached a new peak of destructive anarchy with the attacks on Massangano in 1887 and 1888, the rebellion in Macanga in 1888 and the disorders of the Zumbo district. At the same time Portuguese claims to central African territory were being challenged by British missionaries and adventurers. An immediate settlement of the *prazo* question was vital and so on 18 November 1890 a decree was promulgated which placed the ideas of the *prazo* commission into legal form. However, as the government did not authorise the decree to be put into effect until April 1892, and as the administrative regulations dealing with its practical application in Moçambique were not completed until July 1892 (by Antonio Ennes who was royal commissioner in Moçambique), the legislation is sometimes referred to as dating from this year.

Article One of the decree re-established the *prazos*, which had technically been abolished by the decrees of 1854 and 1880, as divisions of state land. The governor-general was to arrange for

355

a survey of the land and a census of the population but, in drawing the boundaries of the *prazos*, he was instructed to keep as far as possible to the traditional frontiers.

In the administrative regulations for the carrying out of the decree, Ennes laid down an elaborate system of consultations with the African chiefs and headmen and with all other interested parties before the frontiers should be drawn. This was to be conciliatory legislation, not an attempt to revolutionise a very traditional society.

Very large *prazos* were to be divided up but nothing under consideration was as extreme as the measures which had been proposed in the *prazos* decree of 1760 when three square leagues had been made the maximum size of a *prazo*.

Article Two laid down that *mussoco* should be paid by every *colono* between the ages of fourteen and sixty, with the exception of invalids, chiefs, and headmen (*sangires, samocoas, mocasambos*). The *mussoco* was to be paid at the rate of 0:800 *reis* a year and half of this sum was to be paid in labour.

These provisions followed closely Castilho's regulations for the collection of the tax which had been published in 1886, but with one major and one minor exception. The age of exemption in 1886 had been sixteen; it was now lowered to fourteen— presumably to make it easier to distinguish the true minor among the unmarried men posing as minors. The major change concerned labour. In 1886 the African had been *permitted* to pay half his tax in labour; in 1890 he was *obliged* to pay half in labour.

This article was central to Ennes' whole plan; it was the 'gospel' for the Portuguese plantations owners as Castellobranco described it in his report on the *prazos* in 1908. To our eyes it is clear evidence that Portuguese colonial administrators were turning away from the extreme liberalism of the middle years of the century. Slavery was still vigorously condemned but more and more frequently the view is expressed that the African is idle by nature and needs to be compelled to work both for his own moral advancement and for the good of the colony. This conception was to find expression in successive native labour codes which applied throughout Portugal's African territories.

However, it is often forgotten that this article put compulsion also on the European plantation owner. He was bound to receive labour in lieu of tax and was bound to employ this labour. If the African was to be forced to work, so indirectly was the European. It was Ennes' attempt to root out the traditions of three centuries

356

of seigneurial idleness.

The administrative regulations which Ennes published in 1892 altered this part of the decree in one important respect. The decree said nothing about the payment of the *mussoco* in kind instead of money. Ennes thought he could encourage Africans to grow profitable export crops if he allowed them to pay half their *mussoco* in kind and so he appended a list of acceptable products which included ivory, wax, rubber, copra and oil-bearing seeds. The prices paid for these commodities were to be fixed by the government.

This last provision was almost certainly introduced, as we shall see, in a vain attempt to prevent the exploitation of the *colono* by the *prazo*-holder buying below the market price in the traditional Zambesi manner. However, it introduced into the Portuguese colonies an economic principle which has lasted until the present and which allows metropolitan Portugal to dictate prices of raw materials produced in Africa, thereby removing the privilege of exploiting the producer from private hands and making it an act of state.

Article Three divided the *prazos* into two categories; first, those *prazos* which were not pacified and where economic development was impossible; second, the pacified *prazos* where settled conditions existed in which plantations might flourish. This distinction was broadly that made by the *prazo* commission and it certainly corresponded to the realities of the situation. As areas of Zambesia were pacified *prazos* would pass from the first to the second category and the full range of conditions for their development would become operative.

This, at any rate, seems to have been Ennes' idea but the law was not clearly worded and people who later rented *prazos* in the first category took the line that the obligation to cultivate part of the *prazo* did not apply to them (435, 252).

Article Four indicated the terms on which the *prazos* were to be rented. Class one *prazos* could be rented out directly by the governor without public tender for periods of ten years. The contracts could be renewed but could equally be rescinded at any time if the conditions were broken or the security of the state demanded it. These considerations apart, the conditions were to approximate as closely as the situation permitted to the conditions laid down for Class two *prazos*.

Class two *prazos* were to be put up for public auction and rented to the highest bidder for twenty-five years. The minimum rent was to be half the potential yield of the *mussoco*. Every five

357

years the rent was to be reviewed and increased by five per cent or more according to the growth of the population of the *prazo*. The renter was to develop land in proportion to the number of *colonos* available for labour, and he was obliged to take half the *mussoco* in labour. He could employ the *colonos* for longer periods of time at the stipulated rate of 400 *reis* (half the *mussoco*) per week. The *colonos* could only be forced to do unpaid work on government projects, and the renter was obliged to provide them with wood, shelter and water during their service. Otherwise the *colonos* were to be secured in possession of the land needed for their crops and were to be supported by the *senhor* in time of famine. The contract ended if the conditions were not fulfilled.

The provisions of this article were a bureaucratic work of art. At one stroke four things were accomplished which had defied the colonial governments of Portugal for centuries; the African was to be made to work 'productively'; the *prazo*-holders were to be compelled to develop their concessions; a mechanism was created for collecting rents proportionate to the yield of the *prazo*; the problem of finding labour for public and private enterprises was solved.

Ennes elaborated this structure with minute detail in his administrative directions. Receipts were to be given by the *prazo*-renter for money or labour received, the *prazo* inspectors had to check that the area of land scheduled for development did not include the land occupied by houses or other buildings etc. etc. Every crack through which the bad old ways might push like so many weeds through a concrete pavement were closed and cemented over.

Article Five said that one third of the land to be developed had to be farmed within five years—essential, this, to prevent endless procrastination.

Article Six said that any individual might rent land or develop concessions within the *prazos* as long as the *prazo*-holder was given rights of pre-emption in each case. Any European who thus leased an estate became responsible for the payment of the *mussoco* of Africans living on it. This clause underlined the fact that the renter of a *prazo* was renting the right to collect *mussoco* and not the land itself. He was only permitted to rent a small proportion of the actual land.

Article Seven made it impossible for the renter of a *prazo* to claim mineral rights on any land except that actually farmed by himself.

Article Eight allowed *colonos* freedom to sell their surplus

358

products to whomever they wished but it forbade itinerant traders to operate within the *prazos* and made provisions for the holding of regular fairs.

This provision was made with at least half a glance at critical overseas opinion which was always willing to attribute to Portugal the most heinous sins of economic protection. Any hint of commercial monopoly was therefore to be avoided and Ennes laid down elaborate regulations to see that the fairs were conducted openly and equitably, and that the *prazo*-holders had no unfair advantage. The restrictions on the itinerant traders, however, were aimed at the Indians who were the only traders who usually made the effort to travel into the bush to buy from and sell to the African *colonos*. To drive the Indians from the *prazos* was, however, in practice to hand over the local commerce entirely to the *senhors*, so that what this article gave with one hand, it took away with the other.

Article Nine made the *prazo*-holder the agent of local government within his *prazo*. The duties he was to perform were listed by Ennes in 1892 and they read very much like a record of the functions of an English Justice of the Peace of the eighteenth century. He was to report crimes; arrest criminals caught *in flagrante delicto*; report epidemics; keep the roads and river channels clear; provide for any public functionary travelling through the *prazo*; supervise cemeteries and act as sanitary officer; make monthly returns of deaths and births; keep public order and establish schools for Africans wherever the *prazo* had more than 2,000 *colonos*.

As far as these functions of government had ever been performed in Zambesia they had been performed by the *prazo senhor*, so there was no new departure here. Similar duties were also performed by the District Commissioners in British Africa, but District Commissioners did not wield the political, military and economic power that was concentrated in the hands of the renter of the new-style *prazos*.

Article Ten authorised the *senhor* to raise a force of 'sepoys' to police his *prazo*. These men would be armed by the government and would come ultimately under the military commander of the province. They were not to be used outside the *prazo* at all.

Article Eleven established an inspectorate of the *prazos*, to be based on Quelimane, and to be subject to a separate set of regulations. Among his duties, however, would be the establishment of a government agricultural research and advisory service to aid

359

the development of plantations.

Once again there are echoes of the *ancien régime* of the *prazo* system, for one remembers the *tanador-mor*—a creation of the eighteenth century—who was to encourage agriculture and inspect the *prazos*.

Article Twelve ordered the establishment of a service to enable a proper survey of the *prazos* to be made.

Article Thirteen allowed private property to be excluded from the *prazo* when it was put for renting again.

Article Fourteen enabled the government to administer directly any *prazo* which could not be rented.

Article Fifteen ordered the governor to make the regulations necessary for the implementing of the decree and

Article Sixteen revoked all contrary legislation.

Ennes spared no bureaucratic pains to see that his beautiful paper structure was flawless. Tables of fees and licences; regulations for the leasing of land within the *prazos*; regulations covering the fairs; and regulations for the inspectorate of the *prazos* all followed. Within three days of the publication of Ennes' administrative regulations the governor-general issued the first details of the procedure for renting the Quelimane *prazos*. It looked as though, at last, the affairs of the Zambesi were being put in order. But just what had Ennes achieved by his struggles with the hydra of the *prazo* system?

The length and detail of the decree and the regulations at first gives the impression that the new, refurbished *prazo* system was a radical departure from past practice. It became a commonplace—especially among those who wanted to defend Ennes' reform—to say that nothing had remained of the old *prazos* except their name (*431*, 169). But this was not so. The most original of Ennes' ideas had been to overcome Portugal's lack of colonising resources by allowing a *prazo*-holder to derive from the *mussoco* the capital which he was to invest in the development of plantations. However, even this concept had its roots in the past and it is not difficult to see in Ennes' ideas a modernised version of the old captaincies of Brazil and the Atlantic Islands.

For the rest, Ennes had appreciated the full force of traditional attitudes and relationships among the peoples of the Zambesi valley, and had deliberately rejected the idea of instituting a totally different system of government and property. However, he can scarcely have realised just how little he had succeeded in changing the existing situation.

The *prazos* largely maintained their old names and boundaries; they were still to be rented by a single individual who would collect the *mussoco*, command service, do justice and enforce 'law and order' with black irregular troops; there was still the equivalent of the old commercial monopoly of the *senhor* and it was the *senhor* who continued to represent the government to the *colonos* as he had done since the seventeenth century.

Ennes had pinned all his hopes on his plans for a *prazo* inspectorate, a new arrangement, which he thought would prevent the *prazo*-holder from merely living off the taxes he collected from the peasantry. The inspectorate would exist as a special department with a trained staff and it would supervise the carrying out of all parts of the new decree.

But the development of the Zambesi valley depended on peace and the decade following the publication of Ennes' regulations was far from peaceful. Barue and the old da Cruz *prazos* were virtually independent; Maganja and Macanga openly defied the Portuguese and most of the remaining *prazos* in the Zumbo and Sena areas remained outside effective Portuguese control. In these areas the elaborate structure of Ennes' regulations was meaningless and even in the comparatively settled areas of the Quelimane district the government had neither the resources, nor the personnel to act as midwife for the new order. Like a river artificially diverted into a new bed, life on the *prazos* followed the new channels for a year or two and then began to wear back into its old courses.

The final dissipation of Ennes' dream came in 1896 when the *prazo* inspectorate was wound up and replaced by a skeleton supervisory staff working directly under the governor. The reason given for doing this was the expense of the service but the persistent pressure of the *prazo* interests almost certainly helped the government to make up its mind. Without any effective inspection service, the carrying out of the contract obligations was left to the good-will of the renters of the *prazos* and they frequently bore nothing but ill-will towards Ennes and all his works. The corpse of Ennes' *prazo* inspectorate gyrated once or twice before finally disappearing from the scene. In 1901 a land commission was set up to take over the supervisory duties and in 1909 the land commission also disappeared and what supervision there was became vested entirely in the hands of the governor of Zambesia (*304*, 157–158).

Plus ça change, plus c'est la même chose. The new attempt to control the *prazo senhors* had proved less effective even than the *capitaes-mores das terras da coroa* of the early nineteenth century.

361

Ennes had made a deliberate choice of priorities. He had thrust
aside the lure of high revenues to be obtained for the state by the
direct collection of *mussoco* and he had rejected any idea of developing Zambesia by injecting large infusions of foreign capital.
Instead he had devised a plan by which Zambesia would, as it
were, pull itself up by its own boot-straps.

This ideal of self-help may, perhaps, meet with approval in
modern Africa but during the decades which followed 1892 it
increasingly appeared that Ennes' good intentions were making
no impression on the problems of Portuguese Africa. Attempts
to improve on his regulations soon became an indispensable
exercise for every visitor to, or writer on the Portuguese colonies,
although in the event the abolition of the inspectorate was the
only modification to the system of any importance that was made
during the few years that the *prazos* were to remain.

The final chapter of this book will attempt to describe these
last days of the *prazo* system in Zambesia.

Ennes' original vision of the *prazos* reborn had almost certainly
shown him a colony divided into large private estates rented and
run by individual entrepreneurs. The traditional relationships
of Zambesia had been personal ones and Ennes had been concerned to make use of tradition wherever he could; he also used
language in his regulations which shows that he assumed that
the average renter of a *prazo* would be an individual and not a
corporate body. Those eligible to rent a *prazo* were described as
'Portuguese or foreign individuals who enjoy their civil and
political rights' (*438*, 102).

However, Portugal did not have a capitalist class eager to
venture its money in Zambesia and when the *prazos* were put up
for auction in the late months of 1892 they found few takers.

Eventually they fell into the possession of a handful of companies, in part foreign-owned and all under-capitalised. Only two *prazos* were rented directly to individuals—one of these being Carungo which was rented by Francisco Gavicho de Lacerda, a staunch supporter of the *prazo* system and the author of four books of essays and criticism on Portuguese East Africa. Of the companies, two rapidly acquired the greater part of the old *prazo* inheritance—the Moçambique and Zambesia Companies.

The Moçambique Company, as we have seen in chapter 19, had been founded after ten years of entrepreneurial labours by Paiva de Andrada. It began life in 1888 as a mining company with a working capital of only £40,000, but in 1891 it was granted a charter which was confirmed in 1897. By the charter it acquired extensive rights to administer and develop all the country between the Zambesi, Sabi and Luenha rivers, a concession which included all the right bank *prazos*.

Because of the extensive powers which the company enjoyed by virtue of its charter, it was claimed that the *prazo* regulations of 1890–2 did not apply in its territory. Until 1902 Barue, Gorongosa and many of the Sena *prazos* were not effectively controlled by the company at all and in the areas which it could control it either collected the *mussoco* directly through Company agents or sub-leased land to Companies such as the Luabo and Gorongosa Companies. After 1902 the old *prazos* disappeared one by one and were replaced by administrative circumscriptions (districts). The last to go were Luabo and Mulambe which continued to be cited as *prazos* until 1919 when the contract of the Luabo Company expired (*461, 690*).

The refusal of the Moçambique Company to enforce Ennes' legislation meant that the right bank *prazos* developed in an entirely different way from the others or, as Governor Freire D'Andrade put it:

> In this way was divided into two parts a single whole which the *prazo* law had intended for the same process of exploitation, and which would only work harmoniously if it was all subject to the same legislation and the same administration (*355*, vol 1, 155).

The company was content to collect *mussoco* in cash from the Africans and to leave them otherwise unmolested and although this system did not help the development of the region, there being only one agricultural enterprise underway as late as 1907, it did lead to a steady migration of Africans across the Zambesi from the left to the right bank; from an area where labour was compulsory to one where simple payment of the *mussoco* discharged the Africans responsibility to his rulers. The size of this migration clearly discredited Caldas Xavier's claim that Africans would choose to work rather than pay taxes.

This migration caused an increasing shortage of labour north of the Zambesi and swelled the population, and hence the tax returns, south of the river. The population of the Moçambique Company's *prazos* rose from a supposed figure of 47,126 in 1896 to a figure of 115,900 in 1905, and this at a time when the area was torn by the wars of Coutinho against Barue and the last of Sousa's captains (*355*, vol 1, 156–7).

The north or left bank of the Zambesi had, meanwhile, been slipping into the grasp of the Zambesia Company. The Zambesia Company had been inaugurated by a decree of 28 April 1892 for the purpose of developing Andrada's concession north of the Zambesi. This, it will be remembered, had been a mining and forestry concession which limited the concessionaire to holding only 100,000 hectares of land. When the Company drew up its statutes, however, it abrogated to itself far wider powers which made its position not dissimilar to that of the chartered Moçambique Company.

Not content with laying claim to the right to build roads, telegraphs and ports on its concession, the Zambesia Company declared its intention of renting *prazos* and assuming all the obligations listed in Ennes' regulations. In September 1892 it received a concession for ten years of all unrented *prazos* west of the Shire and Luenha rivers. These were the 'class one' *prazos* which were considered 'unpacified' and not subject to the full responsibilities of the new system.

In the next few years the size and scope of the company's undertakings grew apace. Its nominal capital was increased; it contracted to build a telegraph; it undertook to rent Macanga in 1895 and make it into *prazos*; in 1897 it rented the *prazos* of Andone and Anguaze in the Quelimane area; in 1900 it rented Timbue and took over the land between Massingire and the Picos of Namuli (*355*, vol 1, 149–155).

The statistics published by Freire D'Andrade in 1907 showed the Zambesia Company's position north of the river to be one of near monopoly. In the administrative district of Zambesia it rented four out of eighteen *prazos*, these four being among the richest and most populous, having for instance a combined population of 99,758 inhabitants compared with 127,894 in all the others. In the Tete administrative district the company rented 126 out of 136 *prazos* (*355*, vol 1, 220–221).

The Zambesia Company was really equipped only to carry out limited mining operations, and found itself having to digest vast territories which would have taxed the constitution of a Cecil Rhodes. Its *prazos* soon became a by-word for neglect and abuse. It had no money, no men and no technical capacity to undertake the task of development.

The company was forced into a policy of subletting the *prazos* and existing on the rents that it received. Of its 126 *prazos* in the Tete district, sixty-nine containing three-quarters of the population were subrented. The beneficiaries were seventeen individuals and institutions, but the most important of them were Rafael Bivar, Carl Wiese and João Martins, all three men who had fought their way to prominence in the days when the *muzungos* ruled supreme from Zumbo to the delta. They still retained much of their wealth and in the large blocks of land they subrented from the company they continued the old seigneurial regime.

In the Tete district the 'reformed' *prazo* system soon became reduced to a ruthless exploitation of the African *colono*. The company paid a rent for its *prazos* amounting in 1907 to 26,040: 452 *reis*, but received from its subrenting 42,104:565 *reis*. The sub-renters were then faced with the task of making a profit in their turn. This they proceeded to do through extortionate, tax-collecting, fraudulent trading and the sale of labour to contractors—in short by just those means that Ennes had been so anxious to prevent.

The economic prospects of the district were for a long time believed to lie in its supposed mineral riches—its coal, iron ore and gold. But year after year passed without any of these riches manifesting themselves. When Freire D'Andrade toured the country in 1909 he found only three plantations of any kind in the whole district, though for one of these he had great praise (*355*, vol 4, 231). In 1914 there were only 2,598 hectares under cultivation (*304*, 186), while the roads of the Tete district were worse even than the appalling tracks which served as roads in other parts of Moçambique.

Recently an inquiry into the general impact of the Portuguese occupation on the African peoples in the northern part of the Tete district has shown that almost up to the present Portuguese rule has made no impact at all on the traditional way of life, except to depopulate the country by forcing whole families to emigrate to British territory. Economic activity has been virtually nil, roads reach only a small part of the country, there are few schools or clinics—only tax collectors (*339*). When the guerrilla invasion of Moçambique took place in 1964 it met with considerable initial success in the Tete district just because the Portuguese presence there had been so slight.

Nor did the rule of the Zambesia Company even succeed in maintaining public order. The year 1902 had seen the successful final campaigns against Barue and Macanga, after which the latter was divided into *prazos* and rented to Rafael Bivar, while the former was taken from the hands of the Moçambique Company and directly administered by the government through three military command posts.

Barue was soon used by the government as a major recruiting ground for labour. Agents toured the villages armed with pictures, one showing a naked African before going to the mines and the other a well-appointed labourer returning from his contract. But in fact many of the contract labourers did not return and the death rate among the Moçambique Africans on the Rand was seven and a half per cent per annum. Even those who returned, or who never went, found themselves recruited for the unpaid forced labour on government construction projects, under the supervision of black *askari* in the Portuguese service.

With the outbreak of the World War Portugal decided to involve herself on the side of the allies and had to defend a front against the Germans in northern Moçambique—a front which crumbled at the first sign of von Lettow-Vorbeck's army. Carriers were recruited in vast numbers throughout the whole of Zambesia. Francisco Gavicho de Lacerda, who knew Zambesia well having had plantations in the area since the 1890s, estimated that 25,000 men were recruited for the carrier corps of whom only 5,000 ever returned (*366*, 14).

This appalling and totally meaningless loss of life, coming on top of the losses suffered at the mines and the deaths which resulted from the famines that frequently struck the Rivers in the early years of the century, eventually drove the Africans to desperation. In March 1917 a rebellion broke out in Barue, led by surviving members of the two royal houses of Barue and supported by the spirit-mediums (*436*). The rising spread rapidly among the surviving Tonga chiefs on the old Sena *prazos* and many exiles who had fled the country after Coutinho's campaign of 1902 returned to join the movement. On Chemba *prazo* the leader of the revolt claimed to be a descendent of Manuel

Antonio de Sousa (*296*, 128). Within a few weeks the Portuguese had been expelled from all the country between Tete and Sena.

North of the Zambesi the rebels found a response among the Zimba and Pimbe chiefs of the middle Zambesi. Here the leaders of the revolt were Madzombwe and Pangura of the chiefly line which had held out for so long against the *muzungos* in the previous century. The rising does not appear to have been very forcefully led but a number of agents of the Zambesia Company were caught and killed and Portuguese stations at Miruru and Zumbo were sacked and burnt. During the height of the dry season the rebels held much of the country within the angle formed by the Luangwa and the Zambesi and their movements could be easily followed by the British in Feira. But by November the Portuguese had regained control by employing Ngoni mercenaries as they had done in the last war against Macanga in 1902. Father Moskopp's account of the Ngoni warriors in their feathered battle dress and armed with assagai and shield hunting the rebels to the very edge of the Luangwa must be the description of the last traditional Ngoni raid to take place in central Africa—the end of the old military tradition of Shaka and Zwide (*412*).

By 1918 the rising both in Barue and in the Zumbo areas was snuffed out—the last revolt in Africa to be organised on wholly traditional lines. For all their brave talk about German intrigues, even the Portuguese realised that the rebellion was the clearest possible indictment of their neglect of their East African colony.

The prazos and their critics

In the years between 1892 and the First World War the *prazo* system never lacked critics. In fact probably at no time in Portugal's history was debate on colonial questions carried on so publicly and at so informed a level. As a result of this criticism many minor details of Ennes' scheme were adjusted but no fundamental alteration of the general principles of 1892 was attempted until the appearance of Salazar.

Among the early critics of Ennes' plan were the renters of the *prazos* themselves. The companies had taken over the *prazos* during the 1890s in the most unfavourable circumstances. The Zambesi wars were still smouldering and were sufficient to discourage capital investment; Portugal herself was bankrupt and there was no spare money at all for colonial development, and it was commonly believed that Britain and Germany might partition Portugal's empire at any time. In addition to these external factors, the companies found themselves inexperienced in African affairs. It took years for them to learn what crops to grow, how to grow them and how to employ the labour for them. When the first slender profits began to appear on the balance sheets in the early spring of the twentieth century, the *prazo* interests began to put pressure on the government to extend the term of their contracts.

The reasons they advanced were basically three. First they claimed that crops such as coconut took eight to ten years to mature and companies, like the Boror Company, with coastal interests had to plan for a future beyond the twenty-five years envisaged by Ennes. Secondly, they claimed that they could raise no capital with the near prospect of an end of their tenure, while the *mussoco* was not giving them any profit at all. Thirdly, they pointed out that their enterprises would be no use without labour and labour was the really substantial advantage they derived from the contracts.

Within their settlers' limited field of vision these arguments were valid enough and in 1906 the renters of the *prazos* were permitted to extend their contracts by up to another fifteen years. For most of the companies the way now lay open for them until 1930 or 1932 (*461*, *482*).

This success for the ambitions of the *prazo* interests was more than matched, however, by the growing concern over conditions in Zambesia and the failure to implement Ennes' regulations. Once again the *prazo* interests led the way in attacking the operation of the 1890 decree.

Ennes' regulations had been designed to ensure that each plantation had adequate supplies of labour for its needs. The renter of the *prazo* was to cultivate one hectare for every ten *colonos* and the *colonos* were obliged to work every year on the plantations to discharge their tax debts. Far from securing an adequate supply of labour, however, these regulations helped to make it scarce, for Moçambique planters were in competition with their counterparts in Nyasaland and the Rhodesias and with the insatiable demands of the Rand mines.

Ever since the beginning of the century the use of contract and forced labour by Europeans who were meant to be civilising Africa had been attracting increasing attention in the world's press. The recruitment of Chinese and Indian coolie labour for South Africa, the contracting of labourers for the São Thomé

368

cocoa plantations and the techniques used by the agents of King Leopold to extract rubber from the Congo had all exploded as atrocity stories. In 1906 Henry Nevinson published his *Modern Slavery*, denouncing Portuguese contract labour in Angola.

Partly arising out of these events and partly from the concern voiced by many at the situation existing in Zambesia, Carl Wiese in 1907 published an article in the bulletin of the Lisbon Geographical Society on the labour troubles in Portuguese East Africa. Wiese held extensive *prazo* interests as sub-contractor to the Zambesia Company and, in part at least, was speaking for all the *prazo* renters. He drew attention to the massive recruitment of labour in Moçambique by various British interests and pointed out that, although there were a lot of Africans who worked abroad on temporary contracts, there was also a large-scale permanent emigration. In the previous twelve years he thought 50,000 Africans had permanently left Zambesia north of the River. One of the causes was the difference between the taxes demanded in Moçambique and in British territory. If he crossed the frontier, the Zambesi African would find that, instead of paying the equivalent of 6s. in head tax, he would be paying 3s. in hut tax. He would also find himself freed from forced labour either for the *prazo senhor* or for the government and he would not be liable to recruitment as a 'sepoy' in the *senhors'* black militia. Wiese pointed out that in Zambesia an African might have to travel for ten days to reach the plantation on which he was to work off his tax liability. On this journey he would have to support himself and would often have to support himself once he had reached his destination as well (*479*).

Whether or not Wiese was right in his explanations of the shortage of labour, shortage there certainly was, and the plantation owners pestered the government for grants of more land or for labourers from parts of the colony directly under government administration. They also demanded the end of the labour contracts with South Africa which would release an estimated 80,000 Africans a year for work inside Moçambique (*431*).

To the complaints of the *prazo* interests, Governor-General Freire D'Andrade could add the results of his own observations. The situation in Zambesia was far from satisfactory, and in May 1908 the Secretary for Native Affairs, Francisco Xavier Ferrão de Castellobranco, was ordered to carry out investigations and report on the extent of the emigration of Africans from the Quelimane and Tete districts (*435*, 210–211).

Castellobranco reported in March 1909 and although his

369

findings were bitterly criticised by the *prazo* companies, who used every argument they could think of to discredit him, the result of his investigations only seemed to illustrate with a wealth of detail the general points that had already been made by the governor-general himself.

To these reports were shortly to be added two other important works on the *prazos*. In 1915 Ernesto da Vilhena, who had governed the Quelimane district from 1905 to 1907, submitted a report on the *prazo* system to the Colonial Council and the following year Pedro Alvares published his long and detailed analysis of the way Ennes' laws had been administered (*304, 474*). If these four must be seen essentially as critics of white colonisation, its defence in the years before the war rested almost wholly with the director of the Zambesia Company, Portugal Durão.

With the *prazo* inspectorate abolished, the renters were in an extremely strong position. Many of them had obtained their contracts by means not strictly in accordance with the law and in 1901 the Cortes tried to enforce the proper procedures and decreed that it alone had authority to extend the length of any contract. The *prazo* companies, however, took the line that their contracts were inviolable and could not be altered or amended. If they were not in accord with the law, then so much the worse for the law.

In his long report on the *prazos* Pedro Alvares stressed the inability of the colonial authorities to enforce even those aspects of the law which directly affected its own interests. No attempt was made to relate the rent paid to the criteria laid down by Ennes and as a result, he calculated, the *prazo* renters were getting away with paying as little as five per cent of the minimum they should have been paying (*304*, 160). According to his calculations, the state was losing 200 *contos* of revenue every year in under-paid rents. Silva Monteiro, who was governor of the Tete district between 1916 and 1918, made a similar calculation to the effect that some 4,200 *contos* of revenue had been lost in the twenty-five years after Ennes' regulations had come into effect (*454*, 89). Sousa Ribeiro, whose knowledge of Moçambique and its affairs was second to none, also voiced the opinion that the *prazos* were thriving on what amounted to a massive hidden subsidy (*461, 489*).

Portugal Durão, however, wielding his slide rule with great cunning, arrived at rather a different conclusion. The state, he decided, was doing very well out of the system as it was saved

370

the high cost of collecting the *mussoco*. On those *prazos* which were directly administered by the government, he said, the cost of collection was anything as high as 68 per cent (*431*).

However, the defence of the *prazo* companies did not rest there; they pointed at the development of the lower Zambesi which they had been able to achieve and contrasted it with the undeveloped nature of the government land or the concession of the chartered Moçambique Company. Here their ground was stronger, for conditions on the lower Zambesi were very different from those higher up the river or in other parts of the colony.

In 1908 some six companies were operating on the Quelimane *prazos* (*460*, 506) and extensive plantations were being established. These grew until in 1914 some 25,000 hectares were under cultivation in contrast to the 2,500 in the Tete district. The crops grown included rubber, sisal, cotton, coffee, tobacco, sugar and coconuts, but of these coffee and tobacco were little more than experiments and only sugar, rubber, coconuts and sisal were really productive. Almost half the total consisted of the coconut groves of the coastal region—coconuts being a crop which needed a favourable climate but a minimum of labour and capital (*304*, 186). In 1913 some 10,000 tons of coconuts and 25,000 tons of sugar were produced.

How one interpreted these figures depended very much on what one wanted to prove. Some people considered they showed that under the *prazo* system Zambesia was being rapidly developed, for the contrast with the conditions in the 1880s and 1890s was obvious. Some people tried to prove that Zambesia had developed faster than British Nyasaland. Portugal Durão, for instance, used his sliderule with such effect that he proved that on the Quelimane *prazos* 41 hectares had been developed for every thousand of the African population while in Nyasaland a figure of only seven hectares per mil had been achieved (*431*, 185). No one pretended, however, that the *prazo* system had been anything but a total failure in the Tete district.

As with contract labour, the conflict of policy and objective was clear. The colonial exchequer could benefit greatly out of high rents and the direct collection of the *mussoco* and it did benefit from the labour contracts; on the other hand the *prazo* system undoubtedly achieved a measure of economic development for which it needed the labour that was going to South Africa. Either you opted for a full exchequer or economic development in the colony.

As might be imagined, the government took up a position

371

between these two poles. It continued with the labour contracts, though limiting recruiting in the tropical regions of the country, and it continued with the *prazo* system for this after all represented the *status quo* and *quieta non movere* had always been central to the administrative tradition of the Moçambique government.

The colonial debate had not moved very much since the eighteenth century when renting of the *prazos* was suggested as a means of increasing revenue from them and the continuation of the emphyteutic tenures was demonstrated to be a necessity for the development and defence of the colony; or from the seventeenth century when Father Manuel Barreto had recommended ways of increasing royal revenue from the *prazos*; or indeed from the sixteenth century when the crown had tried to wrest the exploitation of the gold mines from the *sertanejos* and draw the profits directly itself.

Criticism of the *prazos*, however, did not confine itself to these broad mathematical considerations of policy. In the protest they registered in 1909 against Castellobranco's report, the *prazo* companies had written 'In his [Castellobranco's] opinion the renters are not much better than parasites living off the *mussoco* and the oppression of the natives. Zambesia lacks little to become another Congolese hell and . . . to require foreign intervention' (*435, 562*). In this the companies revealed, as by some Freudian slip of the pen, the secret preoccupation of all sections of Portuguese opinion. Unless Portugal put her house in order and remedied the abuses which the world, although content to turn a blind eye all through the 1880s and 1890s, now roundly condemned, Portugal would lose her colonies to the greedy powers who were showing every sign of wanting to re-partition Africa.

Castellobranco, and Freire D'Andrade before him, had drawn attention to the endless opportunities which the *prazo* renters had to abuse their extensive powers and turn their *prazos* into rackets for exploiting the African in every conceivable way. As the only defence which the *prazo* holders made to these allegations was either to deny them completely, or to use the centuries-old argument that it was not in the interests of the *prazo* holder to exploit his *colonos* and therefore, self-evidently, these atrocity stories could not be true, murmuring to themselves the while that of course all men are not saints, it is likely that there was a good deal of substance to most of them.

In exacting the *mussoco* every conceivable method of extortion was practised. Some agents registered Africans as minors so that they would be paid at only half the rate; others forced Africans

372

to work for two or three months in the year or sent them on long journeys as carriers for which they had to provide their own food; others employed them at wood-cutting, road-building or canal-clearing and paid little or nothing, alleging that the work was for the government.

Wages were frequently paid months late; sometimes they were paid in cloth or some other commodity like spirit which the *prazo* renter produced himself. If it was alleged that an African was late with his payment of *mussoco* the company's police would raid his kraal and seize his wife and children.

While employed on the *prazos* the Africans were supposed to be fed and housed and their children instructed in company schools. Food was often not provided and the lodgings consisted of one communal sleeping house where the men and girls, who were often only children, employed on the plantations were expected to bed down together. This practice had been forbidden by a *portaria* of May 1907 (*461*, 486) but Castellobranco found it was still common and describes a visit his officers paid one night to one of these communal sleeping houses where they found men and girls sleeping together in complete promiscuity (*435*, 227). Corporal punishment was still common and although there were some schools and missions these were very few and far between.

Like Wiese before him, Castellobranco pointed to the obvious attractions for Africans in slipping across the border and working in British territory. Wages were higher and were paid in cash; taxes were lower and there was reasonable security of the person; there was no conscription into the forces or the police or on government road projects; cloth and other commodities were better quality and cheaper. In areas where there were no plantations the renter or sub-renter of a *prazo* would often encourage this emigration by insisting that *mussoco* was paid in sterling or by secretly contracting with farmers and others in British territory to provide labourers in return for a subsidy.

On the other hand there appears to have been no overall loss of population on the Quelimane *prazos* as opposed to the Tete ones. Figures for the five *prazos* rented by the Boror Company show a rise of almost a third in the adult population between 1904 to 1908 (*435*, 273).

For centuries the *prazo* holders had practised economic extortion, not only in the form of taxation but also by forcing the *colonos* to sell below the market price and by monopolising the means of barter and exchange. Ennes had tried hard to prevent a continuation of these abuses, but they continued in all their virulence. In most *prazos* no attempt was made to set up public fairs and itinerant traders were licensed by the *prazo* company and traded in its interest. As a result the frontier *prazos* had to deal with an extensive smuggling problem and this added to the bad relations that existed between the *colonos* and the company police.

Criticism of this kind suggested remedies departing in varying degrees from Ennes' regulations. Castellobranco made no secret of his belief that the government ought to take over direct administration of Zambesia and in fact there were two attempts in 1910–11 and 1915 to bring forward a plan for setting up civil administration in the area, with the *prazo* holders merely as government agents. As already indicated the *prazo* companies countered this by claiming the inviolable nature of their contracts (*474*, 12–13). Most suggestions for reform, however, were not nearly as drastic and involved only re-establishing the *prazo* inspectorate. Almost all critics of the *prazos* stressed the need for this but the government continued to take the line that the office of the governor of the district was adequate for this purpose.

Other suggestions coming from Alvares and Silva Monteiro called for the setting up of a land bank to find alternative ways of financing development and the introduction of a system of free paid labour which would bring the practice in Zambesia closer to that in British territory and the territory of the Moçambique Company.

In 1915 the Colonial Council reported that the whole question of the *prazos* should be reviewed in its entirety but this herculean task was not undertaken, possibly because of the war, and early in the 1920s the Portuguese had to undertake a defence of the system to the League of Nations. In an official report to the League the government wrote: 'The results of the *prazo* system are well worthy of note. The natives live peaceably following their time-honoured customs, and the country is developing very rapidly.'

The forced labour continued, though its incidence was not confined to Zambesia. All over the Portuguese colonies Africans were obliged to work for nothing on government roads, and the vagrancy laws gave the local administration considerable latitude to round up any labourers they needed. A report of the ILO to the League in 1926 commented unfavourably on the lack of freedom for the Africans and the practice of *chibalo* whereby the rights of the government to recruit unpaid labour were extended

374

by licence to private employers.

The extended *prazo* contracts still had some years to run when, in 1926, the Portuguese Republic was overthrown by a military coup and Dr Antonio de Oliveira Salazar emerged as Portugal's dictator.

Salazar's policy towards the colonies was elaborated only during the 1930s but with the *prazo* question he dealt quickly. In 1928 the *prazo* companies were asked to surrender their contracts to the government in return for compensation and in 1930 those who had not yet availed themselves of the offer found their contracts unilaterally terminated. The end had come abruptly after so many centuries, but the passing of the system went largely unnoticed. The companies retained their plantations and investments and the vagrancy laws enabled labour of an almost unfree kind still to be supplied to them. All that had happened had been the substitution of civil circumscriptions for their administrative duties.

The vigorous action of the *Estado Novo* perhaps requires more comment, however. From the days early in the fifteenth century when the Portuguese crown had granted its overseas possessions to the *Infante Dom* Henrique and he had made them over to the *donatàrios*, the metropolitan government of Portugal had never satisfactorily controlled its empire. There had always existed captaincies and contracts, corporate privileges and franchises which limited the authority of the government at every turn. Add to this the problems of an empty exchequer, inadequate military force and distance and one can appreciate the problem involved. Pombal's attack on the Jesuits had been a drastic and only partially successful attempt to assert the power of the central government and on the narrower stage of Moçambique the era of the Zambesi Wars had represented the desperate struggles of the Portuguese government to assert control. Ennes' system, which appears on the surface so efficiently to have cleaned up the chaos left behind by the wars, proved only to have extended the independence and licence of the old *prazos* for a further forty years.

It is often said that Hitler was the first ruler of Germany ever to have effectively controlled the Prussian army and in the same way Salazar's dictatorship was the first government Portugal had ever had which has effectively controlled the colonies.

But as has so often happened in European history, when the long battle between the central government and the powerful corporations of society has eventually been won by the govern-

375

ment, and all the abuses of privilege, franchise and private jurisdiction have been done away with, the cure has become worse
than the disease. As de Tocqueville pointed out over a hundred
years ago, the great corporations may have been cruel and
corrupt but they did stand up to the central government and
prevent the imposition of a totalitarian dictatorship. For all their
faults the *prazos* had offered relief from the remote government
of Lisbon. It was possible for the *colonos* by good personal
relations with the *prazo* renters and their agents to ameliorate a
regime which was anything but bureaucratic. It was always possible to migrate to another *prazo* in search of a more congenial
regime or to evade in other ways the arbitrary, but essentially
inefficient and corrupt, rule of the companies and their agents.
With the passing of the *prazos* a more modern, a more efficient
and much less humane system of government was gradually
riveted down on the once turbulent and exciting world of the
Zambesi.

Since 1930 there has probably been no more depressed and
inert area of Africa than Zambesia, Barue and Sofala, and the
great river is probably more silent now, more devoid of traffic
and bustle than at any time for a thousand years. All may well be
transformed by the building of the Cabora Bassa dam, but that
is still in the future.

Appendix 1

Table of income from the prazos *1868–1885*

Years	Quelimane	Sena and Tete	Total
1868–9			4.575.000 *reis*
1870–1			6.104.000 ,,
1871–2			4.490,000 ,,
1872–3			4.599.000 ,,
1873–4			5.222.000 ,,
1874–5	6.972.000 *reis*	2.818.000 *reis*	9.790.000 ,,
1876–7	3.691.000 ,,	3.693.000 ,,	7.384.000 ,,
1878–9	3.379.000 ,,	2.140.000 ,,	5.519.000 ,,
1880–1	23.332.000 ,,	3.126.000 ,,	26.458.000 ,,
1882–3	25.756.000 ,,	4.633.000 ,,	30.389.000 ,,
1884–5	32.000.000 ,,	5.629.000 ,,	37.629.000 ,,

Sources—*447 439.*

Appendix 2

What was the correct term for the grantee of a *prazo*? A number of English and American writers (including myself on one occasion) have used the term *prazero* or *prazeiro* on the principle of that if a *fazenda* is farmed by a *fazendeiro*, then a *prazo* must be in the possession of a *prazeiro*. There is, however, no such word in Portuguese as *prazeiro* and English-speaking historians perhaps should not take this liberty with another language.

A wide variety of terms are used to describe the holders of the *prazos*—each of them emphasising a different aspect of their social or political role. For example:

Senhor(a)	seigneur or feudal lord
Donatário(a)	donee. This is the same word used of the holders of captaincies in Brazil or the Atlantic islands.
Dona	lady. This is used of the *prazo* heiresses.
Emfiteute(a)	lessee in a contract of emphyteusis.
Sesmeiro(a)	holder of a *sesmaria*.
Mercenario(a)	receiver of a *prazo* grant.
Morador(a)	resident, this is the commonest word in general use to describe members of the Portuguese community in Zambesia.
Foreiro(a)	lessee.
Agraciado(a)	the recipient of a grant.

Glossary

Adjunto	Assembly of the chief settlers of each Zambesi captaincy.
Aforamento	Lease.
Aldeia	Village. Used to describe the districts into which Portuguese India was divided for tax purposes, and which were leased to individual Portuguese.
Alqueire	Measure equivalent to 13 litres.
Alvara	Royal or vice-regal decree.
Aringa	A very large, fortified stockade used by the Portuguese *senhors* of the nineteenth century as their headquarters.
Arroba	Measure of weight equivalent to 32 pounds. 4 *arrobas* = 1 *quintal*.
Bandazio(a)	Personal attendants of the Portuguese *senhors* and *senhoras*.
Bando	Proclamation.
Banyan	Non-Christian Indian. Term usually used for an Indian trader in eastern Africa.
Bare	Mining camp.
Bare	Measure of weight varying from 16–20 *arrobas*. A measure of cloth containing 400 *panos*.
Bazo	A slave placed in charge of slave gangs. The title of the second-in-command in the great *aringa* of Maganja da Costa.
Bicho	Door-boy.
Botaca (*Butaka*)	Domestic slaves attached to the persons of the Zambesi *donas*.

Canarin	Indian from Goa.
Canhongo	Title of the third in command in the great *aringa* of Maganja da Costa.
Capitão	Commander of the armed slaves in the employment of the *senhor*. Nineteenth century term but widely used today for the foreman of a gang of workers.
Capitão-mor	Captain-major. A title with widely varying usage. Applied to commanders of ships in the sixteenth century; the leaders of foreign communities of the eighteenth century; to commanders of military districts in nineteenth century. The title usually implies judicial powers and is not usually used simply as a military rank.
Capitão-mor das Guerras	Captain-major of the wars. Commander of troops raised for a campaign.
Capitão das Portas	Captain of the Gates. Captain of the Portuguese in the Mashonaland fairs in the sixteenth and seventeenth centuries.
Capitão-mor dos Rios	Captain-major of the Rivers. Chief deputy of the *tenente-geral dos Rios*.
Capitão-mor das Terras da Coroa	Captain-major of the crown lands. Officer charged with supervising defence and justice over districts of Portuguese Zambesia.
Carta da Aforamento	Deed for the lease of a *prazo*.
Carta da foro	Charter setting out the rights of settlers on the land of a lord or a *donatàrio*.
Cazembe (kazembe)	Leader of Zambesi slaves. A nineteenth century usage. Title of the paramount chief of the Lunda of the Luapala.
Chicote	Whip made of hippopotamus hide.
Chikunda	Slave.
Choriro	A weeping. The custom by which Zambesi slaves carried out burning

	and pillage to make people weep for the death of their master.
Chuabo	Fathom of cloth or the value of a fathom of cloth. In the nineteenth century equal to 500 *reis* or 20 strings of beads.
Chuambo	Fortified stockade.
Chuanga	Slave appointed to supervise the revenues of a *senhor*. An official appointed by a Maravi chief to supervise mining operations.
Ciza	Tax of 10 per cent on land sales.
Colono	Free African inhabitant of a *prazo*.
Conselho Ultramarino	Overseas Council.
Conto	One million *reis*.
Corja	Twenty pieces of cloth.
Cruzado	Coin valued at 400 *reis*. In the eighteenth century equivalent to 4/-.
Degredado	Convict.
Direito da Renovação	Right of renewal of a lease.
Dizimo	Ecclesiastical tithe collected by the crown.
Dona	Lady. Title assumed by all women of the Portuguese community, in Zambesia.
Donatàrio	Lord-proprietor.
Em Commisso	Under penalty, forfeit.
Emprazamento	Tenure in emphyteusis limited to one or more lives.
Enfiteute(a)	Holder of a contract of emphyteusis.
Engagé	African labourer recruited under contract to the French.
Ensaca	Company of slaves. According to Gamitto male *ensacas* had ten slaves and female *ensacas* six. Later used for the armed regiments in the service of the *muzungos*.
Esamaçuaca	Same as *bazo*.
Escravo	Slave.
Faraçola	Measure of weight equivalent to 18 pounds.

Feitor da Fazenda	Treasury Factor.
Feitor dos Quintos e Foros	Factor for the collection of rents and fifths.
Feitoria	Factory.
Filho da Terra	A mulatto born in Africa.
Filho do Reino	A Portuguese born in Portugal.
Foreiro	Lessee of a *prazo*.
Foro	Quit-rent.
Forro	Free-man.
Frei	Brother or friar.
Grande	Great one. Used for the most important men in the following of a chief or a *senhor*.
Guta	Fortified stockade. A term used in Barue.
Horta	Garden.
Impi	Regiment of Ngoni warriors.
Incumbe	An African village. Used for territory attached to a *prazo*.
Inhacuava	Senior chief. Used south of the Zambesi.
Inhamacango	Chief. Term used in the Sofala district.
Inhamucangamiza	Custom by which the *prazo*-holders sold to the *colonos* below the market price.
Junta do Commercio	Board of commerce.
Juiz Ordinario	Magistrate.
Kazembe	See *cazembe*.
Luane	Small landed estate or residence.
Liberto	Freed slave who is still bound to work for his former master.
Lei das Sesmarias	Law of the vacant lands. Promulgated 1375 to promote repopulation of the countryside.
Lei Mental	Law of king *Dom* Duarte controlling inheritance of crown lands.

Machilla	Litter or palanquin.
Macoda (*Inhacoda*)	Slave in charge of female slaves.
Madonto	Tribute paid to chiefs for permission to pass through their land.
Mambo	Chief.
Manchillas (*Manxillas*)	Lengths of African-made cotton cloth.
Maprere	Tribute.
Matical	Measure of gold equivalent to .155 oz. Worth in seventeenth century 1.5 *xerafins* or 6 *tangas*.
Mazia-manga	Holy water sent by the Portuguese for use during the coronation of the Macombes of Barue.
Merce nova	New grant of a *prazo*.
Mfecane	Dispersal of the Ngoni people in the early years of the nineteenth century during the era of Shaka's wars.
Michueira	Millet.
Miganos	The traditional boundaries of a *prazo* or of the lands of a chief.
Milando	Breaches of law or custom; cases resulting from these and meetings held to examine allegations of breach of customary law.
Misericordia	Charitable lay brotherhood established in all major Portuguese settlements.
Mitete	An article broken as a symbolic act of servitude.
Mocasambo	Slave placed in charge of part of a *prazo*.
Mossense	Free African. See *colono*.
Muavi	Poison administered as part of a judicial ordeal.
Mucata	Slave in command of other slaves.
Muene	Headman. Term used in the partially Islamised areas of Quelimane.
Mussambaze	Professional class of traders among the slaves of a *senhor* or chief.
Mussito	A stockaded village or the hideout of escaped slaves.
Mussoco (*Missonco*)	Tribute collected by a chief or

	senhor. In the nineteenth century it was the term used for the official head tax collected in Zambesia.
Muzinda	Village of a chief; a term in use north and south of the Zambesi and employed for the divisions of a *prazo*.
Muzungo	Portuguese community and in the nineteenth century specifically members of the old Zambesi families of *prazo senhors*.
Mwanamambo	Slave captains in charge of a *prazo* or of all the slaves of a *senhor*.
Palhota	Hut-tax.
Palmare	Palm plantation.
Palmatoria	A flat piece of wood with holes in it used to beat the hands of offenders.
Panja	Measure of capacity equal to $1\frac{1}{2}$ gallons.
Pano	Fathom of cloth.
Pasta	Measure of **gold** equal to about $16\frac{1}{2}$ oz.
Patricio	Half caste.
Pondoro	Spirit medium. Also *mhondoro*.
Portaria	Government regulation.
Prazo	Land or any right granted on long contracts of emphyteusis. Deriving from the latin *placitum*. Used in Zambesia for the large land concessions made in the seventeenth century to individual Portuguese and which survived until the 1930s. See *emprazamento*.
Prazo da Coroa	Crown *prazo*.
Procurador	Business agent.
Provisão	Provision. Used for the initial grant of a *prazo*, before issue of the patent or the confirmation.
Quintal	Measure of weight equal to 4 *arrobas* or 128 lb.
Quitundo (*Chitundo*)	Basket.

Real	Smallest Portuguese monetary unit worth about one-sixteenth of a penny in the nineteenth century.
Sachicunda	Slave in immediate charge of a slave band.
Sargento-mor	Sergeant-major. Rank of the second in command of a Portuguese infantry regiment. In Zambesia it is used in the same way as *capitão-mor* but with a junior rank.
Senado da Camara	Town council.
Senhor(a)	Lord (Lady). Used frequently to refer to *prazo*-holders.
Serra	Range of mountains.
Sertanejo	Backwoodsman.
Sertão	Interior, backlands.
Sesmaria	Grant of vacant land.
Sura	Palm wine.
Tanador-mor	Inspector of agriculture. A term deriving from Portuguese India.
Tanga	A coin worth 1/6 of a *matical*.
Tenente-geral dos Rios	Title of the governor of Portuguese Zambesia in the eighteenth century.
Terra em fatiota	Perpetual lease, not subject to payment of *foros* and alienable by sale and other means.
Tombo	Register.
Vida	Life. Used as a unit to measure the length of a *prazo* lease.
Xerafim (or *pardão*)	Coin with face value of 300 *reis* in circulation in the Portuguese eastern empire.

Bibliography and References

ABBREVIATIONS

AHU	Archivo Historico Ultramarino
BM	British Museum
CP	Confidential Print
Co	Codice
Cx	Caixa
FO	Foreign Office
GG	Governor general
Moç	Moçambique
PRO	Public Record Office
TG	Tenente-geral

MANUSCRIPTS

AHU Moçambique

1 Cx 2 Letter of Antonio Lobo da Silva, late seventeenth century.

2 Cx 2 *Relação* of Carlos Luis de Almeida, second half of seventeenth century.

3 Cx 3 *Dona* Ursula Ferreira to the king, 22–1–1728.

4 Cx 3 *Relação do Desembargador Duarte Salter de Mendonça*, Lisbon 7–12–1752 printed in Hoppe (217–233).

5 Cx 3 *Provisão* of TG Roberto Homem de Magalães, 17–4–1752.

6 Cx 3 *Memorial do que tenho obrado nestes Rios no Serviço de S. Magestade que Deus Guarde.*

7 Cx 5 Antonio de Brito Freire to viceroy, 8–11–1754.

8 Cx 5 Petition of Manuel Dassa Castellobranco for the post of *capitão-mor* of Zimbabwe, 24–2–1755.

9 Cx 5 David Marques Pereira to viceroy, 30–5–1755.

10	Cx 6	*Auto da Posse* for Martinho Mendes de Vasconcellos of *prazo* Inhamacamba, 23–8–1758.
11	Cx 6	Pedro da Saldanha de Albuquerque GG to the king, 27–12–1758.
12	Cx 7	*Carta Regia* appointing Manuel Caetano Roiz to the post of *tanador-mor*, signed by TG Bernardo Caetano de Sa Botelho, 30–7–1759.
13	Cx 7	*Requerimento* of Antonio Correa Monteiro de Mattos, 3–11–1759.
14	Cx 8	Manuel da Costa to TG Marc Antonio de Montaury, 5–3–1760.
15	Cx 8	Decree dated 3–4–1760.
16	Cx 9	Account of the inheritance of the *prazo* of Luabo compiled by the *feitor dos foros e quintos* José de Mascarenhas, 2–4–1761.
17	Cx 9	Marc Antonio de Montaury TG to the king, 15–7–1761.
18	Cx 9	Pedro da Saldanha de Albuquerque GG to Marc Antonio de Montaury TG, 12–8–1761.
19	Cx 12	João Moreira Pereira to Pedro da Saldanha de Albuquerque, GG, 28–1–1766.
20	Cx 12	João Moreira Pereira to Pedro da Saldanha de Albuquerque, GG, 28–1–1766.
21	Cx 12	Balthasar Manuel Pereira do Lago GG to the king, 20–8–1766.
22	Cx 12	Francisco de Brum to Balthasar Manuel Pereira do Lago, GG, list of lands *em commisso*, 12–2–1767.
23	Cx 12	Antonio Pinto de Miranda to Balthasar Manuel Pereira do Lago, GG, 18–2–1767.
24	Cx 12	Balthasar Manuel Pereria do Lago GG to the king, 18–8–1767.
25	Cx 12	Balthasar Manuel Pereira do Lago GG to the king, 19–8–1767.
26	Cx 12	Patent signed by Inacio de Mello e Alvim TG, 1–12–1767.
27	Cx 13	*Requerimento* of José Mascarenhas, 4–5–1767.
28	Cx 13	Inacio de Mello e Alvim TG to Balthasar Manuel Pereira do Lago GG, 31–1–1768.
29	Cx 13	*Carta de Aforamento* for *prazo* Chatue to Bernardo Roiz de Crasto, 2–4–1768.
30	Cx 13	Balthasar Manuel Pereira do Lago GG to the king, 20–7–1769.

çao e Reparo e Cobertura annual da Fortaleza
desta Villa de S. Tiago de Tette, 16–11–1782.

68	Cx 31	*Balanço da Junta da Fazenda 1794.*
69	Cx 31	Manuel Pereira to Diogo de Sousa GG, 11-1-1795.
70	Cx 31	Carlos José dos Reis e Gama governor of Sofala, to Diogo de Sousa GG, 28-3-1795.
71	Cx 31	Diogo de Sousa GG to João de Sousa e Brito, 16-5-1795.
72	Cx 31	Ignacio Francisco Pinto *inspector da obra do Rio Maindo* to Antonio José Vasconcellos e Sa TG, 30-12-1795.
73	Cx 39	Account of the dependents of the convent of Sena, 23-11-1802.
74	Cx 40	Joaquim de Moraes Rego Lisboa to queen, 29-4-1796.
75	Cx 40	Account of the christians at Sena, 5-2-1802.
76	Cx 40	Petition of Anna Francisca Rangel for *prazo* Inhasererere, 1802.
77	Cx 40	*Termo do Adjunto,* 2-7-1803.
78	Cx 40	*Termo do Adjunto,* 7-8-1803.
79	Cx 40	*Termo do Adjunto,* 20-8-1803.
80	Cx 41	*Mappa circunstanciada do Estado das Povoaçoens dos Brancos, Pardos, e Negros colonos existentes nas Terras da Juridisam de cada uma das Villas do Districto do Governo dos Ryos de Sena,* 4-3-1802.
81	Cx 42	Izidro de Almeida de Sousa e Sa GG to *visconde de Anadia,* 12-8-1802.
82	Cx 43	A. N. de Villas Boas Truão TG to the prince regent, July 1804.
83	Cx 43	A. N. de Villas Boas Truão TG to prince regent, 17-8-1804.
84	Cx 52	*Rendimento da terra Tipue,* drawn up by *Frei* José Barbosa Machado de Aguiar.
85	Cx 57	José Sebastião de Ataide to Marco Caetano de Abreu e Meneses, GG, 15-8-1813.
86	Cx 58	Marc Caetano de Abreu e Meneses GG to Agostinho da Costa TG, 18-9-1814.
87	Cx 58	Marc Caetano de Abreu e Meneses GG to Antonio de Araujo de Azevedo, 5-10-1814.
88	Cx 60	*Balanço da Fazenda Real,* September 1816.
89	Cx 68	Corte Real to Francisco de Mello e Castro GG, 20-4-1752.
90	Cx 68	Corte Real to Francisco de Mello e Castro, GG, 7-4-1755.

91	Cx 68	*Provisão do Concelho Ultramarino*, 29–3–1783.
92	Cx 68	*Instrucção Regia* to Izidro Almeida de Sousa e Sa GG, 28–2–1801.
93	Cx 71	*Balanço da Fazenda Real, 1821.*
94	Cx 71	Judicial inquiry, 14–5–1822.
95	Cx 71	*Bando* of José Francisco Alves Barbosa TG, 16–9–1822.
96	Cx 72	*Balanço da Fazenda Real, 1823.*
97	Cx 73	*Escrivão da Junta da Fazenda de Moçambique* to gov. of Rivers José Francisco Alves Barbosa, 17–3–1823.
98	Cx 73	*Relação dos Prazos da R. Coroa e Fisco do Districto desta Villa de Senna, e quem possue pela maneira abaixo declarado,* 16–1–1824.
99	Cx 73	Proclamation of governor of the Rivers José Francisco Alves Barbosa, 11–5–1824.
100	Cx 73	Faustino José Dias Rego to João Manuel da Silva GG, 6–6–1824.
101	Cx 73	José Francisco Alves Barbosa governor of the Rivers to João Manuel da Silva, 27–7–1824.
102	Cx 73	Manuel Caetano Pereira to Pedro Caetano Pereira, 27–8–1824.
103	Cx 77	Opinion of *desembargador Dom* Carlos Manuel de Macedo Souto Maior Castro e Muito Nobrc, Lisbon, 7–3–1824.
104	Cx 77	Petition of Antonio José Pedroso, 11–10–1826.
105	Maço 25	A. N. de Vilas Boas Truão TG to José Francisco Alves Barbosa, 26–2–1807.
106	Maço 25	Sebastião Xavier Botelho GG to *Conde* de Subserra, 25–12–1825.
107	Maço 25	Manuel Joaquim Mendes de Vasconcelos e Cirne governor of the Rivers to Paulo José Miguel de Brito GG, 30–3–1831.
108	Maço 25	Memorandum of Manuel Joaquim Mendes de Vasconcellos e Cirne governor of the Rivers, 15–6–1831.
109	Maço 25	Paulo José Miguel de Brito GG to *Duque* de Cadaval, 5–11–1831.
110	Maço 26	Manuel Joaquim Mendes de Vasconcellos e Cirne governor of the Rivers to Paulo Miguel de Brito GG, 14–7–1830.
111	Maço 26	Fortunato da Silva *capitão-mor* of Manica to Paulo José Miguel de Brito GG, 23–6–1832.

112 Maço 26 Severino de Almeida *commandante de infantaria* at Manica to José Francisco Alves Barbosa governor of the Rivers, 28–9–1832.

113 Maço 26 Joaquim Xavier Diniz Costa *desembargador ouvidor geral da capitania* to Domingos Ferreira, 8–7–1833.

114 Maço 38 Decree on the reform of *prazo* law dated 2–4–1760.

115 Pasta 1 *Provedor do Concelho* Antonio Francisco Cardoso to emperor, 11–5–1835.

116 Pasta 2 *Junta governativa* to minister, 24–10–1836.

117 Pasta 5 Petition of *Dona* Antonia Rosa Saramago, 12–8–1841.

118 Pasta 13 Galdino Faustino de Sousa to Jeronimo Romero, governor of Quelimane, 10–10–1853.

119 Pasta 13 Isidoro Correia Pereira to Galdino José Nunes, 22–10–1854.

120 Pasta 13 Augusto Pires Gonçalves to J. de Azevedo Alpoim, 30–11–1854.

121 Pasta 32 *Visconde* Paço D'Arcos GG to minister, 18–8–1881.

122 1 Repartição Pasta 1
     Visconde Paço D'Arcos to minister, no 317, 2 Rep., 3–12–1881.

123 1 Repartição Pasta 1
     Visconde Paço D'Arcos GG to minister, 2 Rep., no 35, 30–1–1882.

124 1 Repartição Pasta 1
     Antonio Florencio dos Santos to minister, *Escola Academica*, Lisbon, 26–12–1882.

125 1 Repartição Pasta 2
     Instructions for the new governor of Manica, Carlos Maria de Souza Ferreira Simões, 17–3–1887.

126 Co 212 Theodosio Garcia to the prince, 20–7–1680.

127 Co 1306 Izidro de Almeida de Sousa e Sa GG to A.N. de Vilas Boas Truão TG, 21–1–1805, fol. 90.

128 Co 1310 Francisco de Mello e Castro GG to David Marques Pereira, 2–4–1755.

129 Co 1310 Francisco de Mello e Castro GG to David Marques Pereira, 8–4–1755.

130 Co 1310 Francisco de Mello e Castro to the captain of Sofala, 9–4–1755.

131   Co 1310 Francisco de Mello e Castro GG to David
                          Marques Pereira, 22–10–1755, fol. 127.

132   Co 1317 Pedro da Saldanha de Albuquerque GG to Corte
                          Real, 6–8–1759.

133   Co 1317 Pedro da Saldanha de Albuquerque GG to Corte
                          Real, 9–8–1759.

134   Co 1317 Bernardo Caetano de Sa Botelho TG to Pedro da
                          Saldanha de Albuquerque GG, 22–9–1759.

135   Co 1317 *Lista das terras que possuhião R^{dos} Padres da Com-*
                          panhia, 1759.

136   Co 1317 Manuel Gomes Nobre to Pedro da Saldanha de
                          Albuquerque GG, 12–4–1760.

137   Co 1317 *Copia do Termo do Adjunto* drawn up by the
                          secretary José Francisco Oliveira, 14–6–1760.

       Co 1331 *Registo de Alvaras, cartas patentes, provisões, ses-*
                          marias, quitações etc.

138   1. *Requerimento* of José Caetano de Motta, 27–8–
                          1767, fol. 94.

139   2. *Carta de Aforamento* for Cheringoma to Maria
                          de Mendonça Corte Real, 15–4–1767, fol. 69.

140   3. *Carta de Aforamento* for Sansa Inhaparara to
                          Dona Ines Pessoa de Almeida Castellobranco,
                          9–9–1767, fol. 101.

141   Co 1348 Pedro de Saldanha de Albuquerque GG to *Dom*
                          Frederico Guilherme de Sousa, viceroy of India,
                          4–8–1783.

142   Co 1348 Antonio Manuel de Mello e Castro to *Dom*
                          Frederico Guilherme de Sousa, viceroy of India,
                          12–8–1786.

143   Co 1349 Antonio Manuel de Mello e Castro GG to Antonio
                          Alberto Pereira, captain of Sofala, 18–5–1791.

144   Co 1460 Interim Governor to military commander of Sena,
                          14–11–1876, no 350.

145   Co 1460 Interim governor to *delegado do procurador da*
                          coroa e fazenda, 18–5–1877, no 91.

146   Co 1460 Interim governor of Quelimane to military com-
                          mander of Sena, 8–8–1877, no 167.

147   Co 1460 Governor to *delegado da comarca*, 20–10–77, no
                          245.

148   Co 1460 Governor to Caetano Piedade de Sousa, 17–12–
                          1877.

149   Co 1460 Circular letter to all *prazo*-holders in Quelimane
                          district, 17–10–1878.

150   Co 1460   Governor of Quelimane to Marianno Henrique de Nazareth, 18–9–1879.

151   Co 1460   Governor of Quelimane to governor of Lourenço Marques, 22–11–1880, no 490.

152   Co 1464   Instructions to commandant of Massingire, 13–12–1883.

153   Co 1469   Proclamation of Antonio Marianno da Cunha, governor of the Rivers, 10–3–1833.

154   Co 1469   Antonio Marianno da Cunha, governor of the Rivers to commandant of Sena, 15–4–1833.

156   Co 1469   Antonio Marianno da Cunha, governor of the Rivers to Paulo Miguel de Brito GG, 9–5–1833, fols 35–6.

157   Co 1469   Antonio Marianno da Cunha to Paulo José Miguel de Brito GG, 10–10–1833, fol. 78.

158   Co 1469   Antonio Marianno da Cunha, governor of the Rivers to Paulo José Miguel de Brito, GG 12–7–1833.

159   Co 1469   Proclamation of Izidro Manuel de Carrazedo, governor of the Rivers, 18–2–1835.

160   Co 1477   Izidro Manuel de Carrazedo, governor of the Rivers to minister, 13–9–1835, fols 12–13.

161   Co 1477   Rodrigo Luciano de Abreu e Lima GG to minister, 26–8–1843, fol. 105.

162   Co 1477   Fernandes Carlos da Costa, governor of Quelimane to minister, 15–11–1843.

163   Co 1480   Fernando Carlos da Costa, governor of Quelimane to Galdino Faustino de Sousa, 4–7–1844.

164   Co 1480   Manuel de Abreu Madeira, governor of the Rivers to Anselmo Henriques Ferrão, 11–5–1846.

AHU India

165   Cx 11   *Dom* Felipe Mascarenhas viceroy to the king, 29–12–1636.

Ajuda Library, Lisbon

166   50 v 37   *Orbe Lusitano.*

> *Noticias que se me pedirão no anno de 1677 de Lixᵃ dos Rios de Cuama e da forma que devia ter pᵃ poder concervasse entrando na companhia que se determina fazer pᵃ este Estado.*

167   51–vi–12 (old number 51–vi–28)

> Prince to Denis de Mello e Castro, 22–4–1677.

168 51–viii–43 (old number 51–vii–44)
Anon, Account of the *Rios de Cuama*, 16–3–1683, fols. 473–83.

169 51–ix–3 *Breve informação dos Rios de Cuama, que o P^e Frey Phelipe de Asumpção por andar nas ditas terras quatorze annos, e estado em todas as feiras e ter larga noticia dos vios e costumes dellas.*

170 51–ix–3 King to viceroy, 10–2–1698, fols 18–19, including letter of Manuel Pires Saro, 11–6–1696.

Torre de Tombo Library, Lisbon
Documentos Remittidos da India. Livros dos Monções

171 Livro 40 Summary of the testimonies given in Tete before the *provedor da fazenda* about the mines of Mocranga, fol. 251 and Sena testimonies, fol. 253.

172 Livro 57 King to viceroy, 15–12–1646, fol. 65.

173 Livro 57 King to viceroy, 25–1–1647, fol. 71.

174 Livro 60 Letter of *Dom* Sebastião dated 23–10–1644 enclosed in king to viceroy, 26–3–1649, fols 230–232.

175 Livro 60 *Proposta que o Rey Monomotapa offerece ao V Rey da India pelo seu Procurador, o Padre Frey Manuel da Purificação Religioso da Ordem de São Domingos, em doze de Abril de mil seis centos quarenta e cinco.* fols. 233–5.

176 Livro 60 Viceroy to king, 25–11–1650, fol. 280.

Central African Archives, Salisbury

177 ST/1/1/1 Stewart Correspondence. Nunes to Stewart, Quelimane, 29–7–1877, pages 770–3.

Edinburgh University Library

178 717/10 Scott Papers.
Scott to Robertson, December 1881.

British Museum
Add Mss 28,163 *Indice das Ordens, Leys, Alvaras e Provizões de Sua Mag^{de}* 2 volumes

179 *Provisão* 24–11–1583, fol. 1075, vol. 2

180 „ 25–2–1595, fol. 1078, vol. 2

181 „ 19–3–1623, fol. 1559, vol. 1

182 *Provisão* 20–3–1640, fol. 349, vol. 2
183   „   19–2–1672, fol. 1064, vol. 1
184 King to chancellor, 26–2–1704, fol. 658, vol. 2

Public Record Office, London

185 FO 63 1026 Capt. F. Elton HM Consul Moçambique to
            FO, 22–6–1875.
186 FO 63 1188 Instructions from Augusto de Castilho GG to
            Major Francisco J. G. Moura, Sena, 13–11–
            1885.
187 FO 63 1253 Churchill HM Consul Moçambique to Rose-
            berry, 16–10–1893 enclosing Ross to Chur-
            chill, 10–10–1893.
188 FO 63 1254 Ross to Roseberry, 27–3–1893.
189 FO 63 1277 Macdonell to Kimberley, Lisbon, 16–6–1894.
190 FO 63 1277 Macdonell to Kimberley, Lisbon, 27–6–1894.
191 FO 63 1386 Report of vice-consul de Grijs rewritten by
            acting consul Wallis, Moçambique, 8–5–
            1901.
192 FO 84 1539 H. O'Neill, HM Consul Moçambique to
            Salisbury, Moçambique, 14–10–1879.
193 FO 84 1595 H. O'Neill, HM Consul Moçambique to
            Granville, Moçambique, 14–6–1881 en-
            closing extracts from Nunes to O'Neill
            29–5–1881.
194 FO 84 1616 F. Moir to H. O'Neill, HM Consul Moçam-
            bique, Quelimane, 15–9–1882.
195 FO 84 1671 H. O'Neill to Granville, Moçambique, 1–12–
            1884.
196 FO 84 1662 Foot to Granville, Blantyre, 7–8–1884.
197 FO 84 1662 Goodrich to Kirk, 12–11–1884.
198 FO 84 1901 H. O'Neill, HM Consul Moçambique to
            Salisbury, Moçambique, 20–8–1888.
199 FO 403 143 CP 6061
            Petre to Salisbury, Lisbon, 8–1–1890.
200 FO 403 144 CP 6069
            A. Sharpe to H. Johnson, H.M. Consul,
            Nyasland, March to July 1890. Sent to Lord
            Salisbury, 30–9–1890, pp. 149–59.
201 FO 403 157 CP 4157
            Lt. Com. Keane to Capt. Henderson, 21–3–
            1891.
202 FO 403 157 CP 6178

Central African Company to Salisbury, 28–4–1891 with enclosure no 35 'Deed of Concession and Grant', 18–12–1890, pp. 20–1.

203 FO 403 174 CP 4604
Churchill to Salisbury, Moçambique, 14–3–1892 enclosing Ross to Churchill, Moçambique, 7–3–1892.

204 FO 403 174 CP 4604
Churchill to Salisbury, Moçambique, 15–3–1892.

205 FO 403 174 CP 4604
Churchill to Salisbury, Moçambique, 3–3–1892 enclosing Ross to Churchill, 29–2–1892.

206 FO 403 174 CP 4604
Ross to Kimberley, Beira, 14–6–1894 enclosing 'Report regarding the Slave-trading of Quilimane', pages 17–19.

207 FO 541 25 CP 4914
Nunes to H. O'Neill, HM Consul Moçambique, 14–5–1883 enclosing Avila to Nunes, 2–5–1883.

208 FO 541 26 CP 5165
F. Moir to H. O'Neill, HM Consul Moçambique, 'On board "Dunkeld" south of Quelimane', 27–9–1884.

PRINTED DOCUMENTS

Annaes do Concelho Ultramarino, parte não official, 7 vols (Lisbon, 1854–66), 2nd series 1859–61

209 'A Feira do Aruangua do Norte' extracts from an *oficio* written by J. C. Monteiro, 13–6–1830, pages 203–8.

Archivo das Colonias published in Lisbon between 1917 and 1933.

210 Letter of João de Tavares de Almeida GG dated 7–8–1863 enclosing patent appointing Manuel Antonio de Sousa as *capitão-mor* of Manica, dated 21–7–1863, vol. 2, no 9, March 1918, pages 99–105.

211 'Uma viagem do Missionario Courtois', vol. 2, no 12, June 1918.

212   Pedro da Saldanha de Albuquerque GG to King, 29–12–1758, part 4, pages 125–6.

Archivo Historico de Moçambique. Inventario do Fundo do Seculo xviii, Introdução, Inventario, Sumarios e Transcrições, ed. Caetano Montes (Lourenço Marques, 1958), *separata* from *Moçambique* nos 72–92.

213   Inacio de Mello e Alvim TG to Balthasar Manuel Pereira do Lago GG, 4–2–1769.

214   Inacio de Mello e Alvim TG to Balthasar Manuel Pereira do Lago GG, 24–2–1769.

215   Report of Manuel da Costa, 2–3–1769.

216   *Carta de Aforamento* for *prazo* Condo to *Dona* Maria Antonia Teodora e Carvalho, 28–11–1775.

Archivo Portugues Oriental, ed. J. H. da Cunha Rivara, 9 vols (Nova Coa, 1857–76)

217   King to *Conde* de Sandomil, Lisbon, 9–3–1737, fasciculo supplementos, doc. 1, page 516.

Arquivo Portugues Oriental, nova edição, ed. A. B. de Bragançao Pereira, 11 vols (Bastora Goa, 1936–40)

218   Viceroy to king, Goa, 16–1–1716, vol. 3, part 2, 1709–19, no 152, page 212.

219   *Livro das Plantas de Todas as Fortelezas, Cidades e Povoações do Estado da India Oriental* by Antonio Bocarro, vol. 4, part 1. See also (*321*).

Boletim Official do Governo de Moçambique

220   1889 no 1.   Telegram from Augusto de Castilho GG to minister, 2–1–1889.

221   1889 no 7.   Report from the military command at Guengue, December 1888.

222   1889 no 13. Report of the Tete district, 31–1–1889.

Copia de Documentos Officiaes trocados entre a Companhia de Moçambique e o Governor de Sua Magestade de 21 de Fevereiro de 1888 a 2 de Junho de 1891 (Lisbon, 1891)

223   *Marquez* de Fontes Pereira de Mello to Tito Augusto Carvalho, *comissario regio*, Lisbon, 7–2–1892 enclosing the report of Charles de Llamby and the draft of the

procés verbal I entitled 'Programme des Questions a elucider avec le roi Mutaca'.

Copia de Documentos . . . de 5 de maio de 1892 a 4 de maio de 1893 (Lisbon, 1893)

224 Luiz Ignacio, commandant of Sena to J. Machado, governor of the Company, Sena, 29–9–1892, pages 149–51.

225 Luiz Ignacio, commandant of Sena to J. Machado, governor of the Company, Sena, 17–12–1892, pages 225–226.

Copia de Documentos . . . 5 de maio a 31 de dezembro de 1894 (Lisbon, 1894)

226 Marquez de Fontes Pereira de Mello to Tito Augusto Carvalho, Lisbon, 2–7–1894, page 24.

227 Luiz Ignacio, commandant of Sena to J. Machado, governor of the Company, Sena, 29–4–1894, pages 27–34.

228 Luiz Ignacio to *Juiz Ordinario* of Sena, Sena, 28–4–1894, pages 35–7.

229 Luiz Ignacio to J. Machado, governor of the Company, Sena, 14–8–1894, pages 112–13.

Copia de Documentos . . . de 1896 (Lisbon, 1896)

230 J. Machado, governor of the Company to *Marquez* de Fontes Pereira de Mello, Beira, 6–2–1896, pages 79–80.

231 J. Machado, governor of the Company to GG, Beira, 18–7–1896, pages 222–3.

Documentação Avulsa Moçambicana do Arquivo Historico Ultramarino, edited by Dr. Francisco Santana, vol. 1 (Lisbon, 1964)

232 Maço 1 *Requerimento* of José Francisco Alves Barbosa, Nov. 1827, doc. 16/1, pages 5–6.

233 Maço 1 *Copia da Exposição e Parecer do Concelho Ultramarino sobre a Concessão do Prazo Cheringoma a Francisca Aurora de Araujo Bragança, 10–9–1830*, doc. 100, pages 63–6.

234 Maço 1 *Informação de Sebastião Xavier Botelho, 22–3–1832*, doc. 107/7, pages 73–5.

235 Maço 1A *Carta de Aforamento* for *prazo* Pitta to *Dona* Anna Maria Xavier Vaz, 15–10–1801, doc. 31–2, pages 96–7.

236 Maço 2   *Termo da Abertura da Embaixada do Rei Massa,*
31–5–1827, doc. 133, pages 315–16.
237 Maço 2   *Oficio* of Paulo José Dinis to Francisco Henriques
Ferraõ, governor of the Rivers, 27–9–1827, doc.
145, page 320.
238 Maço 2   Francisco Henriques Ferrão to Sebastião Xavier
Botelho GG, 4–2–1828, doc. 151, pages 440–1.
239 Maço 3   Petition of *Dona* Barbara de Sousa e Brito, 20–5–
1828, doc. 172, page 453.
240 Maço 3   Francisco Henriques Ferrão to Sebastião Xavier
Botelho GG, 28–7–1828, doc. 24, pages 375–6.
241 Maço 3   *Oficio* of Francisco Henriques Ferrão, governor of
the Rivers, 29–10–1828 enclosing *representação
dos arrendatorios dos prazos da coroa*, docs.
7/1, 7/2, pages 366–7.
242 Maço 4   Proclamation of Francisco Henriques Ferrão,
governor of the Rivers, 6–3–1828, doc. 66,
page 501.
243 Maço 9   *Oficio* of José Amante de Lemos, 21–7–1829, doc.
104, page 998.

*Documentação Avulsa Moçambicana do Arquivo Historico Ultra-
marino*, edited by Dr. Francisco Santana, vol. 2 (Lisbon,
1967)

244 Maço 12 José Manuel da Silva's explanation of the case of
the negress Mutibue, 1830, doc. 152/2, pages
203–4.
245 Maço 12 *Parecer de Joaquim Xavier Dinis Costa sobre a
concessão do prazo Tirre a Irmandade da Misericordia de Moçambique*, 14–5–1830, doc. 167,
pages 134–5.
246 Maço 13 *Duque* de Cadaval to Paulo José Miguel de Brito
GG, 27–4–1830, enclosing list of *degredados*,
docs. 56/1, 56/2, pages 311–12.
247 Maço 13 *Duque* de Cadaval to Paulo José Miguel de Brito
GG, 27–4–1830, pages 311–12.
248 Maço 14 Manuel Joaquim Mendes de Vasconcellos e Cirne
to *conde* de Basto, 28–7–1830, doc. 3, pages 328–
331.
249 Maço 14 *Oficio* of Luis Felix, 2–10–1830, doc. 11, page 345.
250 Maço 15 *Oficio* of the provisional governor to Antonio
Manuel de Mello e Castro, TG, 10–5–1784(?),
doc. 6, page 449.

251   Maço 16 *Frei* Antonio da Graça to Joaquim Mendes de
       Vasconcellos e Cirne, 3–6–1830, doc. 95, pages
       608–9.
252   Maço 16 Paulo José de Brito GG to *conde* de Basto, 20–6–
       1830, doc. 21, pages 794–5.
253   Maço 19 Representations of Caetano de Sousa e Vascon-
       cellos, 6–6–1830, doc. 46, pages 880–1.
254   Maço 19 Joaquim Mendes de Vasconcellos e Cirne gover-
       nor of the Rivers, to Paulo José Miguel de Brito
       GG, 18–7–1830, doc. 87, pages 900–1.

Documentos Apresentados ao Cortes na Sessão 1890

255   *Relatorio do Sr. Alexandre Alberto da Rocha Serpa Pinto,
       23–12–1889*, pages 208–16.

Documentos Remittidos da India. Livros dos Monções, 5 vols
(Lisbon, 1880–1935)

256   *Regimento* for *Dom* Nun'Alvares Pereira, vol. 5, page 45.

*Documentos sobre os Portugueses em Moçambique e na Africa
Central 1497–1840. Documents on the Portuguese in Moçambique
and Central Africa 1497–1840.* Vols 1–6, Lisbon 1962–)

Vol. 1, 1497–1506

257   Diogo de Alcaçovas to the king, Cochin, 20–11–1506, pages
       388–401.
258   Instructions to the captain-major D. Francisco de Almeida,
       Lisbon, 5–3–1505, pages 156–259.

Vol. 4, 1515–1516

259   Memorandum of the fleet which the king our Lord is send-
       ing to India this year of 1515, page 21.
260   Expenditure book of Pedro Lopes clerk of the factory of
       Sofala, 1515, pages 25–210.
261   João Vaz de Almada, captain of Sofala to king Manuel,
       Sofala, 26–6–1516, pages 274–95.

Vol. 5, 1517–1518

262   Antonio da Silveira to king Manuel, *c.* July 1518, pages
       538–73.

Fontes para a Historia, Geografia e Commercio de Moçambique,
ed. Luis Carvalho Dias (Lisbon, 1954). See (*333*)

263   *Noticia da Situação das Ilhas de Cabo Delgado*, Joaquim

José da Costa Portugal to King, Ibo, 26-7-1781, pages 275-80.

264 *Mappa do Rendimento da Terra Gorongosa*, pages 345-51.
265 *Mappa do Rendimento da Terra Cheringoma*, pages 352-7.
266 *Carta Regia de Confirmação de terras na Zambezia aos Jesuitas*, 19-2-1745, pages 359-65.

Historia das Guerras no Zambeze, by F. G. Almeida de Eça, 2 vols (Lisbon, 1953-4). See (*299.*)

Vol. 1

267 Nicolau Pascoal da Cruz to José Agostinho da Costa TG, 7-11-1809, doc. 2, pages 400-1.
268 *Oficio* of Domingos Fortunato do Valle GG, Moçambique, 27-6-1849, doc. 21, pages 433-4.

Vol. 2

269 Antonio Tavares de Almeida to GG, Sena, 28-9-1869, doc. 31, pages 611-18.

Moçambique. Documentario Trimestriale

270 Sept. 1941. José Francisco Alves Barbosa to Constantino Pereira de Azevedo, Sena, 30-12-1811, page 123.

Records of South Eastern Africa, edited by G. M. Theal, 9 vols (Cape Town, 1898-1903)

Vol. 1

271 Pedro Vaz Soares, factor of Sofala to king Manuel, Sofala, 30-6-1513, pages 78-85.
272 Francisco de Brito, factor of Sofala to king Manuel, Sofala, 8-8-1519, pages 99-107.
273 Extracts from the account of the wreck of the ship Santiago 1585, pages 330-54.

Vol. 3

274 *Determinação dos Letrados*, 23-1-1569, pages 150-6.

Vol. 4

275 King to *Conde* de Feira viceroy, Lisbon, 21-3-1608, pages 64-74.
276 King to viceroy, Lisbon, 24-3-1612, pages 83-7.
277 King to viceroy, Lisbon, 28-3-1613, pages 108-9.
278 *Alvara* granting the commerce of the *Rios de Cuama* to Ruy

Melo de Sampaio, captain of Moçambique, Lisbon, 20–3–1614, pages 127–9.

279 Report made by the governor-general Diogo da Cunha de Castellobranco, 7–2–1619, pages 147–69.

280 King to viceroy, Lisbon, 17–2–1624, pages 187–8.

281 King to viceroy, Lisbon, 21–3–1625, pages 189–90.

282 King to *Conde* de Linhares, viceroy, Lisbon, 24–1–1629, pages 203–4.

283 King to viceroy, Lisbon, 24–1–1652, pages 314–15.

284 Prince to viceroy, Lisbon, 20–3–1669, pages 344–5.

285 Prince to viceroy, Lisbon, 14–3–1675, pages 366–8.

Vol. 5

286 King to *Conde de* Ericeira, viceroy, Lisbon, 19–2–1718, pages 40–2.

287 *Dom* Luiz de Meneses, viceroy to Antonio Cardim Froes TG, Goa, 21–1–1719, pages 45–52.

288 *Dom* Luiz de Meneses, viceroy to Manuel Gonçalves Guião, Goa, 26–1–1719, pages 63–6.

289 *Dom* Luiz de Meneses viceroy to Manuel Gonçalves Guião, Goa, 26–1–1720, pages 98–9.

290 King to João de Saldanha de Gama, viceroy, Lisbon, 13–2–1727, pages 145–7.

The Times

290A Letter headed 'British Zambesia and the Portuguese Claims' by F. C. Selous, 6–1–1890.

PRINTED BOOKS AND ARTICLES

291 Abraham, D. P., 'The Monomotapa Dynasty', *NADA* (Native Affairs Department Annual), no 36, 1959.

292 Abraham, D. P., 'The early political history of the Kingdom of Mwene Mutapa 850–1589', *Historians in Tropical Africa*, proceedings of the Leverhulme Intercollegiate History Conference held . . . Sept. 1960 (Salisbury, 1962), 61–92.

293 Abraham, D. P., 'Maramuca; an Excercise in the combined Use of Portuguese Records and Oral Tradition', *Journal of African History*, vol. 2, no 2, 1961, 211–25.

294 Almeida, Manuel Antonio de, 'Memorial sobre a Terra do Luabo, 1763', *Relações* . . . ed. Andrade A. A., 225–31.

295 Almeida Costa, M. J. B. de, *Origem da Enfiteuese no Direito Portugues* (Coimbra, 1957).
296 Almeida de Eça, Filipe Gastão de, *Mosaico Moçambicano* (Lisbon, 1943).
297 Almeida de Eça, Filpe Gastão de, *Gamitto* (Lisbon, 1950).
298 Almeida de Eça, Filipe Gastão de, *Lacerda e Almeida Escravo do Dever e Martir de Sciencia 1753–1798* (Lisbon, 1951).
299 Almeida de Eça, Filipe Gastão de, *Historia das Guerras no Zambeze: Chicoa e Massangano (1807–1888)*, 2 vols (Lisbon, 1953–4).
300 Alpers, Edward, *The Role of the Yao in the Development of Trade in East Central Africa*, unpublished thesis in the Senate House Library of the University of London, 1966.
301 Alpers, Edward, 'North of the Zambesi', in Roland Oliver ed., *The Middle Age of African History* (London, 1967), 78–84.
302 Alpers, Edward, 'The Mutapa and Malawi Political Systems' in T. O. Ranger ed., *Aspects of Central African History* (London, 1968).
303 Alvares, Francisco, *The Prester John of the Indies: a true relation of the lands of the Prester John being the Narrative of the Portuguese Embassy to Ethiopia in 1520*, trans. Lord Stanley of Alderley, 1881, revised and edited by C. F. Beckingham and G. W. B. Huntingford, 2 vols, Hakluyt Society (Cambridge, 1961).
304 Alvares, Pedro, 'O Regime dos Prazos', *Boletim da Sociedade de Geografia de Lisboa*, April–June 1916, 137–213.
305 Andrade, Antonio Alberto de, *Relações de Moçambique Setecentista* (Lisbon, 1955).
306 Andrade Corvo, João de, *Estudos sobre as Provincias Ultramarinas*, 4 vols (Lisbon, 1883).
307 Angus, Crawford, 'A Year in Azimbaland and Chipitaland: the Customs and Superstitions of the People', *Journal of the Royal Anthropological Institute*, 1898, 316–25.
308 Anon (perhaps F. R. Morais Pereira), 'Memorias da Costa d'Africa Oriental e algumas reflexões uteis para estabelecer melhor, e fazer mais florente o seu commercio', 1762, in Andrade, *Relações . . .*, 189–224.
309 Anon, 'Descripção da Capitania de Monsambique, suas povoações, e produções', 1788, in Andrade ed. *Relações . . .*, 375–407.
310 Anon, 'Como se estabeleceu em Africa a primeira Com-

panhia de Moçambique', *Revista de Manica e Sofala*, serie 1, no 8, Oct. 1904.

311 Anon, 'Zambezia Portugueza, as Maravias, a Macanga', *Revista Portugueza Colonial e Maritima*, 1904–5.

312 Axelson, Eric, 'Goldmining in Mashonaland in the 16th and 17th centuries', *Optima*, vol. 9, no 3, Sept. 1959, 164–170.

313 Axelson, Eric, *Portuguese in South-East Africa 1600–1700* (Johannesburg, 1960).

314 Axelson, Eric, *Portugal and the Scramble for Africa* (Johannesburg, 1967).

315 Azurara, Gomes Ennes, *Chronicle of the Discovery of Guinea*, extracts edited by V. de Castro e Almeida, trans. B. Miall (London, 1936).

316 Barahona e Costa, Henrique César da Silva, *Apontamentos para a Historia da Guerra da Zambezia* (Lisbon, 1895).

317 Barnard, Frederick Lamport, *A Three Years Cruise in the Mozambique Channel for the Suppression of the Slave Trade* (London, 1848).

318 Barreto, Manuel S. J., 'Informação do Estado e Conquista dos Rios de Cuama', in Theal ed., *Records . . .*, vol. 3, 436–508.

319 Barros, João de, *Decadas da Asia* (Lisbon, 1552). Extracts published in Theal ed., *Records . . .*, vol. 6, 1–306.

320 Birmingham, David, *Trade and Conflict in Angola: the Mbundu and their Neighbours under the Influence of the Portuguese, 1483–1790* (Oxford, 1966).

321 Bocarro, Antonio, 'Livro do Estado da India'. This manuscript history, one copy of which is in the British Museum, was revised by Pedro Barreto de Resende who drew charts for it. Extracts are printed in Theal ed., *Records . . .*, vol. 3, 254–436 and vol. 2, 378–426. See also under *Arquivo Portuguese Oriental (219)*.

322 Boteler, Capt. Thomas R. N., *Narrative of a Voyage of Discovery to Africa and Arabia*, 2 vols (London, 1835).

323 Boxer, C. R., ed., *The Tragic History of the Sea*, vol. 1, Hakluyt Society (London, 1957). Contains:
   (a) 'Narrative of the Shipwreck of the São Thomé', 1959, by Diogo do Couto.
   (b) 'Shipwreck of the Santo Alberto', 1593, by João Baptista Lavanha.
   (c) 'Treatise of the Misfortune that befell the Great Ship São João Baptista', 1622, by Francisco Vaz d'Almada.

324 Boxer, C. R., *The Golden Age of Brazil* (Los Angeles, 1962).
325 Boxer, C. R., 'The Querimba Islands in 1744', *Studia*, no 11, Jan. 1963: Contains:
 (a) 'Ilhas de Quirimba athe o Cabo Delgado', 1744.
 (b) 'Outra descricção anonyma das Ilhas Querimbas em 1744'.
 (c) 'O visorei Marques de Castello-Novo e as Querimbas em 1744'.
326 Brandão, Alfredo César, *A Conferencia do Snr Paiva de Andrada acerca da recente Campanha que poz Termo ao Dominio do Bonga na Zambezia* (Lisbon, 1888).
327 Brelsford, W. V., 'Harrison Clark: King of Northern Rhodesia', *The Northern Rhodesia Journal*, 1954.
327A Brendon, N. J., 'Chiuzingu', *NADA*, vol. 36, 1959, 19–25.
328 Buckland, W. W., *A Textbook of Roman Law* (London, 1909).
329 Burton, Sir F., ed. and trans., *The Lands of Kazembe* (London, 1873). See also Lacerda e Almeida, '*Diario da Viagem de Tette . . .*' (*385*).
330 Caldas Xavier, A. A., 'Factos do Ultima Revolta da Baixa Zambezia em 1884', *As Colonias Portuguezas*, no 10, Nov. 1886, nos 11 and 12, Dec. 1886.
331 Caldas Xavier, A. A., *Estudos Coloniais*, edição official (Nova Goa, 1889). Contains:
 (a) 'A Zambezia'.
 (b) 'A Questão do Nyasa e os Prazos do Chire'.
 (c) 'O Relatorio da Commissão dos Prazos'.
332 Capello, H. and Ivens, R., *De Angola a Contracosta*, 2 vols (Lisbon, 1886).
333 Carvalho Dias, Luis Fernando de, *Fontes para a Historia, Geografia e Commercio de Moçambique (Sec XVIII)*, *Anais da Junta de Investigações do Ultramar*, vol. ix (Lisbon, 1954).
334 Castilho, Augusto de, *Relatorio da Guerra da Zambezia em 1888* (Lisbon, 1891).
335 Chadwick, Owen, *Mackenzie's Grave* (London, 1959).
336 Clark, J. Desmond, 'The Portuguese Settlement at Feira', *The Northern Rhodesia Journal*, vol. 6, 275–92.
337 Conceição, *Frei* Antonio da, 'Tratado dos Rios de Cuama', *O Chronista de Tissuary*, vol. 2 (Nova Goa, 1867).
338 Correa Pereira, João, *João Correa: Colono Zambeziano, 1840–1889, sua Vida e a sua Obra* (1952).
339 Correia de Matos, M. L. M. M., *Portuguese Law and*

Administration in Mozambique and their effect on the customary Land Laws of the three Tribes of the Lake Nyasa Region, 1969, unpublished thesis in the Senate House Library of the University of London.

340 Courtois, Victor S. J., 'Terras de Macanga', *Boletim da Sociedade de Geografia de Lisboa*, serie 5, no 8, 1885, 502–520.

341 Coutinho, João de Azevedo, *Manuel Antonio de Sousa, um Capitão-mor da Zambezia*, pelo imperio no 20 (Lisbon, 1936).

342 Coutinho, João de Azevedo, *Memorias de um Velho Marinheiro e Soldado de Africa* (Lisbon, 1941).

343 Couto, Diogo do, *Decadas da Asia* (Lisbon, 1602 and 1788). Extracts published in Theal ed., *Records . . .*, vol. 6, 307–410.

344 Cunnison, Ian, 'Kazembe and the Portuguese', *Journal of African History*, vol. 2, no 1, 61–76.

345 Diffey, Bailey W., *Portugal Overseas before Prince Henry* (Nebraska U.P., 1960).

346 Duffy, James, *Portuguese Africa* (Harvard and Oxford, 1961).

346A Durand, E., *Une Exploration Française au Zambèze* (Paris, 1888).

347 'Edital da Inquisição de Goa', *O Chronista de Tissuary*, Cunha Rivara ed., vol. 2 (Nova Goa, 1867), 273–5.

348 Fagan, Brian, *Southern Africa during the Iron Age*, ancient peoples and places, vol. 46 (London, 1965).

349 Faria y Sousa, Manuel de, *Asia Portuguesa*, extracts published in Theal ed., *Records . . .*, vol. 1, 1–46.

350 Ferão, 'Account of the Portuguese Possessions within the Captaincy of the Rios de Sena', in Theal ed., *Records . . .*, vol. 7, 371–87.

351 Fernandes, José Augusto Barrahona, 'Barras do Rio Zambesi', *Garcia de Orta*, vol. 6, no 2, 1958.

352 Ferreri, Alfredo Brandão Cro de Castro and Joaquim José Lapa, *Elementos para um Diccionario Chorographico da Provincia de Moçambique* (Lisbon, 1889).

353 Fitzler, M. A. Hedwig, *Os Tombos de Ceilão* (Lisbon, 1927).

354 Foa, Edouard, *Du Cap au Lac Nyassa* (Paris, 1901).

355 Freire D'Andrade, A., *Relatorios sobre Moçambique*, 4 vols (Lourenço Marques, 1907–9).

356 Galante, Pereira, *Martires de Massangano* (Lourenço Marques, 1945).

357 Galvão da Silva, Manuel, 'Diario das Viagens feitas pelas Terras de Manica', in Carvalho Dias ed., *Fontes* . . ., 321–334.

358 Galvão da Silva, Manuel, 'Diario ou Relação das Viagens Philosophicas, que por Ordem de Sua Magestade Fidellissima tem feito nas Terras da Jurisdição da Vila de Tette, e em algumas dos Maraves', in Carvalho Dias ed., *Fontes* . . ., 313–19.

359 Gama, J. V. da, *Almanach Civil Ecclesiastico Historico Administrativo da Provincia de Moçambique para o anno de 1859* (Moçambique, 1859). Contains an itinerary of the route from Quelimane to Moçambique made in 1779 by A. A. de Sousa Vasconcellos, 181–3.

360 Gama Barros, Henrique de, *Historia da Administração Publica em Portugal nos Seculos xii a xv*, 5 vols (Lisbon, 1914).

361 Gamitto, A. C. P., 'Prazos da Coroa em Rios de Sena', *Archivo Pitoresco*, vol. 1, 1857–8, 61–3, 66–7.

362 Gamitto, A. C. P., 'Successão e Acclamação dos Reis do Barue', *Annaes do Concelho Ultramarino*, parte não official, serie 1, 1867.

363 Gamitto, A. C. P., *King Kazembe*, translated by Ian Cunnison, 2 vols (Lisbon, 1960).

364 Garlake, P. S., 'Seventeenth Century Portuguese Earthworks in Rhodesia', *South African Archaeological Bulletin*, vol. xxi, no 84, part iv, Jan. 1967, 157–70.

365 Garlake, P. S., 'Excavations at the Seventeenth Century Portuguese Site of Dambarare, Rhodesia', *Transactions on the Rhodesian Scientific Association*, vol. 54, part 1, 23–61.

366 Gavicho de Lacerda, Francisco, *Cartas da Zambezia*, 2nd edition (Lisbon, 1923).

367 Gavicho de Lacerda, Francisco, *Costumes e Lendas da Zambezia* (Lisbon, 1925).

368 Gavicho de Lacerda, Francisco, *Figuras e Episodios da Zambezia* (Lisbon, 1929).

369 Gibbons, Major A. St H., *Africa from South to North through Marotseland*, 2 vols (London, 1904).

370 Godinho, Vitorino Magalhães, *A Economia dos Descobrimentos Henriquinos* (Lisbon, 1962).

371 Gomes, Antonio S. J., 'Viagem que fez o Padre Antº Gomes da Compª de Jesus ao Imperio de Manomotapa', edited with notes by E. Axelson, *Studia*, no 3, 1959.

372 Gorjão de Moura, F. I., 'Campanha nas Terras do Bire', *Boletim da Sociedade de Geografia de Lisboa*, no 7, 1888–1889, 359–89.

373 Guyot, Paul, 'Voyage au Zambèse', *Bulletin de Société de Géographie de l'Est*, 1882.

374 Haight, M. V. Jackson, *The European Powers and South East Africa* (London, 1967), a revised version of work originally published in 1942.

375 Hammond, R. J., *Portugal and Africa 1815–1910* (Stanford, 1966).

376 Hanna, A. J., *The Beginnings of Nyasaland and North-Eastern Rhodesia* (Oxford, 1956).

377 Hoppe, Fritz, *Portugiesisch-Ostafrika in der Zeit des Marques de Pombal*, biblioteca Ibero-Americana, vol. 7 (Berlin, 1965).

378 ILO, *Draft for a Report on Forced Labour*, 1926. Copy in Rhodes House, Oxford.

379 Junod, Henri, 'Notes on the Ethnographical Situation in Portuguese East Africa, on the South of the Zambesi', *Bantu Studies*, vol. x, 1936.

380 Kirk, John, *The Zambesi Journal and Letters of Dr John Kirk*, ed. R. Foskett, 2 vols (London, 1965).

381 Kirkman, James, *Men and Monuments on the East African Coast* (London, 1964).

382 Knight-Bruce, Bishop G. W. H., 'The Mashonaland Mission', diaries edited by C. E. Fripp, in Fripp and Hillier, *Gold and Gospel in Mashonaland*, Oppenheimer Series no 4 (London, 1949), 5–149.

383 Lacerda e Almeida, Francisco Maria de, 'Noticias dadas por Manuel Caetano Pereira' in *Travessia de Africa*, ed. M. Murias, 1936, 384–95.

384 Lacerda e Almeida, Francisco Maria de, 'Diario da Viagem de Moçambique para os Rios de Senna', in *Travessia . . .*, 79–136.

385 Lacerda e Almeida, Francisco Maria de, 'Diario da Viagem de Tette . . . para o Interior de Africa', in *Travessia . . .*, 149–247.

386 Leite, Bertha, *D. Gonçalo da Silveira* (Lisbon, 1946).

387 Liesegang, Gerhard ed., *Reposta das Questões sobre os Cafres ou Noticias Etnographicas sobre Sofala do Fim do Seculo xviii*, Estudos de Antropologia Cultural, no 2 (Lisbon, 1966).

388 Liesegang, Gerhard, *Beitrage zur Geschichte des Reiches der*

409

Gaza Nguni im Südlichen Moçambique, doctoral thesis presented at the University of Cologne, 1967.

389 Livingstone, David, *Missionary Travels and Researches in South Africa* (London, 1857).

390 Livingstone, David and Charles, *Narrative of an Expedition to the Zambesi and Its Tributaries; and the Discovery of the Lakes Shirwa and Nyasa 1858–64* (London, 1865).

391 Livingstone, David, *The Zambezi Expedition of David Livingstone*, ed. J. P. R. Wallis, Oppenheimer Series no 6 (London, 1956).

392 Livingstone, David, *Livingstone's African Journal*, ed. Schapera, 2 vols (London, 1963).

393 Lobato, Alexandre, *A Expansão Portuguesa em Moçambique 1498 a 1530*, 3 vols (Lisbon, 1954).

394 Lobato, Alexandre, *Evolução Administrativa e Economica de Moçambique 1752–63* (Lisbon, 1957).

395 Lobato, Alexandre, *Colonização Senhorial da Zambezia e outros Estudos* (Lisbon, 1962).

396 Lopes de Lima, José Joaquim, with Francisco Maria Bordalo, *Ensaios sobre a Estatistica das Possessões Portuguezas na Africa Occidental e Oriental e na Asia Occidental na China e na Oceania*, 6 vols (Lisbon, 1859). Volume 4, second series is entitled *Ensaio sobre a Estatistica de Moçambique e suas Dependencias na Costa Oriental de Oriental de Africa ao Sul do Equador* and is by F. M. Bordallo.

397 Lupi, Eduardo do Couto, *Angoche* (Lisbon, 1907).

398 Macdonald, Duff, *Africana*, 2 vols (London, 1882).

399 Main, Sir Henry, *Ancient Law*, Everyman edition.

400 Marchant, Alexander, 'Feudal and capitalistic Elements in the Portuguese Settlement of Brazil', *Hispanic American Historical Review*, vol. 22, 1942.

401 Marwick, M. G., 'History and Tradition in East Central Africa through the Eyes of the Northern Rhodesia Cewa', *Journal of African History*, vol. 4, 1963, no 3, 375–90.

402 Mello e Castro, Dionizio de, 'Noticia do Imperio Marave e dos Rios de Sena, mandada pelo coronel Dionizio de Mello e Castro ao governador Pedro da Saldanha de Alberquerque', Carvalho Dias, *Fontes . . .*, 119–49.

403 Mello e Castro, Francisco de, 'Rios de Senna. Sua Descripção desde a Barra de Quillimane até ao Zumbo', *Annaes do Concelho Ultramarino*, parte não official, serie ii, 1859–62 (Lisbon, 1867).

410

404 Mesquita e Solla, A. de F. de, 'Apontamentos sobre o Zumbo', *Boletim da Sociedade de Geografia de Lisboa*, 1907, 247–57, 274–87, 319–27, 340–56, 382–91, 436–56.

405 Miller, F. V. Bruce, 'A Few Historical Notes on Zumbo and Feira', *Journal of the Royal African Society*, vol. 9, 1910, 416–23.

406 Miranda, Antonio Pinto de, 'Memoria sobre a Costa de Africa', in Andrade, *Relações* . . ., 231–312.

407 Miranda, Antonio Porfirio de, *Noticia acerca do Bonga da Zambesia* (Lisbon, 1869).

408 Moir, F., *After Livingstone* (London, 1923).

409 Monclaro, Father, 'Relação da Viagem QFizerão os P^{es} da Companhia de Jesus com Fran^{co} Barreto na Conquista de Monomotapa no anno de 1569', in Theal, *Records* . . ., vol. 3, 157–253.

410 Montagu Kerr, Walter, *The Far Interior*, 2 vols (London, 1886).

411 Montagu Kerr, Walter, 'The Upper Zambesi Zone', *The Scottish Geographical Magazine*, 1886, no 7, July, 385–402.

412 Moskopp, Father, 'The P.E.A. Rebellion of 1917: Diary of Rev. Father Moskopp', *The Northern Rhodesia Journal*, July 1961, 154–60.

413 Negreiros, Almada, *Le Mozambique* (Paris, 1904).

414 Newitt, M. D. D., 'The Massingire Rising of 1884', *Journal of African History*, vol. 9, 1970, no 1, 87–105.

415 Newitt, M. D. D. and Garlake, P. S., 'The "Aringa" at Massangano', *Journal of African History*, vol. 8, 1967, no 1, 133–56.

416 Nogueira de Andrade, Jeronimo José, 'Descrição em que ficaram os Negocios da Capitania de Moçambique em Fins de 1789 e considerações sobre a decadencia do seu Commercio', *Archivo das Colonias*, 1917–18.

417 Noronha, Joaquim Francisco Correa de, *Memoria sobre a Administração dos Prazos do Districto de Quelimane* (Orlim, 1883).

418 Oliviera, Delfim José de, *A Provincia de Moçambique e O Bonga* (Coimbra, 1879).

419 Oliver, Roland, *Sir Harry Johnston and the Scramble for Africa* (London, 1959).

420 Ornellas, Ayres d', *Collectanea das suas principais Obras militares e coloniais*, 3 vols (Lisbon, 1934–6).

421 Owen, Capt. W. F. W., 'Particulars of an Expedition up the

Zambesi to Senna, performed by three officers of His Majesty's Ship Leven, when surveying the East Coast of Africa in 1823', *Journal of the Royal Geographical Society of London*, vol. 2, 1832, 136–52.

422 Owen, Capt. W. F. W., *Narrative of Voyages to explore the Shores of Africa, Arabia and Madagascar*, 2 vols (London, 1833).

423 Pacheco, Albino Manuel, *Uma Viagem de Tete a Zumbo* (Lisbon, 1883). Printed in instalments in *Boletim do Governo de Moçambique*, 1883, nos 17, 18, 19, 21, 22, 23, 24, 28, 29, 30, 31, 32, 33, 34, 35, 36, 37, 38.

424 Paiva de Andrada, Joaquim Carlos, *Relatorio de uma Viagem as Terras do Changamira* (Lisbon, 1886).

425 Paiva de Andrada, Joaquim Carlos, 'Campanhas de Zambesia, 1887', *Boletim da Sociedade de Geografia de Lisboa*, 1887, no 11, 713–38.

426 Paiva de Andrada, Joaquim Carlos, 'Relatorio do Major Paiva de Andrada', *Boletim da Sociedade de Geografia de Lisboa*, 188–9, no 8, 405–39.

427 Pereira, Francisco Raimundo Morais, *Account of a Journey made Overland from Quellimane to Angoche in 1752*, ed. M. Newitt (Salisbury, 1965).

428 Pereira do Lago, Baltasar Manuel, 'Instrucção que o Illmo e Exmo Sr. Governador e Capitão General Baltasar Manuel Pereira do Lago deo a quem lhe suceder neste Governo', in Andrade, ed., *Relações* . . ., 317–38.

429 Peters, Dr Carl, *The Eldorado of the Ancients* (London, 1902). English translation of the German original entitled *Im Goldland des Altertums*.

430 Philipson, D. W. and Fagan, B. M., 'The Date of the Ingombe Ilede Burials', *Journal of African History*, 1969, no 2.

431 Portugal Durão, A. de, 'O Districto de Quelimane', *Boletim da Sociedade de Geografia de Lisboa*, 1914, nos 5–6, 139–189.

432 Postan, M. M., *The Cambridge Economic History of Europe*, vol. 1, 'The Agrarian History of the Middle Ages', 2nd edition (Cambridge, 1966).

433 Prestage, Edgar, *The Portuguese Pioneers* (London, 1933).

434 T. Price, 'Malawi Rain Cults', in *Religion in Africa* (Edinburgh, 1964).

435 *Provincia de Moçambique. Relatorios annexo ao Boletim Official* (Lourenço Marques, 1909).

436 Ranger, T. O., 'Revolt in Portuguese East Africa', in Kirkwood ed., *St Anthony's Papers*, no 15 (London, 1963), 54–80.

437 Ranger, T. O., *Revolt in Southern Rhodesia 1896–7* (London, 1967).

438 *Regimen dos Prazos da Coroa*, published by the Ministerio da Marinha e Ultramar (Lisbon, 1897).

439 *Relatorios dos Governadores Geraes das Provincias de Cabo Verde, Moçambique e Estado da India*, presented to the Cortes in the session of 1878.

440 Ribeiro, Caetano Manuel, 'O Gouveia', *Moçambique Documentario Trimestral*, no 10, 1937.

441 Rowley, Rev. Henry, 'Slavery among the Portuguese in Eastern Africa', *Mission Life*, March 1868, 197–206.

442 Rowley, Rev. Henry, *Africa Unveiled* (London, 1876).

443 Salter de Mendonça, Duarte de, 'Memoria do Desembargador Duarte Salter de Mendonça', Lisbon, 7–12–1751. Original in AHU Moç Cx 3, printed in Hoppe, *Portugiesisch-Ostafrika . . .*, 217–33.

444 Santa Caterina, *Frei* Francisco de, 'A Dominican Account of Zambesia in 1744', ed. C. R. Boxer, *Boletim da Sociedade de Estudos de Moçambique*, vol. 29, 1960.

445 Santos, *Frei* João dos, *Ethiopia Oriental E Varia Historia de Cousas Notaveis do Oriente* (Evora, 1609). Extracts published in Theal, *Records . . .*, vol. 7.

446 Santos junior, J. R. dos, *Estudo da Antropologia de Moçambique* (Oporto, 1944).

447 Sarmento, Affonso de Moraes, 'Zambezia', *As Colonias Portuguezas*, June 1887, nos 11 and 12.

448 Schebesta, Paul, *Portugals Konquistamission in Südost-Afrika*, Studia Instituti Missiologici Societatis Verbi Divini, no 7 (St Augustin, 1966).

449 Selous, Frederick Courtenay, *A Hunter's Wanderings in Africa*, 1st ed., 1881 (London, 1928).

450 Selous, Frederick Courtenay, 'Twenty Years in Zambezia', *The Geographical Journal*, April 1893.

451 Sena Barcellos, Christiano José de, *Subsidios para a Historia do Cabo Verde e Guiné*, 3 vols (Lisbon, 1899).

452 Seyrig, Henri, *Rapport sur la Situation actuelle e ." Avenir possible du Prazo de Gorongosa* (Lisbon, 1897).

453 Sicard, Harald von, 'The Ancient Barue Accession to the Chieftaincy', *NADA*, no 31, 1954.

454 Silva Monteiro, A. M. da, 'Distrito de Tete', *Boletim da*

Sociedade de Geografia de Lisboa, January–March 1926, 80–9, June–September 1926, 118–43, October–December 1926, 169–210.

455 Silva Rego, A. da, *Portuguese Colonisation in the Sixteenth Century: A Study of the Royal Ordinances* (Johannesburg, 1959).

456 Soares, Augusto Estanislas Xavier, *Villa de Sofala* (Nova Goa, 1855).

457 Sousa, Francisco de, *Oriente Conquistado a Jesu Christo pelos Padres da Companhia de Jesu da Provincia de Goa*, 2 parts (Lisbon, 1710).

458 Sousa Monteiro, José Maria de, *Diccionario Geographico* (Lisbon, 1850), vol. 8 and appendix to *Os Portugueses em Africa, Asia, America e Oceania* (Lisbon, 1851).

459 Sousa Ribeiro, ed., *Regimen dos Prazos de Coroa* (Lourenço Marques, 1907).

460 Sousa Ribeiro, ed., *Anuario de Moçambique* (Lourenço Marques, 1908).

461 Sousa Ribeiro, ed., *Anuario de Moçambique* (Lourenço Marques, 1917).

462 Sousa e Silva, Pedro Augusto de, *Distrito de Tete* (Lisbon, 1927).

463 Summers, Roger, *Zimbabwe: a Rhodesian Mystery* (Cape Town, 1963).

464 *Termos de Vassalagem nos Territorios de Machona, Zambezia e Nyasa 1858–89* (Lisbon, 1890).

465 Tew, Mary, *Peoples of the Lake Nyasa Region*, Ethnographic Survey of Africa, East Central Africa, part 1 (London, 1950).

466 Texugo, F. Torres, *A Letter on the Slave Trade still carried on along the Eastern Coast of Africa* (London, 1839).

467 Theal, George McCall, *Records of South Eastern Africa*, 9 vols (Cape Town, 1898–1903).

468 Thoman, Mauriz, *Reise und Lebensbeschreibung* (Augusburg, 1788).

469 Thornton, Richard, *The Zambezi Papers of Richard Thornton*, ed. E. C. Tabler, Robins Series no 4, 2 vols (London, 1963).

470 Tracey, Hugh, *Antonio Fernandes Descobridor do Monotapa 1514–1515*, trans. with notes by Caetano Montes (Lourenço Marques, 1940).

471 Truão, Antonio Norberto de Barbosa de Villas Boas,

Estatistica de Capitania dos Rios de Senna do Anno de 1806 (Lisbon, 1889).

472 Varella, Joaquim José, 'Descrição da Capitania de Moçambique e suas Povoações e Produções, pertencentes a Coroa de Portugal', in Carvalho Dias, *Fontes* . . ., 281–311.

473 Vasconcellos e Cirne, Manuel Joaquim Mendes de, *Memoria sobre a Provincia de Moçambique* (Lisbon, 1890).

474 Vilhena, Ernesto da, *Regime dos Prazos da Zambezia* (Lisbon, 1916).

475 Vinogradoff, Sir Paul, *Roman Law in Medieval Europe* (London, 1909).

476 Warhurst, Philip, *Anglo-Portuguese Relations in South-Central Africa 1890–1900*, Royal Commonwealth Society, Imperial Studies no 22 (London, 1962).

477 Wellington, John H., *Southern Africa, a Geographical Study*, 2 vols (Cambridge, 1955), vol. 1 'Physical Geography'.

478 Wiese, Carl, 'Expedição Portuguesa a M'Pesene', *Boletim da Sociedade de Geographia de Lisboa*, 1891, 235–73, 297–321, 331–412, 415–30, 465–97; 1892, 373–431, 435–516.

479 Wiese, Carl, 'Zambezia', *Boletim da Sociedade de Geografia de Lisboa*, serie 25, no 7, July 1907, 241–7.

480 Young, E. D., *Nyasa: a Journal of Adventures* (London, 1877).

481 Xavier, Inacio Caetano, 'Noticias dos Dominios Portugueses na Costa de Africa Oriental 1758', in Andrade, ed., *Relações* . . ., 139–88.

Index

421

425

429